DUBLIN'S JOYCE

Drawing of James Joyce 1920.
By Wyndham Lewis.

Dublin's
JOYCE

By

Hugh Kenner

I grieve for the City, and for myself and you
. . . and walk through endless ways of thought

OEDIPUS REX

BEACON PRESS

BOSTON

66-13125

First published in England by Chatto and Windus Ltd. in 1956

First published in the United States in 1956 by Indiana University Press

Library of Congress catalog card number: 56-5486

*First published as a Beacon Paperback in 1962 by arrangement with the
original publisher*

Printed in the United States of America

For
JOSIE
who pushed

ACKNOWLEDGMENTS

To the following pages every writer on Joyce, and notably Frank Budgen, has contributed his quota of details; if most of them are unascribed it is because I take their provenance to be by this time common knowledge. But it is to Wyndham Lewis's chapter in *Time and Western Man* that I owe the challenge of incontrovertible facts that would square neither with the received image of Joyce nor, as he interprets them, with my own conviction of the value of Joyce's work; and to Ezra Pound's neglected " James Joyce et Pécuchet "(reprinted in *Polite Essays*) that I attribute the order my views have ultimately taken.

The material on DeValera and *Finnegans Wake* owes its inception to the work of Mr. Andrew Cass, who staked a modest claim on this lode in *The Irish Times* for April 26, 1947. On the other hand, resemblances between my sixteenth chapter and Mr. J. S. Atherton's " Lewis Carroll and Finnegans Wake " (*English Studies*, February 1952) must be ascribed to the fact that we were both looking at the same object; I first saw a copy of his article four years after writing my chapter. Similarly, it was two years after my chapter on *Dubliners* was completed that Marvin Magalaner's "'The Sisters' of James Joyce" (*University of Kansas City Review*, Summer 1952) came to my attention.

Mr. John Jermain Slocum placed at my disposal in 1950 his magnificent collection of letters, books and manuscripts (now in the Yale University Library) and gave me the benefit of his invaluable conversation on things Joycean. Quotations from Joyce's letters to Harriet Weaver Shaw, recently donated by their recipient to the British Museum, were copied from transcripts furnished by her to Mr. Slocum. Dr. H. M. McLuhan of the University of Toronto has permitted me free use of his unpublished History of the Trivium, on which my thirteenth chapter depends heavily, and afforded the continual stimulus of letters and conversation. I have also to thank Vivian Mercier and Donald Davie for supplying and confirming various Dublin facts.

Vivian Mercier, Kenneth Millar, Donald Pearce, Gordon Ringer, Mrs. Adaline Glasheen and my colleague Marvin Mudrick extirpated a great many errors and inadequacies from the typescript, and the cost of preparing it for the printer was in part met by a grant from the Committee on Research of Santa Barbara College.

Earlier versions of parts of this book have appeared in *James Joyce: Two Decades of Criticism* (Vanguard Press, 1948), *Hudson Review, Kenyon Review, Sewanee Review, Essays in Criticism, Shenandoah,* and *English Institute Essays 1952* (Columbia University Press); I am grateful to the editors concerned for permission to reprint. An early draft of the entire book was written in 1950 as a Yale doctoral thesis, under the guidance of Cleanth Brooks. Though the work has been completely rewritten since then, the effect of his patient counsel has not been obliterated.

But my most pervasive debt is to Mr. John Reid, who devoted countless hours to helping me puzzle out means of presentation for a subject so complex that it seemed at one stage to elude all possibility of orderly treatment, and who in effect showed me how to write the book.

For making possible copious quotation, abridgment of which would have inconvenienced the expositor as much as the reader, I am under grateful obligation to the publishers of Joyce's works: Jonathan Cape Ltd. for the quotations from *A Portrait of the Artist as a Young Man, Stephen Hero, Dubliners,* and *Exiles;* John Lane The Bodley Head Ltd. for the quotations from *Ulysses;* and Faber and Faber Ltd. for the quotations from *Finnegans Wake.*

Messrs. Monro, Saw & Co., on behalf of the Administrators of the James Joyce Estate, have permitted the publication of extracts from certain unpublished letters of Joyce's. In this connection I must also thank Messrs. Faber and Faber Ltd. and The Viking Press, who possess publication rights to the letters of James Joyce, and the Yale University Library, present owners of the letters and copies of letters from which I made my own transcriptions.

In addition, I am indebted to Frank Budgen for quotations from his *James Joyce and the Making of Ulysses;* to Wyndham Lewis for quotations from *Time and Western Man;* to Mrs. W. B. Yeats and Messrs. Macmillan & Co. Ltd. for quotations from *Collected Poems* by W. B. Yeats and *A Vision* by W. B. Yeats; to St. Martin's Press Incorporated for quotations from " The Tables of the Law " by W. B. Yeats; to Mr. Arthur V. Moore of Shakespear & Parkyn, London,

Agent for the Committee of Mr. Ezra Pound, for quotations from *The Cantos of Ezra Pound* and *The Letters of Ezra Pound*; to Faber and Faber Ltd. for quotations from T. S. Eliot's *Prufrock*, *Little Gidding*, and *Selected Essays*; to Macmillan & Co. Ltd. for a quotation from *Alfred Tennyson* by Sir Charles Tennyson; to Thomas Nelson & Sons Ltd. for quotations from W. H. D. Rouse's translation of *The Odyssey*; to George Allen & Unwin Ltd. for quotations from Henrik Ibsen's letters in *The Life of Ibsen* by Halvdan Koht; to John Murray (Publishers) Ltd. for quotations from the Sherlock Holmes stories by Sir Arthur Conan Doyle; to Sheed & Ward Ltd. for quotations from Jacques Maritain's *Preface to Metaphysics* and *Art and Scholasticism*; to Pantheon Books Inc. for quotations from Jacques Maritain's *Existence and the Existent*; to Cornell University Press for quotations from *The New Science of Giambattista Vico*, translated by T. G. Bergin and M. H. Fisch; to the editors of *The Hudson Review* for permission to quote from Felix Giovanelli's translation of " James Joyce: A Memoir ", by Stanislaus Joyce; and to John Lane The Bodley Head for permission to quote Joyce's translation of Verlaine's " Chanson d'Automne ", which was published in Herbert Gorman's biography *James Joyce*.

HUGH KENNER

Santa Barbara College,
Santa Barbara, California

SCHEME OF REFERENCES

A letter followed by two numbers is a page reference to the standard American and English editions of one of Joyce's books. Thus U 51/47 means that the quotation appears on page 51 of the Modern Library edition and on page 47 of the Bodley Head edition of *Ulysses*. References to *Finnegans Wake* carry only one number since the pagination of both editions of that book is identical. The standard editions are as follows:

TITLE OF WORK AND REFERENCE LETTER	AMERICAN EDITION PUBLISHED BY:	ENGLISH EDITION PUBLISHED BY:
D: *Dubliners*	Modern Library	Jonathan Cape
E: *Exiles*	New Directions	Jonathan Cape
F: *Finnegans Wake*	Viking Press	Faber and Faber
P: *A Portrait of the Artist as a Young Man*	Modern Library	Jonathan Cape
S: *Stephen Hero*	New Directions	Jonathan Cape
U: *Ulysses*	Modern Library	John Lane The Bodley Head

Chamber Music is published in the United Kingdom by Jonathan Cape, and is to be found in the United States in Joyce's *Collected Poems*, published by the Viking Press.

" Gilbert " refers to Stuart Gilbert's *James Joyce's " Ulysses "* (Knopf, N.Y., and Faber and Faber, London).

" Gorman " refers to Herbert Gorman's biography, *James Joyce* (Farrar and Rinehart, N.Y., and John Lane The Bodley Head, London).

" Budgen " refers to Frank Budgen's *James Joyce and the Making of Ulysses* (Grayson and Grayson, London).

" Givens " refers to *James Joyce: Two Decades of Criticism*, edited by Seon Givens (Vanguard Press, N.Y.).

CONTENTS

PROLOGUE   Shaking hands with the Corpse   *page* 1

PART ONE *Icarus*

1   Double Writing   7
2   The Unquiet Father   19
3   The Anatomy of " Love "   27
4   Dedalus Abolished   36
5   Dubliners   48
6   Exiles   69
7   Return to Lyric   95

PART TWO *Odysseus*

8   The *Portrait* in Perspective   109
9   The School of Old Aquinas   134
10   Baker Street to Eccles Street   158
11   Homer and Hamlet   179
12   How to Read *Ulysses*   198
13   The Trivium in Dublin   214
14   The Plan of *Ulysses*   225

PART THREE *The Dream of the West*

15   The Stuffed Phoenix   265
16   Alice in Chapelizod   276
17   The Pale of Words   301
18   Vico and History   321
19   Three Dreams   337
20   Two Selves   354

EPILOGUE   Four Burials   371

This is the story of a man, one who was never at a loss. He had travelled far in the world, after the sack of Troy, the virgin fortress; he saw many cities of men, and learnt their mind; he endured many troubles and hardships in the struggle to save his own life and to bring back his men safe to their homes. He did his best, but he could not save his companions. For they perished by their own madness, because they killed and ate the cattle of Hyperion the Sun-god, and the god took care that they should never see home again.

> " *Sero, sero* . . .
> *Nothing we made, we set nothing in order,*
> *Neither house nor the carving,*
> *And what we thought had been thought for too long;*
> *Our opinion not opinion in evil*
> *But opinion borne for too long.*
> *We have gathered a sieve full of water.*"

Prologue

SHAKING HANDS WITH THE CORPSE

...the errears and erroriboose of combarative embottled
history....

Finnegans Wake (F140)

...Even facial characteristics may be distinguished, and most
visitors are particularly impressed by the well-preserved features
of " The Nun ", whose corpse is said to be three hundred
years old. Even more interesting is the corpse of " The
Crusader ", which lies alongside the former. The leather-like
hands of the Crusader have become shiny from the custom,
which most visitors honour, of " shaking hands " with the
corpse.

Dublin Guide-Book

In Dublin guidebooks tourists are directed to " the largest
brewery in the world ". Most Dubliners will guide the
stranger to their city and its past through the open door of a
public house. There talk and alcohol preserve the Seventh
City in Christendom, Dublin a European capital for two thousand years, Dublin which had its present charter from Henry
II, Dublin to which Handel, whom Johnson's London dis-
appointed, presented his *Messiah* " to offer this generous and
polished nation something new ". Within memory of the
bartender's father, the descent of the Irish Kings from Adam
and of their language from the unbabelized true names of the
creatures in Eden was written out, with tables, in a thick green
volume by a pious citizen. Someone remembers his book. He
sent a copy to Queen Victoria, whose secretary acknowledged
it. Within a mile the Dane dwelt who discovered Florida a
thousand years ago and called it " Greater Ireland ". The
soda-water dashed into a stranger's whiskey is bottled from a
miraculous healing spring called forth from the rock by St
Patrick. The locutions of barflies echo the aristocratic gestures
of eighteenth-century Europe. There, turns of phrase remind
us, Jonathan Swift preached and Edmund Burke inquired into
the Sublime and the Beautiful, and Bishop Berkeley refuted
the visible world. Their names are bywords. Oral tradition,
lubricated by gin, preserves the ballads of half a dozen

I

rebellions, the exploits of Buck Whaley who played ball against the walls of Jerusalem, the dying words of Emmett, the proud eye of Parnell. Juxtaposed in a brewer's poster on the wall, Georgian façades line the Liffey in pillared elegance and " The Smiling Face of Dublin's Fair City " beams at the tourist out of the winking foam on a glass of Guinness's stout.

In the street outside, one may hire a Ford, bet on a horse, or buy an American novel. Swift, the pilgrim discovers, has dwindled to a tomb and bust in St. Patrick's and a watch, escritoire and snuff-box displayed in the mental hospital he founded. Tom Moore's birthplace is denoted by a memorial tablet. In this house Sheridan was born; in this house Burke was born; in this house the Duke of Wellington was born. Their fame is English now. Here Daniel O'Connell is buried; here Parnell. Dublin still claims certain graves. Here stood a house where Shelley lived. This square was " once a fashionable residential quarter "; these Assembly Rooms " were the scene of many a fashionable gathering in the colourful eighteenth century ". Here Swift went mad. Here Emmett was hanged. Here *The Countess Cathleen* was hissed. The streets are thronged with vacant urban faces. " Peculiar dessicating qualities in the atmosphere " are credited with preserving down the centuries the corpses in the vault at St. Michan's. " Symbolic of the country's cultural connections with the outside world," a granite boulder with Mediterranean stone-age markings stands at the entrance to the National Museum.

Since the eighteenth century it has been a city of the dead, a person set down in Dublin might reflect. Talk flows on with the Liffey; preserved in its own cadence Berkeley's age, wavering and inverted, stands still in that river's flow. The Liffey, churned by tugs and barges, mirrors shakily swans and Augustan domes—the Customs House and the Four Courts of the judicature which an atavistic chivalry carefully restored after first demolishing them in the fighting of 1921. A lazy tide washes squared stones at the sea-wall.

Through other countries other rivers flowed, bearing away all the past that floats; submerging the rest to be peered at by men averted from factories on the banks who saw down through the waters a cloud, a skylark, a topsy-turvy world for Alice among the debris. Only Dublin had kept its past above the waters; evading the cataclysmic mutation of the Romantic revolt, it had chosen to preserve its form rather than its life. And a man born into that Dublin, exhorted to admire the image of old buildings in the stream, might seek instead to seize the once-living City. Quickened by bar-room voices and enraged by the drinkers' opacity, aroused by the civic traditions and exasperated by their street-walking ghosts, loving his city's leisure and hating the lethargy of the living who cut him off from life, such a man—James Joyce, over fifty years ago, at the pivot of an age—would find himself simultaneously citizen and exile.

The Dublin from which he was exiled, even while he felt its stones beneath his feet, was the paralysed form of the historic City. The Dublin of which he proudly knew himself citizen lay in, behind, around, beneath those stones: *there*, not elsewhere. Its abstracted soul existed in schoolbooks. The *Ratio Studiorum* of St. Ignatius governed Joyce's education. Aristotle's *Ethics* and *Politics*, the *Summa* of St. Thomas Aquinas, the intertwined disciplines of grammar, logic, and rhetoric, trivium and quadrivium, came to him through the musty rote of anachronistic classrooms, solid as they had been when they informed the mind of Europe, realities of the mind evading their jailers the school-masters. He reached for the Philosopher's solid, the rock: τό τι ἐν εἶναι.

The solid was all around him, in Dublin, as nowhere else in Europe. Its voice had rusted, lute and madrigal. Dusty pianos in curtained parlours thudded and tingled beneath olcographs of an obtruded Sacred Heart, *La ci darem* sung by a town buck and a whore, the chamber music of a tinkling pot. Full and clear through this depravity, his father's fine tenor voice, a lost grace shadowed in his father's rich phrasing, reached and stirred Joyce's mind.

Young men write lyrics; Joyce wrote lyrics. His lyric expression dwelt on the symbols of passion he knew, the yellow keys, inclined heads, pale brows and sad farewells of Dublin's love-songs. They were marshalled, however, by a sense of order corresponding to something he did not then see in Dublin: a lost precision of phrase and rhythm drawn from Ben Jonson, a disciplined allotrope of the dim resonant parlour sensibility drawn from Verlaine. Years later he was to see clearly how truly Symbolist France and an older England met in the scene before him. In the first years of his young manhood, however, the function of lyric writing was to draw off as they accumulated the emotional potentials of adolescence, keep his creative daemon occupied, and so deflect the impulse to tamper busily with what he heard as he listened with a fascination he could not explain to the endless talk of Dublin.

PART ONE

Icarus

Phall if you but will, rise you must:
and none so soon either shall the pharce for the
nunce come to a setdown secular phoenish

★

Chapter 1

DOUBLE WRITING

Willy-nilly we are all living inside Joyce's head.... There is a
sort of nightmare quality about not being able to get out of
literature however hard we try.

Letter from a Dublin friend

PEOPLE talking:
- But did you see Miss Bergin?
- O, I saw her . . . with a black and white boa.
- And the two Miss Kennedys were there.
- Where?
- Right behind the Archbishop's throne.
- O, I saw her—one of them.   Hadn't she a grey hat with a bird
in it?
- That was her!   She's very lady-like, isn't she.   S74/62.

Nothing there: gossip, question, response, vacuity; not even
an irony in the application of "lady-like".   Man is distinguished from the brutes by speech, and speech like this
surrounds the citizen from birth.

As a small boy James Joyce strained his imagination after
secret connections between real things and the vocables his
Dublin so prodigally disbursed.   "That was not a nice
expression", P4/9;   "Suck was a queer word", P6/12;
"How could a woman be a tower of ivory or a house of gold?",
P36/40.   The college freshman did not relax this quest:

He read Skeat's *Etymological Dictionary* by the hour and his mind,
which had from the first been only too submissive to the infant
sense of wonder, was often hypnotized by the most commonplace
conversation.   People seemed to him strangely ignorant of the value of
the words they used so glibly.   S26/20.

But there were more deliberate kinds of talk in Dublin:

" Pope Leo, you know, was a great scholar and a poet."
" He had a strong face," said Mr. Kernan.
" Yes," said Mr. Cunningham.   " He wrote Latin poetry."
" Is that so? " said Mr. Fogarty.
Mr. M'Coy tasted his whisky contentedly and shook his head with
a double intention, saying:

7

" That's no joke, I can tell you.". . .

" I remember reading," said Mr. Cunningham, " that one of
Pope Leo's poems was on the invention of the photograph—in Latin,
of course."

" On the photograph! " exclaimed Mr. Kernan.

" Yes," said Mr. Cunningham.

He also drank from his glass.

" Well, you know," said Mr. M'Coy, " isn't the photograph
wonderful when you come to think of it? "

" O, of course," said Mr. Power, " great minds can see things."

" As the poet says: *Great minds are very near to madness*," said
Mr. Fogarty. D213/189.

This isn't nullity like the students' babble, though the grasp
of the subject is still null enough. Words are being chosen,
thought is being directed. The words are words that have a
conventional affinity for each other: *great scholar and poet;
Latin poetry no joke; strong face; photograph wonderful when you
come to think of it; great minds near madness.* The speakers
are manipulating clichés, but they are speaking deliberately,
with a sense of discovering new provinces of thought. Their
minds are at the stretch. Yet they can speak only in quotations,
and despite their consciousness of effort, their thought
runs in grooves. Any two Dubliners are Bouvard and
Pécuchet.

The circumambient language doesn't serve the citizen's
thought but directs it. He inherits locutions that were once
alive, and shapes his mental processes accordingly. Here is
Thomas Chandler meditating a poetic career:

His temperament might be said to be just on the point of maturity.
There were so many different moods and impressions that he wished
to express in verse. He felt them within him. He tried to weigh
his soul to see if it was a poet's soul. Melancholy was the dominant
note of his temperament, he thought, but it was a melancholy tempered
by recurrences of faith and resignation and simple joy. If he could
give expression to it in a book of poems perhaps men would listen.
He would never be popular: he saw that. He could not sway the
crowd but he might appeal to a little circle of kindred minds. The
English critics, perhaps, would recognize him as one of the Celtic
school by reason of the melancholy tone of his poems; besides that
he would put in allusions. He began to invent sentences and phrases
from the notice which his book would get. " *Mr. Chandler has the
gift of easy and graceful verse.*" . . . " *A wistful sadness pervades these
poems.*". . . " *The Celtic note.*" D90/80.

Not just the last phrases, but every phrase that passes through Chandler's mind, from " temperament on the point of maturity " to " the Celtic note ", is reviewers' jargon; quotation is as close to reality as he gets. Yet it was jargon that had a meaning before the reviewers got hold of it. It contains shreds of meaning still. And Chandler is no contemptible gull; he has really felt some wordless emotion stirring within him, and his melancholy is genuine, and he is seriously meditating a career.

Such was Joyce's material: the language of Dublin. Every Dublin phrase has a double focus: the past meaning it locks away, the present vagueness it shapes. It is in language that the dead city is preserved; and it is language that maintains the citizens in deadness. What the Dubliners do is of no special interest; they drink, and walk, and couple. But when they talk to their women the idealized donnas of Europe haunt their locutions, for they have no other locutions for love (" the sun shines on you he said ", U767/741); when they talk in the streets they conjure up the traditions of peripatetic wisdom; when they talk at bars the swagger of a vanished age lights up among the words:

– Their syphilization, you mean, says the citizen. To hell with them! The curse of a goodfornothing God light sideways on the bloody thicklugged sons of whores' gets! No music and no art and no literature worthy of the name. Any civilization they have they stole from us. Tonguetied sons of bastards' ghosts.
– The European family, says J.J. . . .
– They're not European, says the citizen. I was in Europe with Kevin Egan of Paris. You wouldn't see a trace of them or their language anywhere in Europe except in a *cabinet d'aisance*.
And says John Wyse:
– Full many a flower is born to blush unseen.
And says Lenehan that knows a bit of the lingo:
– *Conspuez les Anglais! Perfide Albion!*
He said and then lifted he in his rude great brawny strengthy hands the medher of dark strong foamy ale and, uttering his tribal slogan *Lamh Dearg Abu*, he drank to the undoing of his foes, a race of mighty valorous heroes, rulers of the waves, who sit on thrones of alabaster silent as the deathless gods. U319/309.

The parody of *Ur*-Celtic heroics establishes the exact coordinates of the preceding conversation; the citizen *is* striking an archaic pose, since his mind is shaped by Gaelic League propa-

ganda. He speaks the language that is given him, and entertains the corresponding ideas. No Dubliner acts from his
nature, no Dubliner knows what his nature is; he acts on the
promptings of *idées reçues* and talks in words that have for too
long been respoken. Yet the words and actions can partake of
a passion it would be difficult to call factitious; human spirits
are imprisoned in these husks. Cadence and image crackle
with continual racy unexpectedness, though phrase and action
are drearily conventional.

Confronted by a French provincial society which a similar
decay had overtaken, Flaubert made huge catalogues of
" Opinions chic ":

ACTRICES: La perte des fils de famille.—Sont d'une lubricité
effrayante, se livrent à des orgies, avalent des millions (finissent
à l'hôpital).—Pardon! il y en a qui sont bonnes mères de famille!

ARCHIMÈDE: Dire à son nom: " Eurêka ".—" Donnez-moi un
point d'appui et je soulèverai le monde.". . . .

LUNE: Inspire la mélancolie.—Est peut-être habitée?

MATHÉMATIQUES: Dessèchent le coeur.

MÉLANCOLIE: Signe de distinction du coeur et de l'élévation de
l'esprit.

PYRAMIDE: Ouvrage inutile.

Joyce made similar collections. We hear of a young man's
notebook entitled " Memorabilia ", of phrases gleaned from
newspapers and novels (" Matcham often thinks of the master-
stroke by which he won the laughing witch who now . . .",
U68/62), of lightning jottings from scraps of conversation
being classified and filed in brown paper envelopes by the
trunkful. He saw, however, more deeply into their meaning
than did Flaubert. Flaubert, nauseated by *la bêtise*, catalogued
intellectual junk in a kind of ecstasy of disgust, contemplating
a society of empty dolls conducting their lives in clichés.
Dublin was less dessicated and Joyce was more humane; he
was interested in clichés for their verve as locutions, not their
nullity as doctrines. By the time Flaubert had gotten to
Bouvard et Pécuchet he was concerned to prove a general
thesis about the limits of human knowledge: " Oui, la bêtise
consiste à vouloir conclure. Nous sommes un fil et nous
voulons savoir la trame." But when Joyce makes Bloom
suddenly ask, " Do fish ever get seasick? " we are in the
presence not of an exercise in nineteenth-century pessimism but
of a tribute to the unpredictable creative leaps of the human soul.

Joyce's Dublin was in fact an eighteenth-century parody. The technique he developed, the technique which underlies everything from the first pages of *Dubliners* to the end of *Finnegans Wake*, came out of the subject: parody: double-writing. The music-halls parodied the heroic dramas; Joyce parodied the music-halls. Journalism parodied heroic elegance: Joyce parodied journalism. He focussed, that is to say, on what was actually there, and strove so to set it down that it would reveal itself as what it was, in its double nature: a distortion, but a distortion of something real. All his characters are walking clichés, because the Dubliners were; a Leopold Bloom is simultaneously a " case " and a person. All his dialogue is an assemblage of *locutions reçues* into unexpected patterns: unexpected because he was dealing with human beings, whose natural spontaneity the past could not quite batten down:

> – Grandest number in the whole opera, Goulding said.
> – It is, Bloom said.
> Numbers it is. All music when you come to think. Two multiplied by two divided by half is twice one. Vibrations: chords those are. One plus two plus six is seven. Do anything you like with figures juggling. Always find out this equal to that, symmetry under a cemetery wall. . . . Musemathematics. And you think you're listening to the ethereal. But suppose you said it like: Martha, seven times nine minus *x* is thirty-five thousand. Fall quite flat. It's on account of the sounds it is.
> Instance he's playing now. Improvising. Might be what you like till you hear the words. Want to listen sharp. Hard. Begin all right, then hear chords a bit off: feel lost a bit. In and out of sacks over barrels, through wirefences, obstacle race. U273/264.

The items are commonplace but the configurations are, if explicable, unpredictable. There is a weird creativeness— Aristotle's perception of similarities in dissimilars—in the rhythms with which this caged mind rattles its prison-bars, flashing from numbers to obstacle-races while musing over school-science commonplaces about sound, Pythagoras hovering somewhere in the background.

Pythagoras, in this eighteenth-century fossil city, is only just out of Mr. Bloom's reach: Dublin lower-middle-class conversation is strikingly aware, as it picks its words, of a cultural heritage. That is why the clichés he listened to didn't drive Joyce to despair as those of Rouen and Paris drove

Flaubert. In Dublin words, even dead words, are consciously used. Parasites and travelling salesmen drop polysyllables into place with an air. A tea-taster in *Ulysses* produces " trenchant " and " retrospective ", U90/83, at every opportunity, U237/228. " That takes the solitary, unique, and if I may so call it, *recherché* biscuit ", cries a barfly to a lecher, D59/53. " Very cool and mollifying ", says Uncle Charles of his outrageous tobacco, conceding that to smoke it in the outhouse will be " more salubrious ", P65/67. Joyce was hardly more word-conscious than his characters were. So the usual criterion of style, that it disappear like glass before the reality of the subject, doesn't apply to his pages. The language of Dublin *is* the subject; his books are about words, the complexity is there, in the way people talk, and Joyce copes with it by making it impossible for us to ignore the word on the page. The distinction and falseness of Dublin are alike comprehended in its musty concern for the simulacrum, the metaphor, the word " hung with pleasing wraiths of former masteries ",[1] the thing not seen but refracted " through the prism of a language manycoloured and richly storied ", P194/190. So Joyce embalms in cadences what Dublin embalms in music, and entraps in the amber of learned multiple puns the futile vigour which the Dubliner, gazing into his peat-coloured Guinness, must generate in language because its counterpart has slipped out of life.

That is why Joyce has many voices but no " style ", as T. S. Eliot discerned long ago.[2] The " scrupulous meanness " of *Dubliners* came out of the subject, not the author. In *Ulysses* he has a voice for every episode, in *Finnegans Wake* a voice for every phrase, and they are all Dublin voices.

As his city pivoted on language, so did Joyce's education. If his city was an eighteenth-century time-capsule, the Jesuit schools were mediaeval survivals. Through them the intellectual disciplines radiating from the classical trivium, grammar, logic, and rhetoric, came alive in Joyce while dead in Dublin and abolished everywhere else. " Some of the means I use are trivial ", he remarked to a friend, " and some are quadrivial." Guided by the classical studies for which his Jesuit schoolmasters gave him the orientations if not the insight, he scrutin-

---

[1] William Carlos Williams.

[2] T. S. Eliot, " Lettre d'Angleterre: Le Style dans la Prose Anglaise Contemporaine," *La Nouvelle Revue Française*, xix, July–December 1922, 751–6.

ized talk as the old rhetoricians did, intent on systematizing its gestures into miniature dramatic situations. Cicero, in pedagogical tradition the father of rhetoric, puts every figure in a forensic context;[1] these dramatic configurations (". . . certain attitudes, or I might say gestures of language "— Quintilian, IX. i. 13) emerge from even the baldest Renaissance codifications, like Puttenham's " the disabler " (*Meiosis*), " the broad floute " (*Antiphrasis*) or " the fleering frumpe " (*Mycterismus*). The symbolists rediscovered this principle; Paul Valery tells us how " a literary *langue mandarine* is derived from popular speech, from which it takes the words, figures, and ' turns ' most suitable for the effects the artist seeks ", and effects juxtapositions, contrasts, contractions or substitutions " which excite the mind to produce more vivid imitations than those sufficient for understanding ordinary language. That is the domain of ancient Rhetoric's ' figures ', today regrettably abandoned. . . ."[2]

As the scope of Dublin's double-talk grew clearer to him, as its European roots were more and more exposed, Joyce made his prose increasingly patterned and artificial, transferred more and more energy out of the subject onto the page. But the artificiality is there from the beginning; we always see the language, we never quite see the object. Even in the early short stories everything is scrupulously overwritten, to mirror Dublin's brushed and curried elegance in a faded patent-leather prose that never quite recedes from the reader's attention:

> Every morning, therefore, uncle Charles repaired to his outhouse but not before he had creased and brushed scrupulously his black hair and brushed and put on his tall hat. . . . His arbour, as he called the reeking outhouse which he shared with the cat and the garden tools, served him also as a soundingbox: and every morning he hummed contentedly one of his favourite songs. . . . P65/67.

The studied awkwardness in the phrasing of this is deliberate; it is a careful pastiche of the humble works of fiction whose mode of consciousness is continuous with that of Uncle Charles' world. Uncle Charles *repairs* to the outhouse because in that sort of book people do *repair* to places; and that sort of book is relevant because in Uncle Charles' Dublin people have that sort of writer's conception of elegance.

[1] Cicero, *Orator*, xxix, 134 sqq.
[2] *Variété* III, 28; V, 290.

People do things in *Dubliners*, but their reasons for what they do are obscured among cadences: obscured, that is, from themselves. The plots of these stories are unexpectedly difficult to paraphrase intelligibly. One can put down what happens, but the motivation of the characters is elusive. On inspecting the stories we find that each phase of action is infallibly preceded by passages of introspection or exhortation whose connection with the action is profound but seldom logical. In " The Dead " a consumptive boy is said to have died for love; what really moved him to stand shivering in the rain is as blurred for the reader as it was for him. " But he said he did not want to live ", D285/253—there is no probing behind such words; nothing *is* behind them but an inarticulate emotion that forced itself into a received phrase and a corresponding gesture, and so doomed him. He is like the people in Dr. Williams' *Paterson* who perish because the language fails them. In " A Painful Case " Mr. Duffy repudiates Mrs. Sinico when she tries to translate discussion into passion by pressing his hand; but the reason for his repudiation is hidden among the verbal formulas, centrifugal Hauptmann and warmed-over Nietzsche, by which Mr. Duffy lives; and two months' meditation on the event yields only a new gnomic formula for his notebook.

Because words so govern actions, rhetoric was studied for eighteen hundred years in close association with moral philosophy, and Cicero's ideal orator, the ideal of princes and churchmen, was an educational model for centuries. He was not a Gongorist but a public figure, a ruler, an organizer of popular thoughts and feelings. By his command of language, he simultaneously educed order from Babel, and imposed it. There still existed in Dublin a civilization corresponding, though inertly, to this respect for the orator which Joyce received from his schoolmasters. The civic sense has not perished from a nation that cherishes eloquence, and Joyce's Dublin was full of connoisseurs. This is one more way in which the past feebly lived, and one more sense in which Dublin remained a city, *civitas*, not a suburban agglomeration. No such impressive *peripeteia* as the work of Wordsworth exemplifies in England had obliterated the very assumptions on which Swift, Burke, and the eighteenth-century divines had worked. These men, as every reader of *Ulysses* can testify, were still thought of in Dublin as high water marks of an

unsuperseded culture, and the mediocrity of nineteenth-century
writers and speakers (when it was noticed) was regarded as a
decay of rather than a challenge to their standards.

> – They're only in the hook and eye department, Myles Crawford
> said. Psha! Press and the bar! Where have you a man now at the
> bar like those fellows, like Whiteside, like Isaac Butt, like silver-
> tongued O'Hagan? Eh? . . .
> . . . Why not bring in Henry Grattan and Flood and Demosthenes
> and Edmund Burke? . . . U136/129.

One needn't ask what Demosthenes is doing in that sentence;
Joyce's newspaper office is in fact the scene of genuine connois-
seurship of eloquence.   It isn't meaningful to separate the fact
that these traditions were dead from the fact that they were
there. J. J. O'Molloy recalling an intricate forensic period by
Seymour Bushe, or Professor MacHugh reciting " as well as I
can bring them to mind " Taylor's powerful words on the
language of the outlaw, manifest a conception of public life
and a relish for the organization of words which however
tawdry suffices to unite the Dublin of Tim Healy with the
Rome of Cicero and the Christian West.   And O'Molloy's
quotation enunciates what it illustrates:

> that stone effigy in frozen music, horned and terrible, of the human
> form divine, that eternal symbol of wisdom and prophecy. . . .

The divine analogy in the human form is located in the gift of
speech, which traditionally differentiates men from beasts;
but Bushe and O'Molloy are innocently evoking the Moses
of Michaelangelo, epiphany par excellence of stone imprison-
ing struggling life.   " Stony effigies in frozen music " hits off
exactly these exercises in baroque oratorical impressiveness:

> Here the stone images
> Are raised, here they receive
> The supplication of a dead man's hand.

And Stephen's sudden memory of St. Augustine,

> It was revealed to me that those things are good which yet are
> corrupted which neither if they were supremely good nor unless they
> were good could be corrupted. U140/132.

warns us how we are to take the cultural implications of the
entire " Aeolus " episode.

There was still in Joyce's youth a powerful tradition of
public oratory, ecclesiastical, political, and forensic.   The Irish

public man was regarded, like Agamemnon, Parnell's analogue
in *Ulysses*, as both a *doctus orator* and a tragic hero.   There was
also, diffused among dead-beats, an almost eighteenth-century
awareness of classical instances.   A bar-fly like Lenehan recalls
the way Pyrrhus died accurately enough to make a joke about
it, U132/124.   MacHugh's mention of the Athenian fleets at
Aegospotami strikes no one as being out of context.   Joyce, as
the Stuart Gilbert commentary illustrates at length, wove into
the " Aeolus " episode set examples of every type of oratory
and a whole lexicon of figures and tropes: testimony not only
to his sardonic awareness that the epic properly embraces
every province of rhetoric, but also to his keen understanding
of his Dublin.   His way of indicating the dismembered
presence of something was always to strew the text with its
parts.   In no episode, despite the learned façade, is the material
more studiously low.   The feeble wit and self-conscious gibes
of the protagonists (" Muchibus thankibus "), the relation of
political oratory to daily journalism (" A newsboy cried in
Mr. Bloom's face:—Terrible tragedy in Rathmines!   A child
bit by a bellows! "), the faded eloquence on which this virtuosity is lavished (" a finished orator, full of courteous haughti-
ness and pouring in chastened diction, I will not say the vials
of his wrath but pouring the proud man's contumely. . . .")
illustrate the decorums of the whole book, an articulation of the
city of the dead.

There is no directness in Dublin; no Parnell now acts out
of middle-heart; the great orators are dead, the live ones
degraded.   Every phase of thought and action has a received
analogue or a bookish correspondence.   So Joyce's task was to
take account of the patterns that lie just outside of the corporeal
citizen and his empirical city.   He solved it by being as indirect
as they, coming at them by way of their analogues, parodying
the models according to which they behaved, his attention
focussed on the invisible point of coincidence between half-
living people and half-real literature, opera, oratory, and
music.

He started always from the material nearest to hand.   He
was interested in bad operas because they contained all the
dramatic components listed by Aristotle, still held in some sort
of classical balance, but imaging the soul of Dublin as the
Oresteia had imaged that of Athens.   He was interested in
Mme. Blavatsky, AE, and the " opal hush " poets because

they preserved umbilical connections with the great allegorical traditions of symbolic grammar, which the French symbolists were engaged in recovering. (It is no accident that Yeats was concurrently interested in Blavatsky and Mallarmé). He was interested in advertising and journalism because they both were and were not aligned with classical rhetoric. He was interested in Leopold Bloom because nothing was in that philosopher's intellect that had not first been in his senses, though not exactly as St. Thomas stipulated.

So in presenting a Dublin aesthete—Stephen Dedalus—Joyce parodies Walter Pater (" Where was the soul that had hung back from her destiny, to brood alone upon the shame of her wounds and in her house of squalor and subterfuge to queen it in faded cerements and in wreathes that withered at the touch? ", P198/194) ; in presenting a Dublin dandy he parodies Oscar Wilde (" The plump shadowed face and sullen jowl recalled a prelate, patron of arts in the middle ages. A pleasant smile broke quietly over his lips ", U5/1—Wilde was a faker, and here the falsifying word is " quietly "); in presenting a Dublin *accouchement* he parodies Dickens (" Reverently look at her as she reclines there with the motherlight in her eyes. . . .", U413/402). By the time of his mature work Joyce's realization that his subject was language, the protean empty language of the dead city, had so deepened that the reader is at first conscious of little but words and cadences embalmed:

> Methought as I was dropping asleep somepart in nonland of where's please (and it was when you and they were we) I heard at zero hour as 'twere the peal of vixen's laughter among midnight's chimes from out the belfry of the cute old speckled church tolling so faint a good-mantrue as nighthood's unseen violet rendered all animated great-british and Irish objects nonviewable to human watchers save 'twere perhaps anon some glistery gleam. . . . F403.

This is still parody; the rhythms and phrases come from nineteenth-century Irish fiction (cf. Le Fanu's *Old House by the Churchyard*); but no cautious *trompe l'œil* is any longer in question; we are not for a moment tempted to suppose that we ought to be seeing a subject through a style; what is on the page is quite frankly the subject. The subject is " style " and what style implies.

And what is behind the words we at first see has also gotten onto the page; in *Finnegans Wake* the technique of double-writing is so perfected as to keep the reader's attention constantly on what is never quite real, never so real as to have an unequivocal name; on things that exist only at the suggestion of words, meals of " riceplummy padding . . . and some cold forsoaken steak peatrefired from the batblack night o'erflown ", F405 (Tennyson's *Maud:* " the black bat, Night, has flown "), bottles overflowing with " catharic emulsipotion " when " the pop gave his sullen bulletaction ", F310, a hero who exists only by the copresence of three initials, " Mookses " compounded of moocows, foxes, and mock turtles snapping at " Gripes " (grapes crossed with griffins), and maxims of conduct as inscrutably reasonable as " Goat to the Endth[n^{th}], thou slowguard ", " Practise preaching ", and " Love my label like myself ", F579.

> – Which was said by whem to whom?
> – It wham. But whim I can't whumember.
> – Fantasy! funtasy on fantasy, amnaes fintasies! And there is nihil nuder under the clothing moon. F493.

Double-writing, in Joyce's last work, becomes *n*-dimensional, and reality is monopolized by the precise but inscrutable products of crossbred words, semantic spooks as necessary and as puzzling as *pi* and the root of minus one, peopling a coherent world that isn't there but that speaks with a Dublin accent. Joyce had suspected as a child, and known as a young man that Dublin's civic reality was contained in its language alone; and through book after book had winnowed that truth until in *Finnegans Wake* he could project in language the generic Dubliner's image: a cataleptic dreaming of the waking world, all his reality a dream and a dream made out of words, the stones of Dublin, its smells, its sunlight, everything but its language taken away.

Chapter 2

THE UNQUIET FATHER

...so through the ghost of the unquiet father the image of the unliving son looks forth....

Ulysses (U192/183)

" Jimmy Joyce's father, madam? He was a BOUNDER."

Belvedere College priest, to enquiring pilgrim

THE showpiece of James Joyce's central technique—parody of the once vital to enact a null apprehension of the null—is the fourteenth episode of *Ulysses*, the section given over to the murder of the Oxen of the Sun, the one crime from whose consequences Odysseus could not save his men. Joyce explained that the section was about " the crime committed against fertility by sterilizing the act of coition ". This matches what paraphrase seems to yield. A child is being born in a lying-in hospital. A lightning-flash of conception, U379/368, is followed by forty paragraphs in pastiche of chronologically successive styles, to parallel the forty weeks of gestation; and there is one reference to " those Godpossibled souls that we nightly impossibilise ", U385/372. What actually happens during the episode, however, is interminably eloquent empty tavern-talk in a hospital ante-room, and the nullity that after so many thousand words of contorted evolution gets born and cast out into the void of Dublin is the civilization of nineteenth-century Ireland, a rabble of gesticulating students rushing for a pub named, ironically, " Burke's ". " Coition ", as Joyce is exploiting it in these pages, is the basic Aristotelian and Aquinatian metaphor for the intercourse between the mind and things.

It was a classroom commonplace of his Jesuit schooling that the phantasm gathered by the senses fertilizes the active intellect, and a concept is generated and flung in affirmation out into existence. The word " conception " unites biology and epistemology. We start with sensory beguilements, whether in begetting or in cognizing; we end with an articulated concept, a begotten Logos, word; an affirmation that this

19

or that exists: *is*, is irreducibly there, ineluctable. Things *are* before we known them, that is the first condition; they doubly *are* after they are known, that is the second. The mind is nourished and impregnated by things, the mind affirms the existence of things, the mind by thousands of successive acts of conception generates an intellected order in more or less exact analogy of the intelligible order with which it copulates. It builds a hierarchic city of the known. The verb " to be " is a copula in every sense. " First came the seen, then thus the palpable." Words flourish in the soil of known things. The civilization in which the act of coition has been sterilized shuffles its hoarded phantasms and generates nothing.

The schools of such a civilization conserve a museum of modes of apprehension which they describe as " prose styles ". These are studied and emulated. Nothing is easier than to appear to be writing by the simple manipulation of these husks. Hence the crepitant deadness of the parodies in " The Oxen of the Sun ". They deploy themselves as, in the Dublin of 1904, they were known and taught. They are de Gourmont's " shells of thought "; opinion not opinion in evil, but opinion borne for too long. They are the masks of culture; " education " consists in memorizing their contours, " literacy " consists in strapping one on and speaking one's banalities through its orifice.

Joyce takes the greatest care to stage the episode in just these terms. The intellect is being slowly sterilized by drink ; at the close, language, its minimal props withdrawn, collapses into a babel of slang (" Your attention! We're nae tha fou. The Leith police dismisseth us. The least tholice.") and the disputants scramble through abysms of undiluted sensation : the pubs, followed by the stews (" Change here for Bawdy-house. We two, she said, will seek the kips where shady Mary is. Righto, any old time. *Laetabuntur in cubilibus suis.* You coming long? ") Nobody, from the time the company sits down to talk, places his mind, however inadequately, in touch with anything. The conversation is kept rolling by the mere gross stimulus-response of insult and banter (" Master Dixon of Mary in Eccles, goodly grinning, asked young Stephen what was the reason why he had not cided to take friar's vows and he answered him obedience in the womb, chastity in the tomb but involuntary poverty all his days ", U386/375) and by the rehearsal of received speculations (" Mr. Mulligan . . . expati-

ating on his design, told his hearers that he had been led into
this thought by a consideration of the causes of sterility, both
the inhibitory and the prohibitory, whether the inhibition in its
turn were due to conjugal vexations or to a parsimony of the
balance as well as whether the prohibition proceeded from
defects congenital or from proclivities acquired ", U395/384).
The abstraction and circumlocution of the language derives
from the fact that not a mind in the assemblage is in contact
with any but a sort of spectral colloquial reality. Their
meeting-ground is the *idée reçue*.

The ostensible prime event of the section, the birth of Mrs.
Purefoy's child, is simply alluded to by a succession of messengers. The only event registered on the consciousness of the
topers is a crack of thunder, the grossest stimulus of the
external world. The only response to it is neural.

> And [Costello] that had erst challenged to be so doughty waxed pale
> as they might all mark and shrank together and his pitch that was
> before so haught uplift was now of a sudden quite plucked down and
> his heart shook within the cage of his breast as he tasted the rumour
> of that storm. U388/377.

Costello has recourse to anodyne (" He drank indeed at one
draught to pluck up a heart of any grace for it thundered long
rumblingly over all the heavens "); the rest of the company
laugh it off (" Then did some mock and some jeer "); Madden
makes a hortatory gesture (" so that Master Madden, being
godly certain whiles, knocked him on his ribs upon that crack
of doom "); and Bloom, Odysseus of the ready word, seeks to
offer consolation by explaining the thunder away " advertising
how it was no other thing but a hubbub noise that he heard,
the discharge of fluid from the thunderhead, look you, having
taken place, and all of the order of a natural phenomenon."

There is the nineteenth century in epitome, the lotus-eaters
conducting their strategies of evasion, by anodyne (the poets,
passim); by sneer (Macaulay); by nudge (Carlyle); by
formularization (Huxley). The employment of one dead
rhetorical husk after another doesn't in the least jar against
" the general vacant hilarity of the assembly "; style and matter
are one, because the matter being treated is Dublin's dead style.

THE SINGING GHOST

In Dublin, however, this nineteenth-century floundering was

taking place within a structure of inherited thought and feeling by no means yet abolished as in England and elsewhere it had been abolished. The abolition is coming, and Mr. Leopold Bloom is there to prove it; nevertheless the tang of living speech still confers on Joyce's most elaborate stylizations the appropriateness of cadences not yet utterly obsolete. The mind of Victorian England, in Tennyson's Malory-and-suet articulation, is flaccid for want of that tang. There had been, earlier in the day *Ulysses* embalms, a reading of a piece of Victorian blather—" Or again, note the meanderings of some purling rill as it babbles on its way, fanned by gentlest zephyrs tho' quarrelling with the stony obstacles . . ."—not only empty but, unlike the " Oxen of the Sun " pastiches, as remote as Tennyson from any possible speech; and an instant critical comment from a mind contemporary with Swift's:

> Mr Dedalus, staring from the empty fireplace at Ned Lambert's quizzing face, asked of it sourly:
> – Agonizing Christ, wouldn't it give you a heartburn on your arse? U122/115.

In the Dublin Joyce knew Simon Dedalus still walks.

Simon Dedalus has a sense of style, his world is still in touch with spectral fashionable Dublin. His aristocratic swagger is not pseudo, as his son Stephen's tends to be; masculine gregariousness, as exhibited by him, is not yet pathological, a horror of being alone ; his wit proceeds from a critical alertness, a flexibility of response to social clichés, such as was preserved in contemporaneous England only in parts of Matthew Arnold's prose. And his wit, his aristocratic impulses, his sense of conversation as a function of leisure and conviviality, locate him, with Cunningham, O'Molloy, Ben Dollard, and other cronies and asymptotes, even Lenehan and Pisser Burke, in a twilight prolongation of the eighteenth-century world of Swift and Burke. It is from this world that the shapeless Bloom is excluded; its inhabitants talk about him rather than to him. The brisk idiomatic prose of its conversations is scrupulously differentiated from Bloom's ruminatory tone. With his cat, his statue of Narcissus, his uncontrollable wife, his love of cleanliness and coziness, Bloom is feminine to the culture of Dedalus père.

Yet Bloom, the bag of clichés, is not a cliché, and Simon Dedalus remains the dead man in a dead world. He is alert and witty, but he is not a rich figure; his liveliest *mots* fade from the memory. The great past is extant about him, at hand wherever he walks; his hand grasps it, and pulls it down as a windowshade against reality. The tide of the new century roars in the street. Simon wills to become a garrulous shade. In *Ulysses* he is part of the background; in the foreground, innocently embodying a new world he knows nothing about, is Leopold Bloom, who remains a good man.

THE APOTHEOSIS OF BLOOM

Irony is one-sided; it pushes the characters away from the author. Joyce's presentation of Bloom is far more than mere irony. He is " a good man ", yet his dreams educe the coming apocalypse of *muflisme:*

BLOOM

My beloved subjects, a new era is about to dawn. I, Bloom, tell you verily it is even now at hand. Yea, on the word of a Bloom, ye shall ere long enter into the golden city which is to be, the New Bloomusalem in the Nova Hibernia of the future. U475/461.

This apotheosis was, in 1904, perilously close; and Joyce stood between it and the intellectual order that had sustained Europe, in one way or another, since Pericles. If we want an English analogue for Joyce, it is Pope; their orientations and procedures are surprisingly similar. Pope is conscious of intellectual traditions running back through St. Augustine to Cicero and Homer; and the universal darkness that he predicted at the end of the *Dunciad* fell exactly as he foretold; the mind of Europe entered the Romantic night-world. Nearly two hundred years later, an analogous alarum was in order for Ireland; Ireland had simply undergone some two centuries' arrest on the very brink of the precipice, and Joyce's generation was hailing a suicidal forward stagger as progress.

Joyce, however, was in a position to do more than Pope. He was in touch with a civilization that had not smashed; and he was also in touch with one that had. He was Irish, and he wrote in English. He could maintain communications with the world of Swift, and write a language that had undergone the mutations of Shelley, Newman, and Pater. He could profit, furthermore, by the great labour of reconstitution performed in nineteenth-century France by Flaubert, Rimbaud, and Mallarmé. Yet he could see that if his own Dublin was

Swift's gone stagnant, Swift's was a façade over barbarism, and a façade inadequately conceived; and he could see that the Symbolists at their greatest were insulated from fact, absorbed in their perceiving selves, in decisive ways. His Stephen Dedalus, a Dublin Rimbaud, repudiates Simon the " consubstantial father " only to discover some wordless affinity with the yearning Bloom.

Imposter and yet aristocrat, Simon Dedalus, the witty singing ghost, embodies the double reality on which Joyce's double writing rests. It is no secret that he is modelled on the artist's father. It was through his father, whose portrait he would never be without, whose death he celebrated with deep emotion in the late poem " Ecce Puer " (" O father forsaken "), whose monument he ordered with endless pains (" No man could be worthy of such intense love as my father had for me "[1]), that Joyce came to his Dublin in book after book: " An imposing everybody he always indeed looked, constantly the same as and equal to himself and magnificently well worthy of any and all such universalization ", F32.

" The ghost of the unquiet father " who haunts the ninth episode of *Ulysses* is deeply engaged with Joyce's apprehension of the city. The backbone of the episode is an exegesis of *Hamlet* which identifies Shakespeare with the paternal ghost rather than with the son. The catastrophe of *Hamlet* depends on the slaughter of the father as that of the *Odyssey* turns on the slaughter of the sun-god's oxen. Sol and Pater are analogues (cf. *Le Roi Soleil*); both crimes offend reason, order, tradition, and civilization. Revenge is enjoined on Hamlet, who muffs it as Stephen Dedalus does for four acts and annihilates the entire court in the fifth. (" He lifts his ashplant high in both hands and smashes the chandelier. Time's livid final flame leaps and, in the following darkness, ruin of all space, shattered glass and toppling masonry." U567/550.) Stephen the romantic artist, *thanatos*, is Joyce without Joyce's sense of fact. Though his gesture in fact does no more than dent the brothel chandelier shade and break the lamp chimney, it is a gesture that makes for the night.

THE SIREN SONG

Ethos and *pathos*, the old rhetoricians' distinction between what is done and what is undergone, and between the doing and

[1] Joyce to Alf Bergan, August 5, 1932 (letter in Slocum collection).

suffering personality, elucidate both Joyce's Dublin, cracked mirror of the civic plenum in which the eloquent public man traditionally functioned, and Joyce's writing, conformed with scrupulous irony to the principles of classical rhetoric and psychology. The mode of his first prose work, *Dubliners*, is pathos; the characters suffer, they are pushed about by wives, employers, fashion and fate; they almost never act. In *Ulysses* it is a masculine civilization that is exhibited, of streets and pubs rather than, as in *Dubliners*, of shops and offices. But masculine culture in *Ulysses* is in process of relapse from ethos into pathos: the feminization toward habit and toward matter of the world of purposefulness, eloquence, and factive energies. The frustrations which *Dubliners* had revealed as endemic to Dublin are heaped upon Bloom, while a faded aristocratic elegance adheres to everyone in the book who is in touch with Stephen's " consubstantial father " Simon Dedalus.

Only once Bloom feels community with the Dedalus cluster, during the hour of singing in the Ormond tavern, at the very moment when, as he knows, he is being cuckolded in another part of town. The matrix of this pseudo-community is not ethos but pathos; music; a melting-down, a mingling at levels below the conscious. At the climax of Si Dedalus' singing of " Co-ome, thou lost one! Co-ome thou dear one! " the union of Leopold and Simon is consummated via the Lionel of the song:

> – *Come!* ...
> – *To me!*
> Siopold!
> Consumed. U271/262.

Merging with his absent wife, Bloom is violated by a voice; and in the conflux of emotion the two men who have in different ways lost their wives make passionate fusion, " under sleep, where all the waters meet ": Stephen's two fathers during song for an instant one.

"Co-ome, thou lost one! " is the Siren song, a voice from nowhere, from other days, from the rocks, the golden age of Dublin a tremor in the air, authority reduced to articulating the banal cadences of a derivative opera. All that remains of Goldsmith's Dublin is in that voice, which merely lures the contemporary of H. G. Wells further toward matter, habit, pathos, and the feminine. Since nostalgia is the sole comprehensive emotion now, integrity beckons to death.

When he sings Simon Dedalus' living death is at its richest and livest; when he sings he is most himself. Song is his point of contact with his opposite Bloom and with his son Stephen. When he sings he sums up his age. The cult of song epitomizes Dublin's abolition of the daylight world: Tom Moore followed on the heels of Swift. The murder of the Oxen of the Sun was being plotted in Swift's and Pope's day by the pedagogues and philosophers themselves;

> ... Since man from beast by Words is known,
> Words are Man's province, Words we teach alone. ...

Words, as the more " clear and distinct ", come before things; so Descartes had thought his world into existence. Words, not Language; the former for the Rationalist are atomized concepts, the latter is an untidy slough of sensate analogies. And the Cartesian ghost of metaphysics was soon laid, and the nineteenth-century night-world deepened, with its premium on dream-states and free association, its tap-roots into infant experience, its womb-like drawing-rooms and trance-like poems cluttered alike with diffusely symbolic objects: " Dust on a bowl of rose-leaves." The hypnotic rhythms of *Ode to a West Wind* and *Dolores*, the luscious adjectival evocativeness of " Now sleeps the crimson petal, now the white " and *Jabberwocky*, answer to a kind of consciousness for which Chaucer was philology, Shakespeare a vagrant portrait-painter, and *Eloisa to Abelard* an operatic essay at what the laureate brought off far better in *Lancelot and Elaine*.

" Once, in the dear dead days beyond recall. . . ." The psychic life of Dublin dropped below articulation. Hearts and voices throbbed, the sounding-boards of parlour pianos tingled; on waves of song Dublin was borne toward the hallucination of a lyrical past.

Chapter 3

THE ANATOMY OF " LOVE "

We now romp through a period of pure lyricism of shamebred music ... evidenced by such words in distress as *I cream for
thee, Sweet Margareen*, and the more hopeful *O Margareena!
O Margareena! Still in the bowl is left a lump of gold!*

Finnegans Wake (F164)

What was that One: arms of love that had not love's malignity,
laughter running upon the mountains of the morning, an hour
wherein might be encountered the incommunicable?

Stephen Hero (S37/30)

PIANO: Indispensable dans un salon.

Dict. des Idées Reçues

Joyce's Dublin submerged itself in song; its emotions were
blurred but intrinsic, not synthesized on discs of wax or in cans
of celluloid. The memory of his father festooning a " strange
sad happy air " with " tender tremors ", P99/100, or breaking
with " voice like a muffled flute " amid the soft lapping of the
tide by the sea-wall into fulsome strains:

> Shall carry my heart to thee
> Shall carry my heart to thee
> And the breath of the balmy night
> Shall carry my heart to thee S160/142

—blended in his mind into every aspect of the City in which
women read novelettes while children at play " entangled
themselves in pieces of wire-netting and coils of gas-pipes."
Song was the one art freely and knowingly discussed:

— It's a pretty old air, said Mr. Dedalus, twirling the points of his
moustache. Ah, but you should have heard Mick Lacy sing it!
Poor Mick Lacy! He had little turns for it, grace notes he used to
put in that I haven't got. He was the boy who could sing a *come-all-
you*, if you like. P99/100.

It was a discussion, however, that divided itself between the
praise of dead performers and the techniques of voice-produc-
tion; their aqueous emotional element the humming denizens

took for granted, flora, ooze, and eddies, as men take air for granted.

It was natural, then, when Joyce started writing verses, that the tenor voice sounding amid strings—

> Bid adieu, adieu, adieu,
> Bid adieu to girlish days,

—not the hieratic chant of the young Yeats, should control their rhythms and sounds. It was equally natural that he should strive for technical control of the one component Dublin took for granted, the exact emotional timbre of the poem. He had determined, at about eighteen, that his emotions were highly specialized, and that he would master the means of setting them down undeformed. Verses were written and burned because "they were romantic", S226/202; two books of villanelles and rondels were entrusted to a friend named Clancy who seems to have lost them; by the end of four years Joyce had written the thirty-six poems published in 1908 as *Chamber Music*, with columns, scrolls, and a large harpsichord on the title-page.

He worked hard at verse-writing to prevent the verse from writing itself; the momentum of language will not only carry it across gaps in the writer's attention, it will carry it tangentially away from the writer's purpose into cliché. Most nineteenth-century verse is full of blanks, where the subject isn't coming through because the writer is *talking*. Joyce found the prop he needed in Paul Verlaine.

Verlaine's emotional quality was related to singing Dublin as Laforgue's to Mr. Eliot's Boston. The emotions in which he deals—yearning retrospect anchored in the cozily banal—if they became in his later work a vice of personal sensibility, were in his earlier work articulated with skill and precision sufficiently often to repay the study of a young man who was trying to articulate something very similar.

"A song by Shakespeare or Verlaine," Joyce wrote in 1902 at the age of twenty, "which seems so free and living and as remote from any conscious purpose as rain that falls in a garden or the lights of evening, is discovered to be the rhythmic speech of an emotion otherwise incommunicable, or at least so fitly."[1] What Mr. Pound was to preach tirelessly ten years later—absolute rhythm; the lyric as Image, its totality equating

---

[1] "James Clarence Mangan", quoted in Gorman, II–v.

with an emotion; the apparently artless as careful artifact —is present in its entirety with perfect clearness in that sentence.

The danger, inherent in such songs, of making the rhythms merely plangent, Joyce conquered by technical care. There would have been nothing fuzzy or forced, to his exact mind, about a statement like Pound's " Every emotion and every phase of emotion has some toneless phrase, some rhythm-phrase to express it."[1] He made a careful distinction between lilting gestures of embellishment and the rhythms which imitate those discernible in the subject, S184/163, "the first formal relationship among parts and whole ", P241/234, " the first entelechy ", U425/413:

> . . . the gift of tongues rendering not the lay sense but the first entelechy, the structural rhythm. U425/413.

Whether in fact or in artifact, a thing exists first as a set of relations, then when matter joins proportion or words join rhythm, as a set of articulate relations. (" I shall present my emotions by the arrangement of surfaces ", wrote the sculptor Gaudier-Brzeska from the trenches.) Controlled rhythms afford a continuous matrix to contain what drops through the sieve of discursive denotations. Hence it is always with rhythms, arranged relationships, that artistic imitation begins. Like Flaubert, Joyce always conceives the prose paragraph as a rhythmic unit; it is the component of " absolute rhythm " that explains why so much of *Finnegans Wake* communicates, when read aloud, before being understood.

To render the inarticulate by the non-discursive implied another danger, that of blurring the words, about which Joyce was equally clear-headed.

> A spiritual interpretation of landscape is very rare. Some people think they write spiritually if they make their scenery dim and cloudy. S129/113.

(Some years later Mr. Pound was advising young poets, " Don't use such an expression as ' dim lands *of peace*.' It dulls the image. It mixes an abstraction with the concrete.")[2] The striking juxtaposition quoted by Joyce, Shelley's " Many a lake-surrounded flute ", joins two concretions to achieve, without

---

[1] From an article in the September, 1914, *Fortnightly Review*, reprinted in Pound's Memoir of Gaudier.
[2] " Some Don'ts for Imagists ".

benefit either of paraphrasable meaning or of picturable image, an exact effect " otherwise incommunicable or at least so fitly ".

To connect and control images in this way was the central procedure of Verlaine, who early progressed away from the paraphrasable, from the mapped-out ratiocinative order of the Parnassian sonnet, to the deliberative juxtapositions of the " symbolist " rhetoric of pathos. In the famous " Clair de Lune " that opens *Fêtes Galantes* (1869), " Votre âme " is cognized without being explained. A metaphoric perception (" Votre âme est un paysage choisi . . .") is raised to intelligibility (Joyce's term was " epiphanized ") by articulation of images whose relevance the poet does not need to justify.

> Et leur chanson se mêle au clair de lune,
>
> Au calme clair de lune triste et beau,
> Qui fait rêver les oiseaux dans les arbres
> Et sangloter d'extase les jets d'eau,
> Les grands jets d'eau sveltes parmi les marbres.

In the emergence of the " meaning " to full light with that wonderful final stanza we may discern the " luminous silent stasis of esthetic pleasure " of which Joyce makes Stephen speak:

> The instant wherein that supreme quality of beauty, the clear radiance of the esthetic image, is apprehended luminously by the mind which has been arrested by its wholeness and fascinated by its harmony is the luminous silent stasis of esthetic pleasure. . . . P250/ 242.

" Chanson d'Automne " achieves epiphany in the same way at its last phrase. So it is with all that side of Verlaine's output from which Joyce learned: " Les roses étaient toutes rouges," for instance, or " Le ciel est, par-dessus le toit. . . ." Verlaine discovered, or rediscovered, how to make a mode of passion emerge illuminated without employing the images as mere steps in an argument, and with an action, a *progression d'effet*, that parallels the movement of the mind penetrating— not playing checkers with—the données. To this discovery all Verlaine's much-surveyed techniques—the reduction of familiar landscapes to one or two details, the wistful counter-theme in final lines, the associative drift of images of pathos or nostalgia—are strictly ancillary.

To put these principles into practice was less easy. Joyce worked hard to master Verlaine's procedures. His biographer prints a very early translation of the "Chanson d'Automne" (in *Poèmes Saturniens*) from which we can see what he was trying to do.

Les sanglots longs	A voice that sings
Des violons	Like viol strings
De l'automne	Through the wane
Blessent mon coeur	Of the pale year
D'une langueur	Lulleth me here
Monotone	With its strain.
Tout suffocant	My soul is faint
Et blême, quand	As the bell's plaint
Sonne l'heure	Ringing deep;
Je me souviens	I think upon
Des jours anciens	A day bygone
Et je pleure;	And I weep.
Et je m'en vais	Away! Away!
Au vent mauvais	I must obey
Qui m'emporte	This drear wind,
Deçà, delà	Like a dead leaf
Pareil a la	In aimless grief
Feuille morte.	Drifting blind.

This is the cruellest test to which skill with words can be put. The wonder is not that the translation is faulty, but that it reads as well as it does. Every third or fourth syllable is involved in the rhyme-scheme, which the translator was determined to retain though much of its function vanished. With his third and sixth lines in each stanza Verlaine's altered sound marks a coming to rest; the translation manages this five times out of six, but stumbles at the very first hurdle: " Through the wane/Of the pale year " is not only a seven-word dilutation of " De l'automne " but an unfortunate pro-longation of a movement that should pause with some finality of sense upon " wane ". The rhyme is an impossible task-master. The translator cannot, like Verlaine, lay his poem gently down with " dead leaf ", he is forced to tip that card prematurely and contrive an alternative strong ending. Enforced circumlocutions harass him: " Monotone " is onyx, " With its strain " is paste; " Et je m'en vais " is a sigh, " Away! Away! " is conscripted Keats. It is instructive to see the impossibilities Joyce was willing to wrestle with; one is reminded of his comment on Sullivan's singing:

I have been through the score of *Guillaume Tell* and I discover that Sullivan sings 456 G's, 93 A flats, 92 A's, 54 B flats, 15 B's, 19 C's, and 2 C sharps. Nobody else can do it.[1]

Such labours paid off. Here is the first poem in *Chamber Music:*

> Strings in the earth and air
>   Make music sweet;
> Strings by the river where
>   The willows meet.
>
> There's music along the river
>   For Love wanders there,
> Pale flowers on his mantle,
>   Dark leaves on his hair.
>
> All softly playing,
>   With head to the music bent,
> And fingers straying
>   Upon an instrument.

Joyce has learned Verlaine's first lessons well. There is not a superfluous word, nor a violation of spoken order (" Music sweet," the apparent exception, happens to be sound rhetoric as well as compliant rhyme); the images come through with quiet exactness; the rhythm, without violation of the tone of unearthly luting, shifts gently twice to mark out three allotropic moods. It follows, in the words of the Imagist Manifesto, the sequence of the musical phrase, not that of the metronome. Syntactic phrases are rhythmic blocks. The syntax is exact but unobtrusive; it is neither the plush vehicle of the images nor their Procrustean frame. If Joyce had not learned to write with this economy, he could not have written *Dubliners*.[2]

[1] Quoted by Gorman, XI–ii.

[2] Mr. Pound has often insisted that verse to be spoken, to be chanted, and to be sung, must be carefully distinguished by the critic, and the song, with its own set of technical criteria, not be judged in competition with, say, the *Holy Sonnets*. In this connection his early review of Joyce's poems is of interest:

" The quality and distinction of the poems in the first half of Mr. Joyce's *Chamber Music* is due in part to their author's strict musical training. Here we have the lyric in some of its best traditions, and one pardons certain inversions, much against the taste of the moment, for the sake of the clean-cut ivory finish, and for the interest of the rhythms, the cross-run of the beat and the word, as of a stiff wind cutting the rippletops of bright water . . .

" Here [Poem VIII], as in nearly every other poem, the motif is so slight that the poem scarcely exists until one thinks of it as being set to music. . . ." (reprinted in *Instigations*, 207.)

What Verlaine taught Joyce was the interdependence of rhythm, phrase, and syntax; the elimination of fat; the self-sufficiency of unadorned presentation and constation. Verlaine was good medicine for one wanting to escape from—let us say —Byron's rhetorical facility. There is a sense of métier, of the indispensability at every stage of relevant techniques, behind labour of this kind and results of this kind that distinguishes *Chamber Music* instantly from " the nineties " in which it is otherwise so obviously located. Joyce was separating these emotions from himself by conscious articulation. And between the poem just quoted and the absolutely sure rendition in " The Dead " of what in weaker hands would sprawl into the maudlin:

> Generous tears filled Gabriel's eyes. He had never felt like that himself towards any woman, but he knew that such a feeling must be love. The tears gathered more thickly in his eyes and in the partial darkness he imagined he saw the form of a young man standing under a dripping tree, D287/255;

or between the charged grace of

> Welcome to us now at the last
> The ways that we shall go upon,
> *(Chamber Music,* XXX)

and the famous ending of " Ivy Day in the Committee Room ":

> Mr. Crofton said that it was a very fine piece of writing, D170/152

—between such instances of refusal either to inflate the emotion or to borrow ready-made the expression lies a formulable technical continuity.

IRONIC ELEGANCE AND BEN JONSON

Not everything was to be learned from Verlaine, however; his emotions were the soft ones, of the half-lights:

> She bends upon the yellow keys,
> Her head inclines this way.

The young Joyce felt within himself a steely reserve Verlaine's techniques could not reach. He understood how to learn procedures without taking over, in pastiche, the ready-made language of others. He had turned from Dublin's preferred ready-mades, Tom Moore, Lady Gregory, and the late Laureate, to France; soon, in pursuit of the dryness he still wanted, he was to turn to Norway. Its first approximation, however, he found in Jacobean England, in the lyric poetry of an age when metal quills, not plush hammers, shook the strings. It was Ben Jonson's silver rhetoric that he wanted, alloys and all; not a Dante's passion aspiring amid the viols to the eighth sphere:

> The *Vita Nuova* of Dante suggested to him that he should make his scattered love-verses into a perfect wreath and he explained to Cranly at great length the difficulties of the verse-maker. His love-verses gave him pleasure: he wrote them at long intervals and when he wrote it was always a mature and reasoned emotion which urged him. But in his expressions of love he found himself compelled to use what he called the feudal terminology and as he could not use it with the same faith and purpose as animated the feudal poets themselves he was compelled to express his love a little ironically. This suggestion of relativity, he said, mingling itself with so immune a passion is a modern note: we cannot swear or expect eternal fealty because we recognize too accurately the limits of every human energy. It is not possible for the modern lover to think the universe an assistant at his love-affair and modern love, losing something of its fierceness, gains also somewhat in amiableness. S174/155.

Here is the programme of " double-writing ": the received expression used " a little ironically ". The " feudal terminology " is that proper to Dante's and Cavalcanti's connotations of " Love ": the

> Love in ancient plenilune,
>   Glory and stars beneath his feet,

of *Chamber Music* XII, which points back to

> Love doth not move, but draweth all to him; ...

> There, beyond colour, essence set apart,
> In midst of darkness light light giveth forth
> Beyond all falsity, worthy of faith, alone
> That in him solely is compassion born.[1]

In Joyce's poem the girl to whom the " hooded moon " has whispered such stuff is admonished to

> Believe me rather that am wise
> In disregard of the divine.

[1] Cavalcanti, *Canzone d'Amore*, translated by Ezra Pound.

The self-possessed interlocutor locates beauty in mortal flesh:

> A glory kindles in those eyes,
> Trembles to starlight. Mine, O mine!

" Mine, O mine! " It is a possessable beauty and a practicable love, and the eyes confer romance on the stars, not vice versa. The final lines turn on the beloved with an authority into which much can be read:

> No more be tears in moon or mist
> For thee, sweet sentimentalist.

" Moony misty poetry is passé ", or " sob no more for the ideal, but take what offers ": both are implied, depending on who is supposed to be refraining from tears. Yet the poem seems at first reading as conventional as may be; it is the first example, though cautious and thin, of the double-writing that is characteristically Joyce's.

To turn " Love in ancient plenilune " into the dream of a " sweet sentimentalist " with what was intended for poised equivocalness of feeling was the sort of manoeuvre Jonson could inspire; Catullus' " Rumoresque senum severiorum " become in Jonson's characteristic reshaping " a few poor household spies ". Jonson's façade of aristocratic poise and insolence depends on his careful adjustment of Horatian and Catullan epigrammatic nicety to the linguistic gestures of a Broadside's conventions, a harridan's court, and a groundling's stage:

> . . . Leave things so prostitute
> And take the Alcaic lute;
> Or thine own Horace, or Anacreon's lyre; . . .
> Strike that disdainful heat
> Throughout, to their defeat,
> As curious fools, and envious of thy strain,
> May blushing swear, no palsy's in thy brain.

Joyce used to speak of buying a lute from Dolmetsch and making a Homeric minstrel-tour of the outer counties. This corresponds to the young man's real yearning after bardic status (one of the strands of *Ulysses*), but is more directly rooted in his studied " enigma of a manner ", S27/20. As it turned out, Dublin's own blend of elegance and banality was to permit him a concentrated drama in place of such a centrifugal gesture.

Chapter 4

DEDALUS ABOLISHED

Full oft the riddle of the painful earth
Flash'd thro' her as she sat alone,
Yet none the less held she her solemn mirth
And intellectual throne.

Tennyson

God, we'll simply have to dress the character. I want puce
gloves and green boots.

Buck Mulligan (U18/15)

. . . his face glows green, his hair greys white, his bleyes bcome
broon to suite his cultic twalette.

Finnegans Wake (F344)

IN a book from a quayside cart—

I shall go away in a little while and travel into many lands, that
I may know all accidents and destinies, and when I return will
write my secret law upon those ivory tablets. . . . I know nothing
certain as yet but this—I am to become completely alive, that is,
completely passionate, for beauty is only another name for perfect
passion. I shall create a world where the whole lives of men shall
be articulated and simplified as if seventy years were but one moment,
or as if they were the leaping of a fish or the opening of a flower.

The Tables of the Law & The Adoration of the Magi, privately
printed for William Butler Yeats in 1897, now within a year
or two consigned by Dublin to the quayside barrows like a
carbuncle excreted by a goose.

Just as poets and painters and musicians labour at their works, building
them with lawless and lawful things alike, so long as they embody
the beauty that is beyond the grave, these children of the Holy Spirit
labour at their moments with eyes upon the shining substance on
which Time has heaped the refuse of creation. . . .

. . . that supreme art which is to win us from life and gather us into
eternity like doves into their dove-cots.

36

... and I understood that I could not sin, because I had discovered the law of my own being, and could only express or fail to express my being, and I understood that God has made a simple and an arbitrary law that we may sin and repent!

He turned and said, looking at me with shining eyes: " Jonathan Swift made a soul for the gentlemen of this city by hating his neighbour as himself."

Swans tossed on the wake of the Liffey tugs; this was surely the image of the forgotten Dublin that had set them there? His intellect playing over these words in the city of fish-wives, trams, and broken fanlights, Joyce could soon repeat both stories word for word by heart. There is ardour in the record of his fascination with the monk-errants Aherne and Robartes who " strode through them with great strides ";

Their speeches were like the enigmas of a disdainful Jesus; their morality was infrahuman or superhuman, S178/158,

and his brother remembered for forty years his account of accosting a Capuchin on the beach and reciting to him *The Adoration of the Magi* amid the solitude of sun and roaring waves. " Very beautiful, very beautiful," murmured the monk.

Yeats' own account of the *persona* that mobilized these stories—

I had gathered about me all gods because I believed in none, and experienced every pleasure because I gave myself to none, but held myself apart, indissoluble, a mirror of polished steel.

—makes it sound very plausible; a disdainful arrogance purified of the operatic clangour of continental Byronism. A fructive tranquillity seemed within his grasp. He moved, it seemed, slender amid bristling burghers, aloof and serious. He infuriated Dublin virtually without effort; *The Countess Cathleen* was booed by Joyce's college classmates. The next morning Joyce alone refused to sign their manifesto against the play.

Yeats' *persona* proved more reliable than himself. Two years later his " treacherous instinct of adaptability " was temporarily " making terms with the rabblement," and Joyce took upon himself the responsibility for continuing the war against *muflisme*. He launched a pamphlet against the official taste of " a nation that has never advanced so far as the miracle play ", where " the rabblement, placid and intensely moral, is enthroned in boxes and galleries amid a hum of approval—la bestia Trionfante ". " No man," he began, quoting the outcast Giordano Bruno, " can be a lover of the true or the good unless he abhors the multitude."

Abhorring the multitude, Yeats had done the finest Irish writing of Joyce's time. Joyce accordingly adopted a role of Faustian glamour; in the " enigma of a manner " that he set about constructing he joined the names of Stephen the first martyr, stubborn in his visions against the hurled stones of an infuriated city, and Daedalus the artificer, who being denied safe-conduct off a tyrant's island, *ignotas animum dimittit in artes*, turned to obscure arts and fabricated wings that bore him above the amazed gaze of shepherds and ploughmen. The signature " Stephen Daedalus " appeared three times in print, appended to stories published in AE's *Irish Homestead* in 1904: " The Sisters ", a narrative of sacerdotal paralysis, " Eveline ", portrait of a Dublin girl too terrified by the implications of exile to flee with her sailor lover beyond the seas, and " After the Race ", which images in Jimmy Doyle a possible Jimmy Joyce who remained in Dublin. The priest is a frustrated St. Stephen; Eveline a frustrated Daedalus.

To have become an *esprit libre* seemed a suitable climax for a triumphant novel; so for ten years Joyce wrestled with the life history of Stephen Daedalus. An autobiographical draft puzzled him by the refusal of its lines to converge on the desired heroic climax, and was abandoned in 1908 after a thousand pages. When it became clear at length that the climactic image comported with a more taut, neurotic, and less intelligent character than himself, he created such a character as a dandyish *alter ego*, and in *A Portrait of the Artist as a Young Man* excised the diphthong from the hero's surname so that Dedalus chimed with " dead ".

The struggle of a complex spirit in an unexampled predicament cannot be covered by a paragraph. The Yeatsian postures, for instance, were facile enough—Pater plus French decadence at second hand via Symons—to be sloughed off quickly, before they could interfere with the writing of *Dubliners*. They left superficial marks on " The Sisters ", which Joyce later rewrote with some difficulty. Two other martyr personae—Bruno the burned indicter of the Roman *Bestia Trionfante*; Dick Turpin

(" Turpin Hero "—*Stephen Hero*), picaresque discomforter of lawyers and clergymen—never engaged his interests very deeply. Ibsen, encountered at about the same time as Yeats, afforded a subtler and more dangerous model, because he seemed to have liberated himself from the lyrical dream. All Joyce's ruthless honesty didn't dispose of the Ibsenite temptation to be as a god until the writing of *Exiles* in 1914. During 1903 and 1904 he worked out an Aristotelian aesthetic theory that seemed to set the whole problem in order by clarifying a mode of contemplating Dublin with active vigilance within a total experience not repudiated but possessed; yet the speculative exactness that could regulate the artist's practical problem couldn't solve it, any more than Einstein could blow up Hiroshima with a page of his notebook. The problem of how to liberate himself from Dublin without losing touch with it was thoroughly resolved only in practice, as its phases presented themselves in terms of jobs to be done, books to be written. That took until 1914. The last two books (1914–1939) presented technical problems only, continuously solved from page to page at a technical level: how to render phase by phase material with which he was at last completely in touch. The books up to *Exiles* and *A Portrait* summarize a struggle to get in touch with Dublin in this fruitful way.

YEATS AND CHAMBER MUSIC

The first practical problem was to go on from *Chamber Music*, to get from the lyric phase to the epic, to shift his own emotions out of the foreground without sterilizing them. This meant developing *Chamber Music*, not discarding it; the poems fortunately weren't smeared. Joyce had at no time allowed the " lyrical impulse " to blur a poem into an image of satisfaction; he had set down accurately what he felt, and the paradoxes of that scrupulous empiricism remained as data for subsequent exploration.

The temptations of Yeats were laid almost as they arose. Joyce's poems echo *The Wind Among the Reeds* (1899) often enough to indicate a radical criticism of the elder poet, whose lyrics are, precisely, images of satisfaction, not without a deadened ache at the core. If Yeats[1] had died in 1899, it is

---

[1] It should be understood that what follows isn't a fair view of Yeats but what I take to have been the young Joyce's. It is rather similar to that of Dr. Leavis in *New Bearings in English Poetry*.

unlikely that anyone would feel he had more to do. His early
poems, and especially his early plays, project a full and coherent
world, like the world of Swinburne or Morris apparently
answering to every desire and impulse of their creator. What
he understands is enacted sharply at the centre; what he does
not yet understand but confusedly apprehends is present in his
poetic world as a surrounding greyness, of the order of

> I am haunted by numberless islands, and many a Danaan shore,
> Where Time would surely forget us, and sorrow come near us no
>   more,

which it does not seem incumbent on him or on us to penetrate.
There is a similar evasiveness about his swagger:

TO HIS HEART, BIDDING IT HAVE NO FEAR

> Be you still, be you still, trembling heart;
> Remember the wisdom out of the old days:
> *Him who trembles before the flame and the flood,*
> *And the winds that blow through the starry ways,*
> *Let the starry winds and the flame and the flood*
> *Cover over and hide, for he has no part*
> *With the lonely majestical multitude.*

Neither the fear nor the wisdom gets sharply defined; glamour
—not intrinsic to the verse but imported, along with the key
images, from the Pateresque last prose page of *The Tables of the
Law*—muffles the sense. Yet the glamour is controlled by a
poise of steely dignity; the solemn hieratic rhythm itself
differentiates

> Be you still, be you still, trembling heart

from the bankrupt's lavishness with which Morris and
Swinburne dispense their tinfoil counters. Ten years earlier
William Morris had been able to say to Yeats with truth, "You
write my sort of poetry"; what Yeats had been doing during
those ten years was fusing the aesthete with the aristocrat, a
fusion Morris and Swinburne could never perform. The Irish
tradition of impoverished aristocracy cultivating the arts
furnished him with a home-grown solution for the disabilities
of the aesthete's congenital languor.

In his parallel poem (XXI in *Chamber Music*) Joyce drew on
the analogous strength of Ben Jonson (who contains the whole

tradition of gentleman-poets since Horace) to give this fusion still more stress.

> He who hath glory lost, nor hath
> Found any soul to fellow his
> Among his foes in scorn and wrath
> Holding to ancient nobleness,
> That high unconsortable one—
> His love is his companion.

The first four lines translate Yeats' stage properties into spare directness of presentation, with in the opening phrase a glance at Lucifer.

> Among his foes in scorn and wrath
> Holding to ancient nobleness

is dry beside Yeats' endemic melancholy. But it is the concluding couplet that turns the screw. Yeats' "Lonely majestical multitude" manages to blunt *lonely* by *multitude* and turn flame, flood, and the winds of space from terrors to glories with *majestical*. Joyce's

> That high unconsortable one—
> His love is his companion.

deletes a romantic lady-love with *unconsortable* and turns the Lucifer into Narcissus. He evades neither the attractiveness of the role nor its penalty. He differs from Yeats in understanding exactly what he is saying. Whenever Joyce rewrites a Yeats poem—"Half close your eyelids, loosen your hair" into "Be not sad because all men"; "I hear the shadowy horses" into "I hear an army charging"—we find a poise less assured than Yeats' (who in 1899 was twelve years older than Joyce in 1904) but an articulation considerably more efficient and a sense of the contradictions in the pose considerably sharpened.

THE STRATEGY OF NOBILITY

Joyce didn't set out so much to improve on Yeats as to do what he could—better than the early Yeats did—with the conventions he had to use, which Yeats also had to use: there is in both poets the same fascination with the intrinsically poetical object (dappled grass, pine-woods, fading loveliness and Love hypostatized), the same tendency toward languorous sorrow (but in Joyce sometimes sharpened towards the wry and resigned), the same unreal unspecified fair ladies.

In what sense were these unreal conventions a necessity? To confront that question is to confront the complete debility of taste with which both poets were surrounded, the taste which exalted Tom Moore and " Lawn Tennyson " and committed to the young for admiring memorization the kind of thing parodied in *Stephen Hero:*

> Art thou real, my Ideal?
> Wilt thou ever come to me
> In the soft and gentle twilight
> With your baby on your knee?

—" the ludicrous waddling approach weighed down by an inexplicable infant ", S83/70. It was a situation no poet in that time and place could escape; Yeats could not escape it. And their first strategies for dealing with it are strikingly similar. Joyce applies to the conventions of the popular opera and the music hall (" The music-hall, not poetry, a criticism of life," he wrote in an early notebook) a Jonsonian precision and elegance:

> Nor have I known a love whose praise
> Your piping poets solemnize,
> Neither a love where may not be
> Ever so little falsity.

Let us invest our emotions here, he says, since there is no other place to invest them; but let us preserve our critical consciousness intact, and derive pleasure from that.

While the pleasure becomes less ironic as the materials assume wider connotations, the materials remain the same to the end of Joyce's life. The situations in the *Portrait*, in *Ulysses*, in *Finnegans Wake*, are the tawdry confrontations of melodrama and pulp romance: the conventionality of Bloom's pose, erect, clutching a stick, over the recumbent Stephen, and the sentimental apparition of the dead Rudy in trappings of pantomime innocence, belong to a deliberate technique, the structural counterpart of a *sottisier* texture.

The Yeatsian strategy resembles that of *Chamber Music* with the proportions reversed. Yeats too invests his emotions in roses and long soft hair, not however because the present sings about these things but because the past did. He provides

them, via the pre-Raphaelite poise and the heroic legends of
Ireland, with a distinguished pedigree:

> When my arms wrap you round I press
> My heart upon the loveliness
> That has long faded from the world; . . .
> The roses that of old time were
> Woven by ladies in their hair,
> The dew-cold lilies ladies bore
> Through many a sacred corridor. . . .

This vanished loveliness versus the irredeemable modern is
Yeats' theme; that the Stephen Dedalus of the *Portrait* elects
instead " the loveliness that has not yet come into the world ",
P297/286, doesn't of course diminish the identical aestheticism of his pose. The effort of will by which the inviolable
status of Yeats' illusions is maintained is as evident as his
rejection of contemporary experience.

> Of old the world on dreaming fed,
> Grey Truth is now her painted toy.

They are dreams, he knows, but he is determined to preserve
them; and the aristocratic dignity in which they are articulated
is a preservative, not a criticism.

There is a good deal of mannered dignity in the early Joyce,
of course. It is written across his biography, and traces of it
get into his work. One reason *Chamber Music* doesn't really
come off is that the author for all his irony toward the glamorous
feels an irony still greater toward the quotidian. The Yeats of
1899 did represent in many ways an ideal for the Joyce of 1904.
At nineteen Joyce praised *The Wind Among the Reeds* as " in
aim and form . . . poetry of the highest order ". But the praise
is checked, even then, by the tart phrase, " an aesthete has a
floating will." A few years later, in the act of recording the
fascination of Aherne and Robartes, he indicates their sterility:

> Civilization may be said indeed to be the creation of its outlaws but
> the least protest against the existing order is made by the outlaws
> whose creed and manner of life is not renewable even so far as to be
> reactionary. These inhabit a church apart; they lift their thuribles
> wearily before their deserted altars. . . . S178/159,

and assesses with detachment the sort of person who will
believe in them: " A young man like Stephen in a season of

damp and unrest." In the *Portrait* he devalues the "indissoluble mirror of polished steel" by equipping Stephen Dedalus with waxen wings and a bleeding heart.

THE CATHARSIS

Joyce was never the Stephen Dedalus of his 1914 *Portrait*, mirror of nineteenth-century romantic idealism: Byron, Shelley, Axel, Frédéric Moreau. He was for a time however approximately the Stephen of the 1905 *Stephen Hero*, a gayer though by no means less intransigent being. During those months he was in the greatest danger of his artistic life. Against the more magnetic danger later, he was on guard; but the Stephen Hero role was indefinitely plausible, as Yeats' later career illustrates.

Stephen Hero isn't, as his relations with Cranly and Lynch imply, insulated from human contacts in the manner of his later namesake, and his intransigence is focused on his art. It is focused on his art, however, by way of his *persona*. You cannot contemplate your material and yourself at the same time: by the time he came to copy out the *Stephen Hero* ms., Joyce was sufficiently detached from, or at least uneasy about, the pretensions of his slightly earlier self to insert devaluing phrases like "this fantastic idealist" S34/27, "the fiery-hearted revolutionary", "this heaven-ascending essayist" S80/67. It is a worthwhile guess that the writing-out of *Stephen Hero* was the crucially cathartic labour of his life. The pain of depersonalization was undergone then once and for all. *Stephen Hero* bogged down in 1906 a few pages past the end of the published fragment. Its necessity was past. After several more years Joyce discovered how he could salvage its materials for the great trilogy.

What was achieved in this time of maturation was what Mr. Eliot has described as the separation between "the man who suffers and the mind which creates". The stiffness, the intransigence, was to be reserved for disciplining words and seeing that the printers didn't tamper with them; the personality was to be unbound and deployed as a perceptive medium. How powerful were the impulses forcing Joyce toward the almost inevitable error of *living* the part of artist we may perhaps guess from the degree of technical rigour that at the time of dissociation got transferred from the role to the workroom. Of the components of Stephen Hero, he retained the uncompromising craftsman who out of the infinite number of ways of saying anything was to seek out the best, spending a day on two sentences of Mr. Bloom's, and 20,000 hours (his own estimate) writing the 700-odd pages of *Ulysses*. On the other hand, this kind of thing was purged away:

> Behind the rapidly indurating shield the sensitive answered: Let the pack of enmities come tumbling and sniffing to my highlands after their game. There was his ground and he flung them disdain from flashing antlers. S35/27.

Mr. Spender has somewhere recorded a mild rebuke of Mr. Eliot's which turned on the distinction between wanting to write poetry and wanting to be a poet. To write poetry one bends one's attention, in trusting detachment, upon "these present things", S78/66. To be a poet one concentrates on preserving integrity in a milieu one dare not trust. This means, at its most vulgar, Bloomsbury and *Transition*, a radical inter-corruption of art and life. At its best, it means bringing aristocratic insolence and inner yearning to the highest possible temper, as Yeats to his lasting glory managed to do.

YEATS AS TRAGIC HERO

As we know from his later work, Yeats did not rest as a reader at the turn of the century might have expected. There was nothing to do with that marvellous coherent dream-world but repudiate it in sorrow, and that was the step Yeats took with unprecedented heroism. Thenceforward he became a tragic hero, and himself repudiating illusion, or defiantly entertaining it, became his subject.

This meant not giving up the use of masks, but making a new set. He at length repudiated, like Stephen Dedalus, Robartes' "loveliness that has long faded from the world". Like Stephen he meant by this act that he would repudiate the lilies and roses and in contact with "life" spin a new heroic dream out of his inside. He did something like that in, for instance, *Byzantium*. He regarded the former pose as mistaken; as he shows by his endless tinkering with a theory of masks, he never questions the need for a pose. Joyce, in regretting, as he did to Eugene Jolas, that the materials of *A Vision* hadn't been put into a great creative work, put his finger on Yeats' paradoxical sterility. A mask, he saw, was strictly a technical device, ancillary to other labours. The omniscient showman-narrator in *Ulysses*, " paring his finger-nails ", is one of the most extraordinary masks in literature.

Yeats never saw the *use* of the mask; his integrity consists in his never having been deluded by its sufficiency. He had little vocation for the happiness which another Irishman called the capacity for being perpetually well-deceived; his intelligence was too acute; in *The Tables of the Law* Aherne discovers that the *Lex Secretum* of Joachim Abbas is a snare of " the spirits whose name is Legion and whose throne is in the indefinite abyss "; and in "Lines Written in Dejection" an older Yeats laments,

> The holy centaurs of the hills are vanished;
> I have nothing but the embittered sun;
> Banished heroic mother moon and vanished,
> And now that I have come to fifty years
> I must endure the timid sun.

YEATS, DEDALUS, AND MR. DUFFY

The career of Yeats, then, is that of a Stephen Dedalus who pursued his premises to the end with uncompromising rigour; and the end, as Joyce understood in making use of the Icarus symbol, was cold water. Stephen in *Ulysses* has suffered some such dousing, dropped into the sea of Dublin after his Paris flight under the auspices of a false exemplar. The *Portrait* closes with him poised for the takeoff, invoking Dedalus:

> Old father, old artificer, stand me now and ever in good stead.

And on June 16, 1904, we find him meditating:

> Fabulous artificer, the hawklike man. You flew. Whereto? Newhaven-Dieppe, steerage passenger. Paris and back. U208/199.

In his drunken stupor that night he has " Who will go drive with Fergus now " upon his lips, U592/573. His new condition, " seabedabbled, fallen, weltering ", leaves him, that is, simply where Yeats was a little before 1912, uttering heroic phrases while seething with self-mistrust. There is a legend that on first meeting Yeats, about 1902, Joyce said " You are too old to learn from me." Whether he said it or not,[1] it was

---

[1] Since Joyce always denied this story, the only authority for it is Yeats, who may have invented it to cap a preface he wrote in 1903 but discarded unpublished. (See Richard Ellman, *The Identity of Yeats*, chapter 5.) Joyce isn't named in the preface, which dramatizes a pair of opposing theories, and Yeats' way of making a great anecdotal peacock out of the merest impressions has often been remarked

perfectly true. Nothing lay before Yeats by then but a wonder-
fully resilient dryness. Lacking Yeats' intellectual recklessness,
the most Stephen Dedalus could have hoped for was the drab,
pottering future of Mr. Duffy in " A Painful Case ". Mr.
Duffy is surely Stephen come to a truce with Dublin and grown
old:

> . . . In the desk lay a manuscript translation of Hauptmann's *Michael
> Kramer*, the stage directions of which were written in purple ink,
> and a little sheaf of papers held together by a brass pin.   In these
> sheets a sentence was inscribed from time to time, and, in an ironical
> moment, the headline of an advertisement for *Bile Beans* had been
> pasted on to the first sheet. D134/119.

Joyce in his nineteenth year had in fact translated Hauptmann,
and the *Bile Beans* folio is an ironical fulfilment of Stephen's

> . . . epiphanies on green oval leaves, deeply deep, copies to be sent
> if you died to all the great libraries of the world, including Alexandria.
> U41/37.

The schizophrenia out of which the mature Yeats made art is
represented in Mr. Duffy by a few futile gestures:

> He lived at a little distance from his body, regarding his own acts with
> doubtful side-glances.   He had an odd autobiographical habit which
> led him to compose in his mind from time to time a short sentence
> about himself containing a subject in the third person and a predicate
> in the past tense.   He never gave alms to beggars and walked firmly,
> carrying a stout hazel. D134/120.

He works in a bank.

Mr. Duffy and Yeats are contraries, but like all contraries
they belong to the same species. Joyce here makes it perfectly
clear that the elevation of Dublin into intellectual light is not
the privilege of one who fosters a timid isolation:

> Mr. James Duffy lived in Chapelizod because he wished to live as
> far as possible from the city of which he was a citizen and because he
> found all the other suburbs of Dublin mean, modern and pretentious.
> D133/119.

These words, with the understanding they imply, were written
when Joyce was twenty-three. Too much cannot be made of
such a fact. A just comprehension of his astonishing achievement must begin with a realization that within a year of writing
Chamber Music he was able to write *Dubliners*. His imagination
had arrived at the point Yeats was only to reach at fifty, and
passed beyond it while young enough to profit.

Chapter 5

DUBLINERS

. . . never dented an idea for a phrase's sake. . . .

Ezra Pound

ABOUT 1905 Joyce wrote most of *Dubliners*, a whole which he conceived, with remarkable originality, less as a sequence of stories than as a kind of multi-faceted novel.

He wrote to a prospective publisher:

> I do not think that any writer has yet presented Dublin to the world. It has been a capital of Europe for thousands of years, it is supposed to be the second city of the British Empire and it is nearly three times as big as Venice. Moreover, on account of many circumstances which I cannot detail here, the expression Dubliner seems to me to bear some meaning and I doubt whether the same can be said for such words as " Londoner " and " Parisian ". . . .[1]

Dublin is not, that is, an agglomeration of residents, but a city. In its present paralysis, it remains a ghost, not a heap of bones: the ghost of the great conception of the City which polarizes the mind of Europe from the time of Pericles to that of Dr. Johnson. Mr. Eliot saw London as " a heap of broken images "; Joyce's Dublin had none of the random quality characterized by " heap ". It was a shell of grandeur populated by wraiths. The *integritas* of the aesthetic image corresponds to something still at a minimal level of organization vitally present in the object of contemplation; but it isn't the sort of organization that fuses in a single action or demands a single narrative. This image Joyce fragmented along its inherent lines of cleavage, the parts he disposed to afford one another the maximum of reinforcement. . . .

> My intention was to write a chapter of the moral history of my country, and I chose Dublin for the scene because that city seemed to me the centre of paralysis. I have tried to present it to the indifferent public under four of its aspects: childhood, adolescence, maturity, and public life. The stories are arranged in this order. I have written it for the most part in a style of scrupulous meanness and with

[1] Gorman, V–iv.

48

the conviction that he is a very bold man who dares to alter in the presentment, still more to deform, whatever he has seen and heard. . . .[1]

It is not a sort of photography that the last clause recommends. The precise locutions, gestures, and things out of which the aesthetic image is being synthesized must not be " dented for a phrase's sake " nor reduced to accessory status as bits of " local colour " subserving a conceptual simplification of their meaning. " The artist who could disentangle the subtle soul of the image from its mesh of defining circumstances most exactly and re-embody it in artistic circumstances chosen as the most exact for its new office, he was the supreme artist." S78/65.

POLISHING THE MIRROR

The easiest way to isolate the sort of respect for undented verity that controls these stories is to inspect a few of Joyce's first thoughts. Here is the *à peu près* of the ending of " The Boarding House ", transcribed from the fair copy Joyce wrote out on July 1, 1905 (now in the Slocum collection). The Bovaryste Polly is leaning back on the bed luxuriating in " secret, amiable memories " while her mother presents the ultimatum to Mr. Doran down below:

> Her hopes and visions were so intricate that she no longer saw the white pillows on which her gaze was fixed or remembered that she was waiting for anything. At last she heard her mother calling her and she jumped up and ran out to the banisters.
> – Polly! Polly! –
> – Yes, Mamma? –
> – Come down, dear. Mr. Doran wants to speak to you.
> She remembered now what she had been waiting for. This was it.

This is the precarious instant of focus. The story is at that point of balance where the smallest touch will send its extremes into oscillation. In these final lines the exact mode of understanding that exists between Polly and her mother is to be revealed, and Polly herself is to be exactly placed on the scale between narcissism and acumen. " This was it " implies too crude a prearrangement, and too explicit an awareness of her own feelings. For the printed text, Joyce deleted it, and made the last line read simply, " Then she remembered what she had been waiting for ", D84/75. A few lines earlier, at the

[1] Gorman, V–iv.

point where Polly's reverie is interrupted, the focus is insufficiently sharp. " Jumped " conveys too little. Jumped as at a cue? from vitality? from habit of obedience? And the flat level sentence, its three verbs—" heard," " jumped," " ran "— reduced to equal value, suggests either phases of a continuous action (an unwanted degree of alertness) or a moving continuous with her dreaming (muffling the all-important switch in her level of consciousness). The primary discontinuity Joyce finally indicated by starting a new paragraph. The mode of awakening he defined by substituting for " jumped up ", " started to her feet ". The secondary discontinuity between the call and the start he rendered by dividing the sentence and deleting the specific " her " as object of " calling ". In the printed text, the sentence reads:

> At last she heard her mother calling. She started to her feet and ran to the banisters.

" THE SISTERS "

Laying hold on the subject, not expressing an attitude to it, sometimes gave Joyce more trouble than such minutiae would imply. One story, the first, " The Sisters ", actually got published[1] with traces of beginner's disdain scarring its paragraphs. Two years later, when the manuscript of the sequence was being put in order, the entire story had to be rewritten to get rid of phrases like " a whimsical kind of providence " and adult cadences like " the ceremonious candles in the light of which the Christian must take his last sleep " (compare the revision—" If he was dead, I thought, I would see the reflection of candles on the darkened blind for I knew that two candles must be set at the head of a corpse "). The " two poor women " reading the death notice were originally " three women of the people ". The wonder and the impatience, in the revised version, are placed as those of a boy; in the first draft the boy-persona is an excuse for working in a grown-up commentary of impatience and wonder. The visit to the corpse was originally narrated thus:

> We followed the old woman upstairs and into the dead-room. The room through the lace end of the blind was suffused with dusty

[1] As " Our Weekly Story " in AE's *Irish Homestead*, August 13, 1904. The quotations here are from Joyce's manuscript in the Slocum collection, which lies between the *Irish Homestead* text and the final version.

golden light amid which the candles seemed like pale thin flames. He had been coffined. Nannie gave the lead and we three knelt down at the foot of the bed. There was no sound in the room for some minutes except the sound of Nannie's muttering, for she prayed noisily. The fancy came to me that the old priest was smiling as he lay there in his coffin.

Here the priest's smile images nothing more than the narrator's distaste for noisy prayer. In the final version the first sentence of this becomes half a paragraph, and the prayer-episode itself reads:

Nannie gave the lead and we three knelt down at the foot of the bed. I pretended to pray but I could not gather my thoughts because the old woman's mutterings distracted me. I noticed how clumsily her skirt was hooked at the back and how the heels of her cloth boots were trodden down all to one side. The fancy came to me that the old priest was smiling as he lay there in his coffin. D14/13.

The shift of the boy's attention from prayer to worn boots is something more than a concretization of " I could not gather my thoughts." It is of the very essence of the rewritten story. The story balances a succession of empirical verities—old Cotter's " little beady black eyes ", " children's bootees and umbrellas ", a bowed head scarcely visible above a banister rail, the worn heel of a boot—against a stirring implication of maleficent mysteries. Everything that is not of the order of boot-heels is vague, suggestive, and a little frightening. On the first page the evenly lighted window is set against the evil suggestion of the word " paralysis " (" It sounded to me like the name of some maleficent and sinful being "). The boy's memories of the dead priest " sitting in his arm-chair by the fire ", the green faded garments, the red handkerchief blackened with snuff stains, the discoloured teeth, are set against a current of sinister suggestion: " I felt even annoyed at discovering in myself a sensation of freedom as if I had been freed from something by his death."

In the revised text a thematic statement of hopeless paralysis is the first sentence in the book. The paralysed priest in his arm-chair near the fire is as Stanislaus Joyce confirms[1] intended as " a symbol of Irish life, priest-ridden and semi-paralysed ". By presenting the interactions of this image with the consciousness of a young boy, Joyce introduces at the outset what was to

[1] *Hudson Review*, II-4, 502.

be the scourge of an older boy in a later book: " a malevolent reality behind those things I say I fear ", P287/277. The young boy is a generic Dubliner, or rather the Dubliner is a generic boy, for whom everything beyond the level of reality represented by boot-heels is vaguely dangerous: for a grown-up too dangerous to bear thinking about, though a child may feel the fascination of evil, and if unusually tenacious may grow up capable of recording it. The terrible image on which " The Sisters " closes displays this dimension of Dublin religion exaggerated to a point where it captures the speculation even of adult women:

> "... And what do you think but there he was, sitting up by himself in the dark in his confession-box, wide-awake and laughing-like softly to himself? "
> She stopped suddenly as if to listen. I too listened; but there was no sound in the house: and I knew that the old priest was lying still in his coffin as we had seen him, solemn and truculent in death, an idle chalice on his breast.
> Eliza resumed:
> " Wide-awake and laughing-like to himself. . . . So then, of course, when they saw that, that made them think that there was something gone wrong with him. . . ." D19/17.

This laughter is a dissolution of intolerable tension, as the ego tortured by the strains and responsibilities of mediation with the supernatural retreats into the world of boot-heels and snuff. It is of a piece with the pathic conviviality of the Dublin tavern. " He was too scrupulous always ", the sister says; " the duties of the priesthood was too much for him "; and the boy had wondered how anyone ever had the courage to under-take responsibilities so grave as those the priest outlined to him. D12/11. The old man, " too scrupulous always ", had attempted to serve the supernatural world on its own terms. Relinquishing that attempt in hysterical laughter, he re-lapsed into the mode of the less scrupulous everyday priest: moral predicaments became complicated logical questions, the responses of the Mass were pattered through with a boy by rote, the works of the Fathers were " as thick as the *Post Office Directory* and as closely printed as the law notices in the news-paper ".

It is the *mechanism* of his paralysed life that needs to be pondered. It offers a complex image of what growing up in Dublin amounted to. The old priest had faced, grappled with, and been bested by the world of mysterious malevolence with which the imagination of the small boy is fascinated. Human kind cannot bear even that much reality. Such as he is will, in a different mode, that boy most probably be: a cheerful habitual inhabitant of the boot-heel world. Such as he is the less scrupulous clergy have always been, though no one calls them mad. He tried, and failed. His paralysis foreshadows that of, say, Father Purdon in " Grace ", who without uneasiness speaks the habitual idiom of the business world because he is too coarse-textured ever to have tried:

> But one thing only, he said, he would ask of his hearers. And that was: to be straight and manly with God. If their accounts tallied in every point to say:
> " Well, I have verified my accounts. I find all well."
> But if, as might happen, there were some discrepancies, to admit the truth, to be frank and say like a man:
> " Well, I have looked into my accounts. I find this wrong and this wrong. But, with God's grace, I will rectify this and this. I will set right my accounts." D222/198.

THE PLAN: CHILDHOOD (" The Sisters "; " An Encounter "; " Araby ")

Of Joyce's four divisions, Childhood includes the first three stories, Youth, Maturity, and Public Life four each. These are phases in the onset of the paralysis imaged in " The Sisters "; the final story, " The Dead ", exhibits it as a living death. A developing mode of consciousness is carefully controlled throughout the book.

The theme of the two modes of priesthood runs from " The Sisters " through " An Encounter " to " Araby ", at which point, with the passing of childhood, the scrupulous and imaginative mode loses its resilience for good. In " An Encounter ", Joe Dillon, who used to caper around the garden, " an old tea-cosy on his head, beating a tin with his fist and yelling: ' Ya! yaka, yaka, yaka! ' " D20/18 (like the vested priest at his Latin ritual, or David dancing before the ark) proves to have a vocation for the priesthood: an ebullient young Irishman whom nothing mysterious will much trouble or puzzle. In " Araby ", the boy-narrator imagines himself in the streets " bearing his chalice safely through a throng of foes "—as scrupulous as the paralysed Father Flynn, but more cautious; Father Flynn, we remember, broke his chalice.

"The Sisters" and "An Encounter", moreover, are linked by father-images. The pervert who interrupts the truant boys' expedition to the Pigeon-house with his talk of whipping "as if he were unfolding some elaborate mystery", D31/28, and his ambivalent injunctions concerning love (it is by turns natural, a furtive secret, and an occasion for flagellation) is very much like the "malevolent reality" itself: he and Father Flynn exist in a complex relation to one another. And with this man's appearance the mysterious is deflected towards the sexual. In "Araby" the sexual achieves glamorous awakening, and the chalice of youthful confident enterprise is broken against deglamouring inadequacy—the late arrival, the empty bazaar, impractical porcelain vases and flowered tea-sets, two pennies and sixpence. Every kind of frustration is implied in the last two pages of "Araby". The great empty hall is a female symbol, entered at last; and it contains only sparse goods, the clink of money, and tittering banalities.

> Nearly all the stalls were closed, and the greater part of the hall was in darkness. I recognized a silence like that which pervades a church after a service. D40/35.

It was in a dark deserted chapel late at night that Father Flynn had sat in his confession-box laughing softly to himself. The confessional motif gets its final twist:

> Gazing up into the darkness I saw myself as a creature driven and derided by vanity; and my eyes burned with anguish and anger. D41/36.

THE PLAN: ADOLESCENCE ("Eveline"; "After the Race"; "Two Gallants"; "The Boarding-House")

The next sequence balances two feminine and two masculine modes. Eveline torn between Frank and her father, tugged by the injunction of her dead mother, and reaching at last the automatic decision of inaction, "passive, like a helpless animal"; Polly of the banished father and the unspoken understanding with her mother ("As Polly was very lively the intention was to give her the run of the young men") reclining after her geste with "no longer any perturbation visible on her face" and collaborating in the manoeuvring of the hapless Mr. Doran into her noose: these are the feminine polarities—virgin and temptress—between which all Joyce's women oscillate

Eveline is the book's second thematic image of paralysis.

She is not a protagonist, like Father Flynn, but a mirror. The stress falls less on her intrinsic drabness than on the masculine world (Dublin) in which she is placed and the materials it has given her mind to feed on. It is a choice rather than a judgment that she is called on to make. The substance of the story, her reverie, is entirely in the mode of passion: not a balancing of arguments but the counterposition of the familiar room, the romance surrounding Frank, her father's contrary moods, the music of the distant street-organ.

Between her and the " lively " Polly two male modalities are poised to complete Joyce's generic fourfold pattern. In " After the Race " " life " is imaged as reckless action—Stephen Dedalus' " spell of arms and voices " explicitly geared to the petroleum-reeking Call of the Open Road. " The journey laid a magical finger on the genuine pulse of life and gallantly the machinery of human nerves strove to answer the bounding courses of the swift blue animal ", D53/47: which components are alive in this sentence and which are dead? Zestful technology is shored against Dublin drabness: " At the crest of the hill at Inchicore sightseers had gathered in clumps to watch the cars careering homeward and through this channel of poverty and inaction the Continent sped its wealth and industry ", D49/94. " The French, moreover, were virtual victors." Ah, Paris!

Jimmy Doyle, who becomes infatuated with continental swish and gambles away the patrimony he had intended to invest, is an avatar of Stephen Dedalus and a Dublin's-eye parody of Jimmy Joyce. The motor racing, the dress clothes, the dancing on the yacht (" this was seeing life ", D56/50), the drinking, the wild card games, are all versions of the anti-Dublin, and that is their attraction for Jimmy. The impecunious artist Villona meanwhile follows their follies, entertains them, and lets in epiphanic light at the end: " Daybreak, gentlemen! " (The young Joyce made a few shillings during his first bleak winter in Paris by interviewing a French motor-racing driver for the *Irish Times*.)

Jimmy forsaking the " channel of poverty and inaction " for Ségouin's jet-propelled " life " inverts Eveline's failure to choose life with the " kindly, manly, openhearted " Frank in Buenos Ayres. The connections of the second masculine story in the section, " Two Gallants ", are with the second feminine world, the Boarding House of cynical put-up jobs.

Metaphors of prostitution reverberate through both stories:
Corley and Lenehan, achieving at the end of their adventure
the small gold coin, emerge as male street-walkers; as for Mrs.
Mooney's Boarding House, " All the resident young men
spoke of her as *The Madam* ", D75/67.

By now the archetypal action of every Joyce work is in full
swing. The gentle lyric antitheses of the first pages are growing sharper, as the consciousness divided between the public
fact and the private dream incarnates its conflicting elements
in the two kinds of men and two kinds of women who people
the epic phase. Later these people will start meeting one
another and realize dimly that they are meeting themselves.

THE PLAN: MATURITY (" A Little Cloud", "Coun-
terparts "; " Clay "; " A Painful Case)

The four stories of maturity rearrange the antitheses of the
preceding section. This time two masculine worlds are followed by two feminine ones; more accurately, since the protagonist of " A Painful Case " is a male clerk, two modes of
ethos are followed by two of pathos.

" A Little Cloud " exhibits the components of " After the
Race " in a more complex context. As Bloom and Dedalus,
as Watson and Holmes, the palefaced Little Chandler encounters the Noble Savage Gallaher who has Been Abroad and
Got On, and by osmosis acquires a timid share of his virtues.
The opposites, as always, belong to the same species: the
feminine Chandler with his " quiet voice " and " refined "
manners confronts the *pseudo*-masculine incarnation of irrational know-how. For the first time in the book, the utter
absence of an organic community begins to be insisted on: the
" mansions in which the old nobility of Dublin had roystered "
are " spectral " now, and no memory of the past touches
Chandler, D87/77. Incommunicable loneliness has superseded the bravado of adolescence. Chandler has none of
Lenehan's resilience. His shyness prevents his reading
the poetry-books of his bachelor days to his wife: " At
times he repeated lines to himself and this consoled him ",
D86/77.

As for Gallaher, his positives are those of the impresario only.
The key-words of the paragraph in which he is first allowed
to emerge at length are tellingly vague. We hear first of
" greatness ", and the early sign of that greatness was that

people used to say he was " wild ". But nobody denied him
" talent ". There was " a certain . . . something " in him that
impressed you. Finally it emerges: ". . . he kept up a bold
face ", D88/78.

The osmotic interchange begins in the eighth line of the
story: " It was something to have a friend like that ", D85/76.
As he goes off to meet the anarchic journalist (for that is
Gallaher's profession) Chandler feels " superior to the people
he passed ", D88/79. His ambitions rise toward the Life
Literary in emulation: " He wondered whether he could
write a poem to express his idea. . . . He was not sure what
idea he wished to express but the thought that a poetic moment
had touched him took life within him like an infant hope."
Communion is achieved for half a page; the rift begins with
Gallaher's patronizing preference for liquor neat, D92/82,
widens through the clash of Chandler's wistful dream of
Europe against Gallaher's reportage, and climaxes with
Chandler's discovery that his prudent marriage earns him no
advantage in Gallaher's eyes, D100/90. He remains uneasily
pestered, D102/91 by Gallaher's image of marriage as the poor
man's fornication, D96/86, attempts a Gallaherian gesture of
" living bravely " by shouting " Stop! " to the crying child,
and subsides into tears of remorse.

Thus the dialectic of " A Little Cloud "; " Counterparts "
repeats its action in a more automatic fashion. The employer's
rebuke is exhibited as response-to-stimulus; his fist " seemed
to vibrate like the knob of some electric machine ", D113/101,
and his voice in the first sentence of the story emerges from a
speaking-tube. The context of the story is mechanism.
Farrington is a copying-machine geared to a law-machine.
The human cogs and levers of the story whirr and jerk as the
rebuke administered by the employer passes through them and
emerges at the other end as the flailing of a cane on the thighs
of a small boy. In " A Little Cloud " there was no community,
only loneliness; in " Counterparts " there is a pseudo-
community of drinking, sterile emulation, action and reaction:
a sketch for the monstrous robot body that dominates
Ulysses.

Maria is " Clay " as humanity itself, as susceptible to
moulding, and as death in life. Joe's wife, another Mrs.
Mooney, has eased her into the laundry and one may suspect
will soon ease her into a convent; and Maria, one is sure, will

never quite realize how she got there. The omen she touches
is that of death; when she laughs the tip of her nose nearly
meets the tip of her chin, D125/112—like a Hallowe'en witch
—and like a banished ghost she returns to Joe's fireside,
D129/116, until cockcrow on All Hallow's Eve. The error
in her song, D132/118, parallels her recurrent failure to get
the ring, D125/112; the song should have gone on to treat
of marriage:

> I dreamt that suitors sought my hand
> That knights on bended knee,
> And with vows no maiden heart could withstand
> They pledged their hearts to me.
>
> And I dreamt that one of that noble band
> Came forth my heart to claim
> But I also dreamt, which charmed me most,
> That you loved me just the same.

THE HEART OF THE MATTER: "A PAIN-FUL CASE"

"A Painful Case" occupies the mid-point of the book. It
gathers up, specifically, the implications of the third group:
Chandler's loneliness, Farrington's automatism (Mr. Duffy
"lived at a little distance from his body, regarding his own
acts with doubtful side-glances"), Maria's living death. Mr.
Duffy is carefully presented for three pages as a person of
absolute meticulous voluntary routine. The rare inscribing of
sentences in a commonplace-book (held together by a brass
pin) is as glamourless an action as is the business of the bank
from which at four o'clock daily he is "set free", D135/120.
Passion when it intersects his life proves impossibly circum-
stanced; he rebukes it; he is touched as by a ghost; and his
newly emotionalized mental life, D138/124, brings an eerie
ultimate awareness of the loneliness he has until then accepted
with his intellect only.

Now that the ghosts have begun to swarm (we are entering
the regions of "The Dead") we become aware that it is a
living death that the book is presenting. The action of story
after story has taken place at night or in twilight; and from
"A Little Cloud" to "Ivy Day in the Committee Room" the

season is autumn.[1] " A Painful Case " is the first adumbration
of " The Dead ": passion missed and returning as the phantom touch of a hand, D144/129, a hallucinatory voice, D146/
130, cold air creeping into the sleeves of a coat, D144/129.
The malevolent realities surrounding the innocent protagonist
of the first part of the book are now part of the texture of life;
but the antithesis to the world of boot-heels is no longer the
mysterious power that had cracked the mind of its sacerdotal
servant: rather, the multiplication of spectres of choices
negated, passions unexplored, opportunities missed, aspects of
the self denied. The alter ego who returned in the flesh to
Little Chandler returns as a wraith to Mr. Duffy.

The theme of might-have-been is endemic to Joyce's books:
Richard Rowan's fear lest he deprive his wife of some moments
of passion that ought to have been hers, Stephen's speculation
(" Weave, weaver of the wind ") on the events of history
" lodged in the room of the infinite possibilities they have
ousted ", Anna Livia's disillusion as her Prince Charming's
coach dwindles back into a pumpkin: " I thought you were all
glittering with the noblest of carriage. You're only a bumpkin.
I thought you the great in all things, in guilt and in glory.
You're but a puny. Home! " Its layers of meaning are numerous. It is the paralysis of the City, at one level; the rhythm
of the Dubliners' lives rises to no festivity and is sustained by
no community; in the drabness of mediaeval peasant life without its seasonal joyfulness, they oscillate between bricks and
ghosts. It is the paralysis of the person, at another level,
though it is seldom evident that these persons are so circum-
stanced that they might have chosen differently. But at the
most important level it is metaphysical: the Exiles are exiled
from the garden, and the key to their plight, as *Finnegans Wake*
brings forward, is the Fall. Joyce's world, as the Rev. Walter
Ong has written of Kafka's, " is governed by the sense in
which man's actions are carried on in a setting to which they
are irrelevant ".[2] Father Ong goes on to define " the great

---

[1] With the exception of " Counterparts ", which takes place in a foggy
February dusk. The first three stories (Childhood) span the extremes of June
and December; the next four (Adolescence) occur in summer (though the time
of " Eveline ", a bridge from the childhood section—she is nineteen—isn't
specified; the street organ suggests summer, however). Autumn follows. With
" The Dead " we are plunged into the dead of winter.

[2] Walter J. Ong, S. J., " Kafka's Castle in the West ", *Thought*, XXII–86
(Sept. 1947), 439–460.

fiction of the West; the self-possessed man in the self-possessed
world, the fiction which seeks to erase all sense of plight, of
confusing weakness, from man's consciousness, and which
above all will never admit such a sense as a principle of operation ". Man so constituted, he notes, cannot afford to *give*,
since giving recognizes the fact of *otherness*, of a portion of
being neither susceptible to his control nor violable to his gaze;
this works out alike between man and man, and between man
and God. It is precisely this fiction of self-containment that
Joyce defines in successively more elaborate images, from Mr
Duffy's careful control over every detail of life through the
tightly-bounded ethical world of *Exiles* and Stephen's " All or
not at all " to HCE's solipsistic nightmare. What beats
against all these people is the evidence of otherness: the
ghosts in *Dubliners*, Richard Rowan's voices on the strand at
dawn, Stephen's fear of a " malevolent reality " and his collapse
into Dublin itself (" I have much, much to learn "), the voices
and tappings that derange Earwicker's slumbers like leaves,
twigs, and stones dropped into a pool that craves stagnation.

The focus of Mr. Duffy's plight is achieved in exactly these
terms. During his evenings of intellectual friendship with
Mrs. Sinico,

> Sometimes he caught himself listening to the sound of his own voice.
> He thought that in her eyes he would ascend to an angelical stature;
> and, as he attached the fervent nature of his companion more and more
> closely to him, he heard the strange impersonal voice which he
> recognized as his own, insisting on the soul's incurable loneliness.
> We cannot give ourselves, it said: we are our own. The end of these
> discourses was that one night during which she had shown every sign
> of unusual excitement, Mrs. Sinico caught up his hand passionately
> and pressed it to her cheek. D139/124.

" Her interpretation of his words disillusioned him." Her
touch brings otherness, a world of passion lying outside his
controlled and swept and tidied world, a denial of the voice
which says " We are our own." The " strange impersonal "
quality of that voice is Mr. Duffy's kind of gratuitous illusion,
comparable to the dry detachment with which he had translated *Michael Kramer*, the stage directions written in purple
ink, trying to pretend that someone else did it, some perfected
self disengaged from the tensions of the drama. The voice *is*
his own, as Joyce knew and as Duffy himself half recognizes.

That is what is unforgivable, that she should challenge his self-sufficiency; and he is thrown off balance, breaks off the affair, and after a false quiet steps into hell.

THE PLAN: PUBLIC LIFE ("Ivy Day in the Committee Room "; " A Mother "; " Grace ")

The public life stories are ampler looks round at the same material, with a shift of emphasis to the social manifestations of self-sufficiency. They enact a muted scherzo between the first climax of the book, Mr. Duffy's contact with the dead and his conviction of haunted aloneness, and the long final epiphany, " The Dead ".

In " Ivy Day in the Committee Room " the perspectives of " A Painful Case " begin to expand. The shadow of Parnell to whom they had made years before the one act of faith of which they were capable lies over not just one man but a roomful of paralytics. Political activity in the vacuum left by his departure consists of a few futile gestures, sporadic interviews with voters, and much meditative drinking of stout by an October fire. Edward VII, the surrogate father, is the focus of mild colloquial dissension; the betrayed dead father Parnell stirs into life through a piece of turgidly sincere declamation: our first impressive evidence of Joyce's ability to write just the right kind of bad rhetoric without cynicism. They are the received locutions of Dublin execrably joined, yet a real grief and loyalty break through.

In " A Mother " factitious culture and gratuitous pride collaborate; in " Grace ", gratuitous friendship and factitious religiosity. The absence in these two stories of the circumambient dead, so insistently dominant in the preceding three, is not accidental. We are in touch here with the carapace alone, public life in the boot-heel world. It is not into the communion of saints that his friends' little plot and Father Purdon's urbanely muscular sermon induct Mr. Kernan. " If he might use the metaphor, he said, he was their spiritual accountant ", D222/197; nothing could make the point more clearly than the presentation of redeeming spiritual wisdom in two pages of indirect discourse. From his *selva oscura* at the foot of the lavatory steps, up to the nipping air, then via a sick bed to a Jesuit Paradiso of " decorous atmosphere " on Gardiner Street, where his party settles down " in the form of a quincunx " (Dante's courageous made such a cross, in the

fifth heaven—*Par*. XIV)—Mr. Kernan has been led through
a Dublin *Commedia*.

> The gentlemen were all well dressed and orderly. The light of the
> lamps of the church fell upon an assembly of black clothes and white
> collars, relieved here and there by tweeds, on dark mottled pillars
> of green marble and on lugubrious canvases. The gentlemen sat in
> the benches, having hitched their trousers slightly above their knees
> and laid their hats in security. They sat well back and gazed formally
> at the distant speck of red light which was suspended before the high
> altar, D219/195.

> > O abbondante grazia, ond' io presunsi
> > ficcar lo viso per la luce eterna
> > tanto che la veduta vi consunsi!
> > > > *Paradiso* XXXIII, 82–84

When the preacher enters, they produce handkerchiefs, and
kneel upon them " with care."

" A Mother " and " Grace " bring to maximal articulation
the world which the young narrator of " The Sisters " had
glimpsed in contemplating the untidy hooking of the old
woman's skirt and the heels of her cloth boots trodden down all
to one side: that epiphany, we remember, took place at prayer.

THE DEAD

The motifs of " The Dead " are drawn, in ways we need not
detail, from all the stories in the book, but its peculiar modes of
consciousness are in touch with " The Sisters" at the beginning
and with the " Clay "—" Painful Case "—" Ivy Day " group
in the centre. It is towards the definition of living death, as we
saw in connection with " Clay ", that the entire book is
oriented; the first point to grasp about " The Dead " is the
universal reference of the title. " I had not thought death had
undone so many "; in reading *The Waste Land* aloud Mr.
Eliot puts the stress not on " death " but on " undone ". The
link, through the quotation, with the outer circle of Dante's
hell, the souls who lived without blame and without praise, the
world of the Hollow Men, is an Eliotic perspective of the
utmost relevance to Joyce's story. In " The Dead " everybody
is dead. Its Prufrock-world of dinner-parties, elderly aunts,
young topers, old lechers, and after-dinner wit (" He ran over
the heads of his speech. Irish hospitality, sad memories, the
Three Graces, Paris, the quotation from Browning ", D246/

219) is summed up in the story of the factory horse that exasperated the fashionable pretensions of its rider by walking
round and round the statue of King Billy as around the mill-
shaft, D267/238.   Music, the subject on which these Dubliners
are most articulate, is discussed solely in terms of the good old
days, D255/227.   And the most living influence in the story
is the memory, enclosed in music, of a dead peasant boy.

> We have lingered in the chambers of the sea
> By sea-girls wreathed with seaweed red and brown
> Till human voices wake us, and we drown.

We drown: " His own identity was fading out into a grey
impalpable world: the solid world itself, which these dead had
one time reared and lived in, was dissolving and dwindling ",
D287/255.

Like the first story in the book, the last presents a world of
death dominated by two wraith-like sisters.   The priest who
had been first deranged, then paralysed, then dead had enacted,
we now see in retrospect, a symbolic role of much complexity.
The sisters Morkan are custodians of a ritual order, comprising
every component of the culture of eighteenth-century Dublin,
in whose vitality it is now impossible to feel much faith.   It
does not, we are made to feel, stand of itself; the being of its
world of light, movement, quadrilles, music, and banqueting
is sustained, like an underwater bubble, by the pressure of the
dark snowy boundlessness outside.   Gaiety is oddly unspon-
taneous, a function of custom, habit, and encouragement:

> A red-faced young woman, dressed in pansy, came into the room,
> excitedly clapping her hands and crying:
> " Quadrilles!   Quadrilles! "
> Close on her heels came Aunt Kate, crying:
> " Two gentlemen and three ladies, Mary Jane! ". . .
> As the piano had twice begun the prelude to the first figure
> Mary Jane led her recruits quickly from the room.   D235/209.

The cultural order has shifted, since Swift's time, from the
masculine to the feminine mode.   Art is discussed, D254/226,
in terms of performers.   Creation is unthought of.   The world
of art is an established order which undergoes the homage of
ritual performance.   At the same level of triviality, the discussion shifts from art to religion: the pattern of living death
emerges:

He was astonished to hear that the monks never spoke, got up at
two in the morning, and slept in their coffins. He asked what they
did it for.

"That's the rule of the order," said Aunt Kate firmly.

"Yes, but why?" asked Mr. Browne.

Aunt Kate repeated that it was the rule, that was all. . . . D258/
229.

As for the celebration of artistic mysteries, the respect in which
it is surrounded is one of the polite conventions (cf. " the rule of
the order ") dominated by the Sisters:

Gabriel could not listen while Mary Jane was playing her
Academy piece, full of runs and difficult passages, to the hushed drawing-room. He liked music but the piece she was playing had no
melody for him and he doubted whether it had any melody for the
other listeners, though they had begged Mary Jane to play something.
Four young men, who had come from the refreshment-room to stand
in the doorway at the sound of the piano, had gone away quietly in
couples after a few minutes. The only persons who seemed to follow
the music were Mary Jane herself, her hands racing along the key-
board or lifted from it at the pauses like those of a priestess in momentary imprecation, and Aunt Kate standing at her elbow to turn the
page. D238/211.

The " Academy piece ", the departure of the young men " in
couples " (moral support for unobtrusive defection), the
" priestess " gestures of the performer, the dominating presence of Aunt Kate expediting the mechanism of a culture still
in some sense real to her alone, none of these details is accidental. As for male vitality, we have Mr. Browne:

Then he asked one of the young men to move aside, and, taking hold
of the decanter, filled out for himself a goodly measure of whisky.
The young men eyed him respectfully while he took a trial sip.

"God help me," he said, smiling, "it's the doctor's orders."

His wizened face broke into a broader smile, and the three young
ladies laughed in musical echo to his pleasantry, swaying their bodies
to and fro, with nervous jerks of their shoulders. The boldest said:

"O, now, Mr. Browne, I'm sure the doctor never ordered anything of the kind. " D234/208.

—and Freddy Malins:

Mr. Browne, whose face was once more wrinkling with mirth,
poured out for himself a glass of whisky while Freddy Malins
exploded, before he had well reached the climax of his story, in a kink

of high-pitched bronchitic laughter and, setting down his untasted and overflowing glass, began to rub the knuckles of his left fist backwards and forwards into his left eye, repeating words of his last phrase as well as his fit of laughter would allow him. D237/211.

We are made to feel the artificially fostered isolation of this merriment in countless insidious ways. Physical separation from Dublin is implied not only by the frequent references to the cold and dark out of which the visitors emerge, but by the setting itself, a " dark gaunt house on Usher's Island, the upper part of which they had rented from Mr. Fulham, the corn-factor on the ground floor " D225/199, which emerges oddly during the scenes of leavetaking as a gaslit oasis in Limbo. Death is written on the face of Aunt Julia (" Her hair, drawn low over the tops of her ears, was grey; and grey also, with darker shadows, was her large flaccid face. Though she was stout in build and stood erect, her slow eyes and parted lips gave her the appearance of a woman who did not know where she was or where she was going " D229/204) and life on the face of Aunt Kate suggests comparison to " a shrivelled red apple." Aunt Julia sings *Arrayed for the Bridal*, D247/220, and Gabriel catching the haggard look on her face, D286/254, foresees her death.

It is, significantly, through Gabriel that the anachronistic factitious quality of the evening's merriment emerges in definitive fashion:

One boot stood upright, its limp upper fallen down: the fellow of it lay upon its side. He wondered at his riot of emotions of an hour before. From what had it proceeded? From his aunt's supper, from his own foolish speech, from the wine and dancing, the merry-making when saying goodnight in the hall, the pleasure of the walk along the river in the snow. Poor Aunt Julia! She, too, would soon be a shade with the shade of Patrick Morkan and his horse. . . . D286/254.

Gabriel's emotional organization was completed in his youth, in isolation from their world:

The indelicate clacking of the men's heels and the shuffling of their soles reminded him that their grade of culture differed from his, D229/203.

—and now in isolation from every context. Boots speak as they did to the boy in " The Sisters ". Like Mr. Duffy, Gabriel has constructed about himself an armour of isolation;

his own voice speaks to him in countless forms, as it did to
Mr. Duffy: " We cannot give ourselves, it said; we are our
own ", D139/124. The question, for Gabriel, is only what
posture to adopt for minimal friction:

> He would only make himself ridiculous by quoting poetry to them
> which they could not understand. They would think that he was
> airing his superior education. He would fail with them just as he had
> failed with the girl in the pantry. He had taken up a wrong tone.
> His whole speech was a mistake from first to last, an utter failure.
> D229/204.

Lily, the caretaker's daughter, whose pale name is the first
word in the story, is only the first of the women who rebuff
Gabriel. He is heckled by his wife, D230/205, by his two
aunts, D231/206, by Miss Ivors, D243/216; and his wife at
the end turns from him for a shade. It is his know-how,
chiefly, that commands respect:

> He felt quite at ease now for he was an expert carver and liked nothing
> better than to find himself at the head of a well-laden table. D253/
> 225.

Gabriel, then, and the Morkan party are analogous worlds:
analogous in their incurable autonomy. He is one closed
system. The scheme of values expressed at the annual dance
is another. The enveloping background of both is the snow.
Gabriel emerges into the house from the snow as from an
invigorating medium:

> He continued scraping his feet vigorously while the three women
> went upstairs, laughing, to the ladies' dressing-room. A light fringe
> of snow lay like a cape on the shoulders of his overcat and like toecaps
> on the toes of his goloshes; and, as the buttons of his overcoat slipped
> with a squeaking noise through the snow-stiffened frieze, a cold,
> fragrant air from out-of-doors escaped from crevices and folds.
> D226/201.

Their laughter recedes from him; the snow, the " cold,
fragrant air ", standing for something like Ibsen's envacuumed
Norway, is his element. Between his round of infighting with
Miss Ivors and the necessities of the dinner-table speech in
tribute to the aunts whom he privately reduces to " two
ignorant old women ", D247/219, his mind turns to the snow
again with longing:

> Gabriel's warm trembling fingers tapped the cold pane of the window.
> How cool it must be outside! How pleasant it would be to walk out

alone, first along by the river and then through the park! The snow
would be lying on the branches of the trees and forming a bright
cap on the top of the Wellington Monument. How much more
pleasant it would be there than at the supper-table! D246/218.

The meaning of this desire is clarified much later, when at the
beginning of the walk home Gabriel's imagination yields to
the passion that is to suffer such deflation in the hotel-room:

> Moments of their secret life together burst like stars upon his
> memory. . . . He was standing with her in the cold, looking in
> through a grated window at a man making bottles in a roaring furnace.
> It was very cold. Her face, fragrant in the cold air, was quite close
> to his; and suddenly he called out to the man at the furnace:
> " Is the fire hot, sir? "
> But the man could not hear with the noise of the furnace. It
> was just as well. He might have answered rudely. D275/244.

The invigorating cold stands for something complexly
intrinsic to Gabriel's psychic balance. It is that against which
his animal warmth is asserted: an obeisant medium presenting
no diplomatic puzzles. And it is the brisk vacant context of
his ideal passion for Gretta, once experienced and now remembered, in which they exist alone, in a naked mingling of passions,
separated from the ordinary social milieu by a grated window.
The picturesque spectacle of the man making bottles in a
roaring furnace conveys the spectacular toy-shop quality
Dublin acquires when seen from the centre of their union.
The snow, ultimately, corresponds to the quality of Gabriel's
isolation (" How pleasant it would be to walk out alone by the
river and then through the park! ") It is where he feels at
home. It is anti-communal; it is that against which the Misses
Morkan's Christmas dance asserts warmth and order. Gabriel
imagines, as it proves mistakenly, that Gretta has shared it
with him. Because it is anti-communal it is death; it triumphs
in the end over his soul and, as he foresees, over Aunt Kate and
Aunt Julia, and over all Dublin and all Ireland, reducing " the
solid world itself, which these dead had one time reared and
lived in " to a common level with " the dark central plain ",
" the bog of Allen ", and " the lonely churchyard on the hills
where Michael Furey lay buried." D288/256.

The fragrant air Gabriel had carried into the Misses
Morkan's house is the principle of death; it is his proper
medium, as he comes to see:

A shameful consciousness of his own person assailed him. He saw
himself as a ludicrous figure, acting as a pennyboy for his aunts, a
nervous, well-meaning sentimentalist, orating to vulgarians and
idealizing his own clownish lusts, the pitiable fatuous fellow he had
caught a glimpse of in the mirror. D283/251.

He and his generation of glib middle-class snobbery and book-
reviewing are the exorcism of the ghostly eighteenth-century
order that lingers in the salon of his aunts. " Better pass
boldly into that other world, in the full glory of some passion,"
he thinks, " than fade and wither dismally with age." D287/
255. The dancing-party belongs to that which is fading and
withering; as for himself, there is no question of passing
boldly into that other world. He is already of it. His longing
to be alone in the snow was a longing for this death. His soul
already pursues the " wayward and flickering existence " of the
dead; it has taken very little to cause his identity to fade out
" into a grey impalpable world ". He is named for the angel
who is to blow the last trump; but having released no blast
of Judgment he watches through a hotel window the pale
flakes falling through darkness.

One of Joyce's Trieste language-pupils recalls him gazing
into a glass paperweight of the sort containing floating crystals
and murmuring, " Yes, snow is general all over Ireland."
Snow continued to fall and Ireland continued to be paralysed,
in Joyce's mind, throughout his life. The snow is still falling
in *Finnegans Wake* (" Countlessness of livestories have netherfallen by this plage, flick as flowflakes, litters from aloft, like a
waast wizzard all of whirlworlds . . . likeas equal to anequal
in this sound seemetery which iz leebez luv ", F17), and the
" few light taps " that made Gabriel turn to the window
punctuate the dream of H. C. Earwicker with their recurrent
" Tip ".

The epical narrative has concluded by gathering up the
quality of a whole civilization in the isolation of Gabriel Conroy.
His preferred snow-world suggests Ibsen; it was to the meaning of his ethical absolutism, as elevated by Ibsen into a preferred *modus vivendi*, totally divorced from communal context,
that Joyce now turned.

Chapter 6

EXILES

BERTHA: I will tell you if you ask me.
RICHARD: You will tell me. But I will never know. Never in
this world.

Exiles (F139/146)

Sometime then, somewhere there, I wrote me hopes and buried
the page when I heard Thy voice, ruddery dunner, so loud that
none but, and left it to lie till a kissmiss coming. So content me
now. Lss.

Finnegans Wake (F624)

GABRIEL CONROY yearned for the snows. *Exiles*—an austere
ungarnished play—inspects that pseudo-liberation; its Richard
Rowan is a Gabriel Conroy liberated by Ibsen, the Ibsen with
whom Joyce had been flirting for a dozen years. Having
abolished Dedalus—rebellious *superbia*—as a *point d'appui* for
art, Joyce now abolished him as an ethical theory.

Exiles is not an apologia for Richard Rowan; we should be
prepared to find him suspended in a void, and that is exactly
what we do find. Hence the bewilderment of readers who,
traversing the canon chronologically, come to him fresh from
the soaring close of the *Portrait* instead of from the final pages
of *Dubliners*. The play's roots are in Joyce's first cycle, though
it was written after the start of his second; for reasons that
will soon be apparent, Joyce could not attempt it till he had
completed the *Portrait*, and had to finish it before he could get
on with the already-drafted *Ulysses*. Stephen Dedalus is as
much envacuumed as Richard, but sufficient eloquence of
Byronic revolt surrounds Stephen to make this fact easy to
overlook. Contemplation of Richard Rowan's unequivocally
joyless arrogance makes Stephen-worshippers feel they've been
had.

Exiles frees Joyce from Ibsen the undernourished doctrinaire
whose " wayward, boyish " pseudo-rigours of revolt had for
some years compromised a portion of his spirit. The repudiation of the Norwegian's Utopia-at-the-other-side-of-free-love is
explicit. This must be clearly grasped, because the impossibility

of squaring the play with what Shavian Ibsenism may lead us to believe is its "message" has probably stymied more readers than any other difficulty. We had better turn at once to one of the epiphanic moments. Robert Hand ("with growing excitement") proposes to Richard, with the favours of Bertha as prize, "a battle of both our souls, different as they are, against all that is false in them and in the world":

> All life is a conquest, the victory of human passion over the commandments of cowardice. Will you, Richard? Have you the courage? Even if it shatters to atoms the friendship between us, even if it breaks up for ever the last illusion in your own life? There was an eternity before we were born: another will come after we are dead. The blinding instant of passion alone—passion, free, unashamed, irresistible—that is the only gate by which we can escape from the misery of what slaves call life. Is not this the language of your own youth that I heard so often from you in this very place where we are sitting now? Have you changed?
> RICHARD: (*Passes his hand across his brow.*) Yes. It is the language of my youth. E89/99.

"It is the language of their youth," comments Mr. Francis Fergusson,[1] "and it sounds like the Nietzsche of *The Birth of Tragedy*, or the Wagner of *Tristan*." And, Mr. Raymond Williams adds, it is also the language of Ibsen.[2] It is the language, furthermore, of the *Transition*-sponsored official image of Joyce, and of the Transitionists' intercorruption of art and life. It translates the inherent recklessness of aesthetic juxtaposition and manoeuvre into a *modus vivendi*. "The intense instant of imagination, when the mind, Shelley says, is a fading coal", U192/183, is corrupted by Robert into "the blinding instant of passion . . . by which we can escape from the misery of what slaves call life". This is not to weigh the way of the Heathcliffs against the cautious prudential arrangements of the Lintons. Joyce always weighs the parody against the parody. Robert is a Linton posturing as a Heathcliff. *Exiles* explores a counterposition of modes of insincerity. It weighs against the "scrupulous meanness" of "chairs, upholstered in faded green plush", E1/15, and "Death of the Very Reverend Canon Mulhall", E134/142, nothing more radically antithetical than the Liebestod of Robert Hand:

[1] Preface to the New Directions edition, x.
[2] "The *Exiles* of James Joyce", *Politics and Letters*, Summer 1948, 16.

ROBERT: (*Presses her to him.*) To end it all—death. To fall from a great high cliff, down, right down into the sea.
BERTHA: Please, Robert . . .
ROBERT: Listening to music and in the arms of the woman I love—the sea, music and death. E34/46.

We must not be misled by the plausibility of speech and costume into supposing that this is any less " faded green plush " than the armchairs of the Merrion drawing-room.

Ibsen imagined talk like this to be an absolute and a defiance of the drawing-room. Joyce exhibits them as continuous modes. When Robert proclaims the eternal law of passion:

> ROBERT: (*Still more warmly.*) I am sure that no law made by man is sacred before the impulse of passion. (*Almost fiercely.*) Who made us for one only? It is a crime against our own being if we are so. There is no law before impulse. Laws are for slaves. E116/125.

—he both echoes Ibsen:

> . . . set up voluntary choice and spiritual kinship as the only determining factors for union—that is the beginning of a freedom that is worth something. . . . Who can guarantee that two and two are not five on Jupiter?[1]

—and fulfils the mode in which he is exhibited at the beginning of the second act, ejecting sprays of perfume into the summerhouse from a pump which he keeps behind the piano, E69/80: a context for his passion, one would think, sufficiently ludicrous to prevent anyone supposing that he is voicing the " doctrine " of the play. Mr. Williams acutely remarks that " when quotations are sought by commentators intent on illustrating from this play the ideas which they assume to be the persistent attitude of Joyce, it is from Robert only that they can be found." And Robert is not an univocal antithesis for Richard; Robert is in many respects simply Richard hauled down into visibility. ". . . The audience," Joyce wrote in a note-book, " every man of which is Robert and would like to be Richard."

[1] This and subsequent *obiter dicta* of Ibsen's in the present chapter are from letters printed by his biographer Koht. (Halvdan Koht, *The Life of Ibsen*, trans. McMahon and Larsen.)

IBSEN THE LANGUAGE OF RICHARD'S YOUTH

" It is the language of my youth ", admits Richard wearily of Robert's mauve bravado. It was also the principle of action of his youth, and it betrayed him.

This fact cannot be pinned down too securely. The paradigms of Richard's conduct nine years before—the shunning of his mother, the hegira with Bertha—are those of Ibsen. He had transformed, naively, Ibsen's diagnosis of social dishonesty into a principle of action, exactly as did the impossible Norwegian himself, and as Joyce did in 1904. Richard versus his mother:

> She drove me away. On account of her I lived years in exile and poverty too, or near it. I never accepted the doles she sent me through the bank. I waited, too, not for her death but for some understanding of me, her own son, her own flesh and blood; that never came. E14/27.

Ibsen versus his family:

> Do you know that I have separated myself for life from my parents —from all my kin—because I could not continue in a relation of incomplete understanding?[1]

Ibsen confused the impercipient inertia of much human conduct with the matrix of convention and artifice in which social and familial relationships are necessarily enacted. His irascible catchwords, " ruthless honesty ", " giving oneself wholly and freely ", have paralysed most readers as they paralyse Robert Hand; but they conceal *superbia*, not angelic rectitude. He wrote to his sister Hedvig on hearing of his mother's death, " I cannot write letters; I must be present in person to give myself wholly and completely "; this was meant to look like a desire for honest emotion circumventing the spectre of merely conventional grief, but what comes out is a determination not to appear at all unless he can steal the show.

THE TUG OF IBSEN

In the life of the mind there is no such thing as an unwilling victim. What did Joyce want with such a master in the first place?

Joyce the citizen-exile confronting the dual Dublin, the

[1] Letter to Björnson, 1867.

Dublin of " sordid and deceptive details " and that of civic intelligibility, was filled with " such a sudden despair as could be assuaged only by melancholy versing " and had " all but decided to consider the two worlds as aliens to one another . . . when he encountered through the medium of hardly procured translations the spirit of Henrik Ibsen ", S40/32. That was when he was at college, in the *Chamber Music* days, before he had written any of *Dubliners*.

Ibsen, like Joyce, like Flaubert, was a provincial artist. But the blood of Paris flowed, however sluggishly, through Flaubert's Rouen; it was Ibsen's province that was the more like Joyce's, related to Europe not as a torpid member to a body but as a heatless satellite to an over-rated sun. Like Ireland, his Norway was an outlying province of Europe. Like Ireland, it was vacuous and criss-crossed with parlour-bourgeois suspicion. Like Ireland, it was sustained by prohibitions rather than customs. Like Ireland, it brooded on an epic past (Dublin itself was in fact a Scandinavian settlement). Dano-Norse relations strikingly resembled Anglo-Irish. Both Joyce and Ibsen wrote in a conqueror's tongue, while dialects of the autochthonous language continued to be spoken in the country-side.

" I cannot speak or write these words without unrest of spirit ", P221/215, mused Stephen of an English convert's tongue. The example of Ibsen probably encouraged him to foster this fructive unrest instead of, as a young man, aligning his stubbornness with Yeats, Lady Gregory, and the Gaelic League. Ibsen in his earlier years had been similarly involved in a campaign for a national drama and a purely Norwegian language. Persuading himself of a vocation to recall to the people " the rich imagery of the past " and " the forgotten tales of childhood ", he wrote one popular success, was perplexed by a series of failures, and cut his losses after wasting fifteen years.

Ibsen's willingness to cut a loss exemplified the self-confidence by which Joyce was most strongly drawn to him (" A man of genius makes no mistakes ", said Stephen. " His errors are volitional and are the portals of discovery ", U188/179.) His example, as it proved, almost wrecked Joyce's career, because it was ethical as well as professional. Having first become interested in Ibsen as a man who could help him write through the concrete fact without abandoning it, and set himself to learn Dano-Norse because he sensed a resilience in Ibsen's mind incompatible with the barren Archerese of the translations,[1] Joyce soon became absorbed in the biography—disgust with the homeland, exile, early poems, middle monuments of construction and solidity accompanied by *succès de scandale*, later symbolic experiments denounced by fellow-travellers as madness—which, excepting the ultimate return to homeland fame, was to correspond so strikingly with his own.   A few weeks after his eighteenth birthday he published in the *Fortnightly Review* (April 1, 1900) an account of the recently-issued *When We Dead Awaken;* the opening paean indicates how, in his mind, the stress came to fall:

> Seldom, if at all, has he consented to join battle with his enemies. It would appear as if the storm of fierce debate rarely broke in upon his wonderful calm. The conflicting voices have not influenced his work in the very smallest degree.

In the conversations of about this time, epitomized in the *Portrait*, the dramatic artist is " refined out of existence, indifferent, paring his fingernails ", P252/245. That image suggests a somewhat self-conscious impersonality; in 1901 he wrote Ibsen a birthday letter suffused with confidential discipleship:

> I did not tell them [the Dubliners] what bound me closest to you. I did not say how what I could discern dimly of your life was my pride to see, how your battles inspired me—not the obvious material battles but those that were fought and won behind your forehead, how your wilful resolution to wrest the secret from life gave me heart and how in your absolute indifference to public canons of art, friends, and shibboleths you walked in the light of your inward heroism.

Part of the appeal of this " inward heroism " is ascribable to the fact that Joyce encountered Ibsen at about the time when he was losing his Catholic faith.   " Jeg laegger med lyst torpedo under Arken! " (I'll gladly torpedo you the Ark!) Ibsen had written in *Til min ven revolutions-taleren*, and in *Stephen Hero* we read,

---

[1] " His writing can be understood only in terms of the Norse, with its clear, pungent but concrete vocabulary, its strong live metaphors (' we felt our hearts *beat strongly towards* him '), its lack of reverberations or overtones." Miss M. C. Bradbrook, *Ibsen the Norwegian*. It is, for instance, important to know, apropos of a phrase in *Rosmersholm*, that *kinsmen* in Norwegian are *skyldfolk*, those who share a common guilt: a typical instance of thematic density that defies translation.

Anyway you won't repeat what I say to your confessor in future because I won't say anything. And the next time he asks you " What is that mistaken young man, that unfortunate boy, doing? " you can answer " I don't know, father. I asked him and he said I was to tell the priest he was making a torpedo." S210/187.

It was natural for the Stephen Dedalus *persona*, martyr plus aeronaut, to attach itself to the man who roared at a review of *Peer Gynt*, " My book *is* poetry, and if it is not, it shall be. The conception of poetry shall in our land, in Norway, come to adapt itself to the book "; who at 16 told his sister that his ambition was to attain the utmost perfection of greatness and clarity and after that to die; and who insisted with the vehemence of uneasiness that he did not write only for the immediate future but for all eternity. When a friend rejoined that in a thousand years even the greatest man would probably be forgotten, Ibsen was quite beside himself: " Get away from me with your metaphysics. If you rob me of eternity, you rob me of everything."

FLAUBERTIAN IBSEN

The artist lives in two worlds, the world he understands and the world his characters understand. Insofar as he defines the former by disdaining the latter, his work is fissioned by an Ibsen's centrifugal letch toward eternity. In his best work, Ibsen achieved " the syllogism of art ", the mediation between the two worlds, by starting with the given, " bending upon these present things ", with no corruption of practical passions. This was evident to Joyce from the first. It was Ibsen's solid merit. In a portion of the *Stephen Hero* MS. that can hardly date later than 1904, the following exchange occurs:

> – Ah, if he were to examine even the basest things, said the President with a suggestion of tolerance in store, it would be different if he were to examine and then show men the way to purify themselves.
> – That is for the Salvationists, said Stephen.
> – Do you mean . . .
> – I mean that Ibsen's account of modern society is as genuinely ironical as Newman's account of English protestant morality and belief.
> – That may be, said the President, appeased by the conjunction.
> – And as free from any missionary intent.
> The President was silent. S92/79.

"Naturalism", as Joyce saw instantly, is an essentially ambivalent convention. It parades an ironic obsession with what the characters see in order to express what they ignore. It affords the artist immersed in a provincial society leverage for exhibiting the condition of man. For fallen man the intelligible can be attained only by submission of the intellect to the inherent opacity of matter. Provincial man is doubly fallen. He buries even the intelligible realities available to him in yet more matter. He devotes his frantic concern to clocks and furniture. Hence Joyce's scrupulous prescription, in the *Exiles* stage-directions, of such details as the "floor of stained planking", which has occasioned some surprise in devotees of the Fabulous Artificer. "Respectable" furnishings were par excellence the epiphanizing "present things" of the nineteenth century. "At no other time in history," comments Joyce's good friend Siegfried Giedion, "did man allow the goodly ordering of his surroundings to suffer such decay. . . . Taken one by one, the statues, pictures, vases, carpets, are harmless and insignificant. . . . But viewed in their totality, accumulated museum-fashion, as the custom was, their bastardized forms and materials react upon the spectator and corrode his emotional life."[1] In Richard Rowan's drawing-room a kind of faded elegance has been imposed on these abominations; but Robert Hand's cottage, with its piano and "standing Turkish pipe", is a hothouse for eerie banalities of passion. The century externalized its darkest passions in furniture as nowhere else, as Max Ernst saw (see Giedion's reproductions, pp. 386–7, of a typical interior and an Ernst collage). In *Finnegans Wake* we catch a glimpse of Shem the Penman "self exiled in upon his ego, a nightlong a shaking betwixtween white or reddr hawrors, noondayterrorised to skin and bone by an ineluctable phantom (may the Shaper have mercery on him!) writing the mystery of himsel in furniture." F184. In *Ulysses* Joyce wrote the comic mystery of Bloom in the Ithaca inventories: The existing:

A timepiece of striated Connemàra marble, stopped at the hour of 4.46 a.m. on the 21 March 1896, matrimonial gift of Matthew Dillon: a dwarf tree of glacial arborescence under a transparent

---

[1] S. Giedion, *Mechanization Takes Command*. The entire fifth section of this book deserves careful study in connection with Joyce's elaborate description, compiled from furniture catalogues, of Bloom's dream cottage.

bellshade, matrimonial gift of Luke and Caroline Doyle: an embalmed owl, matrimonial gift of Alderman John Hooper. U692/668.

The envisioned:

> ... bentwood perch with fingertame parrot (expurgated language), embossed mural paper at 10/- per dozen with transverse swags of carmine floral design and top crown frieze ... water closet on mezzanine provided with opaque singlepane oblong window, tipup seat, bracket lamp, brass tierod brace, armrests, footstool and artistic oleograph on inner face of door. . . . U698/674.

The Ibsen technique of turning sordid particulars into numinous symbols was Joyce's point of departure here, though it is obvious that he had assimilated Flaubert's sardonic meticulousness as well. A rotting ship, a captive wild duck in an attic—externals, scrupulously documented, masking psychological and supernatural realities to which, until the catastrophe, the protagonists are indifferent—such is Ibsen's image of the condition of a whole society. When William Archer attributed to senile decline the sacrifice of surface reality to underlying meaning in *When We Dead Awaken:*

> Take for instance the history of Rubek's statue and its development into a group. In actual sculpture this development is a grotesque impossibility. . . .[1]

he betrayed the same notion of naturalism-as-documentation that has caused many readers to attribute to a humourless mania Joyce's statement that " Ithaca " was the best episode in *Ulysses*. There are several indications that Bloom would like to write the sort of book many readers imagine *Ulysses* to be:

> Time I used to try jotting down on my cuff what she said dressing. Dislike dressing together. Nicked myself shaving. Biting her nether lip, hooking the placket of her skirt. Timing her. 9.15. Did Roberts pay you yet? 9.20. What had Gretta Conroy on? 9.23. What possessed me to buy this comb? 9.24. I'm swelled after that cabbage. A speck of dust on the patent leather of her boot. U69/62.

This sort of naturalism is a Bloomian product, by Blooms for Blooms. The documentary fussiness of *Exiles*, as of Ibsen's work from *Pillars of Society* to *The Master Builder*, is oriented not toward " reality " but toward images of paralysis and claustrophobia. The furniture of the elaborate stage-directions is there, so to speak, for the characters to trip over.

[1] Introduction to *When We Dead Awaken*.

PROMETHEAN IBSEN

The techniques of ironic naturalism were less central for Ibsen than they were to be for Joyce. Ibsen invented the problem-play in part to exploit a problem he could not solve: whether the artist was not a Prometheus crucified to " facts ". A stanza of his that the young Joyce used often to quote:

> To live is to war with the troll
> In the caverns of heart and of skull.
> To write poetry—that is to hold
> Doom-session upon the soul[1]

—has *Prometheus Vinctus* implications that an older Joyce elicited in assimilating Ibsen's image to that of the Scandin-avian HCE undergoing, bound to his bed, a nightlong intro-spection looking forward to the (unwritten) epilogue *When We Dead Awaken*: " hungerstriking all alone and holding dooms-dag over hunselv, dreeing his weird, with his dander up, and his fringe combed over his eygs and droming on loft till the sight of the sternes, after zwarthy kowse and weedy broeks and the tits of buddy and the loits of pest and to peer was Parish worth thette mess ", F199. (The last two lines of the stanza read in Norwegian, " At digte—det er at holde / dommedag over sig selv." " To peer ": to Peer Gynt.)

Ibsen unbound Prometheus by dismissing all human bonds as sentiment. The myth that contains his life-work was pro-jected in a poem, *On the Vidda*, written at 32. Its themes reach forward to his last play, *When We Dead Awaken*. In the poem a young man from the valley, conventionally in love, is visited on holiday in the mountain uplands by a strange hunter " with cold eyes like mountain lakes " who induces him to stay on the *vidda* all summer and when his mother's cottage burns points out the beauty of the fire and advises on the best way to get the view. The youth takes to heart this lesson in detachment. When his betrothed finally marries another man, having under-standably tired of awaiting his return, he curves his hand to impose pictorial composition on the wedding procession wind-ing through the valley trees. " Self-steeled he looks on at joy from above life's snow-line. The Strange Hunter reappears and tells him he is now free. . . .

> Now I am steel-set: I follow the call
> To the height's clear radiance and glow.

[1] Miss Bradbrook's translation.

> My lowland life is lived out, and high
> On the vidda are God and liberty—
> While wretches live fumbling below."[1]

The author of *The Holy Office* (1904; aetat. 22) took several gestures from this poem:

> So distantly I turn to view
> The shamblings of this motley crew,
> The souls that hate the strength that mine has
> Steeled in the school of old Aquinas.
> Where they have crouched and crawled and prayed
> I stand, the self-doomed, unafraid,
> Unfellowed, friendless, and alone,
> Indifferent as the herring-bone,
> Firm as the mountain ridges where
> I flash my antlers in the air. . . .[2]

Joyce had this poem printed and mailed to all its victims. Even after the scrupulous writing of *Dubliners* was under way, the Ibsenian Dedalus remained a pose behind which he could most readily mobilize his rhetorical energy. When nearly ten years later he turned the Dedalus aesthete himself into an aesthetic object, Stephen remained for him something more than comic. There is tragic necessity in the spectacle of the aesthete's mask being fused to the young sensitive's flesh: the necessity, for a provincial artist deprived of any respectable traditions, of becoming the enemy of his society in ways incompatible with remaining in touch with human wisdom. The split artist, like Shem the Penman " honour bound to his own cruelfiction ", F192, reflects the split man of the split community. Ibsen got no further than that.

That was enough, however, to energize some remarkable plays. Six years after *On the Vidda* he displayed, in *Brand*, some uneasiness about its naive heroics. Brand as clergyman (a more general statement of the artist as communal scapegoat) makes, like the young man on the heath, one ruthless sacrifice after another in the spirit of self-conscious humility which *Murder in the Cathedral* has focussed as the ultimate, subtlest temptation. Having demanded the supreme sacrifice of his mother, his child, his wife, and his congregation, he winds up

---

[1] The verse translation and the quoted phrases are Miss Bradbrook's; the outline is abridged from hers. No complete English version of the poem seems to be available.

[2] Gorman, V, ii.

among the mountain-peaks of his ambition and in the Ice-Church appropriate to his nature; when finally, renouncing Pride and calling on the God of Love, he melts the ice, he and his troll-lover are engulfed in the ruins.

IBSEN THE DUPE OF HIS PROGRAMMES

The fifth-act writing-off of Brand's whole career as *hubris* doesn't balance the doctrinaire intensity with which it has been presented in the first four. That is an index of Ibsen's problems. His was far from being a unified sensibility. It must strike any reader of his biography that much of his intellectual life was conducted in jejune slogans:

> Undermine the idea of the State, set up voluntary choice and spiritual kinship as the only determining factors for union—that is the beginning of a freedom that is worth something. Yes, my dear friend, it is imperative not to let one's self be frightened by its venerable vested rights. The State has its roots in time, it will culminate in time. Greater things than this will perish: all religions will perish. Neither moral principles nor artistic forms have any eternity ahead of them. How much are we at bottom obliged to hold fast to? Who can guarantee that two and two are not five on Jupiter?[1]

Denial of the rational and political nature of man could scarcely go farther. Ibsen thinks of the State, and by extension all frames of reference for action—religious, moral, aesthetic—as convertible with the police. He was even accustomed to using his question about two and two as a serious argument. This skeletal righteousness deprived of all social, political, or theological context is in sharp distinction from the sense of collective wisdom that secures Wordsworth (who denied its intellectual roots) a dignified place in the English tradition, and that for fifty generations from Cicero through Augustine to Erasmus had nourished a complex communal sense of which Wordsworth furnishes only the death-mask. It is only because he is serious and tenacious, involved by his technique in close scrutiny of mundane existential groupings, and not because he is in contact with even a simulacrum of wisdom not himself, that Ibsen's dramas are saved from anarchy.

Behind Ireland, however, via Rome, stood the past of Christian Europe; behind Norway stood nothing remotely comparable. If Ireland was " the afterthought of Europe",

[1] Letter to Georg Brandes (1871).

it was still European.   And if Norway had little to teach Ibsen,
he learned nothing from leaving it.   His revolt against its
bourgeois frontier-ethics became enfleshed in nothing better
than stern intentions: hence the stiff boniness of *Brand*.

In the five chapters of *A Portrait of the Artist as a Young Man*
Joyce rewrote the five acts of *Brand* in a civic perspective Ibsen
knew nothing about.   It is from Brand (the name means both
" sword " and " fire ") that many of the most humourlessly
arrogant gestures of Stephen Dedalus are derived: his
behaviour at his mother's death-bed,[1] his rejection of the
Christianity of the clergy, his romantic positives expressed in
terms of " the spell of arms and voices " and of " exultant and
terrible youth ", P298/288, corresponding to Ibsen's " flashing
eyes " and his dawn above the ice-fields.   Joyce saw, however,
what Stephen was revolting *from:* from a father in whom the
great past of Europe was depraved, to an ideal father whose
wings were expected to bear him above the depravity.   But
above the depravity was away from the reality; Stephen found
himself allied instead with a third father, Leopold Bloom, in
whom the great past of Europe didn't exist.   In the company
of Buck Mulligan (a variation on Peer Gynt) the new Brand
came to grief beneath the eyes of an author who " examines the
entire community in action and reconstructs the spectacle of
redemption " S186/165.

Before writing *Ulysses* Joyce had to fight Ibsen with Ibsen's
own weapons: in *Exiles* he brings an Ibsen hero to nullity
within the context of an Ibsen play.

THE UNSUCCESSFUL ANGEL

Ethical freedom which shall not be anarchy and utter honesty
which shall not be corrosive are proper, it is not merely wry
to remark, to a society of angels.   Angels strictly speaking:
unfallen beings of perfect comprehension in whose society
there is no marrying nor giving in marriage.   The Exiles to
whom this perfection is impossible are exiled from Eden; that
is the ultimate meaning of the play.

The determination to behave in this unfallen way leads fallen
man to behave as a fallen angel: the oldest of theological
commonplaces.   " To hold you by no bonds, even of love, to
be united with you in body and soul in utter nakedness—for

---

[1] Not a piece of autobiography, as Stanislaus Joyce assures us: *Hudson Review*,
II-4, 491.

this I longed ", E154/162.   But human kind cannot bear that
kind of reality.   Here is what actually happened:

> ROBERT: Richard, have you been quite fair to her?   It was her
> own free choice, you will say.   But was she really free to choose?
> She was a mere girl.   She accepted all that you proposed.
> RICHARD: (*Smiles.*)   That is your way of saying that she proposed
> what I would not accept.
> ROBERT: (*Nods.*)   I remember.   And she went away with you.
> But was it of her own free choice?   Answer me frankly.
> RICHARD: (*Turns to him calmly.*)   I played for her against all that
> you say or can say; and I won.   E41/53.

That he has raised her to coangelic status is a gratuitous pretence: the imposition of will upon will is as sharp as in the
most abstract dealings via a marriage-broker.   The Ibsenite
rebel " emancipates " no one but himself: the " gift " of freedom he claims to confer is as Bertha sees meaningless, as much
so as the analogous gift once offered another woman by Lucifer.
He cultivates a habitual exasperation with whatever is not
reduced to an orbit intelligible to him because imposed by him
—again like Lucifer—and he finally deals with an uncoopera-
tive milieu by banishing it.   Exile is his invariable destination,
as it was for Ibsen.   In writing this play Joyce clarified and
purged this motive among his many motives for leaving Dublin.
In explicating the plight of Richard Rowan, *Exiles* became
Joyce's abolition of the last shreds of Stephen.

SAD *SUPERBIA* THE KEYNOTE OF RICHARD

Richard, paradigm of the way the dignity of naked revolt works
out in practice, is after nine years god-like and wretched.   He
casts off, as he progresses, images of himself, indifferently in
human or in verbal material.   Robert is the creature of his
youth, come to terms a little with Dublin but ethically arrested
at the phase in which Richard formed him in 1903.   Beatrice
he remakes in his book in progress.   As for Bertha, " You
have made her all that she is ", Robert acknowledges.[1]

> RICHARD: (*Darkly.*)   Or I have killed her.
> ROBERT: Killed her?
> RICHARD: The virginity of her soul.

[1] " I am simply a tool for you ", she says herself, E95/105.

ROBERT: (*Impatiently.*) Well lost! What would she be without you?

RICHARD: I tried to give her a new life.

ROBERT: And so you have. A new and rich life.

RICHARD: Is it worth what I have taken from her—her girlhood, her laughter, her young beauty, the hopes in her young heart? E83/94.

In his working notes Joyce glosses " the virginity of her soul ":

The soul like the body may have a virginity. For the woman to yield it or for the man to take it is the act of love. Love (understood as the desire of good for another) is in fact so unnatural a phenomenon that it can scarce repeat itself, the soul being unable to become virgin again and not having energy enough to cast itself out again into the ocean of another's soul. It is the repressed consciousness of this inability and lack of spiritual energy which explains Bertha's menta paralysis.[1]

The definition of love is given (" hesitatingly ") by Richard early in Act II:

ROBERT: But if you love ... What else is it?

RICHARD: (*Hesitatingly.*) To wish her well. E78/88.

Conceived as that and not as a desire to possess her, it is " unnatural " in an exact sense: it transcends appetitive nature. That is the *psychological* basis for the indissolubility of marriage: a psychological orientation corresponding to the metaphysical fact against which the Exiles are dashed.

Richard the ape of God has made Robert; he has made Bertha; and he sets them in a country-house with a garden, his new man and new woman. Unlike the God in Genesis, he imposes no conditions; but she who has united her soul to his in performing the act of love cries out for conditions:

You urged me to do it. Not because you love me. If you loved me or if you knew what love was you would not have left me. For your own sake you urged me to do it.

RICHARD: I did not make myself. I am what I am.

BERTHA: To have it always to throw against me. To make me humble before you, as you always did. To be free yourself. ... E139/147.

The parody of " I AM WHO AM " is too close to be accidental. Bertha and Robert, creatures of a rational idealist, are enacting

---

[1] Facsimile reproduction in the *James Joyce Yearbook*, Paris, 1949, facing p. 49.

the generic rational idealist's resentment at the God who set the baited trap in the Garden: " To have it always to throw against me.   To make me humble before you, as you always did.   To be free yourself."   The " freedom " Richard continually exhibits himself as conferring on her has similar coordinates.   He bestows free will on his creatures:

> RICHARD: *(Controlling himself.)*   You forget that I have allowed you complete liberty—and allow you it still.
> BERTHA: *(Scornfully.)*   Liberty!   E61/73.

and later:

> BERTHA: . . . Am I to go?
> RICHARD: Why do you ask me?   Decide yourself.
> BERTHA: Do you tell me to go?
> RICHARD: No.
> BERTHA: Do you forbid me to go?
> RICHARD: No.

To the garden she goes; but he, an enlightened man understanding the nugatory significance of outward acts, an imperfect god incapable of knowing the inner springs of his creatures' volition, knows that he will never know whether or not she has plucked the fruit.

THE ABOLITION OF THE COMMUNITY

It is in his role as lonely deity that Richard catechizes everyone: both because he must on principle dominate everyone, and because his only hope of palliating " the soul's incurable loneliness " is to bring others to the condition of himself:

> RICHARD: *(With some vehemence.)*   Then that I expressed in those chapters and letters, and in my character and life as well, something in you own soul which you could not—pride or scorn?
> BEATRICE: Could not?
> RICHARD: *(Leans towards her.)*   Could not because you dared not. Is that why?
> BEATRICE: *(Bends her head.)*   Yes.
> RICHARD: On account of others or for want of courage—which?
> BEATRICE: *(Softly.)*   Courage.
> RICHARD: *(Slowly.)*   And so you have followed me with pride and scorn also in your heart?
> BEATRICE: And loneliness.   E8/22.

He must make a convert.   He cannot.   The context of civic society once abandoned, each inquisition of the isolated person exposes that same fact: each is alone. " I am living with a stranger," cries Bertha at the height of the last cross-examination, E141/149; and looking back even on her days in Rome: " I was alone ", E153/161.

It was not Richard of course who abolished the community for Robert and Beatrice, whatever his responsibility toward Bertha. The community Robert serves with diffidence and factitious gusto, arranging luncheons with the vice-chancellor, mobilizing the facile rhetoric of the daily paper, has abolished itself. It provides no context for meaningful living. To that extent it is Irish paralysis that is epiphanized in that chorused affirmation of loneliness.

Yet as much as the man who remains in the paralysed community, the man who abandons the wreckage of the community for the *vidda* above the snow-line comes to a paralysing realization of nakedness, tortured like Richard by the voices of those who say they love him, telling him to despair, E149/157.

THE ULTIMATE FOURFOLD

In *Exiles* the Joycean theme of dual vocations and dual femininity reaches explicit geometrical statement. The lyric mode, *Chamber Music* or the *Portrait*, is enclosed within a single person of whom the others are projections. In the drama, Richard swamps the other characters for reasons that are thematic, not traumatic; not because Richard " is " Joyce, but because the other three characters are being carefully exhibited as versions of Richard because creatures of his. For Richard, the procedures of the lyric poet are a *modus vivendi*. The theme of *Exiles* is Richard's *agon;* Robert, Beatrice, and Bertha may be said to exist to explicate aspects of his mode of being and phases of his plight.

The list of characters, reinforced by alliterating names, maps out the scheme explicitly: the men:

> RICHARD ROWAN, a writer.
> ROBERT HAND, journalist.

Robert the commercialized parody of Richard is a " Hand ", not a mind. As for the women:

> BEATRICE JUSTICE, his cousin, music teacher.
> BERTHA.

Bertha is without status: simply "Bertha". Richard has deprived her not merely of regularized union, but of social meaning: even of a surname. Hence the void in which throughout the play she vibrates. The weight of thematic symbolism rests on Beatrice. Her Christian name and her function as inspiration for Richard's writing point back to Dante; but Dublin, 1912, is a Florence of "scrupulous meanness". This Beatrice is "music teacher". The cardinal virtue contained in her surname is ossified toward Protestant ethical rigidity: what resounds in her ears is not the choir of heaven but "the buzz of the harmonium in her father's parlour. . . . The asthmatic voice of protestantism", E24/36.

These three explicate three aspects of Richard. Robert's naive Wagnerian cheapness, both contrasted with and continuous with his life of practical affairs ("I must see part of the paper through every night. And then my leading articles. We are approaching a difficult moment. And not only here", E37/49), is simply the self-consciously dramatistic component of Richard's autarchic idealism. Joyce headed a page of working notes for the play, "Richard: an automystic. Robert: an automobile." The common factor is "auto". Robert's *superbia* is unglamorous: at one time or another during the play he repeats virtually every action of Richard's, and exposes the sterility of these actions by transferring them to his own kind of emotional material. His epigram about statues, E45/56, echoes Richard's attitude to the vice-chancellor, E37/49. His evening with the divorced wife of a barrister, E147/155, echoes Richard's betrayal of Bertha, E83/93. He thinks of the beautiful as the concupiscible ("the qualities which she has in common with [other women]. I mean . . . the commonest", E43/55) but surrounds his desire with vulgar idealism: a kiss is an act of homage. For Richard a kiss belongs to the practical world, an act of union; above it moves the austere mind, carefully separating, in the mode of Stephen's aesthetic, that which presents the most satisfying relations of the sensible and that which we grossly desire.

Richard's attempt to maintain human relations with his wife at the level of pure apprehension at which he conducts a Dedalian analysis of beauty is as quixotic, and insulting, as Robert's sensuality. Both are idealisms: it is not, despite Robert's attempt to equate promiscuity with "nature", either the natural *vs.* the cerebral or the common *vs.* the refined that is really in question. Bertha's attraction on the one hand towards a husband whom she cannot understand and who does not understand her, E132/140, on the other hand towards a lover the factitiousness of whose genial carnality ("There is no law before impulse. Laws are for slaves. Bertha, say my name!", E116/125) she cannot but suspect, underlines the dislocation of both the masculine natures in the play. Richard respects the privacy of everything but her mind. No more than Robert's beglamoured vulgarity can Richard's desire to live in austere detachment like a novelist among his characters be called integral humanism.

THE CONTEXT OF "GIVING"

The Exiles above the spiritual snowline adhere to the Ibsen-Wagner-Nietzsche image of liberated life as a perpetual passion of reiterated giving, a self-conscious angelic unselfishness. To say that they have no sense of the meaning of community, *civitas*, is to say that human nature for them is a flame asserting itself against a background of shadows. The cold is their element, as it was Gabriel Conroy's. Habit, order, custom, are "for slaves"; in the same way, Stephen in the *Portrait* rejects the support of habit amid the difficulties of uniting his will, instant by instant, with that of God, P283/274; for it is only so that he conceives a valid mode of love. That custom is ignoble is the persistent Romantic illusion; that it is cheating is the Puritan version. Richard's way of neither swearing nor expecting eternal fidelity surrounds himself and Bertha with the constant demands of a moral reality too strong for men. We have neither angelic wisdom nor angelic supplies of energy; we cannot live forever on the passionate *qui vive;* to be neither encouraged nor forbidden at every point is the condition not of human liberty but of human paralysis. Richard rapt himself and Bertha out of a community of paralytics, only to immerse himself and her in a paralysis still more naked; hence the dead stop to which *Exiles* grinds. The guidance of a habitual communal order is not an evasion but a human necessity.

It is perhaps because the image of Richard's state is a little too dispiriting—surrounded not even with a rhetoric of despair —that *Exiles* hasn't been revived as an "existentialist" play. Kierkegaard is the ethical ancestor both of Ibsen and Sartre, and Richard is very like a Sartrian hero, refusing to guide his wife very much as Sartre in his famous parable was unable to advise the young man torn between the Resistance Army and his mother's wishes, because the young man must be left free. We have seen apropos of Ibsen that " revolt " of Richard Rowan's kind depends on all universals being equated with the police. As it is exhibited in *Ulysses*, Dublin society in 1904 furnished persuasive grounds for such an equation; the interpenetration of priest and policeman in the " Lestrygonians " episode, like their juxtaposition in *Dubliners* (" Grace ", *passim*), expresses adequately the context against which Joyce found it important to assert the inscrutable subjectivity of moral action.

That is not the same thing, however, as asserting the unreality of moral law. That is where Kierkegaard comes in.

> Kierkegaard's great error, amid all his great intuitions, was to separate and oppose as two heterogeneous worlds the world of *generality*, or universal law, and that of the unique witness (unjustifiable at the bar of human reason) borne by the " knight of the faith ". Consequently, he had to sacrifice, or at least " suspend " ethics. In reality these two worlds are in continuity; both form part of the universe of ethics, which itself is divided into typically diversified zones according to the degrees of depth of moral life.[1]

The Exile repeats " Kierkegaard's great error "; he talks of " expressing himself ", of " obeying the law of his being ", as though " the world of generality ", just because it doesn't provide adequate support, were meaningless. And abolishing " the world of generality "—Dublin— making, in Maritain's phrase, " the formal element of morality consist in pure liberty alone ", the Exile and his creatures enter not the melodramatic universe of Sartre but a joyless suburban limbo:

> In short, by suppressing generality and universal law, you suppress liberty; and what you have left is nothing but that amorphous impulse surging out of the night which is but a false image of liberty.

> RICHARD: (*Controlling himself.*)   You forget that I have allowed you complete liberty—and allow you it still.
> BERTHA: (*Scornfully.*)   Liberty!

This drama is older than Kierkegaard; it is at least as old as Milton, in whose myth, Mr. Empson remarks,

> The Fall is due to carelessness, letting Reason slip for a moment, not living quite for ever in the great Taskmaster's eye. . . .   Milton

[1] Jacques Maritain, *Existence and the Existent*, trans. Galantiere and Phelan.

uses [the myth] to give every action a nightmare importance, to hold
every instant before the searchlight of the conscious will. It is a
terrific fancy, the Western temper at its height; the insane dispro-
portion of the act to its effects implies a vast zest for heroic action.[1]

Milton's Adam and Eve were exiled from the purlieu of a God
not less dispiritingly self-righteous than the city fathers of
Dublin; they go forth united into a free world amid equivocal
calm:

> Some natural tears they dropt, but wip'd them soon;
> The world was all before them, where to choose
> Their place of rest. . . .

" The world was all before them." The nineteenth century is
strewn with sequels to *Paradise Lost*. Wordsworth:

> The earth is all before me. With a heart
> Joyous, nor scared at its own liberty,
> I look about.

So the first page of *The Prelude;* and we know how that poem
grows arid. Dickens: " The world lay all before him ": so
Pip in sight of London, and we know what became of his
Great Expectations, and what father from the antipodes, the
underworld, he found. Joyce: " How simple and beautiful
was life after all. And life lay all before him ": so Stephen
after his return to the Church, and we know what became of his
pious determination to " unite his will instant by instant with
that of God ", and what father he took cocoa with in Eccles
Street. In *Exiles* the equivocal calm of the close of *Paradise
Lost* becomes the acknowledgment of one exile that he is
irrecoverably wounded, of the other that she yearns for her
prelapsarian strange wild lover. " O my strange wild lover,
come back to me again! " In another context we shall be
describing Bertha's final speech as kittenish malaise. It is that
and it is more. The neurotic woman is a parody of the exiled
Eve.

" The soul being unable to become virgin again " is the
image around which Joyce chose to construct his drama of
beings inadequate to the Miltonic holding of every instant
before the searchlight of the conscious will. He chose that
image because it was the inadequacy of that formulation to
mankind that he sought to display, not just the inadequacy of

[1] W. Empson, *Some Versions of Pastoral.*

mankind to the formulation. " The soul . . . not having energy
enough to cast itself out again into the ocean of another's soul "
is a human fact, not an affront to Ibsenite idealism. " We
cannot swear or expect eternal fealty ", S174/155, but neither
can we unaided perpetually repeat the act of love and giving.
Beatrice cannot perform it at all: Beatrice is " the diseased
woman." But Bertha has performed it once, and Bertha is a
human limit. (There is a superhuman limit, but Joyce omits
the saints.) The " battle of both our souls, different as they
are, against all that is false in them and in the world. A battle
of your soul against the spectre of fidelity, of mine against the
spectre of friendship "—the battle that Robert proposes to
Richard is irrelevant to the context of their plight. It is not
" a victory of human passion over the commandments of
cowardice " that will solve their exile. It is not the commandments of cowardice that inhibit a repetition of the act of love.
The conventional marriage into which Bertha and Richard are
settling down is not a retreat but as much of a fulfilment as is
allowed. As the family, so the City. The City is not a refuge
from the demands of alert living but the context of meaningful
life. The city with a small " c " is " the centre of paralysis ".

BERTHA AND ANNA LIVIA

In *Finnegans Wake*, the dramatic phase of the second cycle as
Exiles of the first, Joyce reversed for the western world that
current that has flowed from Milton's exile-myth into the
romantic night-world. He worked in that last book with the
help of a prime romantic attempt to make the soul virgin again,
Lewis Carroll's, and restored the child in Wonderland to the
City. There is nothing of this sort in the *Wake* that isn't
potentially present in *Exiles*, however, and the last pages of the
later book carefully recapitulate the last pages of the earlier.
The quality of Bertha's yearning is reproduced, but the soul is
allowed finally to cast itself out on the ocean that gave it being.
At last, via its analogies with human affection, the dimension
of sanctity enters. " Highhearted youth comes not again ",
as we are told in " Bahnhofstrasse ", and as it is put in another
poem in *Pomes Penyeach*,

> O hearts, O sighing grasses,
> Vainly your loveblown bannerets mourn!
> No more will the wild wind that passes
> Return, no more return.

" You took me—and you left me ", Bertha tells Richard.
" You left me and I waited for you to come back to me." She
asks him to " Forget me and love me again as you did the first
time. I want my lover. To meet him, to go to him, to give
myself to him." But this can only be done in what would be a
new life, each of them restored to virginity, meeting once more.
This is one meaning of the metempsychosis theme that runs
through Joyce's work: redemption. The river perpetually
reborn, laving the City and returning to the sea, is an image of
daily life perpetually redeemed, as for Bertha and Richard it is
not likely to be redeemed. Here is Bertha's longing at full
length:

BERTHA: Yes, dear. I waited for you. Heavens, what I suffered
    then—when we lived in Rome! Do you remember the terrace
    of our house?
RICHARD: Yes.
BERTHA: I used to sit there, waiting, with the poor child with his
    toys, waiting till he got sleepy. I could see all the roofs of the
    city and the river, the *Tevere*. What is its name?
RICHARD: The Tiber.
BERTHA: (*Caressing her cheek with his hand.*) It was lovely, Dick,
    only I was so sad. I was alone, Dick, forgotten by you and by all. I
    felt my life was ended.
RICHARD: It had not begun.
BERTHA: And I used to look at the sky, so beautiful, without a cloud
    and the city you said was so old: and then I used to think of Ireland
    and about ourselves.
RICHARD: Ourselves?
BERTHA: Yes. Ourselves. Not a day passes that I do not see
    ourselves, you and me, as we were when we met first. Every day
    of my life I see that. Was I not true to you all that time?
RICHARD: (*Sighs deeply.*) Yes, Bertha. You were my bride in
    exile.
BERTHA: Wherever you go, I will follow you. If you wish to go
    away now I will go with you.
RICHARD: I will remain. It is too soon yet to despair. E153/160.

One by one, in Anna Livia's great final speech, the materials
recur: " It seems so long since, ages since. As if you had been
long far away ", F622.

The poor child with his toys—" Or see only a youth in his
florizel, a boy in innocence, peeling a twig, a child beside a
weenywhite steed. The child we all love to place our hope in
for ever ", F621.

The roofs of the city and the river—" Agres of roofs in parshes. Dom on dam, dim in dym. And a capital part for olympics to ply at ", F625.

The sky, so beautiful, without a cloud—" My great blue bedroom, the air so quiet, scarce a cloud ", F627.

You and me, as we were when we met first—" Sea, sea! Here, weir, reach, island, bridge. Where you meet I. The day. Remember! ", F626.

Wherever you go I will follow you—" It's Phoenix, dear. And the flame is, hear! Let's our joornee saintomichael make it. Since the lausafire has lost and the book of the depth is. Closed. Come! Step out of your shell! Hold up you free fing! Yes ", F621.

And the strange wild lover: Bertha's " I want . . . to meet him, to go to him, to give myself to him " becomes Anna Livia's " One time you'd stand forenenst me, fairly laughing, in your bark and tan billows of branches for to fan me coolly. And I'd lie as quiet as a moss. And one time you'd rush upon me, darkly roaring, like a great black shadow with a sheeny stare to perce me rawly. And I'd frozen up and pray for thawe. . . . But you're changing, acoolsha, you're changing from me, I can feel. Or is it me is? I'm getting mixed. Brightening up and tightening down. . . . , F626. And it's old and old it's sad and old it's sad and weary I go back to you, my cold father, my cold mad father, my cold mad feary father, till the near sight of the mere size of him, the moyles and moyles of it, moananoaning, makes me seasilt saltsick and I rush, my only, into your arms ", F627. The father whom she shuns (" Save me from those therrble prongs! "—God's thurible, Neptune's trident, and the generative organs of *der Herr*) is both like and other than the husband who has turned from her. On the natural level, a long-married woman toys with the notion of going back to her people (" I'll slip away before they're up ") but shrinks from the thoughts of a parental interview (an inversion of Eveline in *Dubliners*). On one allegorical level, she shrinks from the husk her husband has become, and longs for his earlier self (" If I seen him bearing down on me now under whitespread wings "—Viking ships entering the Liffey—" like he'd come from Arkangels, I sink I'd die down over his feet, humbly dumbly, only to washup.") She would gladly lave those vessels as Magdalene washed the feet of Christ: the emotions of *time Jesum transeuntem* are

woven into her situation. On the anagogical level, she is borne
ineluctably toward the Face she would not meet. Her husband
was Christ in her life. The two fuse, the one she is leaving, the
one she goes to meet. The keys—" How you said how you'd
give me the keys of me heart. [' My ', not ' your ' heart:
the freedom Richard offered Bertha] And we'd be married till
delth to uspart "—are fused with the keys that were given to
Peter in the " tu es Petrus " on the first page of the book.
" The keys to. Given! ", F628. That is the cry that Bertha
cannot utter.

THE USE OF IBSEN

Joyce wouldn't have taken an ethical ideal from Ibsen if he
hadn't wanted it, and one of the obscurer forces infusing *Exiles*
is the discovery that he had wanted it and couldn't blame Ibsen
for supplying it; the discovery, in short, that what he had
gotten from Ibsen had been an explication of his own unde-
veloped desire to upstage Dublin. The discovery that what
was gotten was wanted is usually attended by a violent repudiation of the scapegoat " influence ": Milton inveighing against
pagan culture, for instance, or Blake the lifelong systematizer
noisily repudiating Locke. Joyce was honest enough to see
that Ibsen had taught him indispensable procedures; that he
had wanted the ideas he had swallowed along with the procedures; and that the desire for those ideas had something to
do with Dublin and deserved externalization as part of his
subject. His primary datum, *Chamber Music* itself, is alloyed.
Part of its sentimentality belongs to singing Dublin, part was
intruded, under the guise of classic discipline, by the same
adolescent Joyce who fell for Ibsen:

> He who hath glory lost, nor hath
> Found any soul to follow his.

Yet the whole of *Chamber Music* is a Dublin product; the
artist, especially in the lyric mode, is part of his subject, and
it is futile to pretend otherwise.

Hence Joyce drew off the rebellious heroics and cast them as
a running sub-plot to his later works: first Richard Rowan,
then Stephen Dedalus, then Shem the Penman; a metamor-
phosis of sham personae containing and controlling all the
errors implicit in the relation between Dublin and its " liberated " victim. These figures, impurities from the chemical

process to which the artist was submitting Dublin, prove to be
of permanent interest, just as Dublin is; the emancipated
victim is not only the nineteenth-century tragic hero, he has
affinities, through Prometheus and Oedipus, with the permanent mind of Europe.

That is why Joyce directed so much labour to the purification of what he had taken from Ibsen. Ibsen was both a
catalyst and a heresiarch: a warning. He understood as did
no one else in his time the burden of the dead past and the
wastefulness of any attempt to give it spurious life: his " I
think we are sailing with a corpse in the cargo!" corresponds
to Stephen Dedalus' apprehension of the nightmare of history
from which H. C. Earwicker strains to awake. But he had
never known, and could not know amid the frontier vacuum
of the fiords, the traditions of the European community of
richly-nourished life; and the lonely starvation of his ideal of
free personal affinity in no context save that of intermingling
wills inspired Joyce with a fascination that generated *Exiles* and
a repulsion that found its objective correlative when Leopold
Bloom, reversing Gabriel Conroy's lust for snow, shuddered
beneath " the apathy of the stars ", U719/694.

Chapter 7

RETURN TO LYRIC

RICHARD: O, if you knew how I am suffering at this moment!
For your case, too. But suffering most of all for my own.
Exiles (E12/25)

A SONG—*The Lass of Aughrim*—precipitates the crisis of
" The Dead "; its old Irish tonality trembles faintly in the air;
the words are half-forgotten, the singer is hoarse:

> O, the rain falls on my heavy locks
> And the dew wets my skin,
> My babe lies cold. . . . D270/240.

Michael Furey had sung it once with shy peasant authority, in
Galway, and had one cold night himself stood in the rain to die.
The " old Irish tonality " had lain sweetly on such a tongue;
the song is profaned in concert-room. The brush of its cadence
profanes Gabriel Conroy, book-reviewer with well-filled shirt-
front and glimmering gilt-rimmed eye-glasses; an antique
delicacy alive in the air exhibits the fatuity of his cardboard
elegance.

The autonomy of just such songs was desecrated by the
author of *Chamber Music*. He lived in Gabriel Conroy's parlour
world (" dust on a bowl of rose-leaves ") and he had tried to
forge something more vital by tidying up the technique of
parlour songs. But old Irish tonalities were beyond the reach
of synthesis. The resulting elegance, bastard-Elizabethan, had
much in common with Gabriel's well-filled shirt-front. Far
from expressing something personal, rarefied, and permanent,
he had produced a patent-leather image of a young Irishman
moving self-consciously from the alone to the alone, determined to accept heroically the transience of passions he has
not undergone.

This account of the defects of *Chamber Music* is exaggerated,
but it corresponds to moods the author of *Dubliners* must
frequently have entertained. *Chamber Music* was essentially a
single-minded production, though the young Joyce was

intelligent enough to admit a critical edge once he found the
sentiment ringing false. Even at the time of writing he had
been vaguely aware that the potentialities of the sequence were
comic; the rare marks of this awareness in the verse perhaps
account for the legend that the title was suggested by
the tinkling of a bawd's pot. *Exiles* is Joyce's explication of
Chamber Music; it contains four lyrical single-minded people
unaware that their every gesture corresponds to the jerking of
great parodying shadows on the wall behind:

> RICHARD: (*Lays his hand on his arm.*) Listen. She is dead. She
> lies on my bed. I look at her body which I betrayed—grossly and
> many times. And loved, too, and wept over. And I know that
> her body was always my loyal slave. To me, to me only she
> gave. . . . (*He breaks off and turns aside, unable to speak.*) E86/96.

That is Richard feeling like a weary Superman and talking like
a Gaiety melodrama. Here is Robert feeling like a poet:

> ROBERT: (*Moves his hand slowly past his eyes.*) You passed. The
> avenue was dim with dusky light. I could see the dark green
> masses of the trees. And you passed beyond them. You were
> like the moon.
> BERTHA: (*Laughs.*) Why like the moon?
> ROBERT: In that dress, with your slim body, walking with little even
> steps. I saw the moon passing in the dusk till you passed and left
> my sight. E26/39.

These are the postures of *Chamber Music*, only a little parodied.
Chamber Music, in fact, contains the entire emotional gamut of
Exiles. If you dissociate the ambivalences of the love-poems
with sufficient delicacy, you get two men (a divided speaker)
and two women (a divided loved one); two absurd men and
two paralysed women, whose absurdity and paralysis partake
of considerable tragic dignity. What is wrong with *Exiles* is
that by 1914 Joyce could neither take the emotions of *Chamber
Music* seriously nor frame a drama that could get outside them.
If he had been less patient he wouldn't have written *Exiles* at
all; the manuscript of a new lyric start, the *Portrait of the Artist
as a Young Man*, was already in his desk, along with sketches
for the final sections of its epic continuation *Ulysses*. He insisted
however on carrying *Chamber Music* into a dramatic phase, to
determine the exact lines along which it would crack. It
couldn't simply be abandoned; it was his one valid document

of the artist victimized by Dublin, a situation of which the *Portrait* was not a document but an image.

Exiles cracks between monomania and farce. It is the least actor-proof of plays. Richard " clenches his hands in the air passionately " crying " Yes, yes. The truth! ", E139/147. Many of the lines partake of uneasy comedy:

> RICHARD: And you gave him your garter. Is it allowed to mention that?
> BEATRICE: (*With some reserve.*) If you think it worthy of mention. E10/23.

And what is the reader or the actress to make of a speech like, " It brought me near death. It made me see things differently "?

The one thing that was clear to Joyce when he wrote *Exiles* was the necessity for staying within the subject, exposing the nature of an Ibsen play by writing an Ibsen play, discovering the limits of Dublin emotions by scrupulously expressing them. He didn't write a parody; he was aware of the danger of fending the subject off.

LYRIC INTO DRAMA

That *Chamber Music* should find its term in *Exiles* exemplifies what Joyce regarded as the natural progression from lyric into drama. Since 1903 he had seen that progression as the rule of the artist's development; by about 1911, when the final writing of the *Portrait* was under way, he had come to see it as part of his subject. In his 1903 Paris notebook (Gorman, III–iii) he had used distinctions from the *Poetics* (iii–1448a, 20–23) to define the lyric, epic, and dramatic forms. Stephen Dedalus clothes the pat symmetry of these definitions in plausible eloquence, but Stephen patently isn't being given any more knowledge about their implications than Joyce had in the *Chamber Music* days of 1903:

> The lyrical form is the simplest verbal vesture of an instant of emotion. . . . He who utters it is more conscious of the instant of emotion than of himself as feeling emotion. The simplest epical form is seen emerging out of lyrical literature when the artist prolongs and broods upon himself as the centre of an epical event and this form progresses till the centre of emotional gravity is equidistant from the artist and from others. . . . The dramatic form is reached when the vitality which has flowed and eddied round each person fills every

person with such vital force that he or she assumes a proper and
intangible esthetic life. The personality of the artist, at first a cry
or a cadence or a mood and then a fluid and lambent narrative, finally
refines itself out of existence, impersonalizes itself, so to speak. . . .
The artist, like the God of the creation, remains within or behind or
beyond or above his handiwork, invisible, refined out of existence,
indifferent, paring his fingernails. P252/244.

This is a fake. Two pages later Stephen composes a lyric,
and despite the definition it is of himself as feeling the emotion,
trying to warm his perishing joy in the scarlet glow of overblown flowers on the wallpaper, that he is then supremely
conscious. The theory in this form, so concerned at every
stage with the artist rather than with the subject, leads through
an epic swarming with personae of the artist into a drama from
which he abolishes himself only by ignoring his own ridiculous-
ness.

The epic stage between *Chamber Music* and *Exiles* is
Dubliners, the one artistic success of the first cycle. Though it
moves, according to theory, from first-person narrative into
third, and abounds in disguised images of the author, its
strength comes not from Joyce's soul but from Joyce's grasp of
what Dublin was. Its recurrent plot is the meeting with the
other self: the boy and the priest, Little Chandler and Gallaher,
Mr. Duffy and his banished passionate life, Gabriel and the
spectre of Michael Furey. The realization that this was his
generic plot made possible the three masterpieces of Joyce's
second cycle. There was a lyric, epic, and dramatic progression not only in writing about Dublin but in experiencing
Dublin. Neither himself nor Dublin was his subject, but
himself encountering Dublin which was his other self; between
lyric and drama the stress shifts from " self " to " other ".

DOUBLE LYRIC

It was necessary, for a new lyric start, to focus a *persona* who
should be unconsciously Dublin. In the *Portrait* Joyce used
the lyric form not because it came naturally but because it was
the right form for exposing the nature of a lyric subject.
Stephen isn't pushed away with ironic phrases as he was in
the imperfect first version; the *Portrait* doesn't achieve
" irony " but simply the truth.

The truth was double; the subject of the *Portrait* isn't
simply Stephen Dedalus but everything that surrounds

Stephen and shapes him. The surroundings are visible to the reader only in the way in which they are visible to Stephen. Joyce bent his attention on finding the exact cadences and textures for registering the sort of consciousness a Stephen Dedalus would imagine himself to manifest; the solution, after many trials, proved to be a thickly Paterian prose in which preciosity and self-consciousness could be held in an exact balance with sentiments whose lavishness the protagonist was unequipped to assess:

> He heard a confused music within him as of memories and names which he was almost conscious of but could not capture even for an instant; then the music seemed to recede, to recede, to recede: and from each receding trail of nebulous music there fell always one long-drawn calling note, piercing like a star the dusk of silence. Again! Again! Again! A voice from beyond the world was calling. P195/191.

Two lines later we hear a voice calling:

> .... Eh, give it over, Dwyer, I'm telling you or I'll give you a stuff in the kisser for yourself. ....

This sort of juxtaposition makes as much comment as the author of the *Portrait* permits himself. His main concern is not dramatically to " place " Stephen but to reveal his lyric reality; to invite an apprehension, not a judgment. In the subsequent epic and dramatic works, *Ulysses* and *Finnegans Wake*, we have ample opportunity to see, as the seeds of the *Portrait* exfoliate and flower, what Stephen is and what Dublin is, and how Stephen and Dublin imply one another.

In the *Portrait* we twice surprise Stephen writing lyrics. The first time, after a farewell on the steps of a tram, he excludes from the scene, " by dint of brooding ", " all those elements which he deemed common and insignificant ": the tram, the horses, the bells, the scattered tickets, the corrugated floorboards, everything that in Joyce's two pages of closely particularized narration has constituted the special reality of the event. " The verses told only of the night and the balmy breeze and the maiden lustre of the moon. Some undefined sorrow was hidden in the hearts of the protagonists as they stood in silence beneath the leafless trees. .... " After this, " having hidden the book, he went into his mother's bedroom and gazed at his face for a long time in the mirror of her dressing table." P78/80.

The second time we see Stephen writing verses is late in the book, when several themes, now fully defined, await symbolic unification. The *Portrait* turns, like *Exiles*, on the Dubliner's twofold vocation, and the wound implied in either choice. This division of appetites implies a twofold woman (angel and whore); the context of " Love " is dominated by the Catholic Church on the one hand and the artist's vocation among fleshly vessels on the other. These themes are latent in the poems of *Chamber Music*, which came out of the most difficult period of Joyce's life, when he was caught in a complex Dublin web of appetites, religious claims, and artistic attitudes, and which touch emotions whose inner violence would have wrecked any attempt at direct presentation. The sequence of thirty-six poems, recording a progression of attitudes to Love, from the romantic-unattached through courtship, union, and disillusion, to ultimate lonely self-torment, continually implies flirtation with the priesthood, fleshly dalliance, and a sort of lonely artistic maturation; but these are reduced in the verse to remote psychic dramas that continually trouble the surface with seismographic traces: slight grammatical ambiguities, rhythms not quite in hand, and conventional symbols rebelling dimly against convention.

All this is summed up in Chapter V of the *Portrait*. Stephen's mind, as he lies on his bed towards dawn, is tossed on a flood of sentimental impressions out of which a poem slowly emerges:

> A spirit filled him, pure as the purest water, sweet as dew, moving as music. But how faintly it was inbreathed, how passionlessly, as if the seraphim themselves were breathing upon him! His soul was waking slowly, fearing to awake wholly. . . .
>
> An enchantment of the heart! That night had been enchanted. In a dream or vision he had known the ecstasy of seraphic life. Was it an instant of enchantment only or long hours and years and ages?
>
> The instant of inspiration seemed now to be reflected from all sides at once from a multitude of cloudy circumstances of what had happened or of what might have happened. The instant flashed forth like a point of light and now from cloud on cloud of vague circumstance confused form was veiling softly its afterglow. O! In the virgin womb of the imagination the word was made flesh. Gabriel the seraph had come to the virgin's chamber. An afterglow deepened within his spirit, whence the white flame had passed, deepening to a rose and ardent light. That rose and ardent light was her strange and wilful heart, strange that no man had known or would know, wilful from the beginning of the world; and lured by that ardent

roselike glow the choirs of the seraphim were falling from heaven.

> Are you not weary of ardent ways,
> Lure of the fallen seraphim?
> Tell no more of enchanted days.

P254/247.

The woman is simultaneously Stephen's faint love " E.C. " and the antique courtesan of Yeats' " Adoration of the Magi ", which Joyce knew by heart at nineteen. " Lured by that ardent roselike glow the choirs of the seraphim were falling from heaven." The music of the choirs descends from heaven to refresh and celebrate the mystical Bride; but the choirs themselves, the seraphim themselves, fall lured by the temptation of a woman. But it was of intellectual pride that the tenth part of the angels fell; the woman is more than flesh; she contains the pride of Stephen's aesthetic vocation as well:

> The verses passed from his mind to his lips, and, murmuring them over, he felt the rhythmic movement of a villanelle pass through them. The roselike glow sent forth its rays of rhyme: ways, days, blaze, praise, raise. Its rays burned up the world, consumed the hearts of men and angels: the rays from the rose that was her wilful heart.

" Blaze, praise, raise " evoke the monstrance and the contrary movement of choiring voices ascending; the rays that burned up the world are rays of love: for Stephen's decadent sensibility, burnings of desire:

> Your eyes have set man's heart ablaze
> And you have had your will of him.
> Are you not weary of ardent ways?

Stephen's heart was set ablaze during the retreat (" His flesh shrank together as though it felt the approach of ravenous tongues of flames. . . . A wave of fire swept through his body: the first. Again a wave ", P143/142.) " And you have had your will of him ": the single surrender of confession and repentance; the ultimate renunciation of the Church. The next stanza places the " flame " in a context of self-obliterating devotion:

> Above the flame the smoke of praise
> Goes up from ocean rim to rim.
> Tell no more of enchanted days.

The smoke of the incense of praise: the smoke of obfuscation resting on the brain: the smoke rising from hell, the torments of whose damned, the priest had said, do but reiterate the praises of God.

THE DUBLIN FOURFOLD

The conflict between vocations—artist and priest—is a real tension but a factitious exclusiveness; in Dante's civilization there was no discontinuity between Beatrice moving on a Florentine street, *vestita di nobilissimo color*, and Beatrice conductor through the spheres of Paradise. Dublin, however, thrives on the vigorous presentation of factitious dichotomies. Every Dubliner's will tugs two ways, as in " Eveline " or " The Dead ". His twofold vocation lies between apprehended immediacy and abstract claims; and by no manoeuvre of election between these vocations can he escape the shadow of what he denies.

Hence the thematic weight of double lover and double loved one; the four lovers in *Exiles;* the *Ulysses* pairing of Shakespeare ghost and Shakespeare Hamlet, Anne and the Dark Lady; the fascination of the divided dreamer of *Finnegans Wake* with men who were divided between two women: Tristram, Swift, Wagner.

In the *Portrait* the " feminine " objects corresponding to the artist/priest dichotomy include such allotropic forms as mother, Church, Ireland, " E.C. ", the shadowy Mercedes (from Dumas) of Stephen's childish dream, the ladies of " Greensleeves " and the solemn pavane, the whores. Stephen imagined that in the arms of Mercedes revelation would come and youth and inexperience fall from him; the fulfilment of that imagining was his lurid encounter with whores: that is the parable in a nutshell.

THE NIXIE'S CHAMBER

Joyce never ceased considering *Chamber Music*. As the years passed his feelings grew less and less mixed. Care for technique in 1904 had kept " thought " out of the verses; the image of a troubled young man's Dublin sentiment was unwarped by what the poet might have supposed ought to be there. In his last work he was capable, as at the *Exiles* stage he had not been capable, of transferring its données wholesale into drama. The tug of the rejected Faith, the sense of compromise in accepting its vocation and betrayal in rejecting it, the sense that the Church in Ireland for its own part both compromises and betrays: such motifs, deprived of contingency and transferred to an ultra-physical incarnation of neurotic malaise, animate the ghastly comedy of the temptress Iseult in *Finnegans Wake*. She is another twofold woman, inseparable from the double in her mirror, and she has two lovers, pseudo-artist and pseudo-priest. The quality of her eroticism:

> Delightsome simply! Like Jolio and Romeune. I haven't fell so turkish for ages and ages! Mine's me of squisious, the chocolate with a soul, F144,

—with its correlative in schoolgirl sentiment, candy advertisements, and, always, eating—doesn't really differ from that of the smug narcissus of *Chamber Music* XXIV who sits silently combing, combing her long hair. Nor does the lacquered mask on her rapid alternations of feeling ever manage to conceal her scorn for men in general:

> Of course I know, pettest, you're so learningful and considerate in yourself, so friend of vegetables, you long cold cat you! Please by acquiester to meek my acquointance! Codling, snakelet, iciclist! My diaper has more life to it! Who drowned you in drears, man, or are you pillale with ink? Did a weep get past the gates of your pride? My tread on the clover, sweetness? Yes, the buttercups told me, hug me, damn it all, and I'll kiss you back to life, my peachest. I mean to make you suffer, meddlar, and I don't care this fig for contempt of courting.... F145.

She urges him to immortalize her in a book—

> Bite my laughters, drink my tears. Pore into me, volumes, spell me stark and spill me swooning. I just don't care what my thwarters think,

recoils from his amorous quotations:

> Ah, did you speak, stuffstuff? More poestries from Chickspeer's with gleechoreal music or a jaculation from the garden of the soul,

converts his serious questions into terms of naked appetite:

> Of I be leib in the immoralities? O, you mean the strangle for love and the sowiveall of the prettiest?

thinks to reassure him by her love for reading:

> Yep, we open hap coseries in the home. And once upon a week I
> improve on myself. I'm so keen on that New Free Woman with
> novel inside.

gets impatient for serious business:

> Let's root out Brimstoker and give him the thrall of our lives. It's
> Dracula's nightout. For creepsake don't make a flush! Draw the
> shades, curfe you, and I'll beat any sonnamonk to love.

and finally chucks him for the Man of Action:

> And because, you pluckless lankaloot, I hate the very thought of the
> thought of you and because, dearling, of course, adorest, I was always
> meant for an engindear from the French college, to be musband,
> *nomme d'engien,* when we do and contract with encho tencho solver
> when you are married to reading and writing which pleasebusiness
> now won't be long for he's so loopy on me and I'm so leapy like since
> the day he carried me from the boat, my saviored of eroes, to the
> beach and I left on his shoulder one fair hair to guide hand and mind
> to its softness. F146.

The " ever so little falsity " of *Chamber Music* looks like this
under the microscope; the " Soft arms that woo me to relent /
And woo me to detain " here speak their explicit language of
fascinated revulsion:

> I am enjoying it still, I swear I am! Why do you prefer its in these
> dark nets, if why may ask, my sweetykins? Sh sh! Longears is
> flying. No, sweetissest, why would that ennoy me? But don't!
> You want to be slap well slapped for that. Your delighted lips, love,
> be careful! Mind my duvetyne dress above all! F148.

Chamber Music once more:

> Dear heart, why will you use me so?
> Dear eyes that gently me upbraid,
> Still are you beautiful—but O,
> How is your beauty raimented! (XXIX)

" Why will you use me so? " The quality of romantic passion
is continuous from *Chamber Music* to *Finnegans Wake.* The
frightening monologue of the temptress explicates both the
ambivalence of " chamber " and the falseness of the Ibsenesque
bravado partially anatomized in *Exiles:*

> It is not in the darkness of belief that I desire you. But in restless
> living wounding doubt. To hold you by no bonds, even of love, to
> be united with you in body and soul in utter nakedness—for this I
> longed. E154/162.

It is this instant of the miserable Richard's maturest insight that Bertha chooses for her final Iseult-like manifestation of kittenish malaise:

> Forget me, Dick. Forget me and love me again as you did the first time. . . . O, my strange wild lover, come back to me again!
>
> (*She closes her eyes*)

What drew the author of *Chamber Music* to Verlaine and Jonson was less a desire for techniques to apply to Dublin than a taste for solid writing: his Dublin afforded no model for exactness of phrase or " the ' sculpture ' of rhyme ". What he was aware of applying these techniques to was his own emotions; he picked the models that vibrated in consonance with his emotions. But his emotions had more to do than he realized with the pianos and parlour tenors of Dublin, or the street harpists and *come-all-yous*. If they seemed at the time exotic—" the evil dream of love which Stephen chose to commemorate in these verses lay veritably upon the world now in a season of damp violet mist ", S36/29—still they were the Dublin emotions, of the songs his father sang.

The city, undifferentiated, thoughts and feelings, was contained in its love-songs. There, uniquely, the sensitive temperament could register Dublin entire in miniature compass. It wasn't necessary for the young Joyce to condense his twenty years' impressions; they presented themselves, in song, already condensed: sentiment, gallantry, sprawl, tarnish, elegance, paralysis. These songs were in his ears as he wrote.

The young man wrote lyrics, because he was young. The banalities were his, and he thought they were unique and important. So phase after phase of the Dublin he imagined he was evading went down on these pages with an exactness later to be cherished. He prized his banalities later because they were Dublin's, and Dublin was the shell of the West.

A faded rose-petal through the microscope assaults the eye with cellular corrugations, abstractly organized, pigmented with kaleidoscopic spatters, aswarm with inert bacteria of corruption arrested in lunar pockmarks. Hence the bizarre slow-motion strangeness of *Ulysses* and *Finnegans Wake*, where the thirty-six small glass slides of the *Chamber Music* collection are enlarged over hundreds of pages at successively higher magnifications.

PART TWO

Odysseus

In a gabbard he barqued it, the boat of life,
from the harbourless Invernikan Okean, till he
spied the loom of his landfall and he loosed
two croakers from under his tilt, the gran
Phenician rover

★

Chapter 8

THE *PORTRAIT* IN PERSPECTIVE

> From wrong to wrong the exasperated spirit
> Proceeds, unless restored by that refining fire
> Where you must move in measure, like a dancer.
>
> > *T. S. Eliot*

> Faites votre destin, âmes désordonnées,
> Et fuyez l'infini que vous portez en vous!
>
> > *Baudelaire*

> And yet he felt that, however he might revile and mock her
> image, his anger was also a form of homage.
>
> > *Portrait* (P259/251)

A Portrait of the Artist as a Young Man, which in its definitive form initiates the second cycle, was some ten years in the writing. A 1,000-page first draft was written around 1904–1906, about the same time as the bulk of *Dubliners*. This was scrapped and a more compressed version undertaken in 1908; the third and final text was being composed in 1911, and was finished early in 1914.[1] About one-third of the first draft (the *Stephen Hero* fragment) survives to show us what was going on during the gestation of this book, the only one which it cost Joyce far more trouble to focus than to execute.

Joyce first conceived the story of Stephen Dedalus in a picaresque mode. The original title was meant to incorporate the ballad of Turpin Hero, a reference to which still survives in the final text P252/244. Turpin spends most of the ballad achieving gestes at the expense of a gallery of middle-class dummies, beginning with a lawyer:

> ... As they rode down by the powder mill,
> Turpin commands him to stand still;
> Said he, your cape I must cut off,
> For my mare she wants her saddle cloth.
> > O rare Turpin Hero,
> > O rare Turpin O.

---

[1] Gorman V–iii, VII–i, VII–iii, VII–vi. See also Theodore Spencer's introduction to *Stephen Hero*.

> This caus'd the lawyer much to fret,
> To think he was so fairly bit;
> And Turpin robb'd him of his store,
> Because he knew he'd lie for more.
>   O rare Turpin Hero,
>   O rare Turpin O.

The lawyer's mistake was to admit the plausible stranger to his intimacy. Stephen in the same way achieves a series of dialectical triumphs over priests, parents, and schoolfellows. The typical dialogue commences amid courtesies:

> Stephen raised his cap and said " Good evening, sir." The President answered with the smile which a pretty girl gives when she receives some compliment which puzzles her—a " winning " smile:
> — What can I do for you? he asked in a rich deep calculated voice. . . .

But cut-and-thrust soon follows:

> — May I ask you if you have read much of [Ibsen's] writing? asked Stephen.
> — Well, no . . . I must say . . .
> — May I ask you if you have read even a single line?
> — Well, no . . . I must admit . . .

Stephen always relieves the interlocutor of his complacence:

> — I should not care for anyone to identify the ideas in your essay with the teaching in our college. We receive this college in trust. . . .
> — If I were to publish tomorrow a very revolutionary pamphlet on the means of avoiding potato-blight would you consider yourself responsible for my theory?
> — No, no, of course not . . . but then this is not a school of agriculture.
> — Neither is it a school of dramaturgy, answered Stephen. S95/81.

The ballad ends with Turpin in jail condemned to the gallows; *Stephen Hero* was presumably to end, as the *Portrait* does, with Stephen Protomartyr on the brink of continental exile, acknowledged enemy of the Dublin people. This Stephen is an engaging fellow with an explosive laugh, S59/49, an image of the young Joyce whom Yeats compared to William Morris " for the joyous vitality one felt in him ", or of the student Joyce who emerges from his brother's *Memoir:*

> Uncompromising in all that concerned his artistic integrity, Joyce was, for the rest, of a sociable and amiable disposition. Around his

tall, agile figure there hovered a certain air of youthful grace and, despite the squalors of his home, a sense of happiness, as of one who feels within himself a joyous courage, a resolute confidence in life and in his own powers. . . . Joyce's laugh was characteristic . . . of that pure hilarity which does not contort the mouth.[1]

When Stephen's uncompromising side occasionally becomes absurd, Joyce the recorder is always at hand to supply a distancing phrase: " the fiery-hearted revolutionary "; " this heaven-ascending essayist " S80/67; " he was foolish enough to regret having yielded to the impulse for sympathy from a friend ", S83/70. Toward the end of the existing fragment we find more and more of these excusing clauses: " No young man can contemplate the fact of death with extreme satisfaction and no young man, specialised by fate or her stepsister chance for an organ of sensitiveness and intellectiveness, can contemplate the network of falsities and trivialities which make up the funeral of a dead burgher without extreme disgust ", S168/150. This clumsy sentence, its tone slithering between detachment, irony, and anger, is typical of the bad writing which recurs in the *Stephen Hero* fragment to signal Joyce's periodic uncertainty of Stephen's convincingness.

The book ran down unfinished in 1906, stalled partly by its own inner contradictions, partly by the far maturer achievement of *Dubliners*. It had never, Joyce saw, had a theme; it was neither a novel, nor an autobiography, nor a spiritual or social meditation. It contained three sorts of materials that would not fuse: documentation from the past, transcribed from the Dublin notebooks; Joyce's memories of his earlier self, transmuted by a mythopoeic process only partly controlled; and his present complex attitude to what he thought that self to have been.

Fortunately, the catalytic theme was not long in coming. In the late fall of 1906, he wrote from Rome to his brother about a new story for *Dubliners*, " Ulysses ". On February 6, 1907, he admitted that it " never got any forrarder than the title." It coalesced, instead, with the autobiographical theme, and both subjects were returned to the smithy. A novel, *Ulysses*, as Joyce told a Zurich student ten years later, began to be planned as sequel to a rewritten *Portrait*. In 1908 *Stephen Hero* was discarded for good, and the job of lining up the two works began. And once the final balance of motifs for the *Portrait*

<hr>

[1] Stanislaus Joyce, " James Joyce: A Memoir ", *Hudson Review*, II. 4, 496.

had been at last struck and the writing of the definitive text completed, the last exorcism, *Exiles*, took only three spring months. *Ulysses* and *Finnegans Wake* took seven and seventeen years, but their recalcitrance was technical merely. The *Portrait* includes their scenario: first " the earth that had borne him " and " the vast indifferent dome " (Penelope, Ithaca), then sleep and a plunge into " some new world, fantastic, dim, uncertain as under sea, traversed by cloudy shapes and beings ", P200/196. These are lyric anticipations of the dense epic and dramatic works to come; the actual writing of those works went forward during the next quarter-century with scarcely a false step.

LINKING THEMES

In the reconceived *Portrait* Joyce abandoned the original intention of writing the account of his own escape from Dublin. One cannot escape one's Dublin. He recast Stephen Dedalus as a figure who could not even detach himself from Dublin because he had formed himself on a denial of Dublin's values. He is the egocentric rebel become an ultimate. There is no question whatever of his regeneration. " Stephen no longer interests me to the same extent [as Bloom]," said Joyce to Frank Budgen one day. " He has a shape that can't be changed."[1] His shape is that of aesthete. The Stephen of the first chapter of *Ulysses* who " walks wearily", constantly " leans " on everything in sight, invariably sits down before he has gone three paces, speaks " gloomily", " quietly", " with bitterness ", and " coldly ", and " suffers " his handkerchief to be pulled from his pocket by the exuberant Mulligan, is precisely the priggish, humourless Stephen of the last chapter of the *Portrait* who cannot remember what day of the week it is, P206/201, sentimentalizes like Charles Lamb over the " human pages " of a second-hand Latin book, P209/204, conducts the inhumanly pedantic dialogue with Cranly on mother-love, P281/271, writes Frenchified verses in bed in an erotic swoon, and is epiphanized at full length, like Shem the Penman beneath the bedclothes, F176, shrinking from the " common noises " of daylight:

> Shrinking from that life he turned towards the wall, making a cowl [!] of the blanket and staring at the great overblown scarlet

---

1 Budgen, 107.

flowers of the tattered wall-paper. He tried to warm his perishing joy in their scarlet glow, imaging a roseway from where he
lay upwards to heaven all strewn with scarlet flowers. Weary!
Weary! He too was weary of ardent ways. P260/252.

This new primrose path is a private Jacob's ladder let down to
his bed now that he is too weary to do anything but go to
heaven.

To make epic and drama emerge naturally from the intrinsic
stresses and distortions of the lyric material meant completely
new lyric techniques for a constation exact beyond irony. The
Portrait concentrates on stating themes, arranging apparently
transparent words into configurations of the utmost symbolic
density. Here is the director proposing that Stephen enter the
priesthood:

> The director stood in the embrasure of the window, his back to the
> light, leaning an elbow on the brown crossblind, and, as he spoke and
> smiled, slowly dangling and looping the cord of the other blind, Stephen
> stood before him, following for a moment with his eyes the waning
> of the long summer daylight above the roofs or the slow deft movements
> of the priestly fingers. The priest's face was in total shadow, but
> the waning daylight from behind him touched the deeply grooved
> temples and the curves of the skull. P178/175.

The looped cord, the shadow, the skull, none of these is
accidental. The " waning daylight," twice emphasized, conveys that denial of nature which the priest's office represented
for Stephen; " his back to the light " co-operates toward a
similar effect. So " crossblind ": " blind to the cross ";[1]
" blinded by the cross ". " The curves of the skull " introduces another death-image; the " deathbone " from Lévy-
Bruhl's Australia, pointed by Shaun in *Finnegans Wake*, F193,
is the dramatic version of an identical symbol. But the central
image, the epiphany of the interview, is contained in the movement of the priest's fingers: " slowly dangling and looping the
cord of the other blind." That is to say, coolly proffering a
noose. This is the lyric mode of *Ulysses'* epical hangman,
" The lord of things as they are whom the most Roman of
Catholics call *dio boia*, hangman god ", U210/201.

---

[1] – You want me, said Stephen, to toe the line with those hypocrites and
sycophants in the college. I will never do so.
    – No. I mentioned Jesus.
    – Don't mention him. I have made it a common noun. They don't believe
in him; they don't observe his precepts. . . ." S141/124.

THE CONTRAPUNTAL OPENING

According to the practice inaugurated by Joyce when he rewrote " The Sisters " in 1906, the *Portrait*, like the two books to follow, opens amid elaborate counterpoint. The first two pages, terminating in a row of asterisks, enact the entire action in microcosm. An Aristotelian catalogue of senses, faculties, and mental activities is played against the unfolding of the infant conscience.

> Once upon a time and a very good time it was there was a moocow coming down along the road and this moocow that was down along the road met a nicens little boy named baby tuckoo. . . .
>
> His father told him that story: his father looked at him through a glass: he had a hairy face.
>
> He was baby tuckoo. The moocow came down along the road where Betty Byrne lived: she sold lemon platt.
>
> > *O, the wild rose blossoms*
> > *On the little green place.*
>
> He sang that song. That was his song.
>
> > *O, the green wothe botheth.*
>
> When you wet the bed, first it is warm then it gets cold. His mother put on the oilsheet. That had the queer smell.

This evocation of holes in oblivion is conducted in the mode of each of the five senses in turn; hearing (the story of the moocow), sight (his father's face), taste (lemon platt), touch (warm and cold), smell (the oil-sheet). The audible soothes: the visible disturbs. Throughout Joyce's work, the senses are symbolically disposed. Smell is the means of discriminating empirical realities (" His mother had a nicer smell than his father," is the next sentence), sight corresponds to the phantasms of oppression, hearing to the imaginative life. Touch and taste together are the modes of sex. Hearing, here, comes first, via a piece of imaginative literature. But as we can see from the vantage-point of *Finnegans Wake*, the whole book is about the encounter of baby tuckoo with the moocow: the Gripes with the mookse.[1] The father with the hairy face is the first Mookse-avatar, the Freudian infantile analogue of God the Father.

[1] Compare the opening sentence: " Eins within a space, and a wearywide space it wast, ere wohned a Mookse ", F152. Mookse is moocow plus fox plus mock turtle. The German " Eins " evokes Einstein, who presides over the interchanging of space and time; space is the Mookse's " spatialty ".

In the *Wake*

> Derzherr, live wire, fired Benjermine Funkling outa th'Empyre, sin right hand son.   F289.

Der Erzherr (arch-lord), here a Teutonic Junker, is the God who visited his wrath on Lucifer; the hairy attribute comes through via the music-hall refrain, " There's hair, like wire, coming out of the Empire."

Dawning consciousness of his own identity (" He was baby tuckoo ") leads to artistic performance (" He sang that song. That was his song.") This is hugely expanded in chapter IV:

> Now, as never before, his strange name seemed to him a prophecy ... of the end he had been born to serve and had been following through the mists of childhood and boyhood, a symbol of the artist forging anew in his workshop out of the sluggish matter of the earth a new soaring impalpable imperishable being.   P196/192.

By changing the red rose to a green and dislocating the spelling, he makes the song his own (" But you could not have a green rose. But perhaps somewhere in the world you could." P8/13)

> His mother had a nicer smell than his father.   She played on the piano the sailor's hornpipe for him to dance.   He danced:

> > *Tralala lala,*
> > *Tralala tralaladdy,*
> > *Tralala lala,*
> > *Tralala lala.*

Between this innocence and its Rimbaudian recapture through the purgation of the *Wake* there is to intervene the hallucination in Circe's sty:

> THE MOTHER
> (*With the subtle smile of death's madness.*)   I was once the beautiful May Goulding.   I am dead. . . .

> STEPHEN
> (*Eagerly.*)   Tell me the word, mother, if you know it now.   The word known to all men. . . .

> THE MOTHER
> (*With smouldering eyes.*)   Repent!   O, the fire of hell!   U565/547.

This is foreshadowed as the overture to the *Portrait* closes:

> He hid under the table.   His mother said:
> – O, Stephen will apologise.
> Dante said:
> – O, if not, the eagles will come and pull out his eyes.—
> > Pull out his eyes,
> > Apologise,
> > Apologise,
> > Pull out his eyes.
>
> > Apologise,
> > Pull out his eyes,
> > Pull out his eyes,
> > Apologise.

The eagles, eagles of Rome, are emissaries of the God with the hairy face: the punisher.   They evoke Prometheus and gnawing guilt: again-bite.   So the overture ends with Stephen hiding under the table awaiting the eagles.   He is hiding under something most of the time: bedclothes, " the enigma of a manner ", an indurated rhetoric, or some other carapace of his private world.

THEME° WORDS

It is through their names that things have power over Stephen.

> – The language in which we are speaking is his before it is mine. How different are the words *home, Christ, ale, master,* on his lips and on mine!   I cannot speak or write these words without unrest of spirit.   His language, so familiar and so foreign, will always be for me an acquired speech.   I have not made or accepted its words.   My voice holds them at bay.   My soul frets in the shadow of his language. P221/215.

Not only is the Dean's English a conqueror's tongue; since the loss of Adam's words which perfectly mirrored things, all language has conquered the mind and imposed its own order, askew from the order of creation.   Words, like the physical world, are imposed on Stephen from without, and it is in their canted mirrors that he glimpses a physical and moral world already dyed the colour of his own mind since absorbed, with language, into his personality.

> Words which he did not understand he said over and over to himself
> till he had learnt them by heart; and through them he had glimpses
> of the real world about him. P68/70.

Language is a Trojan horse by which the universe gets into
the mind. The first sentence in the book isn't something
Stephen sees but a story he is told, and the overture climaxes
in an insistent brainless rhyme, its jingle corrosively fascinat·
ing to the will. It has power to terrify a child who knows
nothing of eagles, or of Prometheus, or of how his own grown-
up failure to apologise will blend with gathering blindness.

It typifies the peculiar achievement of the *Portrait* that
Joyce can cause patterns of words to make up the very moral
texture of Stephen's mind:

> Suck was a queer word. The fellow called Simon Moonan that
> name because Simon Moonan used to tie the prefect's false sleeves
> behind his back and the prefect used to let on to be angry. But the
> sound was ugly. Once he had washed his hands in the lavatory of the
> Wicklow hotel and his father pulled the stopper up by the chain after
> and the dirty water went down through the hole in the basin. And
> when it had all gone down slowly the hole in the basin had made a sound
> like that: suck. Only louder.
>
> To remember that and the white look of the lavatory made him
> feel cold and then hot. There were two cocks that you turned and
> the water came out: cold and hot. He felt cold and then a little hot:
> and he could see the names printed on the cocks. That was a very
> queer thing. P6/12.

" Suck " joins two contexts in Stephen's mind: a playful
sinner toying with his indulgent superior, and the disappear-
ance of dirty water. The force of the conjunction is felt only
after Stephen has lost his sense of the reality of the forgiveness
of sins in the confessional. The habitually orthodox penitent
tangles with a God who pretends to be angry; after a reconciliation the process is repeated. And the mark of that kind of play
is disgraceful servility. Each time the sin disappears, the
sinner is mocked by an impersonal voice out of nature:
" Suck! "

This attitude to unreal good and evil furnishes a context for
the next conjunction: whiteness and coldness. Stephen finds
himself, like Simon Moonan,[1] engaged in the rhythm of

---

[1] Joyce's names should always be scrutinized. Simon Moonan: moon: the
heatless (white) satellite reflecting virtue borrowed from Simon Peter. Simony,
too, is an activity naturally derived from this casually businesslike attitude to
priestly authority.

obedience to irrational authority, bending his mind to a meaningless act, the arithmetic contest.   He is being obediently
" good ".   And the appropriate colour is adduced: " He
thought his face must be white because it felt so cool."

The pallor of lunar obedient goodness is next associated with
damp repulsiveness: the limpness of a wet blanket and of a
servant's apron:

> He sat looking at the two prints of butter on his plate but could
> not eat the damp bread.   The table-cloth was damp and limp.   But he
> drank off the hot weak tea which the clumsy scullion, girt with a white
> apron, poured into his cup.   He wondered whether the scullion's
> apron was damp too or whether all white things were cold and damp.
> P8/13.

Throughout the first chapter an intrinsic linkage, white-
cold-damp-obedient, insinuates itself repeatedly.   Stephen after
saying his prayers, " his shoulders shaking ", " so that he
might not go to hell when he died ", " curled himself together
under the cold white sheets, shaking and trembling.   But he
would not go to hell when he died, and the shaking would stop."
P16/20.   The sea, mysterious as the terrible power of God,
" was cold day and night, but it was colder at night ", P14/19;
we are reminded of Anna Livia's gesture of submission: " my
cold father, my cold mad father, my cold mad feary father ",
F628.   " There was a cold night smell in the chapel.   But it
was a holy smell ", P14/19.   Stephen is puzzled by the phrase
in the Litany of the Blessed Virgin: Tower of Ivory.   " How
could a woman be a tower of ivory or a house of gold? "   He
ponders until the revelation comes:

> Eileen had long white hands.   One evening when playing tig she
> had put her hands over his eyes: long and white and thin and cold and
> soft.   That was ivory: a cold white thing.   That was the meaning of
> Tower of Ivory.   P36/40.

This instant of insight depends on a sudden reshuffling of
associations, a sudden conviction that the Mother of God, and
the symbols appropriate to her, belong with the cold, the
white, and the unpleasant in a blindfold morality of obedience.
Contemplation focussed on language is repaid:

> Tower of Ivory.   House of Gold.   By thinking of things you could
> understand them.   P45/48.

The   white-damp-obedient   association   reappears   when

Stephen is about to make his confession after the celebrated retreat; its patterns provide the language in which he thinks. Sin has been associated with fire, while the prayers of the penitents are epiphanized as " soft whispering cloudlets, soft whispering vapour, whispering and vanishing." P164/163. And having been absolved:

> White pudding and eggs and sausages and cups of tea.   How simple and beautiful was life after all!   And life lay all before him. . . .
>
> The boys were all there, kneeling in their places.   He knelt among them, happy and shy.   The altar was heaped with fragrant masses of white flowers: and in the morning light the pale flames of the candles among the white flowers were clear and silent as his own soul. P168/166.

We cannot read *Finnegans Wake* until we have realized the significance of the way the mind of Stephen Dedalus is bound in by language.   He is not only an artist: he is a Dubliner.

THE PORTRAIT AS LYRIC

The " instant of emotion ", P251/244, of which this 300-page lyric is the " simplest verbal vesture " is the exalted instant, emerging at the end of the book, of freedom, of vocation, of Stephen's destiny, winging his way above the waters at the side of the hawklike man: the instant of promise on which the crushing ironies of *Ulysses* are to fall.   The epic of the sea of matter is preceded by the lyric image of a growing dream: a dream that like Richard Rowan's in *Exiles* disregards the fall of man; a dream nourished by a sensitive youth of flying above the sea into an uncreated heaven:

> The spell of arms and voices: the white arms of roads, their promise of close embraces and the black arms of tall ships that stand against the moon, their tale of distant nations.   They are held out to say: We are alone—come.   And the voices say with them: We are your kinsmen.   And the air is thick with their company as they call to me, their kinsman, making ready to go, shaking the wings of their exultant and terrible youth.   P298/288.

The emotional quality of this is continuous with that of the *Count of Monte Cristo*, that fantasy of the exile returned for vengeance (the plot of the *Odyssey*) which kindled so many of Stephen's boyhood dreams:

> The figure of that dark avenger stood forth in his mind for whatever he had heard or divined in childhood of the strange and terrible. At night he built up on the parlour table an image of the wonderful

island cave out of transfers and paper flowers and strips of the silver and golden paper in which chocolate is wrapped. When he had broken up this scenery, weary of its tinsel, there would come to his mind the bright picture of Marseilles, of sunny trellises and of Mercedes. P68/70.

The prose surrounding Stephen's flight is empurpled with transfers and paper flowers too. It is not immature prose, as we might suppose by comparison with *Ulysses.* The prose of " The Dead " is mature prose, and " The Dead " was written in 1908. Rather, it is a meticulous pastiche of immaturity. Joyce has his eye constantly on the epic sequel.

> He wanted to meet in the real world the unsubstantial image which his soul so constantly beheld. He did not know where to seek it or how, but a premonition which led him on told him that this image would, without any overt act of his, encounter him. They would meet quietly as if they had known each other and had made their tryst, perhaps at one of the gates or in some more secret place. They would be alone, surrounded by darkness and silence: and in that moment of supreme tenderness he would be transfigured. P71/73.

As the vaginal imagery of gates, secret places, and darkness implies, this is the dream that reaches temporary fulfilment in the plunge into profane love, P113/114. But the ultimate " secret place " is to be Mabbot Street, outside Bella Cohen's brothel; the unsubstantial image of his quest, that of Leopold Bloom, advertisement canvasser—Monte Cristo, returned avenger, Ulysses; and the transfiguration, into the phantasmal dead son of a sentimental Jew:

> *Against the dark wall a figure appears slowly, a fairy boy of eleven, a changeling, kidnapped, dressed in an Eton suit with glass shoes and a little bronze helmet, holding a book in his hand. He reads from right to left inaudibly, smiling, kissing the page.* U593/574.

That Dedalus the artificer did violence to nature is the point of the epigraph from Ovid, *Et ignotas animum dimittit in artes;* the Icarian fall is inevitable.

> In tedious exile now too long detain'd
> Dedalus languish'd for his native land.
> The sea foreclos'd his flight; yet thus he said,
> Though earth and water in subjection laid,
> O cruel Minos, thy dominion be,
> We'll go through air; for sure the air is free.
> *Then to new arts his cunning thought applies,*
> *And to improve the work of nature tries.*

Stephen does not, as the careless reader may suppose, become
an artist by rejecting church and country. Stephen does not
become an artist at all. Country, church, and mission are an
inextricable unity, and in rejecting the two that seem to hamper
him, he rejects also the one on which he has set his heart.
Improving the work of nature is his obvious ambition (" But
you could not have a green rose. But perhaps somewhere
in the world you could "), and it logically follows from the
aesthetic he expounds to Lynch. It is a neo-platonic aesthetic;
the crucial principle of epiphanization has been withdrawn.
He imagines that " the loveliness that has not yet come into
the world ", P297/286, is to be found in his own soul. The
earth is gross, and what it brings forth is cowdung; sound and
shape and colour are " the prison gates of our soul "; and
beauty is something mysteriously gestated within. The genuine artist reads signatures, the fake artist forges them, a process
adumbrated in the obsession of Shem the Penman (from *Jim
the Penman*, a forgotten drama about a forger) with " Macfear-
some's Ossean ", the most famous of literary forgeries, study-
ing " how cutely to copy all their various styles of signature so
as one day to utter an epical forged cheque on the public for
his own private profit." F181.

One can sense all this in the first four chapters of the *Portrait*,
and *Ulysses* is unequivocal:

> Fabulous artificer, the hawklike man. You flew. Whereto?
> Newhaven-Dieppe, steerage passenger. Paris and back. U208/199.

The Stephen of the end of the fourth chapter, however, is still
unstable; he had to be brought into a final balance, and shown
at some length as a being whose development was virtually
ended. Unfortunately, the last chapter makes the book a
peculiarly difficult one for the reader to focus, because Joyce
had to close it on a suspended chord. As a lyric, it is finished
in its own terms; but the themes of the last forty pages,
though they give the illusion of focussing, don't really focus
until we have read well into *Ulysses*. The final chapter, which
in respect to the juggernaut of *Ulysses* must be a vulnerable
flank, in respect to what has gone before must be a conclusion.
This problem Joyce didn't wholly solve; there remains a moral
ambiguity (how seriously are we to take Stephen?) which makes
the last forty pages painful reading.

Not that Stephen would stand indefinitely if *Ulysses* didn't topple him over; his equilibrium in Chapter V, though good enough to give him a sense of unusual integrity in University College, is precarious unless he can manage, in the manner of so many permanent undergraduates, to prolong the college context for the rest of his life. Each of the preceding chapters, in fact, works toward an equilibrium which is dashed when in the next chapter Stephen's world becomes larger and the frame of reference more complex. The terms of equilibrium are always stated with disquieting accuracy; at the end of Chapter I we find:

> He was alone. He was happy and free: but he would not be anyway proud with Father Dolan. He would be very quiet and obedient: and he wished that he could do something kind for him to show him that he was not proud. P64/66.

And at the end of Chapter III:

> He sat by the fire in the kitchen, not daring to speak for happiness. Till that moment he had not known how beautiful and peaceful life could be. The green square of paper pinned round the lamp cast down a tender shade. On the dresser was a plate of sausages and white pudding and on the shelf there were eggs. They would be for the breakfast in the morning after the communion in the college chapel. White pudding and eggs and sausages and cups of tea. How simple and beautiful was life after all! And life lay all before him. P168/166.

Not " irony " but simply the truth: the good life conceived in terms of white pudding and sausages is unstable enough to need no underlining.

The even-numbered chapters make a sequence of a different sort. The ending of IV, Stephen's panting submission to an artistic vocation:

> Evening had fallen when he woke and the sand and arid grasses of his bed glowed no longer. He rose slowly and, recalling the rapture of his sleep, sighed at its joy. . . . P201/197,

—hasn't quite the finality often read into it when the explicit parallel with the ending of II is perceived:

> . . . He closed his eyes, surrendering himself to her, body and mind, conscious of nothing in the world but the dark pressure of her softly parting lips. They pressed upon his brain as upon his lips as though they were the vehicle of a vague speech; and between them he felt an unknown and timid pressure, darker than the swoon of sin, softer than sound or odour. P114/115.

When we link these passages with the fact that the one piece of
literary composition Stephen actually achieves in the book
comes out of a wet dream (" Towards dawn he awoke. O
what sweet music! His soul was all dewy wet ", P254) we are
in a position to see that the concluding " Welcome, O life! "
has an air of finality and balance only because the diary-form
of the last seven pages disarms us with an illusion of auctorial
impartiality.

CONTROLLING IMAGES: CLONGOWES AND BELVEDERE

Ego *vs.* authority is the theme of the three odd-numbered
chapters, Dublin *vs.* the dream that of the two even-numbered
ones. The generic Joyce plot, the encounter with the alter
ego, is consummated when Stephen at the end of the book
identifies himself with the sanctified Stephen who was stoned
by the Jews after reporting a vision (Acts VII, 56) and claims
sonship with the classical Daedalus who evaded the ruler of
land and sea by turning his soul to obscure arts. The episodes
are built about adumbrations of this encounter: with Father
Conmee, with Monte Cristo, with the whores, with the broad-
shouldered moustached student who cut the word " Foetus "
in a desk, with the weary mild confessor, with the bird-girl.
Through this repeated plot intertwine controlling emotions and
controlling images that mount in complexity as the book proceeds.

In chapter I the controlling emotion is fear, and the dominant image Father Dolan and his pandybat; this, associated with
the hangman-god and the priestly denial of the senses, was to
become one of Joyce's standard images for Irish clericalism—
hence the jack-in-the-box appearance of Father Dolan in
Circe's nightmare imbroglio, his pandybat cracking twice like
thunder, U547/531. Stephen's comment, in the mode of
Blake's repudiation of the God who slaughtered Jesus,
emphasizes the inclusiveness of the image: " I never could
read His handwriting except His criminal thumbprint on the
haddock."

Chapter II opens with a triple image of Dublin's prepossess-
sions: music, sport, religion. The first is exhibited via Uncle
Charles singing sentimental ballads in the outhouse; the
second via Stephen's ritual run around the park under the eye
of a superannuated trainer, which his uncle enjoins on him as

the whole duty of a Dubliner; the third via the clumsy piety
of Uncle Charles, kneeling on a red handkerchief and reading
above his breath " from a thumb-blackened prayerbook wherein catchwords were printed at the foot of every page." P67/69.
This trinity of themes is unwound and entwined throughout the
chapter, like a net woven round Stephen; it underlies the central
incident, the Whitsuntide play in the Belvedere chapel
(religion), which opens with a display by the dumb-bell team
(sport) preluded by sentimental waltzes from the soldier's
band (music).

While he is waiting to play his part, Stephen is taunted by
fellow-students, who rally him on a fancied love-affair and
smiting his calf with a cane bid him recite the *Confiteor*. His
mind goes back to an analogous incident, when a similar
punishment had been visited on his refusal to " admit that
Byron was no good ". The further analogy with Father Dolan
is obvious; love, art, and personal independence are thus
united in an ideogram of the prepossessions Stephen is determined to cultivate in the teeth of persecution.

The dream-world Stephen nourishes within himself is played
against manifestations of music, sport, and religion throughout
the chapter. The constant ironic clash of Dublin *vs.* the
Dream animates chapter II, as the clash of the ego *vs.* authority
did chapter I. All these themes come to focus during Stephen's
visit with his father to Cork. The dream of rebellion he has
silently cultivated is externalized by the discovery of the word
Foetus carved in a desk by a forgotten medical student:

> It shocked him to find in the outer world a trace of what he had
> deemed till then a brutish and individual malady of his own mind.
> His monstrous reveries came thronging into his memory. They too
> had sprung up before him, suddenly and furiously, out of mere
> words. ... P101/102.

The possibility of shame gaining the upper hand is dashed,
however, by the sudden banal intrusion of his father's conversation (" When you kick out for yourself, Stephen, as I daresay
you will one of these days, remember, whatever you do, to mix
with gentlemen ..."). Against the standards of Dublin his
monstrous reveries acquire a Satanic glamour, and the trauma
is slowly diverted into a resolution to rebel. After his father
has expressed a resolve to " leave him to his Maker " (religion),
and offered to " sing a tenor song against him " (music) or

" vault a fivebarred gate against him " (sport), Stephen muses, watching his father and two cronies drinking to the memory of their past:

> An abyss of fortune or of temperament sundered him from them. His mind seemed older than theirs: it shone coldly on their strifes and happiness and regrets like a moon upon a younger earth.   No life or youth stirred in him as it had stirred in them.   He had known neither the pleasure of companionship with others nor the vigour of rude male health nor filial piety.   Nothing stirred within his soul but a cold and cruel and loveless lust. P107/108.

After one final effort to compromise with Dublin on Dublin's terms has collapsed into futility (" The pot of pink enamel paint gave out and the wainscot of his bedroom remained with its unfinished and illplastered coat ", P110/111), he fiercely cultivates his rebellious thoughts, and moving by day and night "among distorted images of the outer world", P111/112, plunges at last into the arms of whores. " The holy encounter he had then imagined at which weakness and timidity and inexperience were to fall from him ", P112/113, finally arrives in inversion of Father Dolan's and Uncle Charles' religion: his descent into night-town is accompanied by lurid evocations of a Black Mass (Cf. *Ulysses*, 583/565):

> The yellow gasflames arose before his troubled vision against the vapoury sky, burning as if before an altar.   Before the doors and in the lighted halls groups were gathered arrayed as for some rite.   He was in another world: he had awakened from a slumber of centuries. P113/114.

CONTROLLING IMAGES: SIN AND REPENTANCE

Each chapter in the *Portrait* gathers up the thematic material of the preceding ones and entwines them with a dominant theme of its own.   In chapter III the fear-pandybat motif is present in Father Arnall's crudely materialistic hell, of which even the thickness of the walls is specified; and the Dublin-*vs.*-dream motif has ironic inflections in Stephen's terror-stricken brood-ings, when the dream has been twisted into a dream of holiness, and even Dublin appears transfigured:

> How beautiful must be a soul in the state of grace when God looked upon it with love!
> Frowsy girls sat along the curbstones before their baskets.   Their

dank hair trailed over their brows. They were not beautiful to see as they crouched in the mire. But their souls were seen by God; and if their souls were in a state of grace they were radiant to see; and God loved them, seeing them. P162/160.

A *rapprochement* in these terms between the outer world and Stephen's desires is too inadequate to need commentary; and it makes vivid as nothing else could the hopeless inversion of his attempted self-sufficiency. It underlines, in yet another way, his persistent sin: and the dominant theme of chapter III is Sin. A fugue-like opening plays upon the Seven Deadly Sins in turn; gluttony is in the first paragraph (" Stuff it into you, his belly counselled him "), followed by lust, then sloth (" A cold lucid indifference reigned in his soul "), pride (" His pride in his own sin, his loveless awe of God, told him that his offence was too grievous to be atoned for "), anger (" The blundering answer stirred the embers of his contempt for his fellows "); finally, a recapitulation fixes each term of the mortal catalogue in a phrase, enumerating how " from the evil seed of lust all the other deadly sins had sprung forth ", P120/120.

Priest and punisher inhabit Stephen himself as well as Dublin: when he is deepest in sin he is most thoroughly a theologian. A paragraph of gloomy introspection is juxtaposed with a list of theological questions that puzzle Stephen's mind as he awaits the preacher:

> . . . Is baptism with mineral water valid? How comes it that while the first beatitude promises the kingdom of heaven to the poor of heart, the second beatitude promises also to the meek that they shall possess the land? . . . If the wine change into vinegar and the host crumble into corruption after they have been consecrated, is Jesus Christ still present under their species as God and as man?
> – Here he is! Here he is!
> A boy from his post at the window had seen the rector come from the house. All the catechisms were opened and all heads bent upon them silently. P120/120.

Wine changed into vinegar and the host crumbled into corruption fits exactly the Irish clergy of " a church which was the scullery-maid of Christendom ". The excited " Here he is! Here he is! " following hard on the mention of Jesus Christ and signalling nothing more portentous than the rector makes the point as dramatically as anything in the book, and the

clinching sentence, with the students suddenly bending over
their catechisms, places the rector as the vehicle of pandybat
morality.

The last of the theological questions is the telling question.
Stephen never expresses doubt of the existence of God nor of
the essential validity of the priestly office—his *Non serviam* is
not a *non credo*, and he talks of a " malevolent reality " behind
these appearances P287/277—but the wine and bread that
were offered for his veneration were changed into vinegar and
crumbled into corruption. And it was the knowledge of that
underlying validity clashing with his refusal to do homage to
vinegar and rot that evoked his ambivalent poise of egocentric
despair. The hell of Father Arnall's sermon, so emotionally
overwhelming, so picayune beside the horrors that Stephen's
imagination can generate, had no more ontological content for
Stephen than had " an eternity of bliss in the company of the
dean of studies ", P282/273.

The conflict of this central chapter is again between the
phantasmal and the real. What is real—psychologically real,
because realized—is Stephen's anguish and remorse, and its
context in the life of the flesh. What is phantasmal is the
" heaven " of the Church and the " good life " of the priest.
It is only fear that makes him clutch after the latter at all; his
reaching out after orthodox salvation is, as we have come to
expect, presented in terms that judge it:

> The wind blew over him and passed on to the myriads and myriads
> of other souls, on whom God's favour shone now more and now less,
> stars now brighter and now dimmer, sustained and failing. And the
> glimmering souls passed away, sustained and failing, merged in a
> moving breath. One soul was lost; a tiny soul; his. It flickered
> once and went out, forgotten, lost. The end: black cold void waste.
> Consciousness of place came ebbing back to him slowly over a vast
> tract of time unlit, unfelt, unlived. The squalid scene composed
> itself around him; the common accents, the burning gasjets in the
> shops, odours of fish and spirits and wet sawdust, moving men and
> women. An old woman was about to cross the street, an oilcan in
> her hand. He bent down and asked her was there a chapel near.
> P162/160.

That wan waste world of flickering stars is the best Stephen has
been able to do towards an imaginative grasp of the communion
of Saints sustained by God; " unlit, unfelt, unlived " explains
succinctly why it had so little hold on him, once fear had

relaxed.   Equally pertinent is the vision of human temporal occupations the sermon evokes:

> What did it profit a man to gain the whole world if he lost his soul? At last he had understood: and human life lay around him, a plain of peace whereon antlike men laboured in brotherhood, their dead sleeping under quiet mounds.   P144/143.

To maintain the life of grace in the midst of nature, sustained by so cramped a vision of the life of nature, would mean maintaining an intolerable tension.   Stephen's unrelenting philosophic bias, his determination to understand what he is about, precludes his adopting the double standard of the Dubliners; to live both the life of nature and the life of grace he must enjoy an imaginative grasp of their relationship which stunts neither.   " No one doth well against his will," writes Saint Augustine, " even though what he doth, be well; " and Stephen's will is firmly harnessed to his understanding.   And there is no one in Dublin to help him achieve understanding. Father Arnall's sermon precludes rather than secures a desirable outcome, for it follows the modes of pandybat morality and Dublin materiality.   Its only possible effect on Stephen is to lash his dormant conscience into a frenzy.   The description of Hell as " a strait and dark and foul smelling prison, an abode of demons and lost souls, filled with fire and smoke ", with walls four thousand miles thick, its damned packed in so tightly that " they are not even able to remove from the eye the worm that gnaws it ", is childishly grotesque beneath its sweeping eloquence; and the hair-splitting catalogues of pains —pain of loss, pain of conscience (divided into three heads), pain of extension, pain of intensity, pain of eternity—is cast in a brainlessly analytic mode that effectively prevents any corresponding Heaven from possessing any reality at all.

Stephen's unstable pact with the Church, and its dissolution, follows the pattern of composition and dissipation established by his other dreams: the dream for example of the tryst with " Mercedes ", which found ironic reality among harlots.   It parallels exactly his earlier attempt to " build a breakwater of order and elegance against the sordid tide of life without him ", P110/111, whose failure, with the exhaustion of his money, was epiphanized in the running-dry of a pot of pink enamel paint.   His regimen at that time:

> He bought presents for everyone, overhauled his rooms, wrote out

resolutions, marshalled his books up and down their shelves, pored
over all kinds of price lists . . .

is mirrored by his searching after spiritual improvement:

> His daily life was laid out in devotional areas. By means of ejacula-
> tions and prayers he stored up ungrudgingly for the souls in purgatory
> centuries of days and quarantines and years. . . .   He offered up each
> of his three daily chaplets that his soul might grow strong in each of
> the three theological virtues. . . .   On each of the seven days of the
> week he further prayed that one of the seven gifts of the Holy Ghost
> might descend upon his soul. P170/167.

The " loan bank " he had opened for the family, out of which
he had pressed loans on willing borrowers " that he might have
the pleasure of making out receipts and reckoning the interests
on sums lent " finds its counterpart in the benefits he stored up
for souls in purgatory that he might enjoy the spiritual triumph
of " achieving with ease so many fabulous ages of canonical
penances ".   Both projects are parodies on the doctrine of
economy of grace; both are attempts, corrupted by motivating
self-interest, to make peace with Dublin on Dublin's own terms;
and both are short-lived.

   As this precise analogical structure suggests, the action of
each of the five chapters is really the same action.   Each chapter
closes with a synthesis of triumph which the next destroys.
The triumph of the appeal to Father Conmee from lower
authority, of the appeal to the harlots from Dublin, of the
appeal to the Church from sin, of the appeal to art from the
priesthood (the bird-girl instead of the Virgin) is always the
same triumph raised to a more comprehensive level.   It is an
attempt to find new parents; new fathers in the odd chapters,
new objects of love in the even.   The last version of Father
Conmee is the " priest of the eternal imagination "; the last
version of Mercedes is the " lure of the fallen seraphim ".
But the last version of the mother who said, " O, Stephen will
apologise " is the mother who prays on the last page " that I
may learn in my own life and away from home and friends what
the heart is and what it feels ".   The mother remains.

THE DOUBLE FEMALE

As in *Dubliners* and *Exiles*, the female role in the *Portrait*
is less to arouse than to elucidate masculine desires. Hence the
complex function in the book of physical love: the physical

is the analogue of the spiritual, as St. Augustine insisted in his *Confessions* (which, with Ibsen's *Brand*, is the chief archetype of Joyce's book). The poles between which this affection moves are those of St. Augustine and St. John: the Whore of Babylon and the Bride of Christ. The relation between the two is far from simple, and Stephen moves in a constant tension between them.

His desire, figured in the visions of Monte Cristo's Mercedes, " to meet in the real world the unsubstantial image which his soul so constantly beheld " draws him toward the prostitute (" In her arms he felt that he had suddenly become strong and fearless and sure of himself ", P114/114) and simultaneously toward the vaguely spiritual satisfaction represented with equal vagueness by the wraithlike E— C—, to whom he twice writes verses. The Emma Clery of *Stephen Hero*, with her loud forced manners and her body compact of pleasure, S66/56, was refined into a wraith with a pair of initials to parallel an intangible Church. She is continually assimilated to the image of the Blessed Virgin and of the heavenly Bride. The torture she costs him is the torture his apostasy costs him. His flirtation with her is his flirtation with Christ. His profane villanelle draws its imagery from religion—the incense, the eucharistic hymn, the chalice—and her heart, following Dante's image, is a rose, and in her praise " the earth was like a swinging swaying censer, a ball of incense ", P256/248.

The woman is the Church. His vision of greeting Mercedes with " a sadly proud gesture of refusal ":

— Madam, I never eat muscatel grapes. P68/71.

is fulfilled when he refuses his Easter communion. Emma's eyes, in their one explicit encounter, speak to him from beneath a cowl, P76/78. " The glories of Mary held his soul captive ", P118/118, and a temporary reconciliation of his lust and his spiritual thirst is achieved as he reads the Lesson out of the Song of Solomon. In the midst of his repentance she functions as imagined mediator: " The image of Emma appeared before him," and, repenting, " he imagined that he stood near Emma in a wide land, and, humbly and in tears, bent and kissed the elbow of her sleeve ", P132/131. Like Dante's Beatrice, she manifests in his earthly experience the Church Triumphant of his spiritual dream. And when he rejects her because she seems to be flirting with Father Moran, his anger is couched in the anti-clerical terms of his apostasy: " He had done well to leave her to flirt with her priest, to toy with a church which was the scullery-maid of Christendom ", P258/250.

That Kathleen ni Houlihan can flirt with priests is the unforgivable sin underlying Stephen's rejection of Ireland. But he makes a clear distinction between the stupid clericalism which makes intellectual and communal life impossible, and his long-nourished vision of an artist's Church Triumphant upon earth. He rejects the actual for daring to fall short of his vision.

THE FINAL BALANCE

The climax of the book is of course Stephen's ecstatic discovery of his vocation at the end of chapter IV. The prose rises in nervous excitement to beat again and again the tambours of a fin-de-siècle ecstasy:

> His heart trembled; his breath came faster and a wild spirit passed over his limbs as though he were soaring sunward. His heart trembled in an ecstasy of fear and his soul was in flight. His soul was soaring in an air beyond the world and the body he knew was purified in a breath and delivered of incertitude and made radiant and commingled with the element of the spirit. An ecstasy of flight made radiant his eyes and wild his breath and tremulous and wild and radiant his wind-swept limbs.

> – One! Two! ... Look out!—
> – O, Cripes, I'm drownded!— P196/192.

The interjecting voices of course are those of bathers, but their ironic appropriateness to Stephen's Icarian " soaring sunward " is not meant to escape us: divers have their own " ecstasy of flight", and Icarus was "drownded". The imagery of Stephen's ecstasy is fetched from many sources; we recognize Shelley's skylark, Icarus, the glorified body of the Resurrection (cf. " His soul had arisen from the grave of boyhood, spurning her graveclothes ", P197/193) and a tremulousness from which it is difficult to dissociate adolescent sexual dreams (which the Freudians tell us are frequently dreams of flying). The entire eight-page passage is cunningly organized with great variety of rhetoric and incident; but we cannot help noticing the limits set on vocabulary and figures of thought. The em-purpled triteness of such a cadence as " radiant his eyes and

wild his breath and tremulous and wild and radiant his windswept face " is enforced by recurrence: " But her long fair hair
was girlish: and girlish, and touched with the wonder of mortal beauty, her face ", P199/195. " Ecstasy " is the keyword,
indeed. This riot of feelings corresponds to no vocation
definable in mature terms; the paragraphs come to rest on
images of irresponsible motion:

> He turned away from her suddenly and set off across the strand.
> His cheeks were aflame; his body was aglow; his limbs were
> trembling. On and on and on and on he strode, far out over the
> sands, singing wildly to the sea, crying to greet the advent of the life
> that had cried to him. P200/196.

What " life " connotes it skills not to ask; the word recurs and
recurs. So does the motion onward and onward and onward:

> A wild angel had appeared to him, the angel of mortal youth and
> beauty, an envoy from the fair courts of life, to throw open before
> him in an instant of ecstasy the gates of all the ways of error and glory.
> On and on and on and on! P200/196.

It may be well to recall Joyce's account of the romantic
temper:

> . . . an insecure, unsatisfied, impatient temper which sees no fit abode
> here for its ideals and chooses therefore to behold them under insen-
> sible figures. As a result of this choice it comes to disregard certain
> limitations. Its figures are blown to wild adventures, lacking the
> gravity of solid bodies. . . . S78/66.

Joyce also called *Prometheus Unbound* " the Schwärmerei of a
young jew ".

And it is quite plain from the final chapter of the *Portrait*
that we are not to accept the mode of Stephen's " freedom " as
the " message " of the book. The " priest of the eternal
imagination " turns out to be indigestibly Byronic. Nothing
is more obvious than his total lack of humour. The dark
intensity of the first four chapters is moving enough, but our
impulse on being confronted with the final edition of Stephen
Dedalus is to laugh; and laugh at this moment we dare not;
he is after all a victim being prepared for a sacrifice. His shape,
as Joyce said, can no longer change. The art he has elected
is not " the slow elaborative patience of the art of satisfaction ".
" On and on and on and on " will be its inescapable mode. He
does not *see* the girl who symbolizes the full revelation; " she

seemed like one whom magic had changed into the likeness of a strange and beautiful seabird ", P199/195, and he confusedly apprehends a sequence of downy and feathery incantations. What, in the last chapter, he does see he sees only to reject, in favour of an incantatory " loveliness which has not yet come into the world ", P197/286.

The only creative attitude to language exemplified in the book is that of Stephen's father:

> – Is it Christy? he said.   There's more cunning in one of those warts on his bald head than in a pack of jack foxes.

His vitality is established before the book is thirty pages under way.   Stephen, however, isn't enchanted at any time by the proximity of such talk.   He isn't, as a matter of fact, even interested in it.   Without a backward glance, he exchanges this father for a myth.

Chapter 9

THE SCHOOL OF OLD AQUINAS

> so that you cd/ crack a flea on eider wan
> ov her breasts
> sd/ the old Dublin pilot
> or the precise definition
> *Pound, Canto LXXVII*

Now these two—namely eternal and temporal—are related to our knowledge in this way, that one of them is the means of knowing the other. For in the order of discovery, we come through temporal things to the knowledge of things eternal, according to the words of the Apostle (*Rom.* i. 20): *The invisible things of God are clearly seen, being understood by the things that are made.* But in the order of judgment, from eternal things already known, we judge of temporal things, and according to the laws of eternal things we order temporal things.

Summa Theologica, I. q. 79. a. 7. c.

Chamber Music contains real antitheses of emotion similar to those from which Stephen Dedalus never escapes:

Eyes, opening from the darkness of desire, eyes that dimmed the breaking east. What was their languid grace but the softness of chambering? And what was their shimmer but the shimmer of a scum that mantled the cesspool of the court of a slobbering Stuart. P274/265.

The danger of becoming severed by this dichotomy, as Yeats was to be in the years between the Alchemical Twilight and Crazy Jane's bravado—spirit mocking the excremental flesh and flesh mocking the unconsummating spirit—didn't inhere in the lyric phase but in the attempt to get beyond it. The lyric mode, rooted in the artist's apprehension rather than in what he apprehends, raises few problems beyond the exacting technical one of getting down one's feelings unwarped. That is why many artists never, except abortively, transcend it. Joyce in the poems had been projecting the emotions of Dublin in the clear and slightly ironic mode in which he himself felt them. It was some time before he saw clearly that he had not in fact been writing love-verses but registering something more complex. (" It is a young man's book. I felt like that. It is not a book of love-verses at all, I perceive ", he wrote to his brother in 1907.)

To pass, with the epic phase, out into the city required dealing explicitly with the notion that he and his emotions were alive while the gesturing city was contorted in death. Rather, something was alive in him that was dead in the city; something, however, that he could not have quickened unless it had been preserved in the city; and meanwhile the city was exhibiting its own equivocal modes of life.

Cartesian thinkers, Maritain observes, imagine or construe the object as a piece of reified externality, dead, an affront to the mind until the mind has processed it. The artistic equivalent to this is a scornful Byronic shaking off of dust, and romantic self-expression. The problems Joyce faced were philosophic before they were personal.

What does the mind do when it lays hold on something? How is the artist's understanding an understanding *of* something, and not conceit? What does he do when he lays words together? How can his work be continuous with what he perceives, without being correspondingly opaque? These are ways of asking a single question. " The soul is in a manner all that is. The soul is the form of forms," Stephen Dedalus keeps repeating. Since I have my soul, why worry about what, outside it, is? His own soul, surely, was richer and more radiant than the paralysed city. But his own soul was a Dublin product. Self-disgust then?

The clue leading out of this cave is St. Thomas Aquinas' key doctrine that the essence of the genus *homo* is located neither in body nor in soul, but in the composite. To follow it into a sustaining aesthetic theory led Joyce, in one important way, outside his Byronic century, in which the artist's one model was the sulphurous rebel. Dubliners—people—are not juxtaposed essences, rational plus animal, like Swift's Houyhnhnms; that is the supposition that will lead an observer to scorn their shortcomings, and eventually himself, from a Nietzschean height. In a Florence no less ignoble, Dante, sustained by such a structure of thought as Joyce sought, had done something more.

No other modern artist has been so fortunate as Joyce in being born where everything he needed was in suspended animation around him. Mr. Pound had to go to classical China,

Mr. Eliot to symbolist France, for what the Dubliner possessed at his elbow. It needed laborious resuscitation, however. As he received it at school from the Dublin clerics, the thought of Aristotle and St. Thomas was little more than a stockpile of terminology. That his college paper expounding an " applied Aquinas " aesthetic should have been unintelligible and faintly heretical to his professors was only to be expected; they didn't think of philosophic thought as the articulation of a world but as the recitation of a formula. A debased scholasticism underlay both the work of Descartes and the narrower side of the eighteenth-century French *esprit classique;* priests trained in France in that tradition established the Irish seminaries in which Joyce's masters got their education; Irish scholasticism was thus the debasement of a debasing, Thomistic intuition of being first translated into Cartesian rationalism, and then deprived of Cartesian *clarté.* Handbooks constructed on the principle of " Sic dixit Leibniz " and " Sic Leibniz refutatur " preserved the disputatiousness of the scholastic tradition with none of the imaginative thirst for precision that had in its best times justified it.

Mr. Pound in an essay of fundamental importance has characterized " the radiant world where one thought cuts through another with a clean edge, a world of moving energies ' *mezzo oscuro rade* ', ' *risplende in sé perpetuale effetto* ', magnetisms that take form, that are seen, or that border the visible, the matter of Dante's *paradiso*, the glass under water, the form that seems a form seen in a mirror, these realities perceptible to the sense, interacting. . . ".[1] Dante and (pace Mr. Pound) St. Thomas Aquinas belong, in different ways, to this world; but no such articulated world, only a sheaf of definitions concerning whatness and thusness, is infolded by the covers of such handbooks as the *Synopsis Philosophiae Scholasticae ad mentem divi Thomae* conned at University College by Stephen Dedalus, P205/200. The clerical perversion of the Dumb Ox of Sicily's vision is implied in the title of the unread book before which Stephen's classmate Cranly, his ear inclined like a confessor's, leans back in his library chair: *Diseases of the Ox*, P267/258.

To inform the phrases and definitions pickled in Jesuit textbooks with such a creative spirit as had once animated them was for Joyce a release both from Dublin intellectual deadness and from romantic art. Art was always, for him, a job of

[1] Ezra Pound, *Make It New*, 351.

reanimating the given; so was the speculative work that preceded art. St. Thomas underwent a comparable reanimation
some time afterwards, in the work of Jacques Maritain, and
what Joyce at twenty-one or twenty-two was putting into his
notebooks coincides closely with what Maritain expounds in
Art et Scolastique. The young Dubliner's is probably the first
reasoned aesthetic on Aristotelian principles since the ages
when none was needed.

What was formulated for his own use, however, was never
written out as a treatise. Of the speculative work undertaken
in Paris and Pola in 1903 and 1904, recorded in notebooks at
which his biographer gives us no more than a peep,[1] certain
portions were written up in dialogue form for incorporation in
the autobiographical work which became *A Portrait of the Artist
as a Young Man*. It is only by accident that we have the discarded *Stephen Hero* version; and by the time he came to
rewrite the *Portrait* Joyce had decided to make its central
figure a futile *alter ego* rather than a self-image, and revised the
doctrinal exposition to suit. In the *Portrait* the exposition,
correct so far as it goes, has omissions dangerous for the reader
interested in Aquinas rather than in Stephen. The absence of
the crucial doctrine of epiphanies, and the soft-pedalling of the
location of *pulchrum* in *ens*, emphasize Stephen's highly sub-
jective bent; a technically-minded reader might conclude, as
Joyce meant him to, that Stephen's aesthetic is not Thomist at
all but Neo-Platonist. *Ulysses*, which neither Stephen nor any
extrapolation of Stephen could have written, was expected by
Joyce to clinch this point. Fortunately, we need not proceed
on the unbuttressed assumption that Joyce knew both his own
mind and the philosophical orientations he was talking about;
there is plenty of evidence.[2]

Joyce's rejection of the notion that in speaking of *claritas* St.
Thomas had in mind " symbolism or idealism, the supreme
quality of beauty being a light from some other world, the idea
of which the matter was but the shadow, the reality of which it
was but the symbol ", P 249/242, is aimed against the sort of

---

[1] Not even the pertinacity of Mr. Slocum has turned up these notebooks, or
even assurance that they still do or do not exist.

[2] The chief texts are located as follows: Paris Notebook (1903): Gorman,
III–iii. Pola Notebook (1904): Gorman, V–ii. Epiphanies: *Stephen Hero*,
211/188. The dialogue in chapter V of the *Portrait* is supplemented by six or
seven passages in *Stephen Hero*.

neo-platonism represented by Yeats' "Dreams alone are certain good." Every theory of aesthetics depends on a theory of knowledge. It is radically impossible to understand what Joyce is talking about from the standpoint of the post-Kantian conviction that the mind imposes intelligibility upon things. That is the root of the very romantic egoism from which he was liberating himself. Stephen tells Lynch:

> The first step in the direction of truth is to understand the frame and scope of the intellect itself, to comprehend the act itself of intellection. Aristotle's entire system of philosophy rests upon his book of psychology and that, I think, rests on his statement that the same attribute cannot at the same time and in the same connexion belong to and not belong to the same subject. P244/236

That is, the line that joins the Principle of Contradiction to the *Metaphysics* is the backbone of the *De Anima*, and everything else depends on the *De Anima*. Perceiver, thing perceived, and perception belong alike to a world of irreducible existences. This statement has nothing in common with the Cartesian confrontation of an intelligible world articulated by the intellect and an opaque world reported by the senses; nor with the Romantic transposition of this dichotomy, a concupiscible phantom-world of poesy and a tyrannical world of fact (that was the dichotomy Yeats never solved, despite the toughness of articulation his later phantom-world took on).

"SIGNATURES" AND SIGNATE MATTER

The mind, then, literally knows things; it extracts intelligible species from things; it does not *make* its intelligible forms; it does not construct, acting on hints from the senses, its diagrammatic intelligible simulacra of things; it does not content itself with a Kantian metaphysic of things-as-they-appear, in contradistinction to supposedly unknowable things-as-they-are.

The classical account of the mode of knowledge postulated by Joyce is in the *Summa Theolgica*, Part I, questions 84 to 88. Fundamental to this account is the so-called hylomorphic doctrine[1] that created things are composed of signate matter plus substantial form. Signate matter is matter on which, so to speak, a signature has been impressed, as in Dante's repeated simile of wax and seal (Hence " Signatures of all things I am

---

[1] From ὕλη + μορφή; matter + form. See Jacques Maritain, *Introduction to Philosophy*, 167–168.

here to read "; it is unnecessary to look, with one commentator, to esoteric Buddhism for an explication of this celebrated statement). It must be carefully distinguished from the Cartesian identification of substance with geometrical extension. It guarantees the separateness and otherness of things. St. Thomas writes:

> Some have thought that the species of a natural thing is a form only, and that matter is not a part of the species. If that were so, matter would not enter into the definition of natural things. Therefore we must disagree and say that matter is twofold, common and *signate*, or individual: common, such as flesh and bones; individual or signate, such as this flesh and these bones. The intellect therefore abstracts the species of a natural thing from the individual sensible matter, but not from the common sensible matter. For example, it abstracts the species of *man* from *this flesh and these bones*, which do not belong to the species as such, but to the individual, and need not be considered in the species. But the species of man cannot be abstracted by the intellect from *flesh and bones*.[1]

In things, this matter is joined to substantial form. Substantial form is the principle of determination and so of intelligibility: the internal principle which determines the very being of corporeal substances.

The artist who understands this, and believes it, is in a position to control any perception whatever. The trodden-down boot-heel of an old woman at prayer will image the spiritual condition of a civilization, if he believes in it sufficiently to set it down untampered. If he is interested in the boot-heel only as a token of his own sense of disgust, what will come off the page will be not a civilization but, precisely, his own sense of disgust.[2] The book will be fundamentally about

[1] *Summa Theologica*, I, q. 85, a. 2, ad 2m. Also *De Ente et Essentia*, II–6: " materia signata . . . quae sub certis dimensionibus consideratur." *Materia non signata* is not directly accessible to the intellect but as it were hypostatized in general definitions: " In definitione hominis (sc. inquantum homo) ponitur materia non signata; non enim in definitione hominis ponitur hoc os et haec caro, sed os et caro absolute, quae sunt materia non signata." (*Ibid.*) Thus the anti-poetic abstractifying tendencies castigated by Mr. Pound do not touch the Thomistic account of the act of cognition itself, which is perfectly compatible with the " ideogrammic method " of presenting the mind with constellated particulars for contemplation. The mind can contemplate nothing else.

[2] Hence Joyce's advice to critic, ". . . not to look for a message but to approach the temper which has made the work, an old woman praying, or a young man fastening his shoe, and to see what is there well done and how much it signifies." *James Clarence Mangan* (1902), Gorman, II–v.

himself. How Joyce treated an old woman's boot-heel we can
see from " The Sisters " in *Dubliners*. It contrasts instruc-
tively with the nervous intensity of, say, D. H. Lawrence, for
whom nothing is *there* until his ego has possessed it and *used* it.
He animates things. He gets inside them and pushes them.
His distant trains don't move slowly, they crawl doubtfully.
His snowflakes aren't whirled by the wind, they whirl like
doves. Joycean respect for the given is at the opposite pole
from the Dedalian Paul Morel's belief that the outsides of
things are dead crust, that one paints by leaving out the shadows
and rendering, as he tells Miriam, the shimmering protoplasm.

Neither are things intrinsically opaque to the understanding,
nor are they mere material signs related to abstract intelligibles
as a thumb-print to a thumb or a cookie to a cookie-cutter.
The active intellect was held to extract from the phantasms
formed by the senses the intelligible species of the object being
perceived: of this particular pencil or chair, not of writing-
instruments or furniture. Knowledge is neither of ideas nor
of categories, but of things. Categories come after knowledge.
Ideas are not objects of knowledge, but means of knowledge;
not things, but means of contemplating the thing in its rich
singularity.[1]

That is how Joyce in *Stephen Hero* distinguishes, in avoiding
" spiritual anarchy ", the " classical style " from the " romantic
temper ". The latter is

> . . . an insecure, unsatisfied, impatient temper which sees no fit abode
> here for its ideals and chooses therefore to behold them under insen-
> sible figures. . . .

On the contrary, the classical style ". . . is the syllogism of art,
the only legitimate process from one world to another." (The
conclusion of a syllogism is not *added to* but virtually *in* the
premises.)

> The classical temper . . . ever mindful of limitations, chooses rather
> to bend upon these present things and so to work upon them and

[1] For a discussion of the role of the concept or idea or mental word in Thomistic
apprehension, see Maritain, *Formal Logic*, 17–19. The rigorous reader may
require his distinction between the *mental concept* (" something of ourselves by
which we know the object ") and the *objective concept* (" something of the object
by which it is known to us "). But for a preliminary grasp of Joycean-scholastic
vs. post-Cartesian epistemologies, the statement in the text about the concept as
means, not object, of knowledge is sufficiently accurate.

fashion them that the quick intelligence may go beyond them to
their meaning which is still unuttered. S78/66.

That it is *things* which achieve epiphany under the artist's
alchemical power, and not his own soul which he manifests,
cannot be too much insisted upon:

> The artist who could disentangle the subtle soul of the image from
> its mesh of defining circumstances most exactly and re-embody it
> in circumstances chosen as the most exact for its new office, he was the
> supreme artist.

LOCKE AND ROMANTICISM

The " classical temper ", in short, reads signatures, pursues
epiphanies. It does not create a world, it transmutes and
projects a world, not towards the more concupiscible but
towards the more intelligible. " Il a le goût du paradis
terrestre," writes Maritain, " parce qu'il restitue, pour un
instant, la paix et la délectation simultanée de l'intelligence et
des sens." Two pages later he speaks of " cet éclat de la forme,
si purement intelligible qu'il puisse être en lui-même . . . saisi
dans le sensible et par le sensible, et non pas séparément de
lui."[1]

The rival romantic temper has precise philosophic roots. It
disregards " le sensible ". The day-self of the dreamer is the
mathematician. Imitation, *mimesis*, the imaging within the
mind of the phenomena of sensation, had little meaning or
value after Locke had confined judgment to syllogistic functions
and reduced the sensation and intellection of things to a passive
process. Locke himself pronounces the separation between
Judgment, which consists

> in separating carefully, one from another, ideas wherein can be found
> the least difference, thereby to avoid being misled by similitude, and
> by affinity to take one thing for another,

and the monkey-work of Wit,

> lying most in the assemblage of ideas, and putting those together with
> quickness and variety wherein can be found any resemblance or
> congruity, thereby to make up pleasant pictures, and agreeable visions
> to the fancy.

[1] *Art et Scolastique*, 37, 39.

The latter he dismisses as " that entertainment and pleasantry ", whose " beauty appears at first sight, and there is required no labour of thought to examine what truth or reason there is in it ";[1] the quietus, it would seem, of poetry considered as positive nutriment for the affections, in the sense in which Homer was the educator of Greece. Between Locke and Eliot the English poets have worked in covert defiance of official philosophy; Locke's formulations did much to secure the schism between the man of sense and the bohemian with bay-leaves in his hair.

The gullibility of Joseph Addison, as it happens, makes it easy to trace a clear connection from Locke to Leopold Bloom. Addison made earnest attempts to construct an aesthetic on Lockeian bases; he was much intimidated by the éclat with which Locke seemed to have solved all the problems of epistemology. Hence where the essayist on *The Pleasures of the Imagination* seems today most futile he will generally be found to be applying *An Essay Concerning Human Understanding* most syllogistically:

> Nothing is more pleasant to the fancy, than to enlarge itself by degrees, in its contemplation of the various proportions which its several objects bear to each other, when it compares the body of man to the bulk of the whole earth . . . (etc.).[2]

This, of course, is the sort of thing Bloom does all the time; it is the chief significance of his interest in astronomy. And it is, as Addison's next paragraph shows (" Our reason can pursue a particle of matter through an infinite variety of divisions, but the fancy soon loses sight of it . . .") derived with little but emotive modification from Locke II. xvii. 8: ". . . though it seems to be pretty clear when we consider nothing else in it but the negation of an end, yet, when we would frame in our minds the idea of an infinite space or duration, that idea is very confused and obscure because . . . (etc.)." The confused and obscure, of course, soon came to be identified with the poetical; that was the use of Longinus to the eighteenth century. Blake, before Locke's ideas had become very much modified, accurately diagnosed the boundless as supremely *un*-interesting; but it was 250 years before thought accelerating into sterile extension, with its concomitant

---

[1] *Human Understanding*, II.xi.3.
[2] *Spectator*, No. 420.

emotional spectrum, received definitive embodiment in the person of Leopold Bloom.

Swift, of course, performed a similar diagnosis, though his point has been missed. Gulliver's Travels are those of a Bloom; he is immensely impressed by the measurements of everything, and interested in gathering tangible souvenirs. The baboons-at-typewriters Thinking Machine of Lagado (III–5) is closely related to the notions of Hobbes and Locke (". . . wit lying most in the assemblage of ideas, and putting those together with quickness and variety wherein can be found any resemblance . . ."). On the Lagado machine, whenever there turn up " three or four words together that might make part of a sentence ", they are promptly written down. Bloom's notions of literary composition are analogous:

> *The hungry famished gull*
> *Flaps o'er the waters dull.*
> That is how poets write, the similar sounds. But then Shakespeare has no rhymes: blank verse. The flow of language it is. The thoughts. Solemn. U150/141.

This is at one level a parody of Stephen's speculations in the previous chapter about mouth-south and the personified rhymes from Dante, U136/129. At another level it is a fair digest of five hundred respectable " appreciations " of Shakepeare. Bloom's elliptical speculations contain hundreds of condensed presidential addresses, *Atlantic Monthly* articles, sociological surveys, doctoral theses, etc. And for solemnity as the major criterion of art, once one has accepted a mechanical account of its genesis, we have only to return to Addison: *Spectator* 418 contains some relevant remarks. As usual, Addison is most Bloom-like when he is most decorously rational.

This rattling around of superficially similar notions in the head (Locke's " wit " and the behaviourist's " free association ") may be said to be the Lockeian model for the poetic process. Since Joyce was to spend the greater part of his life portraying this process going on, it was important for him to focus it as an aesthetic datum, not an aesthetic mode. According to Aristotle and St. Thomas, the *nous poietikos* or agent intellect extracted the intelligible species from the object as reproduced in the mind. The object provides the intelligible species, and

the mind liberates them from their immediate matter.   The
nous poietikos (cf. " poetic soul ") functions alike in conceiving
an epic or looking at a donkey.   According to Descartes, Locke,
and Kant, the mind dissociates and assembles nothing more
pregnant than its own ideas.   (Locke considers the ideas under
an explicitly atomistic metaphor).   If this work is done with
deliberative earnestness, we have Judgment; otherwise, the
accidental assemblages and gay non-sequiturs of Wit.   (" A
fool, so just a copy of a wit ", gibed Pope, with intricate irony,
from just outside Locke's world.)   Hence the interior monologue, image of a mind on which the key has turned.

THE EPIPHANY

It is no wonder, since Locke, that the meaning of " visa " in
" quae visa placent " has been obliterated; likewise the meaning of " claritas."   These terms are sustained by the analogy
the light on the object bears to the light in the mind.   Colour
exemplifies the reach of the intelligible out into the sensible;
hence St. Thomas' gloss on *claritas*, " unde, quae habent
colorem nitidum, pulchra esse dicuntur ".   The supposition of
more than one commentator that St. Thomas defines *claritas*
as " having a bright colour ", and that Joyce has chosen to
suppress this in order to claim his authority for a subtler
theory (Stephen indeed calls the connotation of *claritas* vague,
and the term inexact) is symptomatic of our divorce of the
mind from the senses.   As for the not uncommon notion that
" art meant little to St. Thomas in any but a very concrete,
obvious way ", we have Stephen's reminder that St. Thomas
was the poet of *Pange lingua*, and the Rev. Walter J. Ong's
fascinating analysis of the metaphysical wit of that and other
Thomistic poems.[1]   Father Ong's essay is required reading for
students of *Finnegans Wake*: " Who knows?—said Stephen
smiling.—Perhaps Aquinas would understand me better than
you ", P246/238.

In his 1904 gloss on " quae visa placent " Joyce translates
and expands with emphasis on the intelligible.

> Those things are beautiful the apprehension of which pleases.   There-
> fore beauty is that quality of a sensible object in virtue of which its

---

[1] ' Wit and Mystery: a Revaluation in Mediaeval Latin Hymnody ", *Speculum*,
XXII.3, 316–320.

apprehension pleases or satisfies the aesthetic appetite which desires to apprehend the most satisfying relations of the sensible.[1]

Apprehension—vision—is threefold: the perception that the object exists self-bounded and selfcontained as *one* thing; the perception that it is a *thing*, " complex, multiple, divisible, separable, made up of its parts, the result of its parts and their sum, harmonious "; the perception that it is *that thing which it is*. Rationalism has denatured this last phrase into a tautology. We think of categories instead of seeing individualities.

> This is the moment which I call epiphany. First we recognize that the object is *one* integral thing, than we recognize that it is an organized composite structure, a *thing* in fact: finally, when the relation of the parts is exquisite, when the parts are adjusted to the special point, we recognize that it is *that thing* which it is. Its soul, its whatness, leaps to us from the vestment of its appearance. The soul of the commonest object, the structure of which is so adjusted, seems to us radiant. The object achieves its epiphany. S213/190.

The object achieves *its* epiphany. What the scrutinizer comes to know is the thing itself in its irreducible otherness: other than himself, other than all other things. Its meaning is discoverable only within itself; it does not function as seed-crystal to jell a private configuration of thought.

> He told Cranly that the clock of the Ballast Office was capable of an epiphany. Cranly questioned the inscrutable dial of the Ballast Office with his no less inscrutable countenance:
> – Yes, said Stephen. I will pass it time after time, allude to it, refer to it, catch a glimpse of it. It is only an item in the catalogue of Dublin's street furniture. Then all at once I see it and I know at once what it is: epiphany.
> – What?
> – Imagine my glimpses at that clock as the gropings of a spiritual eye which seeks to adjust its vision to an exact focus. The moment the focus is reached the object is epiphanized. It is just in this epiphany that I find the third, the supreme quality of beauty. S211/188.

[1] Gorman, V–ii. For " the aesthetic appetite ", called in Stephen's less rigorous *Portrait* version " the imagination ", see Joyce's gloss of the previous week on " Bonum est in quod tendit appetitus "; St. Thomas on the interrelation between *pulchrum* and *bonum* (S.T. I, q.5, a.4, ad 1); and Maritain's delicate exegesis: " Le beau ... diffère du bien en ce qu'il ne fait pas directement face à l'appétit ... cependant il a dans sa définition de délecter en tant que vu, et implique ainsi nécessairement un rapport à l'appétit." (*Art et Scolastique*, 178).

Bloom's intense gaze at a bottle-label, during which he was
" recollecting two or three private transactions of his own ",
U410/398, is the polar opposite of the contemplation of a
thing in its quiddity; Buck Mulligan's comment on this spectacle describes with surprising exactness the antitype of the
epiphany:

> Warily, Malachi whispered, preserve a druid silence. His soul is
> far away. It is as painful perhaps to be awakened from a vision as to
> be born. Any object, intensely regarded, may be a gate of access to
> the incorruptible aeon of the gods. Do you not think it, Stephen?
> U409/398.

The possibility of epiphanies depends on the composite
structure of things, signate matter plus substantial form.
Mulligan is parodying the doctrines of Blake, AE, and the
theosophists, depending on a contrary metaphysic, in which
the gratuitous plurality of the sensible world conceals a
monistic comprehensive insight, " the incorruptible aeon of the
gods ", or Blake's world seen in a grain of sand. It doesn't
much matter what object you select, since you look through it
rather than at it.[1] Hence one's feeling that Blake's symbolic
wheels are turning in a medium offering little resistance. As
his intelligible structure exists behind or beyond the particulars
in which it is perceived, so it fails of radical engagement with
the images, rhythms, and analogies by which it is communicated. The latter become not foci of contemplation but modes
of persuasion: not ideograms but enthymemes. Hence Joyce
rejected a Blakean reading of *claritas:*

> Aquinas uses a term which seems to be inexact. It baffled me for a
> long time. It would lead you to believe that he had in mind sym-
> bolism or idealism, the supreme quality of beauty being a light from
> some other world, the idea of which the matter was but the shadow,
> the reality of which it was but the symbol. I thought he might mean
> that *claritas* was the artistic discovery and representation of the divine

---

[1] Cf. *Summa Theologica*, I, q.88, a.2, " Whether our intellect can come to
understand immaterial substances through its knowledge of material things? "
St. Thomas notes, " This would be true, were immaterial substances the forms
and species of these material things, as Plato supposed." Q.84, a.3 (" Whether
the soul understands all things through innate species? ") and q.76, a.2 (" Whether
the intellectual principle is multiplied according to the number of bodies? ") are
closely related treatises. They offer technical refutation, on the basis of the only
metaphysic in which the theory of epiphanies is meaningful, of a position with
which Joyce's is often confused.

purpose in anything or a force of generalization which would make the aesthetic image a universal one, make it outshine its proper conditions. But that is literary talk. P249/242.

EPIPHANY AND THE INTUITION OF BEING

The artist isn't a metaphysician, nor the metaphysician an artist; but both work in the same way, toward a vision that isn't the less comprehensive for being coloured by their respective intentions. The epiphany is the reward of intense contemplation; not a tranced stare, but precisely the active groping of a spiritual eye seeking to adjust its focus to what is there: precisely like the experience of trying to grasp a poem. The reward is not an " insight " but a grasp of the whole. Though Maritain's precise account of the metaphysician's " intuition of being "[1] isn't oriented toward artistic reproduction, it parallels exactly Joyce's account of the artist seeking to lay hold on his subject:

> It is difficult, inasmuch as it is difficult to arrive at the degree of intellectual purification at which this act is produced in us, at which we become sufficiently disengaged, sufficiently empty to *hear* what all things whisper and to *listen* instead of composing answers.

(Mr. Pound has observed that people generally read his poetry when they want to write articles against it.)

> We must attain a certain level of intellectual spirituality,

(*The true and the beautiful are spiritually possessed, the true by intellection, the beautiful by apprehension, and the appetites which desire to possess them, the intellectual and aesthetic appetites, are therefore spiritual appetites.*"—*Joyce, Pola Notebook, 1904*).

> such that the impact of reality upon the intellect—or to use a less crude metaphor, the active attentive silence of the intellect,

(" *The luminous silent stasis of aesthetic pleasure . . .*" P250/242)

> its meeting with the real—gives the objects received through our senses (whose *species impressa* is buried in the depths of the intellect) a new kind of presence in us: they are present in a mental world of transobjective presence and intelligibility. Then we are confronted within ourselves with the object of this intuition,

[1] *Preface to Metaphysics*, III.

(" *The object achieves its epiphany* ", S213/190)

> as an object of knowledge, living with an immaterial life, with the burning translucence of intellectual nature in act.

THE WORDS ON THE PAGE

In the work of art as in the object contemplated by the artist, " claritas is quidditas ", Joyce had announced. Maritain begins his treatment of *claritas* (*Art et Scolastique*, 37–8) by quoting St. Thomas, " claritas est de ratione pulchritudinis," and " lux pulchrificiat, quia sine luce omnia sint turpia ", only to emphasize that this " light " is " un resplendissement d'intelligibilité."

> " Splendor formae ", says St. Thomas, in his precise metaphysician's language; for *form*—the principle securing in their proper perfection all things that are, constituting and achieving them in their essence and their qualities, the ontological secret they bear within themselves, their spiritual being, their operative mystery—form is above all the proper principle of intelligibility, the proper *clarté* of all things.

The incandescence of the surprising word, the steady light of images appropriately juxtaposed, follows from this. The perceived epiphany, the grasp of a subject external to the artist, comes first; lacking that, syntactic bravura strikes momentary sparks from bits of flint. But the grasp on a subject isn't its reduction to a schema. " L'éclat de la forme doit s'entendre d'une splendeur *ontologique* qui se trouve d'une manière ou d'une autre révélée à notre esprit, non d'une clarté *conceptuelle*.... C'est un contresens cartésien que de reduire la clarté *en soi* à la clarté *pour nous*. En art ce contresens produit l'académisme, et nous condamne à une beauté si pauvre qu'elle ne peut irradier dans l'âme que la plus mesquine des joies."[1]

Given the grasp, however, the words on the page are controlled by it in surprising ways. " The image isn't created by comparing (with inevitable feebleness) two disproportionate realities. The valid image on the contrary arises from juxtaposition, without ' comparison ', of two diverse realities whose relationships have been grasped by the spirit alone."[2]

[1] *Art et Scolastique*, 42
[2] *Art et Scolastique*, 201, note 121; quoted from Pierre Reverdy. The phrase in the text from which this note is appended is, "... la perfection avec laquelle l'œuvre exprime ou manifeste la forme, au sens métaphysique de ce mot, ... la vérité de l'imitation comme manifestation d'une forme." (p. 84).

" Dont *l'esprit seul* a saisi les rapports."   Mill the utilitarian
sponsored the denotation-connotation antithesis to rescue
poetics from the impasse of a philosophy in which " rapports "
were supposed to be seizable only conceptually, in which one
was either making cartesian " statements " or talking nonsense.
Since for some reason poetry is agreed to be valuable, it must
be composed of statements.   But the poet's " statements "
were so made, it was said, as to utilize the shifting auras of
connotation.   His denotations, it was agreed, might or might
not be important.   When important, they were usually of a
legislative character.   Practice, as always, kept touch with
analysis.   The nineteenth-century poet in his search for denota-
tive imprecisions which would allow thrilling novelties of
associated connotation to occupy the centre of attention (in his
attempt, that is, to avoid writing prose) lost all control over
language.

> For winter's rains and ruins are over
> And all the season of snows and sins

makes a kind of evocative sense because *ruins* and *winter*
coalesce in a memory of leafless trees, and *ruins* comes in pat
by assonance with the *rains* proper to winter; while *snows*, also
linked with *winter*, introduce *sins* via the black-white cliché.
Analysis may entangle itself in further ingenuities, but perception really goes and can go no further: Swinburne is not really
interested in such sin/virtue : : winter/spring ratios as he may
seem to be setting up.   This is the kind of writing with which
Joyce's is often confused.   It is important to see that in darkest
Finnegan the metaphorical superimpositions, however intricate,
are always precise.   " The flushpots of Euston and the hanging
garments of Marylebone ", F192, generates such ratios as:

Shem's dreams		Modern London		Hanging garments
———————————	: :	———————————	: :	———————————
Genuine sensuous idealism		Egypt & Babylon		Hanging gardens

while the Shaunian speaker's attitude to any sensuous idealism,
and the fact that *fleshpots*, for instance, are both like and different
from *flushpots* (more dignified because tending to aesthetic
sensuality, correspondingly ignoble in pandering to an animal
function) introduce further complexities into a miniature
epiphanic drama.   The flushpot is like the Egyption fleshpot

a sort of temple to animality; we recall the Englishmen in *Ulysses* who (like the Roman enemies of Egypt) said: " It is meet to be here.   Let us construct a watercloset ", U130/122, and the vision of the " rulers of the waves, who sit on thrones of alabaster silent as the deathless gods." U319/310.

There are plenty of ways of faking vivid prose, when the discipline that makes possible this close engagement of images hasn't been undergone.   Mr. Gilbert has pointed out verbal usages of Oscar Wilde's that resemble those of *Ulysses:* " A rose shook in her blood, and shadowed her cheeks.   Quick blood parted the petals of her lips."   When Joyce read *The Picture of Dorian Gray* in 1906 (oddly enough, in an Italian translation) he saw at once that the felicities were ways of evading, not presenting, the material.   Wilde's wish " to put himself before the world ", Joyce reported in a letter to his brother, caused him to crowd the book with " lies and epigrams " through reluctance to raise the real motifs of the plot to a surface scummed by irridescent prose.   " But it is not very difficult to read between the lines."[1]   The fanciest writing in *Ulysses* is in touch with the subject, with some level of abstraction or of glamour that Dublin has imposed upon banality.

> At each slow satiny heaving bosom's wave (her heaving embon) red rose rose slowly, sank red rose.   Heartbeats her breath: breath that is life.   And all the tiny tiny fernfoils trembled of maidenhair. U281/271.

This isn't Wildean sensuous plush display, though it uses similar techniques.   It is Bloom, with the aid of quotations, sentimentalizing a barmaid.

The peculiarity of Joyce's undertaking is that the phenomena he grasps before seeking appropriate words are themselves so largely linguistic.   A city full of haunted talk, littered with hulks of public rhetoric, required the setting in motion by the artist of words more than of persons.   Though in *Chamber Music* the aesthetic operations had been performed on lovesongs rather than on lovers, Joyce didn't develop the implications of this in the first cycle as clearly as in the second.   The progressive effacement of the writer, from lyric through epic into drama, from *Chamber Music* to *Exiles*, leaves behind a

---

[1] Gorman, VI–iii.

drama of actors, and what is epiphanized in *Exiles* is an aloneness in which they speak words while making no contact with
one another. The comparable progression from the *Portrait*
to *Finnegans Wake* leaves behind a drama of daftly autonomous
words, language, not persons, in action, convoluting in a void
of non-communication, but, by virtue of its tentacular contacts
with things and traditions, richly epiphanic of the fragmented
mind of Europe.

The tentacular complexity of language is as offensive to the
rationalist as is the irreducible existence of things; it should not
surprise us that the principles of an orderly synthetic language
were first outlined in 1629 by Descartes himself. Unlike the
inventors of Volapuk and Esperanto, Joyce wasn't offended by
the makeshifts of daily intercourse. He was too interested in
the real. He saw clearly that for his almost anthropological
purposes a word *is* a " thing " (not to be confused with the
notion that the word " horse " is a horse).

A word is a rich ontological object; its exegesis leads us
towards the semanticist's " referents " (the things it calls to
mind, and to which, for practical purposes, it is firmly attached),
towards contexts of usage (Mr. Empson notes a nascent conflict in " The cat sat on the mat ", in that it might come out of
a fairy-story or out of a spelling-book), towards the historical
perspectives telescoped in its etymology, towards the social
matrix or matrices in which it takes its place. One may find
literal, allegorical, anagogical, and tropological senses in a
single word; the poet juxtaposing words is setting whole
worlds of meaning in vivid analogical tension. Flaubert and
the Symbolists recovered much of this. Mallarmé noted in
Paget's fashion that the sensuous integument of a word, its
" signate matter ", is inseparable from its " meaning ": " Ces
mots comptent également par leur son et pour leur signification qui sont intimement liés d'après tout ce que nous savons
sur les origines du langage. . . ."; and contrived a poem—
Un Coup de Dés (1897) exploiting the position of a word above
or below another, or in relation to the white paper, or hung at
the end of a line out over void, or nestled in the heart of a
closely-printed passage—which whatever its limitations is
perhaps the Michelson-Morley experiment of contemporary
literature.

Mallarmé's Orphic role remains a role, however. There is
more than one consequence to Valéry's observation that the

arch-symbolist "understood language as though he had invented it himself". Joyce's attention was absorbed by the way Dubliners talked: their world of language and the worlds implied by that.

EPIPHANY AND ALLEGORY

Once language comes alive allegory returns. It went out of literature at the same time as existential metaphor, and for the same reasons. When a word is conceived as a geometrical point set in linear relation with other points, an allegorical meaning becomes something superimposed by the writer on a literal meaning by a sort of desperation of artifice. Exegesis can skim it off and exhibit it as a separate object, but nothing can rehabilitate its integrity. It incurs Locke's severest strictures on the accidental juxtapositions of wit. Thus the rationalist critic; and the romantic poet for his part is no more friendly to controlled layers of meaning, because they bring to the fore just that element of artifice which it is his primary concern to submerge as part of his campaign for getting poetics out of reach of the reasonable Philistine. To insist on Homer's primitive sincerity was among other things a device for pushing him away from what were regarded as the symbologizing accretions of his crudely "critical" ("uncreative") successors.

For the poet, however, who conceives his function as that of setting existent beings in apprehensible (not explicable) relationships, various levels of meaning are various perspectives on the richness inhering in poetic order. Hence St. Thomas Aquinas' tip for the exegetist of scripture, that the moral and symbolic senses

> . . . are not multiplied because one word signifies several things but because the things signified by the words can be themselves signs of other things. Thus in Holy Scripture no confusion results, because all the senses are founded on one, the literal, from which alone can any argument be drawn, as Augustine says.[1]

[1] Since Dante's letter to Can Grande della Scala is frequently quoted as though fourfold significance were an invention of his, a few Augustinian references may be apropos. In *De Genesi ad Litteram* I.1 (Migne, *Pat. Lat.*, vol. 34, col. 245) he states that we should read sacred books to discover " quae ibi aeterna intimentur, quae facta narrentur, quae futura praenuntientur, quae agenda praecipiantur vel moneantur ". These are the anagogical, literal, allegorical, and tropological meanings respectively; in connection with Joyce and Vico it is of interest to notice how St. Augustine relates them to eternity and the three kinds of time. In the same place he cites " Omnia autem haec in figura contingebant illis "

In the same way, human actions, as offspring of the embrace of the will (material cause) and the intellect (formal cause), have existential status, and image analogically both the being of things and the activities of the Divine will. (The behaviourist action, which obeys a pre-established pattern or leaps to an appetitive end like iron to a magnet, is of course devoid of such significance.)

St. Thomas was talking about Holy Scripture, not Symbolist poetry, and the Author of Holy Scripture was responsible for the events narrated as well as the text. The poet or novelist, however, is analogically responsible for his grasp of the events narrated by him; thus the Homeric or other analogies in *Ulysses* inhere in the situation rather than in the language; they aren't artifices of executive ingenuity; they don't depend on words being, in the Cartesian sense, imperfect or leaky. This remains true of *Finnegans Wake;* only the situations there are linguistic situations.

Ultimately, for Joyce, all the " meanings " are *in Dublin;* ultimately, for the reader, they are all *on the page.* A complex *integritas* has been seized and transferred. Things are not talked about, they happen in the prose. Appropriate exegesis does not consist in transposing the allegorical to the propositional, but in detailed apprehension of the rich concrete particularity of what has been placed before our eyes.

> Under the sandwichbell lay on a bier of bread one last, one lonely last sardine of summer. Bloom alone. U284.

This is not just a whimsically elaborate way of rendering Mr. Dedalus' opinion of the cuckolded Bloom. The literal sense, from which all the others derive, is not that there was a sardine sandwich on the counter beneath Mr. Dedalus' gaze. The literal sense is what is actually *there on the page.* What is there on the page is an arrangement of nineteen words implying a fusion of Bloom's pathos with the modes of being of an extravagantly sepulchred dead fish, of a rejected sandwich under glass, of a mortuary flower beneath a bell, and of the lachrymose

(I Cor. x, 11) as Scriptural warrant for going beyond the obvious sense. In *De Utilitate Credendi* III.5 (Migne, vol. 42, col. 68) he gives a fuller explanation of these four modes of signification, with examples showing that Christ and the Apostles use all four of them in citing the Old Testament. *De Doctrina Christiana* II.xvi.25 (Migne, vol. 34, col. 48) should be examined by anyone interested in the significance Joyce attaches to numbers.

cadences of the song about the last rose of summer, left bloom-
ing alone. The richness of this fusion includes many relevant
levels of paraphrase.

TRAGEDY AND INTEGRITAS

That the life of the book doesn't enter the material for the
first time only when the words are being found, that execution
is governed by seeing, is the cardinal principle of Joyce's
entire aesthetic. It is possible to impose laughter-and-tears,
or some other factitious vivacity, on material one hasn't
penetrated, but comedy and tragedy in the pure state must have
been *there* and apprehended before they were placed on the
page. The events that feed the artist exist, have being, are
intelligible, not fortuitous. Joyce went to Aristotle's *Metaphysics* for a paradigm of impure tragedy to elucidate his aesthetic of contemplation.

> – Pity is the feeling which arrests the mind in the presence of
> whatsoever is grave and constant in human sufferings and unites it
> with the human sufferer. Terror is the feeling which arrests the mind
> in the presence of whatsoever is grave and constant in human suffer-
> ings and unites it with the secret cause. . . .
> – A girl got into a hansom a few days ago—he went on—in
> London. She was on her way to meet her mother whom she had
> not seen for many years. At the corner of a street the shaft of a
> lorry shivered the window of the hansom in the shape of a star. A
> long fine needle of the shivered glass pierced her heart. She died on
> the instant. The reporter called it a tragic death. It is not. It is
> remote from terror and pity according to the terms of my definitions.
> P239/232.

To see why this is not a tragic death is to grasp the sense in
which the primary condition of a work of art is *integritas*. The
example is a transposition of the one given by Aristotle in the
Metaphysics (VI.3; 1027b) of fortuitous causality. A man
eats salty meat, gets thirsty, goes to a spring, and is murdered
by brigands who happen to be hiding nearby. Aristotle's
point is that no metaphysical account of this event is possible.
Maritain elucidates this further:[1] the man's death, he points
out, was due to the chance intersection of three series of
causes; the history of the brigands, which brought them to the
spring; the state of the man's digestion, which brought him to

---

[1] *Preface to Metaphysics*, VII–7.

the spring; the geological facts which brought a spring to the surface near his house. These are three rigid chains of causality; but their intersection with the man's death is uncaused in the strictest sense. No plot will enclose it. Nothing can make it artistically plausible. " There is no nature, no natural agent predetermined by its structure to this encounter of these three events, nor any created intelligence that designed it."

The death of Aristotle's man, like that of Joyce's girl, isn't, that is, an *intelligible* event, though it can be *accounted for*.

> The encounter has no *being*, save in thought. Certainly it exists. But it is not an essence. It is a pure coincidence, and possesses no ontological unity requiring, to render its existence intelligible, an active structure preordained to it. It is neither a genuine being, nor a genuine unity, and therefore does not possess a genuine cause, in the ontological sense which I have explained.

In the same way the intersecting routes through London, explained by the girl's errand and the lorry's business, and the intersection of the glass's tangent and her heart, explained by the laws of momentum and gravitation, leave her death in the ontological sense uncaused; and it fails to meet Joyce's definition of pity and terror because it neither exemplifies what is grave and constant in human sufferings, nor owns a " secret cause."

That which does not, in Coleridge's formula, possess within itself the reasons why it is so and not otherwise, is not a genuine unity and has no genuine cause, *quia non est vere ens cum non sit vere unum (Summa Theologica*, I, q.115, a.6). It is, though explicable, unintelligible; no *claritas, splendor formae*, leaps from its vesture. The integral plot, the integral line of action, is the emergence of light. That everything dovetails in *Ulysses* doesn't constitute its *consonantia*, nor confer its *integritas;* that everything dovetails is an ingredient in its irony. *Ulysses* is an epiphany of the self-contained, explicable world of mechanism; and it is a prison and an inferno.

Thus Stephen's speculations on causality, U26/22, are relevant to Joyce's elaborate use of efficient causes to weave an iron net around the protagonists. Maritain distinguishes the formula, " Every agent acts in view of an end," from its perversion, " Whatever happens, happens in view of an end." The latter, by excluding chance, defines a determinist prison; the man in Aristotle's example would have been intrinsically fated not only to die but to die at the hand of brigands on that day by that spring. History is in such a view strictly speaking a nightmare from which there is no awakening; the past is a constantly increasing incubus of " branded and fettered " potentialities, realised and exhausted; and the " great goal " toward which all history moves is of no more significance than " a shout in the street ". Stephen's attempt to escape this prison by dominating it—the comfort he draws from " The soul is in a manner all that is: the soul is the form of forms ", U27/23— is rebuked by the context in which St. Thomas places that statement. The statement is Aristotle's (*De Anima* III.8, 431b.21), and in citing it St. Thomas (*Summa Theologica* I, q.84, a.2, ad 2m) rebukes the Platonist misinterpretation which would make it mean that the soul makes it own intelligible order through its essence.

COMEDY THE SUMMIT OF ART

Every detail of Joyce's aesthetic speculations is oriented toward the epiphany—toward the criterion of intelligibility. The artifact is a supremely intelligible object. The plot, when employed, has ontological consistency, not merely the rationalistic consistency which it may or may not exhibit but which the fortuitous always exhibits. The real plot of *Finnegans Wake* is the emergence of light, imaged by the daybreak at the end through chapel windows: the gradual subsumption of particulars into an intelligible order; so is the plot of a story in *Dubliners*. The breaking of this light upon the mind leads, Joyce saw, to comedy. The proper object of comedy is not desire, " the feeling which urges us to go to something," but Joy, " the feeling which the possession of some good excites in us."

> For desire urges us from rest that we may possess something, but joy holds us in rest so long as we possess something. . . . All art which excites in us the feeling of joy is so far comic and according as this feeling of joy is excited by whatever is substantial or accidental in human fortunes the art is to be judged more or less excellent: and even tragic art may be said to participate in the nature of comic art so far as the possession of a work of tragic art (a tragedy) excites in us the feelings of joy.

This is a metaphysical account of *katharsis*. It is in the possession of the tragic work, the intuitive understanding, proper to the mode of aesthetic knowledge, of whatever is grave and constant in human sufferings, that the celebrated purification consists.   The rational nature is affirmed above the appetitive, cognition above passion.

> From this it may be seen that tragedy is the imperfect manner and comedy the perfect manner in art.[1]

Dante conceived the *Inferno* as a portion of a comedy; his comedy ends in, precisely, the archetypal epiphany, the contemplation of the First Cause Himself.   A pupil of St. Thomas startlingly illustrates the relation between joy and understanding in arguing that the blessed rejoice in the punishment of the wicked; for the divine economy is thereby illuminated.[2]

Such an aesthetic ideal desiderates the possession by the reader as by the artist of a trained and unified sensibility which will not be swerved from contemplative vigilance by emotional irrelevance: neither moved by the graveyard rat in *Ulysses* to disgust, nor by Mrs. Bloom to concupiscence.

> It will be seen afterwards how this rest is necessary for the apprehension of the beautiful—the end of all art, tragic or comic,—for this rest is the only condition under which the images, which are to excite in us terror or pity or joy, can be properly presented to us and properly seen by us.   For beauty is a quality of something seen, but terror and pity and joy are states of mind.

It was in this spirit that the transmutation of the stones of Dublin was undertaken:

> ... here the imagination has contemplated intensely the truth of being of the visible world and ... beauty, the splendour of truth, has been born.   S80/67.

[1] Paris Notebook.
[2] *Summa Theologica, Supplement,* 9.94, a.3.

Chapter 10

BAKER STREET TO ECCLES STREET

> *Lucifer:*   What are they which dwell
> So humbly in their pride, as to sojourn
> With worms in clay?
>
> *Cain*:   And what art thou who dwellest
> So haughtily in spirit, and canst range
> Nature and immortality—and yet
> Seem'st sorrowful?
>
> *Byron*

> " Everything comes in cycles, even Professor Moriarty."
>
> *Sherlock Holmes*

" WILL you permit me, Holmes ", I said, " to ask you a question, which I have wanted to ask you for years, and have not asked because we have grown nearly strangers? Why did you refuse the baronetcy, and almost at the last moment? . . ." I had watched through dinner for a moment to put my question, and ventured now, because he had thrown off a little of the reserve and indifference which, ever since his last return from Italy, had taken the place of our once close friendship. He had just questioned me, too, about certain private and almost sacred things, and my frankness had earned, I thought, a like frankness from him.

When I began to speak he was lifting to his lips a glass of that old wine which he could choose so well and valued so little; and while I spoke, he set it slowly and meditatively upon the table and held it there, its deep red light dyeing his long delicate fingers. . . .

These were sentences Joyce knew by heart at nineteen. Two small alterations have been made in transcribing them here. " Holmes " has been substituted for " Aherne ", and " baronetcy " for " berretta ". Yeats' *Tables of the Law* was Joyce's point of contact with the clangorous *Axel* aestheticism popularized for most English readers by Sir Arthur Conan Doyle. One of the keys to *Ulysses* is that Joyce there transposes to the Dublin of sooty bricks and the plane of Holmesian melodrama the tension between aesthete and citizen which Yeats had staged in the precious chapel of Owen Aherne.

Yeats' story depends on his distinction between the child's

world of sin and repentance and the moral worlds of the *esprits libres* who sought beyond good and evil to discover and to fulfil " the law of their own being ".   Aherne the monk-errant has come into possession of the lost *Liber Inducens in Evangelium Aeternum* of Joachim of Flora, who taught " that the Kingdom of the Father was passed, the Kingdom of the Son passing, and the Kingdom of the Spirit yet to come.   The Kingdom of the Spirit was to be a complete triumph of the Spirit, the *spiritualis intelligentia* he called it, over the dead letter ".   The *Liber Inducens* is divided into two parts; the first, called *Fractura Tabularum*, proclaims the free life attainable by inverting the proscriptive Mosaic commandments (" that long third chapter, set with the emblems of sanctified faces, and having wings upon its borders, is the praise of breakers of the seventh day and wasters of the six days, who yet lived comely and pleasant lives. . . .") and the second " is called *Lex Secreta*, and describes the true inspiration of action, the only Eternal Evangel . . .".

The Joachim of Yeats' imagination was no ordinary heresiarch; " He considered that those whose work was to live and not to reveal were children and that the Pope was their Father; but he taught in secret that certain others, and in always increasing numbers, were elected, not to live, but to reveal that hidden substance of God which is colour and music and softness and a sweet odour; and that these have no father but the Holy Spirit."   As for living, their servants will do that for them.

This is the gospel of the great aesthetes: the final chapter of Pater's *Renaissance*, or Lionel Johnson erect at a table amid tavern tipplers proclaiming his allegiance to the Holy Roman Catholic and Apostolic Church.   The once orthodox Aherne of Yeats' story goes forth to live this gospel, and returns after ten years to describe his new life:

" At first I was full of happiness," he replied, " for I felt a divine ecstasy, an immortal fire in every passion, in every hope, in every desire, in every dream; and I saw, in the shadows under leaves, in the hollow waters, in the eyes of men and women, its image, as in a mirror; and it was as though I was about to touch the Heart of God. Then all changed and I was full of misery, and I said to myself that I was caught in the glittering folds of an enormous serpent, and was falling with him through a fathomless abyss, and that henceforth the glittering folds were my world; and in my misery it was revealed to me that man can only come to that heart through the sense of separation

from it which we call sin, and I understood that I could not sin.
because I had discovered the law of my being, and could only express
or fail to express my being, and I understood that God has made a
simple and arbitrary law that we may sin and repent! "

At the last moment the cautious narrator of the tale sees gathered
behind Aherne faint figures robed in purple, " and I saw the
mild eyes and the unshaken eyelids, and thought they were
about to fling their torches upon me, so that all I held dear, all
that bound me to the spiritual and social order, would be burnt
up, and my soul left naked and shivering among the winds that
blow from beyond this world and from beyond the stars." So
he flees to the noise of the street, leaving Aherne to be " driven
into some distant country by the spirits whose name is legion,
and whose throne is in the indefinite abyss, and whom he obeys
and cannot see ".

Unworthiness, as much as prudence, is of course exhibited
in that flight; the prudent narrator is a *persona* engaging with
only part of Yeats' mind; we have already quoted the lyric in
which, as the same imagery of winds and stars assures us, he
speaks with the voice of Aherne in relish of lonely eternal
exclusion: *To His Heart, Bidding It Have No Fear:*

> ... *Him who trembles before the flame and the flood,*
> *And the winds that blow through the starry ways,*
> *Let the starry winds and the flame and the flood*
> *Cover over and hide, for he has no part*
> *With the lonely majestical multitude.*

We have also seen Joyce paraphrasing this poem (" He who
hath glory lost ") with a less blunted sense of what its choices
involve:

> That high unconsortable one,
> His love is his companion.

And we have seen Joyce, whom it cost little pains to pierce the
purple fog of Yeatsian aestheticism, triumphing in a ten-year
agon with Ibsen's much sharper vision of high unconsortability
as a way of life, in *Exiles* disclosing its inefficacy, and in the
Portrait exhibiting one who had discovered, Aherne-like, the
law of his being and could only express or fail to express his
being, composing a lurid *Villanelle* to a Temptress and spread-
ing wings gummed on with wax for a not un-ludicrous flight.
Stephen Dedalus' Temptress, lure of the fallen seraphim, owes

something to the woman in Yeats' companion story, *The Adoration of the Magi*, whom the three very old men with stout sticks attended at her death-bed in Paris, " and wondered at her look, as of unquenchable desire, and at the porcelain-like refinement of the vessel in which so malevolent a flame had burned " (Pater's Gioconda), and who told them the Secret Names.

Joyce was now in a position to control not only the materials and symbols of romanticism, but the nineteenth-century plot, Great Expectations, proud youth confronting dismayed its secret benefactor, the election of the life beyond law and its collapse, and the sweet tragic relish of collapse. Gabriel Conroy gazing at softly falling death, Richard Rowan walking alone on the strand contending with voices, Icarus Stephen plunging into the sea, these were the Dublin versions of Owen Aherne striding through clouds of incense into a bottomless pit of Freedom, or Byron's Lucifer and Cain:

> Souls who dare use their immortality—
> Souls who dare look the Omnipotent tyrant in
> His everlasting face, and tell him that
> His evil is not good!

There was nothing, by 1904 or 1914, particularly novel or daring about any of these plots and gestures. There remained two good reasons for troubling, a century after their first enunciation, to give over seven years' labour to a definite statement. They had become profoundly involved with every phase of civilization, the controlling metaphors of all civic thought; and they underlay all popular art, fiction, melodrama, journalism, poetry, reflecting the assumptions and desires of Dubliners, Londoners, and Minnesotans. The best-seller, like the camera, cannot lie, as Wyndham Lewis noted in *The Doom of Youth*; and since Conan Doyle, the best seller *par excellence* (today one-third of all fiction printed in English) has been the detective story, juxtaposing the insolent amorality of the clue-reader with the trepidant admiration of the decent but muddled citizen: Holmes, Watson; Stephen, Bloom.

THE METAPHORS OF MECHANISM

The artist examines a civilization for its dominant metaphors. (His work is " popular " when he does this too unconsciously to be critical of what he finds.) Joyce ploughed through thrillers, patent medicine tracts, and comic books in search of their metaphorical assumptions as social images. The catalogue of Bloom's library, U693/669, contains a world. So do the budget, U696/672, and the furniture inventory of the dream cottage, U697/673. A letter to Frank Budgen (Nov. 6, 1921; Slocum collection) asks, among other things, for " any catalogue of Whiteley's or Harrod's stores; any catalogue of a Tottenham Court Road furnisher; any bookseller's catalogue, preferably old ". Another asks for all available back numbers of *Bits of Fun*. He lifted from these not only details—phrases, gestures, locutions—but whole congeries of metaphoric assumptions: that mind is mechanism, that the Body Politic is wired together, that human relationships, domestic or civic, are reducible to problems in engineering. His fusion of H. C. Earwicker's brain with a radio: ". . . their tolvtubular daildialler, as modern as tomorrow afternoon and in appearance up to the minute, . . . with a vitaltone speaker, capable of capturing skybuddies, harbour craft emittences, key clickings, vaticum cleaners, due to woman formed mobile or man made static and bawling the whole hamshack and wobble down an eliminium sounds pound so as to serve him up a melegoturny marygoraumd, eclectrically filtered for allirish earths and ohmes ", F309, corresponds to the account of the brain as a super-telephone-exchange in any popular handbook of physiology and reflects a fatally romantic exaltation of the merely sub-human, like Byron's identification of himself with a thunderstorm.

The twentieth century reflects the nineteenth with meticulous accuracy. Immediately after World War II we began to hear a great deal about mechanical brains; a semi-technical book on the subject, Dr. Norbert Wiener's *Cybernetics*,[1] even achieved bookstore popularity. In his introduction Dr. Wiener spoke of the complications introduced into radar mechanisms by the " human gun-pointer . . . coupled into the fire-control system and acting as an essential part of it. It is essential to know their characteristics, in order to incorporate them mathematically into the machines they control." By page 55 he was noting that

> the many automata of the present age are coupled to the outside
> world both for the reception of impressions and for the performance

[1] Norbert Wiener, *Cybernetics: Control and Communication in the Animal and the Machine.*

of actions. They contain sense-organs, effectors, and the equivalent
of a nervous system to integrate the transfer of information from the
one to the other. They lend themselves very well to description in
physiological terms. It is scarcely a miracle that they can be subsumed under one theory with the mechanisms of physiology.

" Subsumed under one theory " is far from being a mere
rhetorical gesture. Not only can the brain be considered as a
complex of electrical circuits and its synapses as switching
mechanisms (" They had used the technique of mathematical
logic for the discussion of what were after all switching problems ", writes Dr. Wiener of two neurological reformers), but
the automaton and the brain as responder-to-stimuli are alike
susceptible of intricate statistical description. This is borne
out by experiments on the muscles of cats; and intellectual
activities of all kinds, in Dr. Wiener's subsequent discussion,
are regarded as prolongations, localized in a spherical box, of
the nervous system's twitches and signals. There are political
bearings as well; networks of communication inform (in both
senses) the machine, the brain, and the community, as is readily
seen in " social communities such as those of ants ". (The
cyberneticist shrinks from confronting human communities
only because while " the main qualities affecting society are . . .
statistical, the runs of statistics on which they are based are
excessively short ".)

One's sense that Dr. Wiener's assumptions grate against his
admirably lucid prose to produce an unintentional resemblance
to Swift's *Modest Proposal* was apparently not shared by
thousands of his readers. They had been standing on their heads
for years, and were eager for a book written upside down. The
bland reassurance that their own brains were, with whatever
deficiencies of speed and intake, at least in the same genus with
ENIAC,[1] the Bush Differential Analyzer, and Harvard's Mark
III, which can chew through several years' human figuring in a
few hours, outweighed completely Dr. Wiener's premonitory
devaluation of human grey matter (" the average human being
of mediocre attainments or less has nothing to sell that it is
worth anyone's money to buy.") Even the sting of implications
like that is eased by contemplating the megalocephalic IBM
machine in New York that earns $300 an hour.[2]

So Watson worships Holmes, and Watson in his picayune

[1] " *Electronic Numerical Integrator and Calculator.*"
[2] *Time*, Jan. 23, 1950, 58.

fashion repeats Holmes. Holmes is the super-brain, Watson the economy size of the same design. The cleavage between Holmes and Watson is a cleavage that passes through each of them. As Holmes is to Watson, so Holmes the sleuth is to Holmes the violinist, and Watson the " bulldog " to Watson the poltroon. Holmes is a thinking-machine, but Watson would think like a machine if he could; Watson is romantic, but Holmes despite his scorn of emotion is a romantic artist. Stephen Dedalus in a flash of prescience expounds, like James in *The Jolly Corner*, the nightmare tramping of historical corridors towards a meeting with oneself, " self which it itself was ineluctably preconditioned to become." U494/479. " He found in his world without as actual what was in his world within as possible ". U210/201. What he meets is Bloom.

LOCKE THE GODFATHER OF ENIAC

To return to the rational world. There is nothing new about the discovery that the brain can't hope to compete with the super-calculator. The Chinese never pretended it could keep up with an abacus. What is relatively new is the supposition that the brain has no other modes of operation, a supposition that can for present purposes be traced back to Locke, though it involves assumptions that had been in cold storage at Oxford for a Locke to defrost at least since the time of William of Ockham. The nominalist assumption that there is an impassable separation between things and knowledge entered, deprived of its Ockhamist subtlety, into the mercantile swagger of Locke's mechanist account of the mind as a combiner of units of sensation. (Fifty years earlier, Pascal had designed an adding-machine.) Hence the rapport between Prof. Wiener's statement that the modern study of automata " whether in the metal or in the flesh " is " a branch of communication engineering ", and Locke's image of the brain, responding to everything and seeing into nothing.

The brain, of course, does just this when it is not encouraged to do anything else. The romantic poets were defying commercial philistines and official philosophy alike at a time when reciprocal modulation was going on between the popular image of " safe " (= the reverse of " Bohemian " or " enthusiastic ") thinking and the moralistic attributes of the soundly-managed counting-house. Lockeian thought seemed " true " because the mechanical brain repeated the structure of the Newtonian clockwork universe (Leibniz indeed compares his monads to clocks, and because miraculously well-made clocks will keep time together for all eternity, he was able to abolish efficient causality and deprive his monads of all connections with the other processes their workings mirror).   Hence the " reasonable " man, like the well-regulated watch, exhibits a high degree of conformity with his fellows, and the Blake, the maverick, can be safely excommunicated.   When reality is regarded as inaccessible, consistency is to be sought rather between mind and mind than between minds and things; hence conformity of thought as a guarantee against anarchy, and the mechanization of the community as well as of the brain. The market-researcher asks the consumer how he chooses to be exploited, and is enabled to exploit him more effectively every time he asks; this corresponds neatly to Dr. Wiener's account of the control engineer's *feed-back* (" When we desire a motion to follow a given pattern, the difference between this pattern and the actually performed motion is used as a new input to cause the part regulated to move in such a way as to bring its motion closer to that given by the pattern."   For " motion " read " notion ".)   In such a milieu, given the stimuli, it soon doesn't take a Joyce to predict the responses.

ULYSSES THE VOICE OF THE MACHINE

Bourgeois fiction depends on the characters' patterns of response being set.   (This is virtually a definition of melodrama, and the key to Joyce's continual recourse to the plots and situations of the melodramas of his time.)   Robinson Crusoe is as conventional as Bloom; hence Joyce's interest in Defoe, on whom he lectured in Trieste.   Defoe's originality consisted in providing unusual stimuli (the naked footprint).   Joyce's consisted in cataloguing the quotidian responses of everyman to the commonplace with cathartic meticulousness.   We are constantly surprised not because Bloom's mental processes are so recherché but because the recording is so crazily minute.   We shall see how Joyce's way of playing these processes against rational norms subserves serious purposes with comic tensions. First, here are the Bloomian wheels whirring:

> Howth a while ago amethyst.   Glass flashing.   That's how that wise man what's his name with the burning glass.   Then the heather goes on fire.   It can't be tourists' matches.   What?   Perhaps the dry sticks rub together in the wind and light.   Or broken bottles in the

furze act as a burning glass in the sun. Archimedes. I have it!
My memory's not so bad. U371/361.

Bloom's "I have it!" echoes Archimedes' "Eureka!"
Archimedes however discovered something new, but Bloom,
like ENIAC, can discover only a misplaced bit of data. Except
for his delay in remembering "that wise man's" name,
Bloom's *Gestalt* here could be expanded by only slightly different prose conventions into a newspaper "science" feature or
into the Robert Lynd type of familiar essay beginning, "The
other evening as I walked by the harbour watching the great
eye of the lighthouse flashing above a shoreline now black and
but a short while ago amethyst, it occurred to me to wonder. . . ."
Such writings conventionally begin with a commonplace
experience or news-event and then rapidly riffle the deck of
related readings and memories. The British press serves them
up as culture, the American as information. By expanding
each phrase of Bloom's to a paragraph an alert journalist could
keep his editorial page filled for years, so much is Bloom's
private world a microcosm of the newspapers' public world, so
compendious is Joyce's anatomizing of these ubiquitous
associative connections.

And here we have the clue to that air of meticulous contrivance remarked on by every reader of *Ulysses:* the hundreds of
motifs pegged, dropped, linked without a fumble, the symbols
that grow out of the text but seem to demand separate acts of
abstraction from the reader, the labyrinth without a loose end
or a blind alley, so scattered with clues that a tenacious memory
(or Prof. Hanley's word-index) will elucidate any obstruction of
the surface. A huge and intricate machine clanking and whirring for eighteen hours—at one level *Ulysses* is just that. Its
characters walking clichés, as Wyndham Lewis had the want of
tact to point out—of course they are. Its psychological
insights dry, hard, somehow obvious, devoid of Freudian
romance—naturally. This tesselated mosaic belongs to a
world of gears and sidewalks, of bricks laid side by side, of
data thrust into a computer and whirled through permutations
baffling to the imagination but always traceable by careful
reason. There is much more to it than that, but that, at one
level, is *Ulysses*. It is essential first of all to see it like that, and
not as a solemn mystery; that is the way to see, ultimately,
its laughter.

" If only someone, if only one reviewer, would say the book was funny ", its author complained to Ezra Pound, when explanations of how this motif tied up with that were being published on every hand.

Joyce is mocking the super-brain with a monstrous parody of its workings. If you were to project an auctorial personality behind *Ulysses*, you would find it mechanical and craftsmanlike and unreflective, gifted at transcription with minimal distortion, gifted at tesselation, gifted with anything but the sense to rush with a cry out of this nightmare of correspondence and recurrence, this superimposition of a thousand detective stories (" Potato I have ", U56/50. What about potato? We are told nearly four hundred pages later, U428.) You would find, in fact, if you insisted on feeling for a personality, just the personality sketched by Wyndham Lewis in his brilliant misreading of the book: " not so much an inventive intelligence as an executant ":[1] a thinking-machine, in short, the incarnation of quasi-industrial " know-how ". Joyce has been at great pains to build up this persona behind his book. The Eniac-daemon is not the author; it is behind *that*, rather than behind the obvious façade of the work, that the author stands indifferent, paring his fingernails. Most critics, of course, Watsonian Holmes-worshippers to a man, have reached into the *Portrait* for a clue and found this persona " god-like ". Certainly, the god of industrial man. It is essential to the total effect of *Ulysses* that it should seem to be the artifact of a mind essentially like Bloom's, only less easily deflected; a mind that loses nothing, penetrates nothing, and has a category for everything; the mind that at length epiphanizes itself in the catechism of " Ithaca " (it seems never to have been asked whether it is Joyce *in propria persona* who is asking and answering these droning questions, and if not, what are the implications for the rest of the book). Lewis notes that Bloom seems a disguise of the author rather than a character: Bloom is in fact a low-powered variant on the mode of consciousness that imparts substantial form to the book. It is by the insane mechanical meticulousness of that mode of consciousness, the mode of consciousness proper to industrial man, that in *Ulysses* industrial man is judged. *That* is, in a way, the " meaning " of the book, the form in which it remains as a whole in the memory. One of Joyce's greatest creations is the character of this

[1] *Time and Western Man*, 106.

sardonic impersonal recorder, that constantly glints its photo-
electric eyes from behind the chronicle of Bloomsday.

CONTAMINATION OF GENIUS BY POWER-HOUSE

We have, then, as a sort of ideogram of the modes of consciousness *Ulysses* is exploring, the following:

> Thought as response-to-stimulus.
> Private and collective thought reproducing one another's contours.
> Model of brain-work in mechanical processes.
> Emphasis on *succession* of ideas ("stream of consciousness") rather
> than *penetration* of intelligible objects.
> Emphasis on multiplicity of impenetrable objects. Life amid a
> clutter of *things*.
> Equation of the true and the respectable.
> Art a hallucination-catharsis mechanism; also "romantic"
> (romance = action plus pathos).
> Artist an outcast.
> Social and intellectual entropy.

The speculative changes on these themes are rung in Wyndham
Lewis' *Time and Western Man*, to which the reader is referred
for fuller exposition. One of the prime exhibits of that book
is an analysis of the mind that informs *Ulysses*, which Lewis
unfortunately mistook for the mind of James Joyce. And one
of its most valuable explications concerns the liaison between
mechanism and romance. Mind-as-machine enjoys peculiar
rapport with Shelleyan art, a master-key to the sense in which
Bloom turns out to be Stephen's spiritual father. This is
naturally the sort of perception which the Dedalian aesthete
would prefer to have wrapped in as many veils of Isis and
Karma as possible; hence one of the most curious becloudings
in the Joyce legend.

Not only is mind-as-machine Shelley's point d'appui (the
role he cuts out for himself in the *Defense* would be meaningless
had he not the Lockeians to defy, as Prometheus would be
meaningless without Jove); more important, the antithesis
within his own personality—Prometheus / Narcissus; skylark /
sensitive plant; wild west wind / bleeder on the thorns of life—
depends, as does the Bloomesquely associative proliferation of
his images, on a universe informed by the *libido dominandi*.
The "romance" of romantic art, like the romance of action in
the gasoline advertisements, depends less on its deliquescent

swoon-images than on its insanely accelerated change, inherent as much in its psychological states as in the very structure of its language. "... an exasperated, mercurial form of the flux of Heraclitus ..." writes Lewis: this of the world of Bergson, which is that of Whitehead and Alexander, which is that of the behaviourists, which is that of the calculating machines, which is that (as Whitehead himself rapturously points out) of Shelley's Nature, "changing, dissolving, transforming as it were at a fairy's touch".

The human components of a society so ordered, complexly interlocking and elaborately meaningless, are reduced by assembly-line education and Jesuitic "vocational guidance" (sorting out the products) to the status of replaceable parts.

> The whirr of flapping leather bands and hum of dynamos from the powerhouse urged Stephen to be on. Beingless beings. Stop! Throb always without you and the throb always within. Your heart you sing of. I between them. Where? Between two roaring worlds where they swirl, I. Shatter them, one and both. But stun myself too in the blow. U238/229.

"Beingless beings"—phenomena without *Ens:* Picasso's marriages of collage and cubism, in which a human semblance, like the mind of Leopold Bloom, takes shape through a jumble of vases, guitars, and newspaper clippings. "Throb always without you and the throb always within" betrays Stephen's unwilling recognition that as a contemporary man he has the machine in his guts (Mr. Eliot remarks somewhere that the internal combustion engine has altered our very perception of rhythm); hence "your heart you sing of", he muses half to himself and half to the dynamo, standing outside the throbbing heart of Dublin. The mediaeval metaphor of the Body Politic hovers over every episode, Lungs in the newspaper office, Blood in the corpuscular citizens circulating the streets, Stomach in the crowded eating-houses ("Pungent meat-juice, slop of greens. See the animals feed", U166/157). The Body that emerges from Joyce's epic is that of a gigantic robot; the intricate correspondences and theme-words have a more than accidental connection with a philosophy of making that glories in the assemblage of standardized parts, while the strains to which the language is subjected have, as the eminently technological eye of Moholy-Nagy did not fail to observe,[1] a

[1] Moholy-Nagy, *Vision in Motion.*

real affinity with the processes of welding, riveting, and casting.

Bloom, immersed in this sensate world, is the father of Stephen exactly as the Watsonian Conan Doyle is the father of Sherlock Holmes.

HOLMES AND WATSON: THE SPLIT-MAN

The mythology of the nineteenth century is summed up in two stories: the partnership of Sherlock Holmes and Dr. Watson, and the tumble of Alice into a schizoid mathematician's womb-world. The first underlies *Ulysses*, the second *Finnegans Wake*.

Holmes and Watson epitomize humanity dissected into ratiocinative violence and sentimental virtue, the latter avid of absorption into the former. So Stephen and Bloom.

That Bloom's interior monologue consists so largely of nouns—that Joyce was able to focus him so completely through a catalogue of urban miscellany—signalizes his complete, narcotic immersion in his environment. The sea of matter surges round him like amniotic fluid, and in his last conscious moment he assumes the foetal attitude, " reclined laterally, left, with right and left legs flexed, . . . the childman weary, the manchild in the womb ", U722/697. That matter is narcotic for Bloom is the point of the Lotus-eaters episode, which inflects the familiar panorama with metaphors of dreams and drugs. Opium is the religion of the people.

In Stephen, the other half of the split man, taste and intellect have brought about sterile scorn for the civic and domestic virtues which persist, despite the want of suitable evoking objects, in Bloom's sensibility. For Stephen, Dublin is equally narcotic, since he can scrutinize it endlessly for epiphanies whose import reinforces his scorn: hence the Parable of the Plums, U143/135. His body is characteristically an impediment, as it was for Shelley; his weak eyes and aching teeth transfer to comic terms the " shadow of our night " which he would " outsoar ". That he descends into Mabbot Street in search of bodily pleasures represents a weakening of his perilous integrity, a rapprochement to the Bloomian premises, that pre-figures their ultimate wordless union when Stephen has sunk to a drunken husk of matter on the littered street.

Never, throughout the time the two are together in Bloom's home, is there a line of direct discourse. The long painful scene exploits through the caustic impartiality of its catechism Bloom's mute affection for Stephen and Stephen's impatient,

tolerant scorn of Bloom. That Stephen declines, against his
host's suggestion, to wash his hands, U657/633, is the only
overt rebuff, but the naive abundance of Bloomian details,
which so little engage the concerns of Stephen that he is barely
to be perceived hovering through their midst like a grin without
a cat, steeps the tragic antipathy of the two men into the very
texture of the episode.   " Not only will the reader know everything and know it in the baldest coldest way ", Joyce com-
mented,[1] " but Bloom and Stephen thereby become heavenly
bodies, wanderers like the stars at which they gaze."

The masochistic abysses of the Bloom-Watson sensibility
are neatly illustrated by Sir Arthur Conan Doyle's naive crisis
in " The Three Garridebs ", when Holmes, alarmed at
Watson's narrow escape from death by gunfire, flings wiry
arms of compassion around him:

> It was worth a wound—it was worth many wounds—to know the
> depth of loyalty and love which lay behind that cold mask. The
> clear hard eyes were dimmed for a moment, and the firm lips were
> shaking. . . . All my years of humble but single-handed service
> culminated in that moment of revelation.

After years of supplication, the god condescends to manifest
himself.   Stephen grants Bloom no such epiphany, chiefly
because " the depths of loyalty and love which lay behind that
cold mask " were not there to epiphanize.   Sir Arthur Conan
Doyle simply wanted them to be there, very badly.

AESTHETE PLUS THINKING-MACHINE

Bloom is " society " at the level of hurrying, interlocking,
kaleidoscopic Dublin.   Stephen is the outlaw, accumulating
dangerously undischarged potential, a sour and scornful
thundercloud brooding above Dublin: " Shatter them, one
and both.   But stun myself too in the blow." The Enemy of
the People.   The Savage Noble.

The intellectual as anarchic aesthete is clarified by Sherlock
Holmes, of whom the most cogent character-sketch is Huxley's
celebrated definition of the Educated Man:

> . . . so trained in youth that his body is the ready servant of his will,
> and docs with ease and pleasure all that, as a mechanism, it is capable
> of; whose intellect is a clear, cold logic engine, with all its parts in
> smooth working order; ready, like a steam engine, to be turned to

[1] Letter to Frank Budgen, Feb. 28, 1921. Slocum collection.

any kind of work . . .; whose mind is stored with a knowledge of
the great and fundamental truths of Nature and the laws of her
operations; one who, no stunted ascetic, is full of life and fire, but
whose passions are trained to come to heel by a vigorous will, the
servant of a tender conscience; one who has learned to love all
beauty, whether of Nature or of art, to hate all vileness, and to
respect others as himself.

The body a mechanism, the intellect a steam-engine; Y.M.C.A.
cold-shower hard-mattress virtues; a business man's redaction
of Sterne's sentimental ethics; Baden-Powell his mentor and
Fearless Fosdick his ideal—set beside this some worshipful
phrases from Sir Arthur Conan Doyle. The thinking-machine:

> All emotions, and [love] particularly, were abhorrent to his cold,
> precise, but admirably balanced mind. He was, I take it, the most
> perfect reasoning and observing machine the world has ever seen. . . .
> Grit in a sensitive instrument, or a crack in one of his own high-
> power lenses, would not be more disturbing than a strong emotion
> in a nature such as his.

As for the " lover of beauty, whether of Nature or of art," we
have Holmes' response to the gathering dawn:

> " How sweet the morning air is! See how that one little cloud
> floats like a pink feather from some gigantic flamingo ",

the violin playing, the monograph upon the Polyphonic
Motets of Lassus " printed for private circulation and said by
experts to be the last word upon the subject ". As for " the
great and fundamental truths of Nature ", Holmes is simply
the Victorian geologist harnessed to melodramatic machinery.
His habit of adducing analogous crimes (" The cases of Dolsky
in Odessa and of Leturier in Montpellier will occur at once to
any toxicologist ") derives from the paleontologist's eye for
skeletal resemblances between apparently diverse species, and
he reads the record of the cigar-ash and the footprint with the
confident efficiency of his prototype reading the record of the
rocks. (Joyce's epiphanies, Stephen's signatures; incidentally,
the phrase treasured by Stephen in the *Portrait*, " A day of
dappled seaborne clouds ", comes from a book called *The
Testament of the Rocks*.)

Holmes' parents, it is clear, were the male and female halves
of Sir Arthur Conan Doyle's divided nineteenth-century mind.
His medical training and brisk hapless up-to-dateness aligned
him with the professional scientists, and saddled him with their

materialism, their cult of infallibility, their aestheteish detachment from human concerns, and their desperate anxiety to
enchain in suitable dogmas a settled order that seemed on the
point of falling apart.   On the other hand, he retained some
Bloom-like shreds of middle-class sentimentality, respectability,
and delight in the more complacent forms of emotional self-
indulgence.   These are two phases of Holmes; more clearly
differentiated, they are Holmes and Watson.   In the same way,
Bloom's constant scientific preoccupation with principles he
can never quite remember and inventions he never manages to
perfect is simply his way of making overtures towards his ideal,
like Watson's fumbling efforts at deduction; indeed, towards
the end of the book we find him, anxious for Stephen's approval,
" Sherlockholmesing " the sailor in the cabman's shelter,
U620/597.
    The nineteenth-century scientist vaunted himself on a
detachment parodying that claimed by Flaubert for the artist,
and Holmes is nothing if not an aesthete.   His grandmother
was " the sister of the French artist Vernet ", on which he
remarked, à propos of his profession, " Art in the blood is liable
to take the strangest forms."

> He had the impersonal joy of the true artist in his better work,
> even as he mourned darkly when it fell above the high level to which
> he aspired.

Offered a place on the next honours list, he smiles a Paterian
smile and protests that he plays " the game for the game's own
sake ".   In every way he approximates the popular image of the
lounging artist: " His cigars in the coal-scuttle, his tobacco in
the toe-end of a Persian slipper, and his unanswered correspondence transfixed by a jack-knife into the very centre of his
wooden mantelpiece " are orthodox Bohemian props.   So is his
habit of spending several days in bed from time to time, and
his alternation " between cocaine and ambition."
    Stephen's frequentation of the bordellos of Paris and Dublin
resembles Holmes' cocaine, a cynical defiance of a pleasureless
world.   We find him in bed shrinking from " common noises,
hoarse voices, sleepy prayers ", and turning his face toward
" the great overblown scarlet flowers of the tattered wallpaper ",
P260/252.   The flowers are like overblown whores, the voices
" the commonplaces of existence " that drove Holmes to
desperation and drugs.

The sleuth's bric-à-brac of erudition is notorious. Stephen
in the library dialogue achieves an intricate fusion between his
own dilemma, Hamlet's, Shakespeare's, and the heresies of the
Church, propped with analogies from Milton, Swinburne,
Socrates, Maeterlinck, Drummond of Hawthornden, Brunetto
Latini, St. Thomas Aquinas, and others. In a single novel, *The
Sign of Four*, Holmes recommends Winwood Reade's *Martyr-
dom of Man*, quotes Goethe twice, cites Richter and alludes to
his connection with Carlyle, and talks in a single brilliant
session of miracle plays, mediaeval pottery, Stradivarius violins,
the Buddhism of Ceylon, and the warship of the future,
" handling each as though he had made a special study of it."
Joyce of course knew his hero's mind, and Sir Arthur Conan
Doyle didn't; we are never allowed to hear what Holmes has to
say on these topics. Stephen's virtuosity, like the multilingual
erudition of *The Waste Land* (" I read, much of the night, and
go south in the winter "), is the calculated image of an over-
ripe culture in despair, constantly examining its own mind in
its past literary manifestations:

> And you who wrest old images from the burial earth! The brain-
> sick words of sophists: Antisthenes. A lore of drugs. U238/229.

These fragments, it is true, Stephen has shored against his
ruins. As Bloom's mind is a compost of objects, so is Stephen's
a fabric of quotations. Literature is a dictionary of sensibility,
its study a sanction for resonant grim satisfaction. The Conan
Doyle who created Holmes shared with Stephen this frantic
appetite for mastery of the past (hence his historical novels).
He coveted that in Holmes which readers are meant to
admire. That he sought by casual lists of topics to impress his
audience with the Holmesian virtuosity shows simply that he
was a Bloom writing for Blooms.

SLEUTH AND AESTHETE AS GOD

Something of the Bloom in Sir Arthur Conan Doyle contributed to the tacit judgment, at odds with his admiration for the
sleuth, that Holmes was essentially a specialized criminal.
" Burglary ", remarks Sherlock, " has always been an alternative profession, had I cared to adopt it, and I have little doubt
that I should have come to the front." Detection is as a-moral
as geometry (it is not for nothing that he so often refers to a
case as " a pretty little demonstration "). Whenever they

become components in a problem, human beings become numbered points, devoid of rights and autonomy, like the gunner whose response characteristics the cyberneticist incorporates mathematically into the radar mechanism.   To Watson's horrified protest at his quasi-seduction of a housemaid with information to give, Holmes calmly replies, " You must play your cards as best you can."   So Stephen Dedalus flung himself into a prostitute's arms in quest of experience useful to the artist.

The pride that underwrites these reductions of moral problems to aesthetic ones reaches back through the Byronic postures to Rousseau's savage.   The sleuth, the artist, stands apart from society and interferes when he sees fit.   In about half his cases Holmes as judge supplements the work of Holmes as sleuth in permitting the criminal to escape.   On at least one occasion he snubs a king, as Stephen in the Circe hallucination snubbed Edward VII.   He damns " the public, the great unobservant public, who could hardly tell a weaver by his tooth or a compositor by his left thumb " (Cf. Stephen about to pay Bella Cohen: " This silken purse I made out of the sow's ear of the public ", U542/526), and draws an analogy with his beekeeping retirement " when I watched the little working gangs as once I watched the criminal world of London ".   Nor are his judgments reserved for others.   He " cannot agree with those who rank modesty among the virtues " and in the face of death abrogates to himself the highest judgment seat:

> " If my record were closed tonight I could still survey it with absolute equanimity.   The air of London is the sweeter for my presence.   In over a thousand cases I am not aware that I have ever used my powers on the wrong side.   Of late I have been tempted to look into the problems furnished by Nature rather than those more superficial ones for which our superficial state of society is responsible."

The last sentence enforces his dual pedigree: by Huxley, out of Rousseau.

THE " CLUE " A BOGUS EPIPHANY

Stephen with his " signatures of all things I am here to read " displays the same eccentric ancestry.   Stephen may be thinking of Jacob Boehme's *De Signatura Rerum*, but Joyce's mind is on Aquinas' " signate matter ".   The epiphany, as understood by

Joyce, represents the elevation of matter to a degree of intelligibility proper to the mode of being which it possesses. Stephen, however, as he is presented in the *Portrait* and *Ulysses*, is much less interested in the intelligibility of *Ens* than in his own status as " Priest of the Eternal Imagination ". " From before the ages He willed me and now may not will me away or ever ", U39/35.

These material gestures of eternal intangibles, Augustine's *Vestigia Dei,* offer metaphysical insights corresponding to the clarification introduced into a Holmes case by a " clue ". " It has long been a maxim of mine ", pontificates Sherlock, " that the little things are infinitely the most important." One of his impatient rebukes to Watson might be an explicit vulgarization of the aesthetic credo of a Joyce or a Flaubert:

> " I can never bring you to realize the importance of sleeves, the suggestiveness of thumbnails, or the great issues that can hang on a bootlace."

In another place Holmes sets the clue explicitly in its ratiocinative context:

> " As Cuvier could correctly describe a whole animal by the contemplation of a single bone, so the observer who has thoroughly understood one link in a series of incidents should be able to state all the other ones both before and after."

The clue is a bogus epiphany. In itself it has no ontological significance. It doesn't open to contemplative penetration the intelligible depths of some object; rather it suggests to the quick deductive wit discursive attention to the superficies of a dozen other objects. The clue and the chain of reasoning function, like a jigsaw puzzle, in two dimensions. The sleuth's reconstruction of a crime works at the level of efficient causes only; the epiphany implies an intuitive grasp of material, formal, and final causes as well. Though it resembles " Araby " or " The Dead " in that the significance of the whole becomes clear on the last page, the detective story remains a two-dimensional parody of the Joycean short story, as Holmes is a parody of Stephen, as Stephen is a parody of Joyce, and as discursive analysis, once it deserts its job of arranging data in the line of efficient causality, becomes a parody of metaphysical intuition, or of allied aesthetic modes of knowledge. The " meaning " of " The Dead " cannot be reasoned out, as a whole generation of commentators has had opportunity to discover.

Since the clue is a piece of the puzzle so shaped as to make the contours of adjacent pieces particularly obvious, the sleuth must carry in his head a catalogue of all possible relevant shapes. For reliable results, the isolated object should be seen in a context of omniscience. As Holmes calmly remarks,

" It is necessary that the reasoner should be able to utilize all the facts which have come to his knowledge, and this in itself implies . . . a possession of all knowledge."

The philosophical extension of this, that you can know nothing until you know everything, deserves attention. The Holmesian self-apotheosis is curiously connected with the doctrine of Averroes, that as we collect and relate sensible facts, the agent intellect, which he regards as a sort of world-soul, becomes more and more perfectly united to us, until we come eventually to understand all things material and immaterial. St. Thomas beats him into the ground with no fewer than eleven arguments (*Summa Theologica*, I, q.88, a.1.).

As though in emulation of Joyce with his famous trunkfuls of brown paper envelopes, Holmes trusts to a filing system to make up for the lack of innate omniscience.

DOUBLE VISION

All these things seem to parody Joyce because Joyce, with a detachment greater than irony, parodies them. He had long known that the way to do his job was to work within the things he saw: Dublin's drabness in prose of " scrupulous meanness ", lyric to expose the nature of lyric, and Gerty MacDowell in her own words.

Joyce's mature double-writing rests on double vision: a vision of duality. Sherlock Holmes has his dignity, and Owen Aherne his quota of the bogus; they imply one another. Owen Aherne is a Yeatsian idealization of Lionel Johnson; the Lionel Johnson Yeats saw was a decadent poet idealized as misplaced priest by himself. Stephen Dedalus is a prism so fashioned and placed by Joyce as to catch and gather all these multiply-reflected rays.

In the same way Dublin's letch toward the forms of classical culture was part of the Dublin swill; but it was through the forms of classical culture—working within the thing he saw—

that Joyce presented Dublin. In the wilderness of mirrors in which the artist is placed, the empirical given is his only datum; but the given has fashioned itself on its own images of dignity, and those images—the dominant metaphors of society —are wavering repetitions of permanent human dreams. " Out of the material and spiritual battle which has gone so hardly with her ", Joyce wrote in 1903, " Ireland has emerged with many memories of beliefs, and with one belief—a belief in the incurable ignobility of the forces which have overcome her."[1] Parnell's triumphant return from beyond the seas was widely expected long after the sod was laid over his coffin, U111/105. Parnell, Holmes, Monte Cristo, Hamlet's father, Odysseus: the myth of some returned avenger to rout incurably ignoble usurpers came naturally to Dublin's appetite for the heroic. Such a myth haunted Dublin, and Joyce, working within what he saw, educed a Dublin Odyssey.

[1] " The Soul of Ireland " (a review of Lady Gregory's *Poets and Dreamers*), Dublin *Daily Express*, March 26, 1903, p. 11 (Slocum Collection). This piece was located by Mr. Richard M. Kain.

Chapter 11

HOMER AND HAMLET

... Couldn't you do the Yeats touch?
He went on and down, mopping, chanting with waving graceful
arms:—The most beautiful book that has come out of our country
in my time. One thinks of Homer.

Ulysses (U213/207)

Ukalepe. Loathers' Leave. Had Days. Nemo in Patria.
The Luncher Out. Skilly and Carubdish. A Wondering
Wreck. From the Mermaids' Tavern. Bullyfamous. Naught-
sycalves. Mother of Misery. Walpurgas Nackt.

Finnegans Wake, 229.

THE myths endure. In years of exile from Ithaca, observing
many cities—Paris, London, Trieste, Pola, Rome, Zurich—
enduring troubles and hardships in the struggle to save fellow-
citizens who were determined to perish of their own madness,
Joyce could not have failed to see his own plight and that of
Ulysses repeated in the situation of any man of good will in
Dublin. Ulysses had been his favourite hero in a classroom
essay of his Belvedere schooldays; he had thought of writing
a story, "Ulysses", about the wanderings of a citizen named
Hunter, for the *Dubliners* series but the project "never got
any forrarder than the title"; at another time he had intended
to call the collection of stories *Ulysses at Dublin*, and even
accumulated some Homeric parallels, but he lost interest in
what was proving a none too satisfactory structural device half
way through the writing of a book that was assuming what we
have seen to be a compulsive unity of its own.[1] His homage to
the *Odyssey* was not to be performed for another ten years,
though he had vaguely realized from the time he completed
Chamber Music that the *Odyssey* held the clue to much of his
job.

[1] Such is my reading of the facts set forth by Richard Levin and Charles
Shattuck in their article, "First Flight to Ithaca" (*Accent*, Winter, 1944,
reprinted in Givens, 47–94). They attempt to force the parallel to the end,
though admitting that it falters. It seems to me to have been sustained by Joyce
about as far as "Clay".

179

His error in starting to hang the stories in *Dubliners* from a string of incidents in Homer had been to suppose that the *Odyssey* was a book to be *used*. Its function was to give him, the writer, a scaffolding. He was building (was he not?) an ordered book out of chaos, and needed a plan. It was only after the image of artist as imposer of order, lawgiver to his limp materials, had been lived to the dregs and discarded (*Exiles*) that he could understand with his whole mind how Homer could control the *treatment* of Dublin material because it illuminated the *subject*; because there was a subject to illuminate, not just a jumble of impressions. *Dubliners* was saved by Joyce's willingness to abandon a contrived order the moment he realized that he understood it only as contrivance; *Ulysses* was made a monument and a triumph through his determination to stay with the idea of a Homeric parallel until he saw why it had been right.

For it had been a sound intuition. Homer afforded a situation through which Joyce could control the whole of Dublin's daylight life. It is to this situation that the title of *Ulysses* points; to the situation the elaborate paralleling of incidents and characters is firmly subordinated.

This has never been gotten into focus. The most qualified readers have been put off by a misleading critical tradition. *Ulysses* is habitually regarded as a photograph of Dublin, 1904. Homer's world is somewhere else, in another book; and it is with the greatest impatience that one remarks Joyce or his exegete Mr. Gilbert making incidents tally off. To accustom ourselves to the idea that the Homeric situation—Homer's world—is *in Joyce's text*, because Joyce found it in Dublin, we may consider the implications of one of his letters to Harriet Weaver: T. S. Eliot had just written, " Instead of narrative method, we may now use the mythological method. . . . It has the importance of a scientific discovery."[1]

I suppose you have seen Mr. Eliot's article in *The Dial*. I like it and it comes opportunely. I shall suggest to him when I write to thank him that in alluding to it elsewhere he use or coin some short phrase, two or three words, such as the one he used in speaking to me, " two plane ". Mr. Larbaud gave the reading public about six months ago the phrase " interior monologue " (that is, in *Ulysses*). Now they want a new phrase. They cannot manage more than one

[1] T. S. Eliot, " Ulysses, Order, and Myth ", *The Dial*, Nov. 1923. Reprinted in Givens, 198–202.

such phrase every six months—not for lack of intelligence but because they are in a hurry.[1]

The subsequent history of *Ulysses* criticism consists in the fact that the requisite phrase—" double-writing ", perhaps—was never coined, nor put in circulation. So the public and their middlemen moved only as far as " interior monologue ", and stuck fast. The Homeric substructure has been either haggled over in detail, or brushed aside as a nuisance, by readers settling down, cutlery in hand, to a slab of bleeding realism. That the fundamental correspondence is not between incident and incident, but between situation and situation, has never gotten into the critical tradition.

Joyce is exploring a situation full of quite serious analogies with the Homeric situation. The action of *Ulysses* is an action of emerging intelligibility, progressive epiphanization, to which the doings and details of the characters are subservient. The main situations—the intelligible forms—of the two books coincide. The details are freely disposed, never without point. Joyce doesn't even confine himself to the corresponding Homeric episode for materials; for the Sirens, for instance (Homer's Book X) he borrows the singing minstrel from Book VIII.

THE SITUATION

The basic analogies are clear enough by the end of the first episode. Ireland is the kingdom usurped. It is usurped by Buck Mulligan, as stage Irishman vis-à-vis the autochthonous wit of Simon Dedalus' now ageing and dying generation, and as priest of the body vis-à-vis folk wisdom (the milk-woman) and spiritual order (the artist and the priest of God). No. 7 Eccles Street, correspondingly, is usurped by the merry adulterer, Blazes Boylan. The avenger, the dispossessed paternal principle, point d'appui of hierarchic order, has been absent, tossed about by the sea-god (Ireland's difficulties in Joyce's generation were in part due to the long struggle with the politics and commerce guaranteed by English sea-power). Odysseus' enemy is Poseidon; the Poseidon of *Ulysses* is the *dio boia* presiding over the sea of matter in which Bloom is tossed all day, nearly submerged, clinging to enthymemic planks and clambering onto occasional treacherous rocks or into situations (the newspaper office, the tavern, the lunch-house) that merely delay and betray. The quest for the father is the

[1] Joyce to Harriet Weaver, Nov. 19, 1923. Transcript in Slocum collection.

quest for the masculine and rational, of which Bloom is a paradigm at one level, though hopelessly inadequate on several others.

The detailed correspondences are largely comic—Mr. Bloom's "knockmedown cigar" brandished, like Odysseus' sharpened and heated club, in the Cyclops' face; Nausicaa's cartful of laundry and Gerty MacDowell's airing and blueing of her "four dinky sets" of undies; Corley recommended to apply for the master's job in Deasy's school, and Melanthius castrated for dog-meat.

The larger correspondences are more usually serious, in the sense that they recognize Homer's registration of a permanent mode. Navel-gazing in a bath-tub *is* Lotus-eating. They are two metaphors for one psychological state. Aeolus the wind-god makes an apt counterpart for the journalist, and it is the sort of figure that illuminates wherever explored. (Compare Bacon's way of exposing, in *The Wisdom of the Ancients*, the configurations of Elizabethan polity in classical myths.)

Finally, Homer is constantly employed in a critical mode. He provides a measure of what the Dubliners *don't* do. The new Penelope isn't faithful, Telemachus doesn't refuse to cast out his mother for fear of being haunted by her curses, Nausicaa's father isn't a king but a drunkard and she doesn't take Ulysses home with her, and so on. Both Mr. E. B. Burgum's statement that "it is not simply a parallel but a parallel in reverse—the opposite of everything that happens in *Ulysses* happens in the *Odyssey*"[1] (Dublin unequivocally inverting an ideal order) and Mr. Stuart Gilbert's timid acknowledgment that Bloom "is no servile replica of his Homeric prototype, for he has a cat instead of a dog, and a daughter instead of a son"[2] (Joyce playfully altering a few trifles in the interests of variety) deflect attention from the fundamental seriousness with which the main analogies are to be regarded. The variations exist within a norm; they are neither capricious nor mechanical. The awakening of Telemachus at the opening of Homer's Book II ("He dressed himself, slung a sharp sword over his shoulder, strapt a stout pair of boots on his lissom feet, and came forth from the chamber like a young god")[3] reminds

---

[1] E. B. Burgum, "Ulysses and the Impasse of Individualism", *Virginia Quarterly Review*, xvii-4 (October 1941), 561–573.

[2] Stuart Gilbert, *James Joyce's Ulysses*.

[3] All Homeric quotations from the translation of Dr. W. H. D. Rouse.

us that Stephen has his ashplant, Mulligan's castoff shoes, and his weary walk: an ineffectual artist, a comically inadequate Telemachus, but reduced to a plight that genuinely images the status of the arts in our time. When these perspectives are grasped, the numerous corroborative details such as Antinous Mulligan sponging "twopence for a pint" from Telemachus, the only person in the tower with any money, drop into place as echoes of a situational correspondence, not as a structure of links on the accretion and cohesion of which the entire parallel depends.

MANY DIMENSIONS

It is impossible to draw a reliable map. Joyce uses and reuses the same Homeric material at various levels. At the end of Book IV of the *Odyssey* we read about Telemachus' enemies:

> But the plotters embarked and sailed over the waters, with foul murder in their hearts for Telemachus. There is a rocky islet between Ithaca and the cliffs of Samos, quite a small one, called Asteris, and harbours in it for ships on both sides; there they lay in wait for him.

The primary correspondence is with Stephen's appointment to meet Mulligan, Haines, & Co. in a significantly-named tavern: "—The Ship, Buck Mulligan cried. Half twelve ", U24/20. If Stephen had not evaded this ambush, as he did by sending a mocking telegram, U197/188, he would have been relieved of his money, gotten drunk by early afternoon, and (for what the encounter is worth) never met Bloom. That is one part of Joyce's use of the Homeric passage. At the end of his Telemachia (Part I), however, he uses it again in another mode (it occurs at the end of the Telemachia of the *Odyssey*). Stephen is about to leave the beach:

> He turned his face over his shoulder, rere regardant. Moving through the air high spars of a threemaster, her sails brailed up on the crosstrees, homing, upstream, silently moving, a silent ship. U51/47.

This is, as we later discover, " the threemaster Rosevean from Bridgwater with bricks ", U609/587. It is part of the pattern of usurpation; it comes from the usurping land, bringing yet more matter to obliterate the soul of Dublin. *This* ambush is not to be evaded; the bricks are discharged, the bricks will constitute yet another patch of ignobility on the betrayed realm. And there is yet another parallel: with the ship that brought Telemachus' father back to Ithaca. The *Rosevean* bears W. B. Murphy, Ulysses Pseudangelos, the garrulous sailor of the cabman's shelter, to his native shore.

At no time is Joyce crossing off common factors as he disposes of them. In the Proteus section, for instance, the principal perspective comes from Homer's characterization of Proteus as a source of universal information: hence " signatures of all things I am here to read ", and the philological art of reading the Book of Nature in search of clues to the intelligible order abolished after Eden. (Telemachus went to Lacedaemon to seek clues to the whereabouts of his father; the missing father, Ulysses, is at one level God, at another the rational principle of social, aesthetic, and philosophical order.) The binding of Proteus as accomplished by the artist compels intelligible form out of the flux of things: " He will turn into all sorts of shapes to try you, into all the creatures that live and move upon the earth, into water, into blazing fire; but you must hold him fast and press him all the harder ": the intense contemplation by which the epiphanic insight is wrested. Telemachus doesn't wrestle with Proteus, nor in any significant sense does the egocentric Stephen; his skirmish with appearances does yield an enigmatic poem,

> On swift sail flaming
> From storm and south
> He comes, pale vampire,
> Mouth to my mouth. U131/123.

—which images the return of the father who will take revenge on him (for his adoption of a feminine role of egocentric pathos) rather than on the suitors.

As usual, Joyce employs the Homeric episode at many levels. The wrestler with Proteus in the *Odyssey* is Menelaus, who finds out from him how to get home, what has happened to his companions, and the nature of his own end. The Dublin Menelaus is Kevin Egan, like his prototype a cuckolded exile, whose tales of the revolutionary movement—" Of lost leaders, the betrayed, wild escapes. Disguises, clutched at, gone, not here "—imply that he has been engaged in furthering, not binding, the Protean (in the absence of coherent principles, political activity in Ireland increased rather than dissipated

confusion). Egan, a Menelaus in reverse, has helped unbind
Proteus, cannot get home, knows the fate of his companions as
he knows nothing else (" How the head centre got away,
authentic version ", U44/40) and already inhabits a mockery
of the " Elysian plain at the end of the earth where golden-
headed Rhadamanthys dwells . . . for you are Helen's
husband."—" Loveless, landless, wifeless. She is quite nicey
comfy without her outcast man, madame, in rue Gît-le-Coeur,
canary and two buck lodgers." Proteus' prophecy to Menelaus
is fused with Tiresias' to Odysseus in Stephen's reflections on
" sea-death, mildest of all deaths known to man." Odysseus
went to Hades to see Tiresias, and Bloom is at this moment in
the cemetery; but a Tiresias is the one Homeric figure he does
not meet there. No external wisdom guides him. As his
mutations of sex in Circe's palace imply, he is Tiresias himself,
an Eliotic Tiresias foresuffering all.

Bloom's relations with Odysseus are complex. In the second
book of the *Odyssey* the soothsayer rehearses his prediction, that
the hero will wander 19 years, that all his companions will be
lost, and that no one will know him on his homecoming.
Bloom's day lasts 19 hours, the litany of his lost comrades—
" Martin Cunningham (in bed), Jack Power (in bed), Simon
Dedalus (in bed) . . . Paddy Dignam (in the grave) "—
resounds at the end of the day, U689/665, and his adopted son
knows him not. Odysseus, as Zeus acknowledged, is the wisest
man alive; Bloom is the incarnation of contemporary lore and
know-how. But Odysseus is thwarted by the sea-god Poseidon
because he blinded the Cyclops. Bloom, analogously, is a
wandering Jew because of his role in the denial of Christ. (His
unintentional pretensions as secular Messiah—blinding of
Cyclops—enrage the eponymous Citizen, U339/329.) The
curse God has laid on the Jewish people, according to Jacques
Maritain, is immersion in matter: the correlative of their very
efficiency in practical affairs. The equation of the sea with
matter is one of the master keys in the analogical structure of
Ulysses.

As Odysseus leaves the island of Calypso, Poseidon lashes
the waves in a furious tempest. In the Calypso episode of
Ulysses, the storm is reduced to a little cloud covering the sun,
but the effect on Bloom is not less marked: his mind turns to
the Dead Sea, he thinks " No wind would lift those waves,
grey metal, poisonous foggy waters. . . . Grey horror seared

his flesh ", U61/54. This evocation of the Dead Sea, the Cities of the Plain, utter exhausted sterility, is both a counterpoint to Poseidon's bracing tempest and an epiphany of the plight of Dublin, a sea-evocation proper to the sea in which the modern Ulysses is cast adrift.

It is unnecessary to heap up detailed parallels for the reader who can extract them from the text or from Mr. Gilbert's commentary; our object is to indicate their multivalent modes of functioning. Sometimes they are jokes: in line with Joyce's Aeolus symbolism, we find Odysseus satisfying Aeolus' thirst for news with a full account of what happened in Troy. Sometimes they are comic inversions: Penelope recognizes Ulysses by the secret of the marvellous bed's construction, but the secret of Bloom's bed is known to all Dublin—it jingles. Sometimes they are correspondences of fact inflected with a pathetic divergence of intention: Odysseus the disguised returned avenger takes pleasure in Penelope's behaviour, " to see how she attracted their gifts, while she wheedled them with soft words and had quite other thoughts in her mind ", while Bloom's pathetic pride in Molly's charms for other men (he displays her picture at any opportunity, U636/614) somehow assuages the fact that whatever other thoughts she has in her mind they are not of him. Sometimes they are bits of symbolic opportunism; Odysseus when young was wounded in the thigh by a boar, which image, with its Freudian overtones of castration complex, is applied to Shakespeare (another Ulysses avatar) by Stephen, U194/185, and has obvious relevance as well to Bloom's unprotesting effeminacy. Sometimes, finally, they are structural: as Homer, for instance, has the story retold in Hades from the viewpoint of the suitors, Joyce retells it, in analogous coda, from that of Penelope.

THE CHARACTER OF ULYSSES

Butcher and Lang's *Odyssey*, not only " not Homer " but not even " a very pretty poem ", registers the Odysseus whom representative nineteenth-century minds perceived in the Greek: a sort of Tennysonian Arthur, " ideal manhood clothed in real man." Every translation is a contemporary poem, and the contemporary poets of that age were Tennyson and, say, Lewis Carroll. So the Victorian Ulysses is an important part of Joyce's subject-matter.

It is useful to think of Joyce as a sort of twentieth-century

Homeric translator, at least to get one's lines of sight pegged down. A twentieth-century perspective on Odysseus is given by Mr. Pound—no irreverent Homerist, as Canto I and the opening of Canto XLVII testify—in his correspondence with Dr. W. H. D. Rouse concerning that scholar's remarkable translation:

> As to character of Odysseus. Anything but the bright little Rollo of Chamber's Journal brought up on Sam Smiles. Born un po' misero, don't want to go to war, little runt who finally has to do all the hard work, gets all Don Juan's chances with the ladies and can't really enjoy 'em. Circe, Calypso, Nausicaa. Always some fly in the ointment, last to volunteer on stiff jobs.[1]

This Odysseus resembles a demi-god much less than he resembles the irreducible ethical structure of Mr. Bloom:

> Decent quiet man he is. I often saw him in here and I never once saw him, you know, over the line.
>
> — God Almighty couldn't make him drunk, Nosey Flynn said firmly. Slips off when the fun gets too hot. Didn't you see him look at his watch? Ah, you weren't there. If you ask him to have a drink first thing he does he outs with the watch to see what he ought to imbibe. Declare to God he does.
>
> — There are some like that, Davy Byrne said. He's a safe man, I'd say.
>
> — He's not too bad, Nosey Flynn said, snuffling it up. He has been known to put his hand down too to help a fellow. Give the devil his due. O, Bloom has his good points.... U175/166.

Thus the Bloomesque *ethos;* it is in the mode of *pathos* that Mr. Bloom is un-Homeric, that he exhibits a sordid shapelessness that *is* continuous with the poetic world of Butcher and Lang. Bloom combines permanent virtues with a nineteenth-century sensibility.

Here, for comparison with Mr. Pound's, is Joyce's image of Odysseus (the interlocutor is Frank Budgen):

> " Your complete man in literature is, I suppose, Ulysses? "
>
> " Yes ", said Joyce. .... " Ulysses is son to Laertes, but he is father to Telemachus, husband to Penelope, lover of Calypso, companion in arms of the Greek warriors around Troy and King of Ithaca. He was subjected to many trials, but with wisdom and courage came through them all. Don't forget that he was a war dodger who tried to evade military service by simulating madness. He might never

---

[1] *The Letters of Ezra Pound*, ed. D. D. Paige.

have taken up arms and gone to Troy, but the Greek recruiting
sergeant was too clever for him. . . . But once at war the con-
scientious objector became a jusqu'auboutist. When the others
wanted to abandon the siege he insisted on staying till Troy should
fall."

I laughed at Ulysses as a leadswinger and Joyce continued:

" Another thing, the history of Ulysses did not come to an end
when the Trojan war was over. It began just when the other
Greek heroes went back to live the rest of their lives in peace. And
then "—Joyce laughed—" he was the first gentleman in Europe.
When he advanced, naked, to meet the young princess he hid from
her maidenly eyes the parts that mattered of his brine-soaked,
barnacle-encrusted body. He was an inventor too. The tank is his
creation. Wooden horse or iron box—it doesn't matter. They are
both shells containing armed warriors." [1]

Joyce, it is evident, had no difficulty in evading the nineteenth-
century illusion of the Achaean hero's inviolable grandeur.
That there is an impassable gulf of 3,000 years between Bloom
and Odysseus is the error of a reader who has had the *Odyssey*
served up to him as something archaic and alien, invested with
the glamour of an infinite remove: the Greek Dream. Joyce
placed in his text, as point of reference, a reader precisely so
blinded; Buck Mulligan, for whom poetry means " Swinburne ", hankers after " the Attic note. The note of Swinburne,
of all poets, the white death and the ruddy birth." In 1920,
when about half of *Ulysses* had appeared in *The Little Review*,
Mr. Eliot wrote,

> We need a digestion which can assimilate both Homer and Flaubert.
> . . . We need an eye which can see the past in its place with its
> definite differences from the present, and yet so lively that it shall
> be as present to us as the present. This is the creative eye. . . .[2]

HOMERIC EXEGESIS

" My Ulysses," Joyce told Frank Budgen, " is a complete
man as well—a good man. At any rate, that is what I intend
that he shall be."

Joyce's habitual Aquinatian view of evil as privation opens
into less formularized issues. Both Bloom and Odysseus
contain all the natural virtues in some sort of laudable balance

[1] Budgen, 16–17.
[2] *Selected Essays*: " Euripides and Professor Murray."

(much of Bloom's ignobility is a function of the ignoble
materials with which his prudence, charity, temperance,
fortitude, justice, etc. are engaged).   There is a sort of decorum,
furthermore, in both men's ready perception of the applicable
means and stratagems for every situation.   It is as gadgeteer
that Bloom fulfils the nineteenth-century epithet, " man of
many devices" ("He was an inventor too," Joyce slyly remarked
of Ulysses).   In his public actions Bloom fulfils Dr. Rouse's
translation of the same epithet, quite literally " never at a loss ":
unhesitatingly adaptable to such varied demands as guiding the
blind stripling through traffic, helping to arrange the speedy
payment of Mrs. Dignam's insurance, or rescuing Stephen
from Nighttown, with admirably unselfconscious tenacity and
prudence.   It is only in the managing of his interior life that
his gestures become absurd.   Lenehan's tribute isn't at all
ironical:

> – He's a cultured allroundman, Bloom is, he said seriously.   He's
> not one of your common or garden ... you know. ....   There's a
> touch of the artist about old Bloom.   U231/222.

Homer was the educator of Greece primarily because his
poems provided a lexicon of states of moral and emotional being,
and of modes of prudence in exemplary action.   Respect for
the completeness of Odysseus' paradigm of civic and domestic
prudence is echoed by commentators of almost every generation from the age of Plato to that of Pope.   Pope's preface to
the *Odyssey* throws valuable light on the continuity of this
tradition: he remarks, quite in the mediaeval way, on Homer's
competence as historian, antiquary, divine, and professor of the
arts and sciences.

The analogy with Joyce's arts, symbols, and bodily organs is
obvious.   *Ulysses* is an epic in the Renaissance sense, a manifestation of every province of rhetoric and a compilation of every
form of learning.   Commentators too often forget that allegorical exegesis of Homer was not a Blavatskyesque underground
but the central and most respected tradition of poetic studies
from Theagenes of Rhegium (fl. 525 B.C.)[1] through the middle
ages to Chapman's explicitly allegorized translation of the
Odyssey (1615) and beyond.   Homer was thought of as
presenting a multi-faceted solid whose planes had only to be

---

[1] Sandys, *History of Classical Scholarship*, I, 7.

projected to make contact with every portion of the surrounding empirical, moral, and metaphysical world.

Via the Cynic moral exegesis the figure of Ulysses assumed
an important role in education; after a millennium and a half
Shakespeare, presenting him in the conventional Renaissance
light, gives us an incarnation of copiously eloquent wisdom and
prudence, yet another version of the Ciceronian ideal orator.
At one point in their conversations Joyce drew Mr. Budgen's
attention to the Ulysses of Shakespeare; the major difference
is that Bloom's endless encyclopaedic monologue is heard by
no one. There was nothing accidental in Joyce's choice of the
Odyssey as theme for a brightly keyed compendium of twentieth-
century folklore, know-how, art and wisdom.

ODYSSEY AS COMEDY

> I come from Wonderland, where I have good estate, and I am the
> son of my lord Neverstint Griefanpain; my name is Battledown.

From *Ulysses*, somewhere in the Cyclops episode? It is not.
It is from Homer himself (*Od.* xxiv, 304) as rendered *ad
verbum* by Dr. Rouse. The usual practice of translators is to
leave these proper names impenetrable: Alybas, Apheidas
Polypemonides, Eperitos; they sound so much more majestic,
and the whimsical etymologies are (surely!) a mistake. But
Dr. Rouse (in an essay appended to his *Odyssey*) introduces
much evidence that Homer's diction is colloquial and often
ingeniously comic. The decorum of the stock epithet is often
comic (refusal to believe that this can be so accounts for the
frequent assertion that the epithets are often introduced without
regard for context). Thus " I cannot help thinking that the
company laughed when he introduced Eumaios as δῖος ὑφορβός,
pigman by divine right." Homer, it appears, did his share of
guying the epic conventions; Dr. Rouse calls attention to the
battlefield epithet by which the pigherd is made to chop wood
with a pitiless blade. It has not, of course, been possible for
anyone to suppress the pun by which Odysseus deceives the
Cyclops; Dr. Rouse indicates many more; Athena makes one
to sting Zeus (*Od.* i, 62). Finally, he fills three pages with
examples of words, often used only once like much of Joyce's
vocabulary, as colloquial as the Dublin " gave me the wheeze "
and " chucking out the rhino ".

Thus Joyce in the Cyclops episode offers an explicit critique of Homer-as-he-is-read:

> And lo, as they quaffed their cup of joy, a godlike messenger came swiftly in, radiant as the eye of heaven, a comely youth and behind him there passed an elder of noble gait and countenance, bearing the sacred scrolls of law and with him his lady wife, a dame of peerless lineage, fairest of her race.
>
> Little Alf Bergan popped in round the door and hid behind Barney's snug, squeezed up with the laughing. . . . I didn't know what was up and Alf kept making signs out of the door. And begob what was it only that bloody old pantaloon Denis Breen in his bathslippers with two bloody big books tucked under his oxter and his wife hotfoot after him, unfortunate wretched woman trotting like a poodle. U293/283.

The first version is a fair pastiche of Butcher and Lang; we may be sure that if Homer had used an epithet meaning " trotting like a poodle " a scholiast would have been found to explain it as a stock metaphor meaning " fairest of her race ". (Hasn't the significance of " ox-cyed Hera " been lost in purple clouds of " poetic " preconceptions? " Stupid bitch Hera has her bull eyes ", Mr. Pound remarks apropos of Homer's epithetic rightness.) Joyce had no difficulty exhibiting the relation of the slack poetizing of Idyllized Homer to the never-never Celtic twilight, U288/279, Yeats-Blavatsky spiritualism, U296/286, pseudo-Ossianics, U291/281, journalistic pathos, U301/291, etc. There isn't really a great deal of difference between this, from one of the parodies:

> The *nec* and *non plus ultra* of emotion were reached when the blushing bride elect burst her way through the serried ranks of the bystanders and flung herself upon the muscular bosom of him who was about to be launched into eternity for her sake, U304/294,

and this, from Butcher and Lang's *Odyssey:*

> But the daughter of Cadmus marked him, Ino of the fair ankles . . . and sat upon the well-bound raft and spake: " Hapless one, wherefore was Poseidon, shaker of the earth, so wondrous wroth with thee? . . . "

Dr. Rouse's version of the latter runs,

" Poor Odysseus! You're odd-I-see, true to your name! Why does· Poseidon Earthshaker knock you about in this monstrous way? "

On surge-and-thunder principles, naturally, the pun on Odysseus and ὠδύσατο had to be overlooked. *Ulysses* is at this level a comment on the age that had allowed its perception of Homer to get into such a state.

Pope, who predicted the Universal Darkness in which the contours of Homer were blotted out, affords valuable evidence of the persistence of stylistic discrimination from the age of the Alexandrian scholiasts to the early eighteenth century; the reader who imagines that Dr. Rouse, abetted by the irreverent Mr. Pound, is just a cynical modern making things up should check Pope's account of the matter. Pope quotes Longinus' statement that the *Odyssey* is partly comic, Ulysses being shown not in the full light of glory but in the shade of common life. The Cyclops he adds, is explicitly comic, and Calypso and the suitors " characters of intrigue " (a cross-light on stately, plump Buck Mulligan thus comes from Restoration comedy). The themes, as he lists them, are strikingly Dublinesque: banquets, sports, loves, and the pursuit of a woman. With a glance at *Don Quixote*, he notes that the perfection of the mock-epic is the employment of pompous expressions for low actions. And finally, with his usual prescience, Pope hands us the key to Arnold's Homer lectures, Lang's translations, Tennyson's *Idylls*, all the tushery of the century that was to follow: the sublime style, he says, is of all styles the easiest to fake.

The moment we stop thinking of Homer's sweaty and quarrelsome Achaeans as unrelaxingly heroic posturers, much comes into focus. As Mr. Pound does Propertius, so Joyce presents Homer as a modern and in some respects comic poet. Odysseus, like Bloom, it is not always realized, contends with his milieu as much as he illustrates it. His men are constantly hanging back, running out, falling asleep, getting drunk, and letting the winds out of the bag.

Once more, Joyce is in a tradition coterminous with the disciplines of the trivium. He sees Homer much as Pope saw him, and much as did Pope's predecessors for over two thousand years. The immediate source of his Homeric insight is a mystery. He didn't know much classical Greek, though he was fairly fluent in modern Greek (it was always *spoken* languages that interested him). From schoolroom days, he had no difficulty seeing the *story* in modern terms (he first read it in Charles Lamb's version), and as for the language, he was perfectly capable of looking up a few etymologies. Victor Bérard's researches, as Mr. Gilbert copiously if somewhat over-solemnly demonstrates, made it easy to smell out the (Phoenician: hence Semitic) seafaring yarns underlying the epic, and the Joyce who had hung around the quays of Dublin and Trieste had ample experience of the conversation of sailors. Whatever crib he employed had disappeared by the time the relics of his working library were catalogued in 1949. We have here, it would seem, another instance of the kind of poetic insight that was manifested when Mr. Pound wrested his wonderful *Cathay* from a somewhat unreliable crib to ideograms he couldn't at that time make a pretence of reading.

HAMLET

The stories of Dedalus and Hamlet reinforce the Homeric situation, just as such local analogies as the Parnell case and the biography of Shakespeare furnish modes of special emphasis in line with the main form of the book.

Dedalus, of course, had engaged Joyce's attention for many years. In *Les Dieux Antiques*, a translation and adaptation of George Cox's small English handbook of mythology, Stéphane Mallarmé gives a note on his name:

> What does his name signify? Simply the wise or resourceful work-man; and the same idea occurs in the epithet πολύμητις, which is constantly applied to Odysseus. . . . The wisdom of Dedalus is in fact only another form of the wisdom of Phoebus or Odysseus. As for Icarus, behold in him a feeble reflection of his father, as Phaethon is of Helios, and Telemachus of Odysseus.[1]

That Icarus might be the son of Ulysses is implicit, that is, in the very etymology of his surname, Dedalus. A feeble reflection of one father, imagining that the situation will better itself if he hunts out another: that is Stephen. Having employed the Dedalus situation throughout the *Portrait*, Joyce simply switches its materials onto a main-line track of the same gauge.

[1] Mallarmé, *Oeuvres*, Pléiade, Paris, 1945, 1244. (My translation.)

As for the *Hamlet* situation, it is easy to see how it reinforces that of the *Odyssey*:

Hamlet	Stephen	Telemachus	Dispossessed heir
Ghost	Rational Principle	Ulysses	Ghost through death or absence
Claudius	Mulligan, Rome	Antinous	Usurper
Queen	Ireland	Penelope[1]	The usurped
Ophelia	Stephen's sister		Drowned innocent[2]

The shift from the *Odyssey* into *Hamlet* is accompanied by a great increase in psychological intensity: the shift, between Classic and Renaissance, from the civic to the personal (a similar theme underlies Mr. Pound's first thirty *Cantos*). There is also a displacement of centre, from errant father to tortured son. *Hamlet* is in this sense simply the *Odyssey* narrated from the viewpoint of an introverted Telemachus. (There are fragmentary allusions in Joyce's text to *Don Giovanni;* Mozart's opera repeats the same plot from the point of view of the doomed usurper). Hence, although Bloom is allowed at one point to declaim, " Hamlet, I am thy father's spirit ", U150/141, the *Hamlet* correspondences centre on Stephen. The scene in the Tower begins, like Shakespeare's play, on the upper platform. The mummers then descend the stairs and Mulligan plays Claudius, twitting Stephen on his black costume and delivering sententious wisdom on the inevitability of death (" I see them pop off every day in the Mater and Richmond and cut up into tripes in the dissecting room. It's a beastly thing and nothing else.") The Ghost beheld by Stephen is that of his mother, " her wasted body within its loose brown graveclothes giving off an odour of wax and rosewood ". Having planted the correspondence firmly in the first episode, Joyce drops its detailed development and shifts his attention to the character of Stephen / Hamlet.

---

[1] Queen Gertrude who gives in and Queen Penelope who doesn't comprise Joyce's familiar bipolar feminine, just as the Ghost and the triumphant Ithacan give us the bipolar masculine. The tensions between Shakespeare's and Homer's worlds are exploited as much as the analogies.

[2] " She is drowning. Agenbite. Save her. Agenbite. She will drown me with her, eyes and hair ", U239/230. As the " agenbite " and the emblematic " salt green death " imply, sister Dilly is simply Stephen's mother over again. Ophelia in the same way repeats the spiritual death of the Queen. The death of Stephen's mother parallels that of Ireland.

His projection of Hamlet seems significantly related to the meditations of two French poets, Mallarmé and Laforgue. Mallarmé's phrase, quoted to Stephen by Mr. Best, " Il se promène, lisant au livre de lui-même ", U185/175, comes from a page on *Hamlet et Fortinbras* which deserves further quotation:

> ... he walks, that is all, reading the book of himself, a high and living Sign; he scorns to look at any other. Nor will he be content to symbolize the solitude of the Thinker among other men; he kills them off aloofly and at random, or at least, they die. The black presence of the doubter diffuses poison, so that all the great people die, without his even taking the trouble, usually, to stab them behind the arras. Then, evidently in deliberate contrast to the hesitator, we see Fortinbras in the role of general, but no more efficaciously lethal than he; and if Death deploys his versatile appliances—phial, lotus-pool, or rapier—when an exceptional person flaunts his sombre livery, that is the import of the finale when, as the spectator returns to his senses, this sumptuous and stagnant exaggeration of murder (the idea of which remains as meaning of the play, attached to Him who makes himself alone) so to speak achieves vulgar manifestation as this agent of military destruction clears the stage with his marching army, on the scale of the commonplace, amid trumpets and drums.[1]

Mallarmé's insistence on Hamlet's otherness runs counter to the English Romantic critical tradition of " Hamlet is ourselves ". Hamlet is alien to the namby-pamby " so French, don't you know " world of the Dublin aesthetes, but equally alien to the rational masculine world epitomized by his own father. Hamlet, furthermore, is the very incarnation at once of creativity and of death. And Hamlet, like Stephen, reads no book but his own nature, his soul in some manner all that is, the form of forms, U27/23.

Stephen is continuous with Dublin, as his relation of sonship with Bloom emphasizes; Fortinbras, the conquering general, is a vulgarized Hamlet, that is all. Hamlet's kingdom is not of

---

[1] Mallarmé, *Oeuvres*, 1557. Joyce was digging in the very apparatus criticus of the *Divagations* volume (1897) when he found this. It was a paragraph contributed to *la Revue Blanche*, salvaged by Mallarmé in the " Bibliographie " of *Divagations* because, as he says, he wasn't able to work it into his main Hamlet essay. The most evident failure of my translation is its omission of the multiple senses of " autour de Qui se fait seul." French word-order permits this to mean both " Him who makes himself alone " and " Him who alone makes Himself ": Hamlet the epitome of Life and Death, Creator and *dio boia*.

this world.   Stephen's image of himself as a destroying force ("Shatter them, one and both.   But stun myself too in the blow", U238/229) is allied to Mallarmé's emphasis; English criticism has given the gloomy prince a contrary build-up as Thinker.   The propensity for slaughtering suitors, it is worth noting, is transferred from Ulysses to Telemachus by this Hamlet interposition.   Stephen has lethal thoughts all day ("Hired dog!   Shoot him to bloody bits with a bang shotgun, bits man spattered walls all brass buttons", U43/38);   Bloom rejects them ("Assassination, never") but does toy with "Exposure by mechanical artifice (automatic bed) or individual testimony (concealed ocular witness)", U718/694.   The lines from *Don Giovanni* that he hums after lunch belong to the marble avenger in the opera: *a cenar teco m'invitasti.*   An X-ray version of "exposure" is comically juxtaposed: "have to stand all the time with his insides entrails on show.   Science", U177/168.

As for Laforgue's Hamlet, he is introduced to us in *Moralités Légendaires* high in a tower by a stagnant arm of the sea (cf. the opening of *Ulysses*) contemplating his own soul and his Works. The castle is hung with "completely accurate views of Jutland", Academy Art at which Hamlet invariably spits as he passes.   He is very much the Artist Manqué, exhibited as comic adolescent.   He is also a homicidal maniac.   His longing is "To be the hero of a play!   And to reduce all of the other plays to little curtain-raisers!"   He dazzles, or imagines he has dazzled, the self-sufficient little actress Kate with visions of a flight to Paris "this evening under the extremely lucid moonlight", pauses to gather from his father's grave "a flower, a simple paper-flower, which will serve us as a bookmark when we interrupt the reading of my drama to kiss each other", encounters Laertes, and dies with a Neronic "*Qualis* . . *artifex* . . . *pereo!*"[1]

The comic dimensions of Joyce's treatment of Stephen are aligned with Laforgue's.   Laforgue's genius was for the exposé, and in his *Hamlet* he exposed the self-sufficient posturings of Romantic aestheticism, and its lethal substratum.   The difficulty the reader experiences keeping Stephen in focus depends, as a look at Laforgue may convince us, on the fact that the arty adolescent, incapable of separating with exactness

[1] *Six Moral Tales from Jules Laforgue*, ed. and trans. Frances Newman, N.Y., 1928, 140, 190, 200.

his *persona* from himself, can't keep himself in focus; he resembles the kind of picture puzzle in which the perspective suddenly snaps into reverse and foreground becomes background.

In so far as he is a serious figure, Stephen's alignments are with the Hamlet of Mallarmé; in so far as he is the object of satire, they are with the Hamlet of Laforgue. A final dimension comes from the *Odyssey*. As Mr. Deasy brings forward the Parnell case, $U_{35/32}$, so Nestor in the third book of Homer relates the betrayal of Agamemnon by his wife. What he presses on Telemachus, however, is the role of Orestes the avenging son. Homer is evidently quite aware of the parallel between the situations of Telemachus and Orestes. There is, so to speak, a Hamlet in the *Odyssey*, and a successful one.

Chapter 12

HOW TO READ *ULYSSES*

It would have diverted, if ever seen, the shuddersome spectacle of this semidemented zany amid the inspissated grime of his glaucous den making believe to read his usylessly unreadable Blue Book of Eccles ... but what with the murky light, the botchy print, the tattered cover, the jigjagged page, the fumbling fingers, the foxtrotting fleas ... he was hardset to mumorise more than a word a week.

Finnegans Wake (F179)

In narratione ergo rerum factarum quaeritur utrum omnia secundum figuratum tantummodo intellectum accipiantur, an etiam secundum fidem rerum gestarum asserenda et defendenda sint.

St. Augustine, De Genesi ad Litteram, I–I.

Reads it backwards first.   Quickly he does it.   Must require some practice that.

Ulysses, U 121/114

WHILE we no longer suppose, with an early reviewer, that " Mr. Joyce transfers the product of his unconscious mind to paper without submitting it to his conscious mind," we have been encouraged to think that reading the book amounts to determining why one notion of Bloom's follows another. Joyce's interest in this kind of *consonantia* is however much more sardonic than scientific.   While he takes care that Bloom's thought shall be, at Bloom's level, continuous, he takes even greater care that the work as a whole shall be, at Joyce's level, intelligible.   Dublin is being presented in a hundred simultaneous perspectives, with the aid of numerous controlling images.

One of the major perspectives is the analogy of Bloom and Stephen; it is an analogy much more than it is a contrast. Parallels between their meditations proliferate; if these are not too readily dismissed (or admired) as tokens of Joyce's concern for " structure " they will yield a great deal of the book's meaning.

This means reading Bloom's reveries fairly closely, with an eye on the progression of motif from motif.   It is Stephen who

tends to get the close reading, but the higher potential of
Stephen's thought is more apparent than real; the Stephen
monologues are a highly original pastiche of the decadent
sensibility, with a tang of smoking lamps and relished corruption. Bloom's mind, if he could manage to do something with
it, is far more inventive. Bloom, amid his associative driftings,
is ironically oblivious to the patterns in which his thoughts are
cast. Here, for example, after his vastly longing onanistic
tryst with Gerty MacDowell, is Bloom on the shore which
Stephen had visited nine hours before:

> Mr. Bloom stooped and turned over a piece of paper on the strand.
> He brought it near his eyes and peered. Letter? No. Can't read.
> Better go. Better. I'm too tired to move. Page of an old copy-
> book. All those holes and pebbles. Who could count them? Never
> know what you find. Bottle with story of a treasure in it thrown
> from a wreck. Parcels post. Children always want to throw things
> in the sea. Trust? Bred cast on the waters. What's this? Bit of
> stick. U374/364.

This moment is one of the many points of rapprochement
between Bloom and Stephen. It is also a rapprochement of
both to rationally directed aesthetic and perceptive activity.
The analogy of multiple parody runs:
Bloom : Stephen :: Stephen : Artist :: Artist : Unfallen Man.
Each strives uselessly towards an ideal conceived in pathetic
circumscription—Bloom strives to function as a romantic
artist; the romantic artist Stephen strives towards hiero-
phantic power, a Solomon's facility at reading the signatures of
all things; the artist whom Stephen cannot be strives towards a
prelapsarian efficacy, imposing names according to the essences
of things and functioning in a freedom contingent but quasi-
divine amid the luminous forms of an inexhaustibly intelligible
world. It is from this multiple perspective of inadequacy that
the swooning pathos of the latter half of the Nausicaa episode
derives. Stephen's

> Me sits there with his augur's rod of ash, in borrowed sandals, by
> day beside a livid sea, unbeheld, in violet night walking beneath a
> reign of uncouth stars. I throw this ended shadow from me, man-
> shape ineluctable, call it back, U49/45,

marks a Nietzschean-hermetic vision of magnetic power

conceived on a level not really distinct from Bloom's less-focussed musings; and it is Stephen's

> Who ever anywhere will read these written words?

that is echoed by Bloom's encounter with the copybook:

> He brought it near his eyes and peered. Letter? No. Can't read. Better go.

Bloom next echoes *King Lear:*

> All those holes and pebbles. Who could count them?

—as Stephen had echoed, more accurately, that morning:

> His boots trod again a damp crackling mast, razorshells, squeaking pebbles, that on the unnumbered pebbles beats.[1]. . . U41/37.

And as Stephen had read in terms of Conradian romanticism the signature of the bottle—

> A porterbottle stood up, stogged to its waist, in the cakey sand dough. A sentinel: isle of dreadful thirst, U42/38,

so Bloom in terms of *Treasure Island*

> Never know what you find. Bottle with story of a treasure in it thrown from a wreck. Parcels post.

These are modes of consciousness comparable in their inadequacy, in their anxiety to cover the object with a thick veil of dramatic sentiment; the ironies of Joyce's analogical vision are however not yet exhausted. Stephen's occasional devaluations of this sentiment (" When one reads these strange pages of one long gone one feels that one is at one with one who once . . .", U41/37) are wry, masochistic. He lives imprisoned in his own rhetoric of pathos. Bloom, as befits the Ulyssean wisdom, *polúmetis*, displays modes of sensibility haplessly inadequate to, but at least analogous with, genuine critical mobility. His " parcels post " as a reflection on messages cast from bottles is not only a shift of perspective, made innocently, that Stephen could only have made with corrosive irony, it is a genuine devaluation of schoolboy heroics. He goes on in unconscious correlation with the artist's primary urge:

> Children always want to throw things in the sea. Trust? Bred cast on the waters.

[1] *King Lear*, IV.vi.21.

The artist casts his bottles into the sea with an innocence of rhetorical intention analogous to that of the child; Stephen on the other hand glooms bitterly about the unlikelihood of finding a reader. The Scriptural analogy of trust—" Cast thy bread upon the waters "—receives from the loss of a letter an inflection shifting the whole train of speculation from the level of human communication to that of human generation with its ideal concomitant, implicit trust in Providence: children bred, cast upon the waters, found, as Bloom that night is to find the image of his Rudy, after many days. Bloom's thoughts return from the riddling tension of faith, bread cast on the waters, children bred and cast upon the sea of Dublin; messages from ships, from the sea of being, Treasure Island and the Kingdom of Heaven, as his eyes move from the eloquent bottle to the more inscrutable signature, perhaps the " damp crackling mast," genuine souvenir of a shipwreck as the bottle almost certainly is not, on which Stephen had trodden that morning:

What's this? Bit of stick.

Its inscrutability casts his thoughts in on himself, the themes of return, reduced now to the clichés of romantic fiction, continuing to reverberate:

O! Exhausted that female has me. Not so young now. Will she come here tomorrow? Wait for her somewhere for ever. Must come back. Murderers do. Will I?

Bloom, according to the analogies of the next section, has murdered the Oxen of the Sun, his coition with Gerty sterilized by some dozens of intervening yards of space. Oblivious of this implication, he shifts from the cadres of Ouida (" Wait for her somewhere for ever ") to those of Wilkie Collins (" Must come back. Murderers do.").

Mr. Bloom with his stick gently vexed the thick sand at his foot. Write a message for her. Might remain. What?
I.
Some flatfoot tramp on it in the morning. Useless. Washed away.

The echoes of Stephen's meditations grow still more insistent; the message writ in sand (" What? ") parallels the epiphany scribbled on the torn end of Deasy's letter (" Who ever anywhere will read these written words? ", U49/45). What

Bloom writes, of course, is the central romantic fact: " I ".
The parallel grows more intimate still:

> Tide comes here a pool near her feet. Bend, see my face there,
> dark mirror, breathe on it, stirs. All these rocks with lines and scars
> and letters. O those transparent!

What he contemplates as he addresses himself to literary composition, his doomed message to a hypothetical posterity, is a
distorted image of himself.[1] Hard by beckon the ontological
signatures he is powerless to read: " All these rocks with lines
and scars and letters." A further analogy intrudes itself,
Victorian science aping the artist as the doctor apes the priest:
the testament of the rocks, which however Bloom cannot read
even at the level of the Holmesian geologist with a magnifying
glass, still less at the level of the metaphysician. It is the
metaphysical level that is faintly suggested by the next phrase,
" O those transparent ": matter encasing form, Stephen's
" diaphane ", yielding layer after layer of intelligibility to the
penetrating contemplative vision. But this is only further
depth of irony—the referent of Bloom's phrase is silk stockings,
a " signature " which as a passage ten pages previous reminds us
he can read expertly:

> Swell of her calf. Transparent stockings, stretched to breaking
> point. Not like that frump today. A.E. Rumpled stockings. Or
> the one in Grafton Street. White. Wow! Beef to the heel.[2]

From " O those transparent " his mind moves to the misprint
in Martha's letter of the morning:

> Besides they don't know. What is the meaning of that other world.
> I called you naughty boy because I do not like.

Martha's letter had begun,

[1] Cf. Stephen's first recorded composition. Having celebrated " night and
the balmy breeze and the maiden lustre of the moon," he " went into his mother's
bedroom and gazed at his face for a long time in the mirror of her dressing
table ", P78/80.
[2] The loosestockinged frump with A.E. appears on page U163/154; Bloom
remarks appositely that aesthetes are usually tasteless. Joyce implies also that
A.E.'s vision penetrates no diaphane. Stephen's reflection on the lapidary, Old
Russell, burnishing his gem, " Grandfather ape gloating on a stolen hoard ",
U238/229, is perhaps a parallel allusion to the bearded prince of hermetists.
The beefy-heeled Grafton St. woman of Bloom's second reminiscence is on page
U165/156.

I am sorry you did not like my last letter. Why did you enclose
the stamps? I am awfully angry with you. I do wish I could
punish you for that. I called you naughty boy because I do not like
that other world. Please tell me what is the real meaning of that
word.... U76/70.

Her mis-type, " world " for " word ",[1] unconsciously echoes
the opening of St. John's gospel in a way that gives point to its
recurrence in Bloom's pattern of thoughts here. " That other
world "—the world of metaphysical signatures to which his
exegetical skill is inadequate, ludicrously parallels the word in
his letter that puzzled Martha the typist; like the god-like
artist, he has uttered a Word of power. No words of power,
however, present themselves now; his writing continues:

AM. A.
No room. Let it go.
Mr. Bloom effaced the letters with his slow boot. Hopeless thing
sand. Nothing grows in it. All fades. No fear of big vessel coming
up here. Except Guinness's barges. Round the Kish in eighty
days. Done half by design.
He flung his wooden pen away. The stick fell in silted sand,
stuck. Now if you were trying to do that for a week on end you
couldn't. Chance. We'll never meet again. But it was lovely.
Goodbye, dear. Thanks. Made me feel so young.

The significant moment here is the occurrence of the word
" Chance ", suggested to his mind by the behaviour of the
stick and suggesting to him in turn the fortuitous graces of the
quasi-meeting with Gerty. " Chance " is a node of intersecting themes; Bloom's continual inability to decide which
events have an intelligible pattern in them and which have not
is at the root of much of his pathos. He plays with ideas of
chance and destiny, the fortuitous and the ineluctable, as his
mood dictates; the scholastic definition of chance (see above,
Chapter 9) controls many of the ironies of Bloomsday.

Short snooze now if I had. Must be near nine. Liverpool boat
long gone. Not even the smoke. And she can do the other. Did
too. And Belfast. I won't go. Race there, race back to Ennis.

[1] Botched by the printer in the Random House and John Lane editions. Also
" write " four lines from the end of her letter should read " wrote ", and the slip
should be echoed by Bloom two paragraphs later: " Wonder did she wrote it
herself."

Let him. Just close my eyes a moment. Won't sleep though. Half dream. It never comes the same. Bat again. No harm in him. Just a few.

Thoughts of chance have brought him to total resignation: Bloom has reduced himself to the conditions of the " hopeless " sand in which nothing grows. He contemplates with equanimity the departure of the mailboat bearing Nannetti, on whose word had depended the ad from the proceeds of which he had planned to buy petticoats for Molly. He cares now neither to woo Molly nor to blame her; he decides not to dash from Ennis, where he is going for his father's anniversary, up to Belfast where Molly will be staying on her concert tour with Boylan, to enjoy a night with her:[1] " Let him." So deciding to surrender himself to daydream for " just a few " minutes, and dismissing as it flicks across his mind the idea of recapturing the Turkish dream, U374/364, of the previous night (" It never comes the same ") he dismisses the bat (" no harm in him ") as casually as he has just dismissed Boylan and relapses from his brief career as speculative philosopher and reader of metaphysical signatures into the world of " sweets of sin ":

> O sweety all your little girlwhite up I saw dirty bracegirdle made me do love sticky we two naughty Grace darling she him half past the bed met him pike hoses frillies for Raoul to perfume your wife black hair heave under embon *señorita* young eyes Mulvey plump years dreams return tail end Agendath swoony lovely showed me her next year in drawers return next in her next her next.

FLAUBERT AND DOUBLE PERSPECTIVE

With the aid of Senecan prose and the exploded period of the Renaissance rhetoricians, Joyce got a long way beyond

---

[1] Molly speculates on this contingency too: " then this day week were to go to Belfast just as well he has to go to Ennis his fathers anniversary the 27th it wouldnt be pleasant if he did suppose our rooms at the hotel were beside each other and any fooling went on in the new bed I couldnt tell him to stop and not bother me with him in the next room ... then he wouldnt believe next day we didnt do something its all very well a husband but you cant fool a lover after me telling him we never did anything of course he didnt believe me no its better hes going where he is ...", U732/707. The scrambled " he's " and " him's " make it, as Joyce intended, a little less than obvious which of the two Molly intends to deceive. Evidently, however, the shame she would avert is having Boylan know her husband has made love to her; Bloom might be inspired by a new bed to renew the ardours that lapsed late in 1893. U720/696.

Flaubert, but Flaubert's systematic incongruities remained his Archimedean fulcrum for altering the perspective of thought and feeling from phrase to phrase. In Flaubert this happens rather less sharply, but it continually happens:

> Peu importait à Bouvard le procédé. Il voulait s'instruire, descendre plus avant dans la connaissance des mœurs. Il relut Paul de Kock, feuilleta de vieux ermites de la Chaussée d'Antin.
> — Comment perdre son temps à des inepties pareilles! disait Pécuchet.
> — Mais par la suite ce sera fort curieux, comme documents.
> — Va te promener avec tes documents! Je demande quelque chose qui m'exalte, qui m'enlève aux misères de ce monde!
> Et Pécuchet, porté à l'idéal, tourna Bouvard, insensiblement, vers la tragédie.[1]

The rapid shifts—self-help to " la connaissance des moeurs " to Paul de Kock (Molly Bloom's favourite author); defense in the name of documentation and rebuttal in the name of " uplift "; the magnificently ironic " porté à l'idéal " of Pécuchet's deflection of Bouvard, " insensiblement ", to tragedy—need no comment. Their resemblance to the texture of Joyce's prose is still more readily seen in Flaubert's working notes for the unwritten ending of *Bouvard et Pécuchet:* it was the incongruities to be deployed that Flaubert schematized before undertaking a new sequence:

> ... si les convulsions qui existent depuis 89 continuent, sans fin entre deux issues, ces oscillations nous emporteront par leurs propres forces. Il n'y aura plus d'idéal, de religion, de moralité.
> L'Amérique aura conquis la terre.
> Avenir de la littérature.
> Pignouflisme universel. Tout ne sera plus qu'une vaste ribote d'ouvriers.
> Fin du monde par la cessation du calorique.[2]

The progression from total Americanization to workingmen's drunken revelry (" pignouflisme universel ") to " fin du monde " (according to current astronomical eschatology) is pure Bloomian association, corresponding to Joyce's naturalistic facade. The comic disparities on the other hand are pure Flaubertian irony: the transition from " Tout ne sera plus qu'une vaste ribote d'ouvriers " to " Fin du monde par la

[1] Flaubert, *Bouvard et Pécuchet*, V; *Oeuvres*, Pléiade, ii, 785–786.
[2] *Ibid*, ii, 941.

cessation du calorique " is made via one common element (each would be a Bad Thing) in Bloomesque disregard of the disparity between political malaise (conviction that the working classes, if only slightly encouraged, would riot) and apocalyptic despair (gloomy certainty that the sun will burn out).

The critical consciousness that controls the bushels of documentation in *Ulysses* constantly manifests itself in similar rhetorical non-sequiturs. Here is an assemblage of novelistic postures belonging to Gerty MacDowell's day-dream; the better to spring the trap of the example I omit for the nonce the one devaluing word:

> Her words rang out crystalclear, more musical than the cooing of the ringdove but they cut the silence icily. There was that in her young voice that told that she was not a one to be lightly trifled with. As for Mr Reggy with his swank and his bit of money she could just chuck him aside as if he was so much filth and never again would she cast as much as a second thought on him and tear his silly (——) into a dozen pieces. U356/346.

This is authentic enough novelese; the pace perhaps a bit spurious, gotten by under-punctuation; the musical coo of the ringdove is a trifle out of key with silence cut icily; " there was that in her young voice which " is a gesture a little shopworn. A careful reader might smell parody. But the surprising *peripeteia* comes with the word omitted from the last line of our quotation. The word is not " missive " or " epistle ". It is not even " letter ". The word is " postcard ".

This double perspective is typical of Joyce's thematic complexity. Gerty is as inadequate to the decorums of the bad novel as these are inadequate to rational behaviour. The novelist's gestures amid Bernhardtian stage-props are already sufficiently incongruous in terms of the genuine passions they invoke. And Gerty invokes *them* in connection with an amorous postcard.

The second half of the same paragraph employs a different device; self-conscious passion is broken up into units of incongruity by a scrupulous mixing of metaphors that indicates Gerty's reliance on unsorted clichés (italics mine):

> Miss puny little Edy's *countenance fell* to *no slight extent* and Gerty could see by her *looking as black as thunder* that she was simply *in a towering rage* though she hid it, the little kinnatt because *that shaft had struck home* for her *petty jealousy* and they both knew that she

was something aloof, *apart in another sphere*, that she was *not of them* and there was *somebody else too* that knew it and saw it so they could *put that in their pipe and smoke it.*

This is not simple, and nothing in *Ulysses* is simpler. We have not merely a transcription of Gerty's thoughts. We have a delicately-adjusted relationship between mature emotion, novelistic clichés, Gerty's way of perceiving her own feelings, and Gerty's feelings themselves.

"IDEAS" IN THREEFOLD ANALOGY

In the same way, Bloom's thoughts are not naturalistically transcribed, but held in a matrix of irony. The naturalistic façade consists in a strong probability inhering in their sequence; the critical effect consists in the patterns of intelligibility their juxtaposition generates. Bloom has just read the letter from Martha:

> Flat Dublin voices bawled in his head. Those two sluts that night in the Coombe, linked together in the rain.
> *O, Mairy lost the pin of her drawers.*
> *She didn't know what to do*
> *To keep it up*
> *To keep it up.*
> It? Them. Such a bad headache. Has her roses probably. Or sitting all day typing. Eyefocus bad for stomach nerves. What perfume does your wife use? Now could you make out a thing like that?
> *To keep it up.*
> Martha, Mary. I saw that picture somewhere I forget now old master or faked for money. He is sitting in their house, talking. Mysterious. Also the two sluts in the Coombe would listen.
> *To keep it up.*
> Nice kind of evening feeling. No more wandering about. Just loll there: quiet dusk: let everything rip. Forget. Tell about places you have been, strange customs. The other one, jar on her head, was getting the supper: fruit, olives, lovely cool water out of the well stonecold like the hole in the wall at Ashtown. Must carry a paper goblet next time I go to the trottingmatches. She listens with big dark soft eyes. Tell her: more and more: all. Then a sigh: silence. Long long long rest. U77/71.

That these connections are made by associative drift is of the texture of the irony. The données—bawling voices recalling the song about " Mairy " that fuse with his thoughts of Martha and so, via Martha and Mary of Bethany, with the memory of the Bible picture—are simple enough. They undergo astonishing permutations of feeling that reach by analogy far outside Bloom's consciousness. The Protagonist of the picture is never mentioned; the rhythm of Bloom's thought quickens as he considers its cultural status (" old master or faked for money ") and as he recalls cold water at Ashtown (" must carry a paper goblet next time I go to the trottingmatches "); for the rest he reclines in a lotus-eaters' peace which parodies the Peace that passeth understanding that was brought into the house at Bethany:

> And Jesus answered and said unto her, Martha, Martha, thou art careful and troubled about many things: but one thing is needful: and Mary hath chosen that good part, which shall not be taken away from her.[1]

Bloom is never more alert than when he is troubled about many things; Martha's typing, faked old masters, trottingmatches; the good part which another segment of his being chooses is not the contemplation of the Word but postcoital languor: " Let everything rip. Forget." The East and the dissolution of volition he muddles with his sensuous approximations to divinity, with his masochistic compulsions, a Prufrockian " Tell her: more and more: all ", with his feeling for " big dark soft eyes." Yet this is the moment when he is most explicitly concerned with the Imitation of Christ, as Stephen 28 pages earlier had aspired in his capacity of artist to the Imitation of God:

> *Et vidit Deus. Et erant valde bona.*[2] Alo! *Bonjour,* welcome as the flowers in May. Under its leaf he watched through peacock-twittering lashes the southing sun. I am caught in this burning scene. Pan's hour, the faunal noon. Among gumheavy serpent-plants, milkoozing fruits, where on the tawny waters leaves lie wide. Pain is far. U50/46.

These passages are not to be read as lulling fruity oozings of sensuality. The critical alertness that has shifted the modes of consciousness of this prose from plane to plane in portrayal not of minds gripped by intuited reality but of sensibilities waiting upon inturning appetites, needs to be met with a like

---

[1] Luke X, 41–42.
[2] Genesis I, 31.

alertness of response.   Stephen and Bloom are visited all day long by teasing fragments of ideas, and it is easy to read *Ulysses* in a mood of languid assent to these incompatible and unrealized modes of thought.   Wyndham Lewis' assertion, correct in one sense, that the book contains no " ideas " whatever, the contrasting excesses of Stuart Gilbert's Bloomesque introductory chapters on its esoteric philosophy, should warn us that it is precisely the pathetic absurdity of Bloom's and Stephen's bits and pieces of speculation that is being exposed.   Such conceptions as Karma and Metempsychosis apply with ironic punctilio both to Bloom's and Stephen's quasi-hypnotized actions and to the emotional quality of their thought.   And these conceptions are implicitly evaluated by the quality of those actions and that thought.   This evaluation in turn brings us into the realm of the controlling ideas of the book, the rational ethics and metaphysics of the free intelligence, gestured towards by Stephen in his sententious appeals to Aquinas and Aristotle, and by Bloom in the fidelity of his thought, despite its negligible penetration, to empirical reality; belied by Stephen and Bloom alike in their, respectively, hubristic and masochistic narcissism.   The controlling ideas are never stated.   They exist, like magnetic fields, behind and around the words, apprehensible through perspectives of triple analogy.   Joyce's irony goes deep indeed.   Not only does Bloom not know that he is Ulysses (the meaning of his own actions);   he does not know that he is an analogue of Christ inhabiting a sacramental universe (the meaning of his own thoughts).   Stephen on the other hand is aware that he is Hamlet, but his awareness is put to the wrong uses.   It provides him with no insight.   It merely feeds his morbidity.   It is a role in which he is imprisoned.   He is constantly aware of an infinitely extending perspective of future selves to be traversed and assimilated.

> The existing monuments form an ideal order among themselves, which is modified by the introduction of the new (the really new) work of art among them.   The existing order is complete before the new work arrives;   for order to persist after the supervention of novelty, the whole existing order must be, if ever so slightly altered. . . .[1]

For works of art read men and cultures.   The various cultural

[1] T. S. Eliot, *Selected Essays:* " Tradition and the Individual Talent."

organisms which for the contemporary sensibility constitute
aesthetic objects form an ideal order which is totally overhauled
by the arrival among them of the contemporary culture
represented by Leopold Bloom. This is true of Homer, it is
true of *Hamlet*, it is true of nineteenth-century complacency,
it is true of the various modes of consciousness epiphanized
in turn in " The Oxen of the Sun ". The graveyard monuments constitute such an order:

> The high railings of Prospects rippled past their gaze. Dark
> poplars, rare white forms. Forms more frequent, white shapes
> thronged amid the trees, white forms and fragments streaming by
> mutely, sustaining vain gestures on the air. U99/92.

A few pages later this is modulated into the individual talent
of Mr. Bloom confronting the buried traditions of Ireland:

> Mr. Bloom walked unheeded along his grove by saddened angels,
> crosses, broken pillars, family vaults, stone hopes praying with upcast
> eyes, old Ireland's hearts and hands. U111/105.

That " saddened " brings to life the stones of " Cormac's
ruined house; " that " unheeded " locates Bloom in several
frames of reference. And this graveyard which bespeaks the
presence of the past and the stony immortalization of the
temporal:

> (Those are pearls that were his eyes. Look!)

—epiphanizes the Dublin amidst whose similar relics Mr.
Bloom walks all day: Dublin an immense graveyard of buried
hopes, heroic promises dead, promised Homeric heroisms
shrunken to the fulfilment of a Bloom:

> And I Tiresias have foresuffered all
> Enacted on this same divan or bed
> I who have sat by Thebes below the wall
> And walked among the lowest of the dead.

" In a peculiar sense ", Eliot goes on, " he will be aware also
that he must inevitably be judged by the standards of the past."
So it is with Joyce's contemporary Dubliner as with the contemporary artist: the one unheedingly, the other by willed
baptismal immersion, plunged into the presence of the past.

> I say judged, not amputated, by them: not judged to be as good as,
> or worse or better than, the dead; and certainly not judged by the
> canons of dead critics. It is a judgment, a comparison, in which
> two things are measured by each other.

DEATH BY WATER

One ambivalent theme-word illuminates a great deal of the book: "Agenbite of inwit" opens into a twofold drowning, death by water as extinction and as redemption, exactly as in *The Waste Land*. Its real meaning (again-bite: re-mordere) is "remorse of conscience"; but by a fancifully plausible etymology, mistakenly perpetrated by the first modern editor of Dan Michel's treatise, it can signify again-buying, redemption, of the soul. An editorial note in the standard Early English Texts Society edition, which softens its rebuke to the early editor by citing Wyclif's use of "Agen-buying" for "redemption", probably suggested this ambiguity to Joyce; Stephen, who twice refers to Christ as "Agenbuyer", U195/186, U385/374, seems to have looked into the same edition.

Bloom undergoes extinction in a metaphorical sea, presided over by the storm-bringer, *dio boia*, of the sea of matter. The sea at last becomes amniotic fluid for his foetal attitude at the end of the day; but until then the ominous rumble of the thunder-god is heard and feared. Only once Christ as Bread of Life appears darkly, behind Bloom's gift of Banbury cake to the sea-gulls:

> They never expected that. Manna. Live on fishy flesh they have to, all sea birds, gulls, seagoose. U151/142.

(The Christian connotations of "fish" are of course employed here by Joyce, if not by Bloom.)

It is in Stephen Dedalus' meditations that the motif of drowning is most strongly developed. In the second chapter, an Icarus who has fallen into Dublin sea, he hears a schoolboy recite *Lycidas*:

> Weep no more, woeful shepherd, weep no more
> For Lycidas, your sorrow, is not dead,
> Sunk though he be beneath the watery floor.... U26/23.

The interrupted quotation is taken up at the next key line:

> Through the dear might of him that walked the waves.

Christ who walked the waves and whose baptismal water redeems from drowning in matter is Stephen's avowed analogue when he determines in the *Portrait* to be a "priest of the eternal imagination" and a Saviour of the conscience of his race. But water he fears, and his Christian inadequacy is confessed under this figure (" I've been born and once is enough! "). Mulligan the doctor (priest of matter, saviour of the body) had rescued a drowning man. Not only has Stephen no hope of such an exploit, but from his own spiritual drowning, when he has sunken to the pavement of Mabbot Street, he has to be rescued by Bloom:

> Would you do what he did? A boat would be near, a lifebuoy. . . . Would you or would you not? The man that was drowned nine days ago off Maiden's rock. They are waiting for him now. The truth, spit it out . . . I would want to. I would try. I am not a strong swimmer. . . . If I had land under my feet. I want his life still to be his, mine to be mine. A drowning man. His human eyes scream to me out of horror of his death. I . . . with him together down . . . I could not save her. Waters: bitter death: lost. U46/42.

Stephen's mother (" I could not save her ") fuses with the drowning man from the horror of whose fate he shrinks:

> She is drowning. Agenbite. Save her. Agenbite. All against us. She will drown me with her, eyes and hair. Lank coils of seaweed hair around me, my heart, my soul. Salt green death.
> We.
> Agenbite of misery. Inwit's agenbite.
> Misery! Misery! U240/230.

Agenbite—remorse for Stephen. Agenbite—redemption for the mother. " I pray for you in my other world ", U566/548.

And it is in connection with drowning, physical dissolution into circumambient matter (the death which Tiresias prophesied for Odysseus, " mildest of all deaths known to man ", which Bloom has gradually long since undergone), that the theme of eternal recurrence (the Wheel of Mme. Sosostris' pack), the metempsychosis which puzzled Molly Bloom, achieves its sharpest definition:

> Bag of corpsegas sopping in foul brine. A quiver of minnows, fat of a spongy titbit, flash through the slits of his buttoned trouserfly. God becomes man becomes fish becomes barnacle goose becomes featherbed mountain. Dead breaths I living breathe, tread dead dust, devour a urinous offal from all dead. Hauled stark over the gunwale he breathes upward the stench of his green grave, his leprous nosehole snoring to the sun.
> A seachange this, brown eyes saltblue. Seadeath, mildest of all deaths known to man. Old Father Ocean. *Prix de Paris*: beware of imitations. Just you give it a fair trial. We enjoyed ourselves immensely. U51/47.

The material cycle, the perpetual transmigration of matter into other and other bodies, parallels here the cultural cycle which obsessed Joyce through Vico, and which Eliot explores in *East Coker*. " God becomes man "—the Incarnation—" becomes fish "—the redeemed Christian, joyous inhabitant of water—" becomes barnacle goose "—the popular name for an exile from the Irish community—" becomes featherbed mountain." The mountain: inert rock: a phallic masculine totem. Featherbed: the feminine bed of lust. Featherbed Mountain it is that dominates Dublin.

The " urinous offal from all dead " is precisely what Mr. Bloom, as we are told at his first appearance on the next page, most delectates. " Most of all he liked grilled mutton kidneys, which gave to his palate a fine tang of faintly scented urine." Sufferer of that degrading seachange, he " enjoys himself immensely ".

The agen-buying, redemption, of rebirth by water chooses another form as *better;* the appetite of matter in its perpetual metamorphoses (death by water) is for form as *other*. The distinction is crucial.

Chapter 13

THE TRIVIUM IN DUBLIN

> Sllt. The nethermost deck of the first machine jogged forward
> its flyboard with sllt the first batch of quirefolded papers. Sllt.
> Almost human the way it sllt to call attention. Doing its level best
> to speak. That door too sllt creaking, asking to be shut. Every-
> thing speaks in its own way. Sllt.
>
> *Ulysses* (U120/113)

Ulysses, like a Renaissance epic, embraces every province of
rhetoric. All of them smell of the counterfeiter's ink, however,
and the succession of pastiches in episode 14 brings tokens of
contrivance frankly to the surface. Joyce is carefully repro-
ducing the spurious Dublin life of an embalmed past. Furthermore, the three men who dominate the book afford lunar
reflections of the three disciplines of the trivium Joyce had from
his Jesuit masters. He was interested in grammar, logic, and
rhetoric because he always started from what was before him,
and dwarfed mutants of these three modes were there before
him, in the Dublin of 1904. Stephen, Mulligan, and Bloom
are respectively a reader of signatures, a master of ironic disputation, and a frustrated *doctus orator*.

1. MR. BLOOM AND RHETORIC AS
PRACTICAL POLITICS

Rhetoric in its best ages was safeguarded by a sense of civic
responsibility. That is what underwrites Cicero; that is what
made him an educational model for centuries. That was the
area in which there still existed in Dublin a civilization corresponding, though inertly, to what Joyce received from his
schoolmasters. The orator united civic learning with wide
practical experience:

> ... Hear him debate on commonwealth affairs,
> You would say it hath been all in all his study. ...

Bloom is the Ciceronian *doctus orator* in final decay. He goes
through the day uttering an immensely intricate monologue

that no one hears. A speech that Joyce specially indicated to Frank Budgen establishes this orientation clearly:

> I declare to my antimacassar if you took up a straw from the bloody floor and if you said to Bloom: *Look at, Bloom. Do you see that straw? That's a straw.* Declare to my aunt he'd talk about it for an hour so he would and talk steady. U311/301.

This is from the Cyclops episode, the "art" of which is Politics. Bloom is at his most loquacious here, on capital punishment, physiological phenomena, Irish rebels, Gaelic, drink, trust funds, diseases of cattle, violent exercise, lawn tennis and the circulation of the blood, etc., etc., though little of his eloquence is allowed to come through to us. Joyce's comment on the passage about the straw was,

> " You see, ' I ' is really a great admirer of Bloom who, besides being a better man , is also more cunning, a better talker, and more fertile in expedients. If you reread *Troilus and Cressida* you will see that of all the heroes Thersites respects only Ulysses. Thersites admires Ulysses." [1]

That Joyce regarded Shakespeare's Ulysses as relevant is a most important fact. Shakespeare's Ulysses is a Renaissance perspective on Homer's—the Ciceronian ruler once more, copiously eloquent wisdom combined with great practical experience and insight. Bloom's background of experience is carefully documented: he has worked for a stationer, U153/143, the directory publishers, U153/144, cattle dealers, U59/52, and now "cadges ads", U419/408. Each of these jobs is of the sort that brings a wide variety of public contacts. In his hallucinated progression to the rank of King Leopold the First, it is on his eloquence that stress continually falls:. he orates as workman, U469/455, as alderman, U468/455, as King, U474/460. And like Shakespeare's Henry V (" Hear him but reason in divinity . . .") he administers " free medical and legal advice, solution of doubles and other problems ", U577/463. (Since the material in which the ruler worked, so to speak, was the Commonwealth, he was expected to have a grasp of the principles of every human pursuit.)

Joyce said too that Bloom was " a complete man—a good man."[2] Eloquent master of every province of learning, capable

---

[1] Budgen, 169.
[2] Budgen, 18.

of continuous flexible response to every possible human situation, paradigm of all the moral virtues as enumerated by rational psychology—these are the Ciceronian notes of complete humanity. As the old commentators saw, Odysseus, *polúmetis*, never at a loss, exemplified this ideal admirably. So did Christ, with whom Bloom is connected by a tissue of analogies. The early Christian conception of *Christus Rhetor*[1] indicates once more the moral completeness that was felt to inhere in the eloquent ideal.

BLOOM AND SENECA

Bloom's discourse isn't civic and expansive, however. It coagulates into aphorism. Mottos are conned. Reflection seldom goes a sentence beyond observation. Self-improvement, a domestic rather than a civic bias, a boundless curiosity about how things are worked, define a mind the polar opposite of the Irish public man or the Ciceronian Odysseus of the Renaissance. It is with the anti-Ciceronians in fact that Bloom is aligned. They are not " moderns ". Their pedigree extends from the exponents of Attic severity contemporary with Cicero himself.

The anti-Ciceronian ideal was modelled on Seneca, who in the middle ages came to stand for private virtues and aphoristic wisdom leavening the *res publica*, rather than public virtue and eloquent wisdom.[2] Bacon's axioms, and his defense thereof, are Senecan; so is the epigrammatic moralism of Pope's couplets; so is the prose of Montaigne. The Enlightenment, which drew on Montaigne and nourished Pope, had a core of Senecan wisdom to which the eighteenth-century discovery of Confucius, who also recommended the perfection of personal virtue as the foundation of public order, and employed an epigrammatic delivery of insights, proved thoroughly congenial.

The Enlightenment has its comic side. It parodies itself in the saws of Poor Richard and the pollyannaism of Soame Jenyns, whom Johnson trampled. After 150 years the cancerous nuclei had so far displaced the organized tissue as to fill Christendom with twenty million Blooms. The status accorded

---

[1] See Christopher Dawson, *The Making of Europe*.
[2] This was naturally congenial to the Christian distrust of magnificence. For the Senecan bias of the mediaeval view of the theologian, see Gilson's *Héloïse et Abélard*, Paris, 1938, 61 ff.

by Anglo-Saxonry to Bloom's elder contemporary H. G. Wells is a major sociological datum.

Bloom is a parody of the Enlightenment which was itself a slicking-up of the idealized Seneca. His domestic orientations imply a Senecan bias, and his penchant for tinkering and boundless curiosity give us the Enlightenment in a mocking mirror. The very texture of his inner speech resembles the special prose developed by the Renaissance anti-Ciceronians, whose " dependence on casual and emergent devices of construction might sometimes be mistaken for mere indifference to art or contempt of form " (cf. the early reviews of *Ulysses*), and whose " purpose was to portray, not a thought, but a mind thinking, or in Pascal's words, *la peinture de la pensée* "[1] (a phrase which may save our being staggered by the novelty of the interior monologue). Dr. Croll quotes a characteristic " exploded " period from Sir Henry Wotton:

> Men must beware of running down steep places with weighty bodies; they once in motion, *suo feruntur pondere*; steps are not then voluntary.

" The members of this sentence stand farther apart one from another than they would in a Ciceronian sentence, there are no syntactic connectives between them whatever; and semicolons or colons are necessary to its proper punctuation; in fact, it has the appearance of having been disrupted by an explosion from within." Joyce disrupts the Bloomian periods yet more:

> Rusty wreaths hung on knobs, garlands of bronzefoil. Better value that for the money. Still, the flowers are more poetical. The other gets tiresome, never withering. Expresses nothing. Immortelles. U112.

Full stops instead of colons and semicolons; but it is still a sophisticated rhetoric Joyce is employing, with a long tradition; not a mechanical reconstruction of associative processes. Each paragraph has its finely-intuited cadence.

2. STEPHEN DEDALUS AND GRAMMAR AS SCIENTIFIC METHOD

Stress should fall on the utility, rather than the oddness, of Joyce's student researches in Skeat's *Etymological Dictionary* and of the experiments with words recalled in *Stephen Hero*.

[1] M. W Croll, " The Baroque Style in English Prose ", *Studies in English Philology*, ed. K. Malone and M. B. Rand, Minneapolis, 1929, 429–430.

He sought to empty words of their " instantaneous meaning "
and restore them to the status of "wonderful vocables",
S30/23, not in quest of dadaist unmeaning but through a
determination to implicate the meaning in the word's expressive gesture.   There is nothing esoteric about this.   The writer
can only use words when he knows them.   Writing is solid
when the word sticks close to the thing; in Bacon's market-
place it gets attached merely to contiguous words.   The
terminology that will bear stress is anchored to things by etymology, or to social usage by intrinsic gesture.   The war on
cliché involves grammatical scrutiny of words and things alike:
in the previous paragraph of *Stephen Hero* we hear of Joyce's
morning walk to the college:

> He got down off the tram at Amiens St Station instead of going on
> to the Pillar because he wished to partake in the morning life of the
> city.   This morning walk was pleasant for him and there was no
> face that passed him on its way to its commercial prison but he
> strove to pierce to the motive centre of its ugliness.   S30/23.

In the streets he was collecting the materials of *Dubliners;*
in the library, laying hold on a relation between language and
reality which would give him leverage to expose the gaps
between Dublin words and Dublin facts.   The artist defines,
pins down, what is there.   What is there includes, in addition
to what he can see, the language he hears and reads.   Joyce is
never far from lexicography, whether converting a slogan like
" sex appeal " into " Silks apeel ", F508, or pinning down the
Dublin meaning of " good wife ":

> But she never weakened in her religion and was a good wife to him.
> At some party in a strange house when she lifted her eyebrow ever
> so slightly he stood up to take his leave and, when his cough troubled
> him, she put the eiderdown quilt over his feet and made him a
> strong rum punch.   D172/154.

A phrase like " Lugubru Blooloohoom ", U426/414, not only
extends the expressive gestures of the words, it precisely defines
the caressing self-pity of lugubrious Bloom.   Such exactitudes
are not obtained by absorption in the arrangements of sounds
and letters alone; nor by the neglect of such attention.   Joyce
early became conscious of a universe of words containing
potentially all the rhythm and order of which man is capable,
littered in fact with the flotsam and jetsam of order inter-
mittently achieved, and ruffled and tossed by every squall

and catspaw, every inequality of pressure in the social order moving above it. By systematizing such studies he made contact with classical grammar, an art whose assumptions underlie every part of his work.

No word has grown more debased; what grammar meant in Shakespeare's grammar-school in Stratford was the art of reading; more generally, exegetical technique: the scrutiny and elucidation of the materials in which one proposed to work, whether scripture, literature, the book of creation, or human nature. What held this art together was the great doctrine of the Logos, which takes an eighteenth-century curtain-call in the role of Pope's reason-and-nature. It is unnecessary for the reader of Joyce to become embroiled in the mystique with which this conception was from time to time surrounded: suffice it to say that from Plato's *Cratylus* till the Cartesian revolution language was seen as simultaneously linking and harmonizing all the intellectual and physical functions of men with the order of the universe. By the Neo-Platonists and Augustine, by Bonaventure and Francis Bacon, the world was viewed as a book, the lost language of which was analogous to human speech.

GRAMMAR AND THE SYMBOLISTS

Mallarmé's great lines toward the climax of *Toast Funèbre* register the degree of recovery of patristic grammar in nineteenth-century France:

> Le Maître, par un œil profond, a, sur ses pas,
> Apaisé de l'éden l'inquiète merveille
> Dont le frisson final, dans sa voix seule, éveille
> Pour la Rose et le Lys le mystère d'un nom.
> Est-il de ce destin rien qui demeure, non?
> Ô vous tous, oubliez une croyance sombre.
> Le splendide génie éternel n'a pas d'ombre.

[" Ce destin " is not simply that of the dead poet, but that of Eden, whose marvellous inquietude, significances urging to be appeased by elucidation, testifies to the survival, beneath the opacities induced by the Fall, of the " splendide génie éternel " of the Creator's intelligible order. " Ses pas ", likewise, are both the footsteps of the peripatetic voyant and Augustine's *vestigiae Dei*, the imprint left on every detail of creation. The capitalized " Maître " fuses the poet as elucidator with *Christus Rhetor*.]

The Yeats who absorbed Arthur Symons' tidings of Mallarmé was also interested in theosophy and Blakean

exegesis; and Dublin being what it was, attached his real
enthusiasms to the latter group of interests rather than to the
former.   The theosophy with which *Ulysses* is saturated is the
Dublin version of the Symbolist concern with " le mystère d'un
nom ".   Historically the lunatic fringe of grammar, it was the
mode in which, via Yeats and AE, grammar presented itself in
Dublin, just as rhetoric presented itself via J. J. O'Molloy and
Professor MacHugh.   An error that deforms Mr. Gilbert's
entire study of *Ulysses* is the supposition that alchemy and
theosophy represented the most serious mode in which these
studies had ever existed.

France, however, has never lacked patristic scholars, and
within a generation the interests adumbrated by Hugo's
Cabbalism had recovered their true co-ordinates, phoenix
emerging from the Cartesian bonfire.   Hugo lacked orientations.   He simply swallowed the Cabbala.   Baudelaire tran-
scended a hermetic paraphernalia of cats and mummies to
intuit the " ténébreuse et profonde unité " of *Correspondances*,

> La Nature est un temple où de vivants piliers
> Laissent parfois sortir de confuses paroles ;
> L'homme y passe à travers des forêts de symboles
> Qui l'observent avec des regards familiers,

which has puzzled many teachers of French but to grammarians
like St. Augustine or Francis Bacon (cf. his Salomon's House)
would have seemed a perfunctory gesture toward the familiar
and orthodox.   Rimbaud's instinct rightly placed alchemy,
without hermetic bric-à-brac, in the same context—the
Alchimie du Verbe (" Each element, detached from the surroundings in which we are accustomed to see it placed, instead
of just belonging to a set of classified things, acquires a
personality and a soul.   By and by the whole world seems to
become queerly animated.").[1]   Mallarmé, finally, installed
himself in the heart of the tradition, the poet interpreting
vestigiae Dei and manipulating the analogies between the world
of words and the world of things to illuminate once more the
obliterated pre-Adamite order:

> Une agitation solennelle par l'air
> De paroles, pourpre ivre et grand calice clair,
> Que, pluie et diamant, le regard diaphane
> Resté là sur ses fleurs dont nulle ne se fane,
> Isole parmi l'heure et le rayon du jour!

[1] Georges Lemaitre, *From Cubism to Surrealism in French Literature.*

THE WORLD AS BOOK

Man, then, is placed in the world as before a book. That is the tradition to which Joyce refers when he makes Stephen say of his vocation qua man and qua artist, " Signatures of all things I am here to read ", U38/33. As the writer of a mediaeval Franciscan *Ars Concionandi* tells us,

> Verily, if God has set his creation before men's eyes, it is not only to nourish them but also to instruct them: thus we read in the Evangelist, " Consider the lilies of the field, how they grow; consider the fig-tree, and all the other trees." And in Solomon, " Go to the ant, thou sluggard." Or Job, " Ask the animals, and they shall answer." David alludes to this mode, when he says, " Thy works have rejoiced my soul "; for what he here calls the works of God, is the world.... Now whoever would busy himself with this kind of development, has at his disposal a useful book, the world, whose every part instructs him and leads him to God."[1]

In Renaissance England, to take but one example, we find Donne referring to " that great Library, those infinite volumes of the Books of Creatures ", and remarking that " a Beehive, that an Ant-hill is the same book in *Decimo sexto* that a Kingdom is in *folio* ".[2] And if things are books, books are things. In orienting his readers toward the grammar-school of Quintilian, Professor Colson writes of the Christian-Roman promoters of the Logos:

> ... The analogist argues from the unchanging order which prevails in the heavenly bodies, in the tides, in the continuity of species ... language is conceived as a world in itself, much as we conceive of the visible world ... he is as confident ... as the scientific man of today ... as impatient of the suggestion of disorder.... The world of words had a glamour and a wonder for them which it cannot have for us.[3]

It isn't necessary to emphasize how in Leopold Bloom the ideal orator, Ciceronian or Senecan, is both thwarted and debased. What is more fundamental, Bloom's rhetorical activities are deflected towards exegesis of phenomena, in which he is still less proficient. On the beach at nightfall, he contemplates the " signatures "—rocks, sand, bottle, mast, U374/364—which Stephen in the morning has read, if not

---

[1] Quoted by E. Gilson, *Les Idées et les Lettres*, Paris, 1932, 142.
[2] L. P. Smith, *Selections from the Sermons of John Donne*, 234.
[3] F. H. Colson, *Quintilian, Book I*.

with Adamite ease, at least with impressive flexibility of insight. Throughout the day it is grammatical activity that is forced on him; every object on which his eye lights prompts a question or suggests a significance he never quite manages to grasp. At one point a witty exegesis of one of Molly's puns delights him, U152/143, but it is a comic phantom of the subtleties of patristic etymology.

As Bloom is a comic *doctus orator*, so is Stephen a comic grammarian. Grammar is his métier. The Art assigned to the long monologue (" Proteus ") that opens with the sentence about reading signatures is Philology, which seems a pedantic joke until we realize that Joyce is indicating the relevance to art and metaphysics of linguistic science in the classic sense. These are the bearings of the role Stephen would like to play; it is unbalanced by the defect of sincerity which shifts Stephen's centre of gravity from things to Stephen. Thus as Bloom is a rhetorician forced dumbly towards grammar, so it is as dialectician in the library that Stephen the protogrammarian gives the most expert account of himself.

3. MULLIGAN AND DIALECTICS AS DISPUTATION

Mulligan, to complete this round robin, is a dialectician[1] enjoying rhetorical functions as stage Irishman. He is a dialectician via his irresponsible plausibility, in touch with nothing but his own wit (" I remember only ideas and sensations ", U10/6, is his tellingly Lockeian confession). This is the contemporary mode of dialectics: not logic-chopping so much as insulation from fact. Despite superficial " Irish " resemblances, Mulligan must be carefully distinguished from Dedalus père, an exhibitionist of another and aristocratic order. Mulligan's aristocracy—" Why don't you play them as I do? ", U18/14—is as facile as his other poses. He is the archetype of the social engineer.

The Art of the section of *Ulysses* he dominates (significantly,

[1] " The difference between the method of Erasmus and that of Abailard may therefore be stated as that between a use of the three arts oriented to an understanding of a passage (that is, the three arts arranged in accordance with the needs of grammar) and the use of the three arts oriented to a comparative estimation of a variety of arguments (that is, the three arts arranged under the dominance of dialectic)." R. P. McKeon, " Renaissance and Method in Philosophy ", *Studies in the History of Ideas*, N.Y., 1935, III, 81.

the first one in the book) is Theology; the Technic of the section in which he appears at his extravagant wittiest, stealing the latter end of the show from Stephen, is Dialectic. The collocation should be noted. As we shall see later, Mulligan in the first episode is primarily priest (as doctor, the priest of matter, saviour of the body). And dialectical theology was regarded from the twelfth to the eighteenth centuries both as the perversion of theology and as the enemy of humane letters (this is one meaning of the antipathy between Mulligan and Stephen). The twelfth-century rise of the University of Paris and the achievement of men like Abelard engendered the " scholasticism "—dialectics escaping from its Augustianian subordination to rhetoric and grammar—which until recently historians have allowed us to imagine as blotting out the entire middle ages between the fifth century and the fifteenth. It did blot out, as far as it could, the allegorical methods with which it is often confused. For the upholders of the latter, the dialectician, like Buck Mulligan, is the perennial *usurper* and the Grand Renaissance, like the renaissance of the Carolingian epoch, was a renaissance of grammar and rhetoric against his domination.[1]

The role of Irish scholars like Erigena in the Carolingian renaissance indicates how thoroughly the patristic, allegorical, grammatical tradition was intertextured with the early Irish Church. The elaborate iconography of Irish illuminations, as in the *Book of Kells* with which, as Joyce indicates, *Finnegans Wake* is analogous, is the visual counterpart of the intricacies of patristic scriptural exegesis. The quarrel of dialectics and grammar is one dimension of the fable of the Mookse and the Gripes. The Mookse, like a disputatious scholastic dialectician, gathers together his voluminous authorities and delivers 111 proofs " by Neuclidius and Inexagoras and Mumfsen and Thumpsem, by Orasmus and by Amenius, . . . by the binomial dioram . . . and all the mummyscrips in Sock Boke's Juncroom and the Chapters for the Cunning of the Chapters of the Conning Fox by Tail ", F155. The motto of the Irish Gripes, however, " My spetial inexshellsis the belowing things ab ove ", F154, is a hermetic grammatical formula, exploring the connections of things below, tracing

---

[1] The documentation behind this exceedingly compressed account was collected by Prof. H. M. McLuhan in his unpublished History of the Trivium, which he has generously placed at my disposal.

their ontological hierarchies *ab ovo*, and expounding their relationships with things above.

In modern times the theology of the Irish clergy, in sharp contrast to the patristic flourishing of earlier centuries, has been almost exclusively dialectical. This perversion, traceable to the time when the proscribed clergy got their training in seventeenth-century French seminaries, sorts with the philosophy of Descartes and Locke, a web of propositions whose analogies with the sensate culture of Joyce's Dublin are profound.

It should be noted that Joyce makes Theology and Religion separate arts in modern Dublin. When the former turns its face towards categories and disputation, the latter slips toward lotus-eating.

In the library scene, Stephen is tortured by the dialectical role he finds forced on him:

> What the hell are you driving at?
> I know. Shut up. Blast you! I have reasons.
> *Amplius. Adhuc. Iterum. Postea.*
> Are you condemned to do this? U205/196.

Meanwhile Mulligan, the supple master of propositional superficies, the " usurper ", U24/21, as for the humanists the schoolmen were usurpers, is fulfilling the role of artist:

> Wait. I am big with child. I have an unborn child in my brain.
> Pallas Athena! A play! The play's the thing! Let me parturiate!
> He clasped his paunchbrow with both birthaiding hands.

With the abolition of grammar and rhetoric as valid modes rooted in the analogy of being, the mode of aesthetic creation becomes parthenogenesis. And while the poet wrestles with the polemic of his art, Shelleyan Defenses of Poetry and the like, the plausible mummer in touch with the dominant science of the day produces " national immoralities " without apparent effort.

Between this Scylla and this Charybdis, perverted dialectic, perverted grammar, Mr. Bloom the rhetorician passes, " bowing, greeting ", to resume his place at the apex of the triangle.

Chapter 14

THE PLAN OF *ULYSSES*

– That's all done with a purpose, Martin Cunningham
explained to Hynes.
– I know, Hynes said, I know that.
– To cheer a fellow up, Martin Cunningham said.   It's pure
goodheartedness: damn the thing else.

Ulysses (U 106/99)

THE hundreds of interpenetrating arches in this cathedral of
metaphor were reduced by Joyce, with commendable ingenuity,
to a page of memoranda, a codification of his chief working
notes.   This guide and mnemonic was circulated among
friends, and in 1930 a portion of it found its way into a book, of
which, as the one page of indubitable reliability, it is the only
part that has been much called in question by later epigons.
Much energy has been expended in ascertaining that as the
word " green " appears eight times in the first episode, the word
" gold " only once, Mr. Gilbert should have given the Colour
of the episode as green.   Mr. Gilbert may be absolved of
responsibility.   Copies of Joyce's complete tabulation survive,
including the Homeric portion which Mr. Gilbert reserved
for expansion into a book; and since Joyce gave the Colours
of the first episode as white and gold, it is worth a little trouble
to find out why.

Joyce's complete table, first, is given herewith, adapted
from a photograph in the Slocum collection.   Before rushing
to embrace it as Sinaitic antidote to all mysteries, the reader
should reflect that the object of reading the book is not to
reconstruct the schema, any more than one eats a dinner to
reconstruct the recipes.   It is not a set of answers to a puzzle;
Mr. Gilbert deserves credit for not giving it that kind of
emphasis.   It was, while the book was a-writing, *affaire de
cuisine;* its usefulness to the reader who happens to have access
to it now that the book is completed should consist in helping
him focus his apprehension.

THE SYMBOLS IN TELEMACHUS

These statements are readily illustrated.   The first episode opens:

TITLE	SCENE	HOUR	ORGAN	ART	COLOUR	SYMBOL	TECHNIC	CORRESPONDENCES
1. Telemachus	The Tower	8 a.m.		Theology	White, gold	Heir	Narrative (young)	*Stephen:* Telemachus, Hamlet. *Buck Mulligan:* Antinous. *Milkwoman:* Mentor.
2. Nestor	The School	10 a.m.		History	Brown	Horse	Catechism (personal	*Deasy:* Nestor. *Sargent:* Pisistratus. *Mrs. O'Shea:* Helen.
3. Proteus	The Strand	11 a.m.		Philology	Green	Tide	Monologue (male)	*Proteus:* Primal Matter. *Kevin Egan:* Menelaus. *Cocklepicker:* Megapenthus.
4. Calypso	The House	8 a.m.	Kidney	Economics	Orange	Nymph	Narrative (mature)	*Calypso:* The Nymph. *Dlugacz:* The Recall. *Zion:* Ithaca.
5. Lotus-eaters	The Bath	10 a.m.	Genitals	Botany, Chemistry		Eucharist	Narcissism	*Lotuseaters:* the Cabhorses, Communicants, Soldiers, Eunuchs, Bather, Watchers of Cricket.
6. Hades	The Graveyard	11 a.m.	Heart	Religion	White, black	Caretaker	Incubism	*Dodder, Grand, and Royal Canals, Liffey:* the 4 Rivers. *Cunningham:* Sisyphus. *Father Coffey:* Cerberus. *Caretaker:* Hades. *Daniel O'Connell:* Hercules. *Dignam:* Elpenor. *Parnell:* Agamemnon, Ajax.
7. Aeolus	The Newspaper	12 noon	Lungs	Rhetoric	Red	Editor	Enthymemic	*Crawford:* Aeolus. *Incest:* Journalism. *Floating Island:* Press.
8. Lestrygonians	The Lunch	1 p.m.	Esophagus	Architecture		Constables	Peristaltic	*Antiphates:* Hunger. *The Decoy:* Food. *Lestrygonians:* Teeth.

Episode	Scene	Hour	Organ	Art	Colour	Symbol	Technic	Correspondences
9. Scylla & Charybdis	The Library	2 p.m.	Brain	Literature		Stratford, London	Dialectic	*The Rock:* Aristotle, Dogma, Stratford. *The Whirlpool:* Plato, Mysticism, London. *Ulysses:* Socrates, Jesus, Shakespeare.
10. Wandering Rocks	The Streets	3 p.m.	Blood	Mechanics		Citizens	Labyrinth	*Bosphorus:* Liffey. *European Bank:* Viceroy. *Asiatic Bank:* Conmee. *Symplegades:* Groups of Citizens.
11. Sirens	The Concert Room	4 p.m.	Ear	Music		Barmaids	Fuga per Canonem	*Sirens:* Barmaids. *Isle:* Bar.
12. Cyclops	The Tavern	5 p.m.	Muscle	Politics		Fenian	Gigantism	*Noman:* I. *Stake:* Cigar. *Challenge:* Apotheosis.
13. Nausicaa	The Rocks	8 p.m.	Eye, Nose	Painting	Grey, blue	Virgin	Tumescence, detumescence	*Phaeacia:* Star of the Sea. *Gerty:* Nausicaa.
14. Oxen of the Sun	The Hospital	10 p.m.	Womb	Medicine	White	Mothers	Embryonic development	*Hospital:* Trinacria. *Nurses:* Lampetie, Phaethusa. *Horne:* Helios. *Oxen:* Fertility. *Crime:* Fraud.
15. Circe	The Brothel	12 midnight	Locomotor Apparatus	Magic		Whore	Hallucination	*Circe:* Bella.
16. Eumaeus	The Shelter	1 a.m.	Nerves	Navigation		Sailors	Narrative (old)	*Skin the Goat:* Eumaeus. *Sailor:* Ulysses Pseudangelos. *Corley:* Melanthius.
17. Ithaca	The House	2 a.m.	Skeleton	Science		Comets	Catechism (impersonal)	*Eurymachus:* Boylan. *Suitors:* Scruples. *Bow:* Reason.
18. Penelope	The Bed		Flesh			Earth	Monologue (female)	*Penelope:* Earth. *Web:* Movement.

> Stately, plump Buck Mulligan came from the stairhead, bearing
> a bowl of lather on which a mirror and a razor lay crossed.   A
> yellow dressinggown, ungirdled, was sustained gently behind him by
> the mild morning air.   He held the bowl aloft and intoned:
> – *Introibo ad altare Dei.*   U5/1.

These are perhaps the most familiar lines ever written by
Joyce.   Thousands will recognize their unforgettable clarity
who have progressed very little farther in the book before
starting to skip.   Can the reader be induced to put aside their
familiarity long enough to see what they mean?

Within six lines, with the words of Mulligan's intonation,
the double-exposure becomes apparent.   The details fall into
their sacramental places with something more than chance
realism.   Mulligan stands at the head of his altar steps, atop
the tower, with a vacancy for an altar.   The narcissist mirror
and the slaughterer's razor make a bitter cross on his chalice;
the razor introduces the theme, later to receive enormous amplifi-
cation, of the priest as butcher; as a tool of barbers it reminds
us of Mulligan's surgeon's vocation (the barber, as his red
and white pole still affirms, was the original phlebotomist).
His yellow dressinggown is a gold chasuble, "ungirdled"
because the priest's cincture symbolizes un-Mulliganian
chastity; it is sustained by air instead of by a server.

By this time the "art," Theology, and the colours, white
and gold, have manifested themselves.[1]   When the colours of
the sacred vestments are explicitly mentioned some twenty-five
lines later, it is in an image of shark-like rapacity forecasting
the priest-king-cannibal motifs of the Lestrygonians episode:
". . . his even white teeth glistening here and there with gold
points."   The parody-mass runs throughout the chapter.
Stephen, reluctant server at these mocker's rites, recalls,
carrying down the bowl which has been left forgotten on the
parapet:

> So I carried the boat of incense then at Clongowes.   I am another
> now and yet the same.   A servant too.   A server of a servant.   U13/9.

He is "another now and yet the same" in terms both of

---

[1] Gold (on a white ground) is the generic colour of sacerdotal vestments.   With
certain exceptions, it may be worn at all masses, except during Advent and Lent
and at masses for the dead.   The 16th of June, 1904 (St. John Francis Regis in
the liturgical calendar) is no exception.   White is prescribed, with gold optional,
because of the feastday of a Confessor.

personal identity and of function: Mulligan whom he serves
now mocks God's priesthood as (but far from exactly as) the
opacity of the Clongowes Jesuits had mocked it.   The next
paragraph displays Mulligan resuming his sacerdotal function
in a Gothic setting, before a homelier altar:

> In the gloomy domed livingroom of the tower Buck Mulligan's
> gowned form moved briskly about the hearth to and fro, hiding and
> revealing its yellow glow.   Two shafts of soft daylight fell across
> the flagged floor from the high barbicans; and at the meeting of
> their rays a cloud of coalsmoke and fumes of fired grease floated,
> turning.   U13/9.

A moment later he bears from the smoking altar the consecrated elements to the faithful:

> ... Then he carried the dish and a large teapot over to the table,
> set them down heavily, and sighed with relief.
> — I'm melting, he said, as the candle remarked when ...   But
> hush.   Not a word more on that subject.   Kinch, wake up.   Bread,
> butter, honey.   Haines, come in.   The grub is ready.   Bless us,
> O Lord, and these thy gifts.   Where's the sugar.   O, jay, there's no
> milk.   U13/10.

Stephen, in his capacity of server, fetches and carries loaf,
honey-pot, butter-cooler.   Mulligan distributes his morning
communion:

> Here, I can't go fumbling at the damned eggs.   He hacked through
> the fry on the dish and slapped it out on the three plates, saying:
> — *In nomine Patris et Filii et Spiritus Sancti.*[1]

The milk is brought in for the tea as water is added to the wine;
Stephen at the locker recalls the server at purification; Mulligan
as he produces a florin for the milkwoman cries " A miracle ";
the meal over, he removes his dressinggown with a ceremony of
dramatic resignation, U18/14, recalling the prayers of unvest-
ing, and slings his towel " stolewise " around his neck, U19/16.
    Stephen's reflection on the milkwoman's deference to
Mulligan makes the priest-doctor connection specific:

[1] These words at the distribution of the eggs mark the first of many mutations
of the trinity-theme: Mulligan the usurping father (pseudo priest), Stephen the
betrayed son, Haines the descended dove of an inverted Pentecost, acquiring the
gift of one tongue and representing the race that has bestowed the unwanted gift
of another.

— Are you a medical student, sir? the old lady asked.

— I am, ma'am, Buck Mulligan answered.

Stephen listened in scornful silence.   She bows her old head to a
voice that speaks to her loudly, her bonesetter, her medicineman:
me she slights.   To the voice that will shrive and oil for the grave
all there is of her but her woman's unclean loins, of man's flesh made
not in God's likeness, the serpent's prey.   And to the loud voice
that now bids her be silent with wondering unsteady eyes.   U16/12.

" Medicineman " unites doctor and priest; medical functions
are concealed in sacerdotal metaphors—" shrive and oil for
the grave "; the old lady's deference to " her gay betrayer "
reflects Ireland's submission to the double-crossing clergy[1]
who over and over again as Stephen can remember from the
speeches at that memorable Christmas dinner in the *Portrait*[2]
have in pursuit of unimpeachable spiritual ends betrayed the
political health of that " priestridden Godforsaken race ",
P39/42.

The first section of *Ulysses* goes far beyond the political
anticlericalism of the *Portrait*.   To cast the doctor as priest is to
strike at the outset the note of materialistic transposition that
runs through the book.   The body usurps the room of the soul,
theology gives way to associationist psychology, visions become
hallucinations, the metaphors of scripture receive bitterly
literal realization in matter, in an inferno whose apotheosis is
the debris-crammed brain of hapless Leopold Bloom.

EXAMINATION OF TWO MORE OPENINGS

In this manner the action of each episode proceeds in a frame
of running metaphors of which the table of themes furnishes
a useful concordance.   The arts, colours, symbols, organs, are
rubrics for modes in which the material of the episode is

---

[1] Cf. the inflection of the x's at the end of the famous letter in *Finnegans Wake*:
" With Kiss. Kiss Criss. Cross Criss. Kiss Cross. Undo lives 'end. Slain."
F11 Kiss Christ as did Judas, double-cross Christ, then in pharisaical submission
kiss a symbolic cross; unto life's end undo lives' end; and the echo of the " Amen "
is " Slain ".   The indictment of misguided clericalism has never been more
succinct.

[2] "—Didn't the bishops of Ireland betray us at the time of the union when
Bishop Lanigan presented an address of loyalty to the Marquis Cornwallis?
Didn't the bishops and priests sell the aspirations of their country in 1829 in
return for catholic emancipation?   Didn't they denounce the fenian movement
from the pulpit and in the confession box?   And didn't they dishonour the ashes
of Terence Bellew MacManus? " P39/43.

epiphanized. And the whole complex is generally set in motion on the first page. Here is the opening of " Nausicaa ":

> The summer evening had begun to fold the world in its mysterious embrace. Far away in the west the sun was setting and the last glow of all too fleeting day lingered lovingly on sea and strand, on the proud promontory of dear old Howth guarding as ever the waters of the bay, on the weedgrown rocks along Sandymount shore and, last but not least, on the quiet church whence there streamed forth at times upon the stillness the voice of prayer to her who is in her pure radiance a beacon ever to the stormtossed heart of man, Mary, star of the sea. U340/329.

The very first image is erotic (" embrace ") and religiose (" mysterious "). This sentimental sunset is a twilight of masculine and feminine civilization. The Head of Howth guards the bay in the mode of God become rock, assimilated to policemen and castled bulk; the Protean strand of early morning has set and hardened, like the souls of Dubliners, into " weedgrown rocks "; and the voice of prayer to the Virgin Mary leads into an exploration of a feminine world (Gerty MacDowell's) in which her cultus is as perverted as was the priestly function in episode one. Religion, too, has hardened into sentiment. Our Lady's " beacon to the stormtossed heart of man " receives its material transposition, later in the episode, as Bloom strains after a glimpse of Gerty's knickers.[1]

Here is the opening of " The Oxen of the Sun ":

> Deshil Holles Eamus. Deshil Holles Eamus. Deshil Holles Eamus.
> Send us, bright one, light one, Horhorn, quickening and womb-fruit. Send us, bright one, light one, Horhorn, quickening and wombfruit. Send us, bright one, light one, Horhorn, quickening and wombfruit.
> Hoopsa, boyaboy, hoopsa! Hoopsa, boyaboy, hoopsa! Hoopsa, boyaboy, hoopsa. U377/266.

Mr. Gilbert glosses:

> The first of these formulas means simply: " Let us go south to Holles Street." The second is an invocation to the Sun, Helios, personified by Sir Andrew Horne, the head of the Lying-in Hospital,

---

[1] Mr. Eliot has perhaps profited by this collocation, as by so much in *Ulysses;* his Siren in *The Waste Land* displays " Out of the window perilously spread/ Her drying combinations touched by the sun's last rays." The sailor has been called home from sea three lines previously.

the " House of Horne." The third is the triumphant cry of the
midwife as, elevating the new-born, she acclaims its sex.[1]

This is true enough, but not very helpful, unless we concede the
relevance of a cryptoanalytic approach. Much more to be
marked is the liturgical chant of the prose, strongly set off by
the " Tacitean-Sallustian " amorphism that follows. It is a
miniature liturgy ending with the elevation of an achieved
body, a materialist mass in a new mode, parallelling the elevation of the shaving-bowl on the first page. The gulf between
" Hoopsa, boyaboy, hoopsa " and " Hoc est enim corpus
meum " is negligible beside that between the consecrating
words and Buck Mulligan's " One moment. A little trouble
about those white corpuscles." It is at least, in Holles Street,
a body and not a bowl of lather that is elevated. Yet the procession of the tripartite liturgy, from Latin to Jacobean English
to slang, parallels that of the whole chapter, from the language
of Christian mystery downward to that of demotic earthiness;
not merely three Viconian ages but three steps, via a vernacular
middle term, from a world in touch with the supernatural to a
world obsessed with the " vicous cicle " of pullulating accouche-
ments. " Horhorn " of course echoes the name of Sir Andrew
Horne; much more does it echo the " Horn. Hawhorn "
motif of Blazes Boylan, U252/242. Bloom is still in quest of
a son, even one begotten by his supplanter.

WHO ARE THE CANNIBALS?

A more intricate opening is that of the " Lestrygonians "
episode. Everyone knows why it is so called—it has to do with
eating. But why the art should be architecture, and the symbol
the constables, has puzzled everyone from Mr. Gilbert (who
ignores the question) to Mr. Kain (who is annoyed by it). As
usual, the necessary alignments are given on the first page,
which runs as follows:

> Pineapple rock, lemon platt, butter scotch. A sugarsticky girl
> shovelling scoopfuls of creams for a christian brother. Some school
> treat. Bad for their tummies. Lozenge and comfit manufacturer
> to His Majesty the King. God. Save. Our. Sitting on his throne,
> sucking red jujubes white.
> A sombre Y.M.C.A. young man, watchful among the warm

---

[1] Gilbert, 277. " Deshil " means *deisiúl*, Gaelic for clockwise, walking to the
right hand. A magical ritualistic movement, imitating that of the sun.

sweet fumes of Graham Lemon's, placed a throwaway in a hand of Mr. Bloom.

Heart to heart talks.

Bloo ... Me? No.

Blood of the Lamb.

His slow feet walked him riverward, reading. Are you saved? All are washed in the blood of the lamb. God wants blood victim. Birth, hymen, martyr, war, foundation of a building, sacrifice, kidney burntoffering, druid's altars. Elijah is coming. Dr. John Alexander Dowie, restorer of the church in Zion, is coming.

Is coming! Is coming!! Is coming!!!
All heartily welcome.

Paying game. Torry and Alexander last year. Polygamy. His wife will put the stopper on that. Where was that ad some Birmingham firm the luminous crucifix? Our Saviour. Wake up in the dead of night and see him on the wall, hanging. Pepper's ghost idea. Iron nails ran in.

Phosphorous it must be done with. If you leave a bit of codfish for instance. I could see the bluey silver over it. Night I went down to the pantry in the kitchen. Don't like all the smells in it waiting to rush out. What was it she wanted? The Malaga raisins. Thinking of Spain. Before Rudy was born. The phosphorescence, that bluey greeny. Very good for the brain. U149/139.

What runs through this entire section, as these initial motifs insist, is the note of blood-sacrifice, adumbrated on the very first page of the book in the account of the glistening teeth of the pseudo-priest. In the first paragraph above, scoopfuls of creams are ladelled to a clerical schoolmaster, and the King sits on his throne sucking red jujubes white: a fee-fi-fo-fum giant sucking the blood out of his Hibernian subjects, in the mode of the " Cyclops " section whose " art " is politics. Bloom is handed a " Blood of the Lamb " tract, and in his capacity as subject of church and state and analogue of Christ, momentarily confuses its topic with himself.

" God wants blood victim. Birth, hymen, martyr, war, foundation of a building, sacrifice, kidney burntoffering, druid's altars." The policemen are the guardians of this brutal order; the art of architecture rears its head for a moment as the catalogue rolls by. The cities of such a dispensation, we are later reminded, are heaps of stones reared on the corpses of slaves, a sacrificial victim, as Sir James Frazer noted, buried under the cornerstone.

This Dublin, this city, reared by this architecture, is an immense blasphemy against the New Jerusalem of the faith of Christ: the savage parody rises to a preliminary climax as Bloom scans the pamphlet, with its apocalyptic imagery implying the second coming of Christ, or of antichrist in His guise.

> Dr. John Alexander Dowie, restorer of the Church in Zion, is coming.
>
> *Is coming!   Is coming!!   Is coming!!!*
> *All heartily welcome.*

Bloom's comment reduces this apocalypse to its true dimensions: " Paying game."

The blood-victim theme now takes a new twist; Joyce evokes a parody of the eternal luminous transfigured presence of the Saviour, blood-victim of the Sanhedrin:

> Where was that ad some Birmingham firm the luminous crucifix? Our Saviour. Wake up in the dead of night and see him on the wall, hanging. Pepper's ghost idea. Iron nails ran in.

This new transfiguration is sponsored by the ad-man and assimilated to a circus-act, *Pepper's Ghost*. Bloom's muddled exegesis of I.N.R.I. exhibits by comparison an innocent sort of inadequacy; the commercial appetites that have engendered this travesty (and that of Dr. John Alexander Dowie) are a variation on the cannibal motifs of the episode.

In this sensate and appetitive world the Mystical Body has rotted; this transmogrification of an early Christian symbol underlies the evocation in the next paragraph of a rotting fish[1] emitting the pale luminosity of corruption, " that bluey greeny. Very good for the brain." Bloom's innocent associative shift, phosphorescence-fish-brainfood, parallels the descent of Christian culture into a brainless world of associative logic and material conceptions of nutriment; all that was in fact once good for the brain has gone out of it. The organ of the episode is the stomach; it is into a vast stomach, seat of the appetites, the belly usurping the functions of the members, that the Body Politic has declined. Movement is peristaltic, involuntary: Mr. Bloom's " slow feet walked him riverward; " the throwaway is thrust into " a hand of Mr. Bloom " that seems to have lost all connection with his will.

[1] Later we hear of a man who can't write his own name making a fortune ripping the guts out of fish, U173/164: commerce *vs*. Christ again.

Church parallels state throughout the section; a "priesty-looking chap," Penrose, is exhibited as a peeping tom, U153/144; he later turns out to have been one of Molly's lovers, U716/692. The police are correspondingly presented as spies, U161/152, "Egging raw youths on to get in the know. All the time drawing secret service pay from the castle." Priests and constables serve the English King and the Hangman God. The cannibal constables emerge from their barracks gorged:

> Foodheated faces, sweating helmets, patting their truncheons. After their feed with a good load of fat soup under their belts. Policeman's lot is oft a happy one. U160/151.

A communal kitchen makes a suitable symbol of Church Union, U168/159; as reference to "our incorporated drinkingcup" implies, the appetitive is the level on which an enduring union of church and state could be consummated as well, the tin cup mocking the function of the chalice.

> Have rows all the same. All for number one. Children fighting for the scraping of the pot.

"Number one" is proverbially oneself; here it is also God, who has become man in the image of laissez-faire democracy.

> Soup, joint and sweet. Never know whose thoughts you're chewing. Then who'd wash up all the plates and forks? Might be all feeding on tabloids that time. Teeth getting worse and worse.

"Never know whose thoughts you're chewing." Bloom is still speculating on the community kitchens of the future, but the metaphor is still that of an immense rapprochement of the state and all churches. The hungry sheep look up and are fed tenth-hand thinking, tabloids, pre-processed food, predigested sensational news. "Teeth getting worse and worse:" the ingestive faculties, the teeth that bite into food and into ideas, undergoing steady decay.

> Religions. Christmas turkeys and geese. Slaughter of innocents. U169/160.

The rapprochement is not toward Christ but toward Herod.

The tiniest details of the episode bear out these themes. The "puffball of smoke" from the brewery barge, U150/141, suggests an edible fungus; but like the journalistic "puff" over which Bloom agonizes in the "Aeolus" episode, it is made

of wind.   The wind that vacant shuttles weave, U22/19, is the
only intellectual or spiritual nutriment available to the Dubliner.
As fish, once the symbol of Christ, has become the brain-food
of folklore, so every religious symbol is devalued:

> Kosher.   No meat and milk together.   Hygiene that was what they
> call now.   Yom Kippur fast spring cleaning of inside   U169/160.

The sacraments of the Church turn up reflected in mocking
mirrors: Baptism—the defecation of pigeons, U160/151;
Confirmation—the newborn children having the Blood of the
Lamb washed off them, U162/153;   Eucharist—Bloom's
manna cast to the seagulls, U151/142; Penance—the Hely's
sandwichmen whose scarlet letters proclaim " we have sinned:
we have suffered ", U152/143; Matrimony—the groaning
plight of Mrs. Purefoy, U159/150; Holy Orders—the
" paying game " of Dr. Dowie, U149/140; Extreme Unction
—" Dignam carted off ", U162/153.

The arts, organs, and symbols appear in *Ulysses* in a mode of
parody, which is perhaps why so many have sought in vain for
their relevance.   Architecture appears in the " Lestrygonians "
episode in connection not with the free expression of the human
spirit but with the infernal cities, erected by slaves, whose
dumb stones have crushed their builders and which mock in
their ponderous permanence the peristaltic Viconian cycle of
passing generations bound to the appetitive wheel: the New
Jerusalem become Blake's city of " dark Satanic mills ".

> Cityful passing away, other cityful coming, passing away too:
> other coming on, passing on.   Houses, line of houses, streets, miles
> of pavements, piledup bricks, stones.   Changing hands.   This owner,
> that.   Landlord never dies they say.   Other steps into his shoes
> when he gets his notice to quit.   They buy the place up with gold
> and still they have all the gold.   Swindle in it somewhere.   Piled up
> in cities, worn away age after age.   Pyramids in sand.   Built on
> bread and onions.   Slaves Chinese wall.   Babylon.   Big stones left.
> Round towers.   Rest rubble, sprawling suburbs, jerrybuilt, Ker-
> wan's mushroom houses, built of breeze.   Shelter for the night.
> No one is anything.   U162/153.

" Landlord never dies they say."   The one thing as permanent
as the piled stones is usurious ownership, the belly lord of the
members.
    These motifs exfoliate through *Finnegans Wake* in connection
with the Viconian cycle:

Countlessness of livestories have netherfallen by this plage, flick as flowflakes, litters from aloft, like a waast wizzard all of whirlworlds. Now are all tombed to the mound, isges to isges, erde from erde. Pride, O pride, thy prize! F17.

On the same page " babylone the greatgrandhotelled " is brought to the level of " tit tit tittlehouse ". A parody-eternity freezes the vital development of vegetable time:

> Till tree from tree, tree among trees, tree over tree become stone to stone, stone between stones, stone under stone forever. F259.

The tree-postures are those of hierarchic society, the stone-postures those of copulation: the act of life itself become an automatic death. Again, the sprawling jerrybuilt suburbs, Kerwan's mushroom houses of Bloom's contemplation, are evoked near the end of the *Wake* as an image of temporal pullulation seen through the eyes of eternity:

> Mch? Why, them's the muchrooms, come up during the night. Look, agres of roofs in parshes. Dom on dam, dim in dym. And a capital part for olympics to ply at. F625.
> [*Agre*=acre plus Lat. ager, territory. *Parshes*=parishes, and *roofs in parshes*=the divine Work in Progress, the eschatological process. *Dom*inus on *dam* breeds the cosmos, *dim* in its *dym*amics; and the *capitals* on the columns of this mansion of eternity—in human form: caput, head—which destiny shapes out of the ruins of time (the New Jerusalem as the aesthetic form of the entire divine and human achievement) are set in place by Olympian forces plying their tasks with the joy of cosmic *olympic* games (ply/play).]

Joyce connects the art of architecture always with the erection of eternal forms. In the " Lestrygonians " episode of *Ulysses* it is oppressive parodies of these forms that get built.

FURTHER NOTES ON THE SYMBOLS

The rationale of this sequence of symbols is the vision of Dublin as a mechanization both of the Body Politic and of the Mystical Body of Christ. In Shakespeare's *Coriolanus*, the vision of the Body Politic, expounded by Menenius in the first scene, is continually present in the imagery and continually denied by the facts. Three centuries later its denial by the facts is so strident that its presence is attested only by rubric and gloss. The genitals of Dublin are gelded, its heart is a grave-yard, its lungs inflate and deflate to the rhythm of giant presses, its corpuscular bodies circulate, discrete entities, to the rhythm of the art of mechanics, through an arterial labyrinth of stony streets; all in the sharpest possible contrast to the pulsating universe of *Finnegans Wake*, one level above the *Ulysses*-world of eternal fixity. It is no reproach to the techniques of *Ulysses* that the correspondences are frequently of the most mechanical kind; the more mechanical the better, for Joyce's purposes.

The mechanization of the body politic in *Ulysses* is closely connected with the speculations of Stephen on act and potency:

> Had Pyrrhus not fallen by a beldam's hand in Argos or Julius Caesar not been knifed to death. They are not to be thought away. Time has branded them and fettered they are lodged in the room of the infinite possibilities they have ousted. But can those have been possible seeing that they never were? Weave, weaver of the wind. U26/22.

Act in this universe (the scholastic *actus existentiae*, not to be confused with " action ", *actus operationis*[1]) is a fetter, potency a ghost, and history, the congeries of inescapably realized potentialities, an ineluctable incubus. " History is a nightmare from which I am trying to awake." The actualizing power is a principle not of realization but of death, fettering and branding potencies into frozen states, like the museum of statues of marble goddesses without entrails of Mr. Bloom's delectation, or like the cemetery full of " white forms and fragments streaming by mutely, sustaining vain gestures on the air ", U99/92. Everything has become all that it can ever be, the past is exhausted, the passage of time simply crams the museum of history fuller and fuller of Laocoonic tableaus, nothing can be willed away, nothing can change, nothing is of the slightest intrinsic interest, and that is hell.

The huge human form that is Dublin, to shift these observations into another analogy, is articulated as it were with bolts and axles, it resounds with circulating clanging tramlines, its thought is carried on by IBM associative processes, every idea so to speak on a little punched card susceptible not of modification but only of re-shuffling. And the parody of free intellectual operation is the all-but-random shuffling of motifs that takes place in Bella Cohen's brothel, in the " Circe " episode whose organ is the locomotor apparatus and whose technique is Hallucination. All the day's tag-ends of perception and

---

[1] See Maritain, *Introduction to Philosophy*, 244.

verbalization are dealt out in a new order which has the advantage over the old of at least exhibiting an insane logic. The irrepressible comic vitality of the writing confers a sense of hallucinated liberation from the world of high-grade hats, 11/- trousers, legal rhetoric, pork kidneys, parallax, potatoes, and plaster goddesses; but the mocking mirrors are reflecting the same dead catalogue of objects amid which the deadened spirit has moved all day. It is from this hell of ineluctable categories that the daft metamorphoses of the *Wake* are a liberation. The dream of H. C. Earwicker marks an illusory escape from the Ulyssean day-world; but the relation between Bloom's day and Earwicker's night is analogous with the relation between infernal and purgatorial states, between shuffled cards and thought continuously inflected by the contours and densities of the existences it plays over and penetrates.

ARTS

The arts are perverted in a similar way. We have examined Mulligan's mockery of theology (" My mother's a jew and my father's a bird ", U20/16), and the anti-Viconian incubus of History. Philology, in the ancient grammatical sense of reading the book of nature, is practised by Stephen with indifferent because self-conscious success, and by Bloom with less. Religion is the art of perfunctory burial, Rhetoric is subverted from Augustinian to journalistic ends, Architecture rears Moloch-cities and Walls of China, Literature is a playground for dialectical ingenuity, the running metaphors of Politics are drawn from the cattlepen and the slaughterhouse, Painting is degraded to the lush descriptive banality of " Nausicaa " and provides the picture of " halcyon days " on the grocer's Christmas almanac for Gerty MacDowell to hang in the outhouse, U349/338.

COLOURS

Of the eight episodes to which colours are assigned, six use the schemes of liturgical vestments. *White* and *Gold* have been explained. *Red* (the symbol of blood and fire) is used for the Pentecostal mass of the Holy Ghost, to commemorate the descent of the Holy Spirit, like a mighty wind rushing, bearing tongues of fire and imparting the gift of tongues. Hence its ascription to the windswept " Aeolus " episode of many-tongued rhetoric. How *Black* (Good Friday and masses for the dead) attaches itself to the "Hades" episode is obvious. Subdued by the *Grey* of Dublin's, Bloom's, and civilization's twilight, *Blue*, the colour of the Virgin Mary, is the assigned colour of the "Nausicaa" episode, which counterpoints Bloom's flirtation with the virgin Gerty and Father Hughes' Litany of Our Lady of Loreto.

Green is more complicated. In Catholic iconography it is a symbol of hope, prescribed for a sequence of Sundays after Epiphany and another sequence after Pentecost. As the colour of the "Proteus" episode, it focuses several levels of irony. Liturgically, it registers as *fait accompli* a comprehensive Epiphany which has not taken place (Cf. "Dublin. I have much, much to learn", U142/134) and a descent of Pentecostal tongues which Stephen's dictionary-erudition ("She trudges schlepps, trains, drags, trascines her load", U48/44) merely parodies. The bard with his Hamlet hat, his rotting teeth, his missing handkerchief, his "epiphanies on green oval leaves, deeply deep, copies to be sent if you died to all the great libraries of the world, including Alexandria", U41/37, inhabits with acute self-consciousness a speculative prison which he is inclined to mistake, under the liturgical green sign of hope, for a magically flowering garden of liberation in which with a gesture his shadow can be sent beyond the stars:

> No white nor red was ever seen
> So am'rous as this lovely green. . . .
> Meanwhile the mind, from pleasure less,
> Withdraws into its happiness;
> The mind, that ocean where each kind
> Does straight its own resemblance find,
> Yet it creates, transcending these,
> Far other worlds, and other seas;
> Annihilating all that's made
> To a green thought in a green shade.

And it should not be forgotten that Green denotes the Erin from which ("Remembering thee, O Zion") is exiled the cuckolded Menelaus, Kevin Egan, protagonist of the most moving pages in the episode.

The colours *Brown* ("Nestor") and *Orange* ("Calypso") are nonliturgical. Brown is a mystery, unless it places a brown study (Deasy's) between the golden words ("his even white teeth glistening here and there with gold points. Chrysostomos") of Mulligan in "Telemachus" and the green thought of Stephen in " Proteus ". As for Orange, suffusing " Calypso ", where the charms of sun-warmed orange-groves of Jaffa impel Mr. Bloom's *Drang nach Osten*, the clue is simple. It was the colour of Greek harlots' dresses.

SYMBOLS

Each symbol marks the point from which Dublin as a whole is being epiphanized: as a cemetery under the mayoralty of a caretaker, as a cannibal realm dominated by policemen, as a mild grey-blue Phaeacia under the ambivalent tutelage of the virgins in which its capital of sentimental reverence is invested (the cult of the sanctity of Irish girlhood incarnate in a crippled flapper) as a brothel under the whoremistress, as a bellows pumped by the editor.

TECHNICS

These, again, provide clues for apprehending the structural rhythms of the book. As Mr. Gilbert points out, Narrative, young, mature, and old, initiates each of the three main divisions. Furthermore, the prologue—Narrative (young), Catechism (personal), Monologue (male), is meant to be seen in relation to the threefold epilogue—Narrative (old), Catechism (impersonal), Monologue (female). As the day runs on, everything moves towards death. Entanglement in matter, in cliché, and in weariness, has in " Eumaeus " overtaken the high-keyed narrative prose of " Telemachus ". The impersonality of the " Ithaca " catechism is on the one hand an immense parody of pseudo-Flaubertian " scientific " detachment, on the other hand an inflation of Stephen's classroom techniques vis-à-vis his pupils (the journalist's " questions of the day " catechise the citizen with identical perversity). The female monologue circulates about the speaker's body as the male monologue had played over presented existences.

There is more to the prologue-epilogue relationship than this, however. Epilogue is not simply to Prologue as parody to exemplar. It is also as *reductio ad absurdum* to thing reduced. The social matter (Bloom's menage) vulgarizes the intellectual matter (Stephen's mind) because the latter already contains seeds of perversion. In passing from the Martello Tower to 7 Eccles Street we have simply penetrated deeper into the same

modes of being. Stephen's persona is formed not with reference to impersonal reason but with reference to the Dublin to
which it is antithetical. Hence with only a little manipulation
of the " mocking mirrors " we can scrutinize Stephen and see
Dublin; dig beneath the *Telemachia* and discover the *Nostos*.
The social clichés of " Eumaeus " drive into every detail of
casual conversation the perversions implied in the parodied
theological clichés of " Telemachus ". The relationship of
catechizer to catechized in " Nestor "—not a cooperative
interest in the subject under discussion but a barbed antithesis
of personalities—becomes that of the inane impersonal
catechizing voice to the thoroughly abstract and abstracted
respondent in " Ithaca ". Catechism runs smoothly once the
persons are abolished. The impersonality of " Ithaca " is a
pseudo-impersonality; it preserves all the alignments of
Stephen's and his students' contempt for one another, but
merely dissolves into terminological inanity the obviously
personal features of their mutual tension. As for the male and
female monologues, Stephen's is only superficially oriented
toward circumambient being. " Proteus " circles around its
protagonist just as does " Penelope ". Molly has merely
resolved the tensions of the earlier episode by accepting with
smug satisfaction the body with which Stephen is at once so
obsessed and so displeased. " What a thing is when fully
developed, that we call its nature." *Ulysses* adheres to this
Aristotelian precept. The epiphanies are achieved, as always,
by allowing the introductory seeds to sprout. From the familiar
sensuous mask we move to the invincible opacities of the underlying will.

The techniques of the Odyssey proper (episodes 4–15) fall
into similar groups of three, as the following scheme will show:

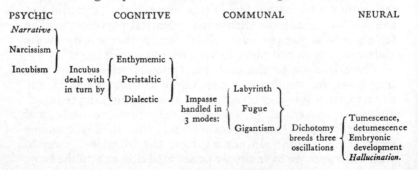

The progression of styles enacts a drama even at this tabular level of abstraction.   As the technique shifts from Narrative to Hallucination the focus shifts from Bloom's household to the " ruin of all space " in the brothel.   But as the headings imply, the arena of the ultimate epiphany is neural rather than cosmic; at the moment when the rhythms have become most centrifugal, the drama is most of all concentrated within the skull. The structure of each of the four groups deserves a word.

Narrative—Narcissism—Incubism.   The collection, as his day on earth progresses, of further and further materials on which to work does not enlarge the mind of industrial man. First his thoughts turn inward, then he reduces his surroundings, with a gesture of helplessness, to the status of meaningless statuary, " sustaining vain gestures on the air."   And this incubus (in Stephen's phrase, the nightmare of history) he bears piled on top of himself, an irremovable Pilgrim's burden.

Enthymemic—Peristaltic—Dialectic.   The Enthymeme is the syllogism of rhetoric;[1] its result is the probably true, its province that of persuasion rather than demonstration.   A preliminary clue to its function in the present context may be found in Aristotle's remark,

> An Enthymeme is a syllogism dealing with practical subjects.   It is therefore roughly true that the premisses or conclusions of Enthymemes, considered apart from the rest of the argument, are maxims.[2]

The Enthymemic technique as adopted by a Bloom or an editor arranges and rearranges bits of proverbial wisdom into maxims of conduct, and in this way derives some nugatory sustenance from his plight.   The mutations of sententious wisdom and second-hand wit in the newspaper office parody the classical enthymeme, the " peristaltic " rumination of Bloom's mind en route to lunch parodies the digestion of facts, the virtuosity with which Stephen proves a theory he doesn't believe parodies classical dialectics.   At the same time, the emergence of the Stratford / London (Stephen / Bloom, mind / matter) dichotomy brings the generic dialectical impasse of the book to focus.

Labyrinth—Fugue—Gigantism.   Faulty relation of the mind with things parallels faulty relation of the man with other social beings.   The intersections and correspondences of the labyrinth are as mechanical as may be, as mechanical as all social

---

[1] Aristotle, *Rhetoric*, 1356b.

[2] *Rhetoric*, 1394a, 25.

intercourse in a dialectical milieu. The Fugue in the " Sirens "
episode is simply a more complicated shuffling of the same
materials; something like genuine community of interests
seems temporarily achieved, only because this music melts down
minds into merging pools of sentiment. In the "Cyclops"
episode the materials of the labyrinth and Fugue are employed
in alternation: racy slang and sentimental or mock-heroic
inflation, the same pair of obsessions that turn up in " tough "
novels or news-magazines.

   *Tumescence, detumescence—Embryonic development—Hallu-
cination.* Tumescence and detumescence mark an extension of
the " Cyclops " technique : the alternation of irreconcileables
acquires sexual connotations. Masturbation in the presence of
a pseudo-virgin parodies orientation of the will toward the
Mother of God; contraception mocks fertility; the brothel
assumes the role of marriage-bed. The embryonic development of the " Oxen " episode, which as Joyce wrote to Frank
Budgen[1] recapitulates that of the book itself, runs the gamut
from Narrative to Gigantism once again, realizing in quotidian
material each successive stage of the historical incubus. The
issue, and the ultimate solution of all the day's tensions, is
Hallucination.

   Thus the action of the book resembles the running down of
an immense clock. The sharp conflict in the sharp daylight of
the opening episode becomes slacker and slacker as the book
goes on. By " Proteus " Stephen has become immersed in
himself. With " Calypso " we are transported into the mind
of Mr. Bloom, and a noticeable slackening of tensions takes
place. By the " Wandering Rocks " the people have become
discrete mechanisms; in " Cyclops ", with the appearance of
interspersed parodies, they are being put on display and guyed
as comically animated dolls. By the " Oxen of the Sun "
nobody is talking to anyone else, despite the amount of disputation; all is conveyed by indirect discourse, and external
descriptive phrases like " general vacant hilarity." " Circe " is
a gesticulating clockwork charade of private worlds, animated
by the Locomotor Apparatus alone. " Eumaeus " immerses
Stephen and Bloom in cliché; " Ithaca " is utterly deperson-
alized; Molly in "Penelope" has no direction but that imposed
by the vagaries of her appetites, and no audience but herself.

[1] " This progression is also linked back at each part subtly with some foregoing
episode of the day. . . ." Letter of March 2, 1920. (Slocum collection).

THE NAMES

Each proper name imposes an additional perspective on the common world, somewhat as follows:

Stephen Dedalus: St. Stephen, the first martyr; Dedalus, the exiled builder of labyrinths. Our Stephen of course is his son, who fell into the sea.

Simon Dedalus: The affiliation of Simon is with St. Peter: the Rock. By extension, his faded aristocratic impulsiveness is the cornerstone of the secular church that is Dublin. The Rock also as Father, though Stephen is looking elsewhere.

Leopold Bloom: Lion plus flower; the King of Beasts devalued into vegetable life. Molly's nickname for him, " Poldy," is the symbol of their relation: it unlions him and leaves him polled. Cf. the function of the " Lionel " song in Sirens, and Molly's Boylan—Lion equation in " Penelope ", U761/735.

Molly Bloom: Molly from *mollis*, soft; St. Thomas said the philosopher should be *mollis carne*. Her maiden name, Tweedy, alludes as Mr. Gilbert says to Penelope's web; also to her masculine orientation vis-à-vis her husband.

Millicent Bloom: " Molly. Milly. Same thing watered down ", U88/81.

Malachi Roland St. John (" Buck ") Mulligan: The book of Malachi (last in the Old Testament) is (a) an indictment of profane priests—cf. our account of Mulligan as parody-priest; (b) a prophecy of the Sun of Righteousness. Roland's horn (cf. *Finnegans Wake*, F74), is an apocalyptic trumpet, plus a reinforcement of Mulligan's John-the-Baptist phase. St. John, the evangelist of the Logos, whose role Mulligan the dialectician usurps; also the writer of the apocalypse. Mulligan: stage Irishman. Buck: lecher, dandy.

Blazes Boylan: Hellfire.

Numerous iconographic configurations emerge when we step back from the book for a view of the tableau entire. To mention only three, Bloom as advertisement canvasser spends the day selling something that doesn't exist (the ad with the design of the crossed keys) on behalf of someone who isn't anxious to sell it (the Editor) to someone who doesn't want to buy it: a deep-cutting epiphany of commerce. And much of the day he has a book called *Sweets of Sin* in one pocket and a cake of soap in another. He and Stephen spend the day clad in mourning, and the cab that took Bloom to the cemetery in the morning brings their deliverance from the snares of Mabbot Street at night.

TELEMACHUS

The situation exhibited here is simply: Mulligan—the clown as priest. Stephen—the artist as clown.

The tower and the sea are primordial male and female symbols. The sea, Mulligan's " great sweet mother " and for Stephen the reminder of his mother's corruption, U7/3, signifies Joy and Destiny in the *Portrait*, the feminine, material, and corrupting in *Ulysses*, father and home in *Finnegans Wake*. It becomes the sea of matter into which Stephen has fallen and over which Mr. Bloom navigates.

The transaction with the mirror, U8/4, should be observed.

1. Mulligan uses it to flash tidings abroad, in the mode of Shaun the Post.
2. Mulligan as pseudo-artist offers it to Stephen (holding the mirror up to nature).
3. Stephen inspects himself in it (Narcissus).
4. Stephen sees his own image, " cleft by a crooked crack, hair on end. As he and others see me."
5. Stephen calls it " a symbol of Irish art. The cracked lookingglass of a servant."

Haines the Englishman has spent the night " raving and moaning to himself about shooting a black panther " U6/2; *panther* is the generic beast: etymologically, " all beasts."[1] As we learn in the *Castle of Otranto* parody, U405/394, Haines is driven through his mumming mutations by this spectre much as Stephen/Hamlet by the murdered father's ghost: " The black panther was himself the ghost of his own father." The tradition that the father of Christ was one Panther, a Roman centurion,[2] is alluded to by Virag in the brothel, U510/495; Virag (the ghost of Bloom's father) himself runs through innumerable animal mutations (all the beasts). The panther-theme exfoliates into an image of paternity *secundum carnem*, laying its curse on all the inhabitants of this animal hell. As the Englishman is the usurper of Ireland, as Mulligan is the usurping priest, so Panther the Centurion is the usurping God.

NESTOR

Several themes receive important statement here. The fall of

---

[1] " Panther: all animals," remarked Joyce of the metamorphic dog in " Proteus " U47/43. (Budgen, 54.)

[2] Origen, *Against Celsus*, 1. 19. 1.

Lycidas into the sea parallels that of Stephen, U26/23; but for Stephen " the dear might of him that walked the waves " is just another phase of the nightmare: " Here also over these craven hearts his shadow lies and on the scoffer's heart and lips and on mine."

History is a nightmare from which Stephen seeks to awake, U35/31; the ghost of the unquiet father arises however to lay unwelcome duties on him. The incubus of childhood is tied up, Vico-wise, with that of national history: " Secrets, silent, stony, sit in the dark places of both our hearts ", U29/26.

Deasy's study is synchronized with this blighted static world, and Deasy with God-become-Caesar: " Stale smoky air hung in the study with the smell of drab abraded leather of its chairs. As on the first day he bargained with me here. As it was in the beginning, is now. On the sideboard the tray of Stuart coins, base treasure of a bog: and ever shall be. And snug in their spooncase of purple plush, faded, the twelve apostles having preached to all the gentiles: world without end ", U30/26. " On the first day " God made a bargain which Adam failed to keep. The world was delivered into the hands of commerce: " and ever shall be " is linked to a hoard of coins; the sun itself flings " dancing coins ", U37/33. And via his thrice-repeated wage paying (cf. Stephen's three masters, U22/18) Stephen fuses Deasy with the hangman God: " Three nooses round me here ", U31/37.

PROTEUS

Matter is the prime symbol of *Ulysses*; Proteus is " Primal Matter." " God becomes man . . . &c.", U51/47, is the note not of redemption but of the metempsychotic material cycle. Man on the other hand plays God: Stephen in the centre of his world sends his shadow/soul forth into eternity and calls it back, U49/45. On the next page he leans back in the attitude of God contemplating creation. The entire episode is a careful epiphany of Shelley's world, with its polarities (a Bergsonian material flux accorded pseudo-spirituality, the spectator as pseudo-God) clearly indicated. Stephen in the *Portrait* not only quotes Shelley with approbation, he professes a Shelleyan rapturous atheism and has a Shelleyan interest in birds and clouds. This theme is always related to his contempt of the body and so of existent being. He refers to sound and shape and colour as " the prison gates of our soul ", P242/235, and even his bad eyesight and rotting teeth and clothes are comic transliterations of " the shadow of our night " which he would " out-soar." His Icarian flight of course follows the modes of the *Skylark*.[1]

The Fall and Death are two other important motifs here. The former is developed apropos of the cocklepicker and his wife, U48/44. First they are gypsies (cf. Picasso's harlequins, and the Adamite connotations of Rilke's *Fifth Elegy*, inspired by a Picasso *Saltimbanques:* " Du, der mit dem Aufschlag, / wie nur Früchte ihn kennen, unreif / täglich hundert Mal abfällt vom Baum der gemeinsam / erbauten Bewegung " [41–44]). Then they become Adam and Eve expelled, bearing their burdens.[2] Then the sun's flaming sword (cf. that of the archangel over Eden) suggests that the woman is the moon and her burden the tides: the tides become the cycle of female blood, and so the generative cycle (metempsychosis of human descent). The wet sign that calls her menstrual hour assimilates with the vampire of death; as " Behold the handmaid of the moon " indicates, this image of human generation is to be seen as a dark perversion of the coming of the Holy Ghost to the womb of Mary. " Bridebed, childbed, bed of death, ghostcandled " (all summonses involving blood) are the generative cycle of " Proteus " once more; cf. the four ages of *Finnegans Wake*.

The death motif is developed apropos of " the cold domed room of the tower ", U45/41 (Bloom is at this moment in the cemetery). The tower is the grave, and the skull; Mulligan and Haines dormant troubling forces in the brain; the barbicans eyes through which light, creeping over the " dial floor," brings tidings only of impending death. (In " Circe ", this tower room becomes the amphitheatre of a black mass, U583/565, paralleling Mulligan's parody-mass of the morning.)

[1] On the other hand, Joyce's estimate of Shelley is contained in his characterization of *Prometheus Unbound* as " the Schwärmerei of a young Jew " (Budgen, 13). He gave his own romantic a middle-aged Jew for spiritual father. Cf. also Budgen 182: " No doubt there is much beauty in *Prometheus Unbound* and *Hellas*, but I feel that it's all on the wrong track."

[2] In Joyce's Homeric list, the Cocklepicker is Megapenthus, son of Menelaus by a slave-woman, who is a surrogate for the faithless and hence now barren Helen. (See the opening lines of *Odyssey* IV.) Joyce equates Menelaus (who once bound and questioned Proteus) with Adam, who had formerly the ability to read the Book of Nature. Helen's infidelity is Eve's fall, the slave-girl is the fallen Eve. Megapenthus thus becomes the symbol of Adam's disinherited sons, and so of fallen Adam himself. Joyce's Menelaus, Kevin Egan, is also, like Adam, in exile.

CALYPSO

The time-sequence of the next three episodes, " Calypso "—
" Lotus Eaters "—" Hades ", parallels that of the first
three, "Telemachus"—"Nestor"—"Proteus". In addition,
Stephen in the " Proteus " episode has passed through
Calypso, Lotus-eating and Hades phases. There are trans-
positions of detail, and the motifs of ensnarement, navel-gazing,
and death are continually superimposed, but " Calypso " in a
disengaged state is evident, for instance, at U49/45, " Lotus-
Eaters" at U50/46, "Hades" in the seadeath passage, U51/47.

Upon his introduction, however, Bloom is explicitly contrasted with Stephen; his relish of " grilled mutton kidneys
which gave to his palate a fine tang of faintly scented urine "
U55/48, counterpoints Stephen's shrinking from the " urinous
offal from all dead ", U51/47. The " inner organs of beasts
and fowls ", U55/48, interest the haruspex as legible signatures
and Mr. Bloom as food.

It isn't necessary to enumerate the nymph-avatars: Molly,
Milly (" my looking glass from night to morning ", U62/55),
the girl next door, the cat, the " laughing witch." The picture
over the bed from " the Easter number of *Photo Bits* ",
U64/58, gathers up their significance. More important is the
juxtaposition, in the Dance of the Hours, U69/62, of seduc-
tion (girls in grey gauze) and death (night hours with daggers).
Sex in *Ulysses* follows this apocalyptic mode; Vico's age of disintegration, paralleling twilight, is nigh; compare Stephen's
premonition of the " ruin of all space ", U25/21.

LOTUS EATERS

This episode is an anatomy of contemporary dreams and drugs.
A batch of soap ads, clippings on the religious pronouncements
of screen stars, *National Geographic* colour plates, and *Readers'
Digest* uplift would furnish complete documentation paragraph
by paragraph. The slip in Martha's letter, " I do not like
that other world ", U76/70 orients the refusal of the Lotus-
Eaters to contemplate eternity except in terms of spooning in a
yellow convertible under California starlight.

Thus all the Christian material in the section is systematically perverted: " Safe in the arms of kingdom come. Lulls
all pain. Wake this time next year ", U80/73. By an ironic
twist of which Bloom is not quite aware, his mind slips from

the law of floating bodies to the law of falling bodies, U71/64. The chap " in the dead sea, floating on his back, reading a book with a parasol open " is a pseudo-Adam drifting in a narcissist analogue of Eden; the next thing we hear of is the Fall.

Analogies with Stephen's meditation on the beach turn up in unexpected ways: Stephen's " faunal noon " and " floating foampool ", U50/46, appear as Bloom's " Nice kind of evening feeling " and his vision of an inundation of porter: " lazy pooling whirl of liquor bearing along wideleaved flowers of its froth ", U78/72.

HADES

" Hades " presents Dublin as the Kingdom of the Dead; we have already indicated how many features of the cemetery are analogous to those of the adjoining city. " The Irishman's house is his coffin.", U108/102. Watching the coffin being borne into the cemetery, Bloom thinks, " So much dead weight. Felt heavier myself stepping out of that bath ", U100/93. He has stepped, that is, from Lotus-Land into the land of the Dead, which as the trans-section of the entire city by the funeral procession implies, includes all Dublin.

Death is as material a phenomenon as happiness. The priest croaks like a frog, balances his book against a toad's belly, reminds Bloom of a rhyme about a rook, looks " bully about the muzzle ", has a " belly on him like a poisoned pup ", and according to Mr. Dedalus will some day " burst sideways like a sheep in clover ", U102/95. The cemetery is the kingdom of defunct animals: dead hearts are " old rusty pumps ", U104/98, translation to glory consists of " Bam! expires. Gone at last. People talk about you a bit; forget you ", U109/103. The shades clustered on the bank of Hades turn out to be statues " The best obtainable. Thos. H. Dennany, monumental builder and sculptor ", U98/92. The keeper of the Two Keys is not St. Peter but the custodian, U105/99. " Nothing between himself and heaven " turns out to be a periphrasis for baldness, U101/94. The " dead letter office " that pops into Mr. Bloom's mind, U106/100, is as comprehensive a symbol as any in the episode.

AEOLUS

We have already indicated the main alignments of this episode in terms of the traditions of public oratory still thriving in

Ireland and still preserving a nominal connection with the great rhetorical tradition of Christian Europe. Matter, as in " Hades ", is still the incubus. The rhetoricians of the opening pages are all machines: trams, barrels, presses, the squeaking door. The continuity with the " Hades " episode is explicit: the trams shunt " In The Heart of the Hibernian Metropolis " (the organ of " Hades " is " heart "), and Dignam in the grave is fused with the presses that turn out the account of his death:

> Hynes here too: account of the funeral probably. Thumping thump. This morning the remains of the late Mr. Patrick Dignam. Machines. Smash a man to atoms if they got him caught. Rule the world today. His machineries are pegging away too. Like these, got out of hand: fermenting. Working away, tearing away. And that old grey rat tearing to get in. U117/110.

The " spiritual " that is suddenly set chock-a-block with this materiality is Dan Dawson's panegyric on " Our Lovely Land ", U122/115. Joyce always sets Romantic poetry in close touch with mechanism. In the discussion that follows, collocation of Rome/England/Egypt with Ireland/Jewry needs no comment. The Mosaic " language of the outlaw " that welded together the straggling Israelites is of course intended by the orator for Gaelic; though Stephen we may surmise has other thoughts. The vision he enunciates is a parable of infertility: plumstones dropping over Dublin from a phallic monument. (Boylan, as Mr. Bloom muses much later, " gets the plums and I the plumstones ", U370/360.)

LESTRYGONIANS

The images now shift from mechanism to cannibalism; we have already detailed the anthropophagist modes of Caesar and Christ. Bloom dives out of this dog-eat-dog peristaltic order, brought for him to culminating intelligibility by the sight of Boylan, into the " artifice of eternity " represented by the frozen goddesses: this is the transition into the world of art, dialectically explored in the following episode.

SCYLLA AND CHARYBDIS

This, the most intricate episode in the book, deserves a chapter for which we have not space. Perfunctory equations have been offered at various times, and there is no need of adding to their number: the analogical relationships here set in motion among Stephen, Shakespeare, Bloom, Hamlet, and the persons of the Trinity is too complex for epigram or diagram. All we would draw attention to is the analogy between the modes of theological paternity mentioned by Stephen on U22/18, and the various patterns of fatherhood surveyed in the present episode.[1] Sabellius, who " held that the Father was Himself His Own Son ", U205/196, describes a relationship of spiritual identity such as exists between Stephen and Dedalus the artificer. Arius, " warring his life long on the consubstantiality of the Son with the Father," proposed a relationship of adoption such as is to subsist between Stephen and Bloom. The orthodox consubstantial doctrine describes the relationship between Stephen and his " consubstantial father ", U39/35, Simon Dedalus.

These three paradigms of paternity are first enunciated in Stephen's image of Shakespeare acting the ghost in Hamlet. The character Hamlet is the son of his soul, the dead Hamlet Shakespeare is the consubstantial son of his body, the player Burbage (surrogate manifestation to the audience) his son by adoption. These paradigms function in two ways. The Shakespeare example is enunciated from the standpoint of the father. It is an analogy for the processes of artistic creation, the relation of the artist to his artefact, his experience, and his materials. The Stephen example is enunciated from the standpoint of the son. It is an analogy for modes of intellectual and spiritual loyalty. Much of the difficulty of the episode is reduced if we stop trying to fit all the examples to one another as though they all illustrated the same thing.

It may be worth reiterating that Stephen is and isn't Joyce in just these two modes. Shakespeare is the paradigm of Stephen[2] and Joyce qua artist, transmuting consubstantial experiences into an adopted[3] language to create a spiritual image. But Stephen's scorn of the consubstantial father—that is, Stephen's pattern of loyalties—isn't to be confounded with

---

[1] For more details see Edward Duncan, " The Unsubstantial Father, a Study of the *Hamlet* Symbolism in Joyce's *Ulysses*," University of Toronto Quarterly, Spring, 1950, 126–140. Mr. Duncan was kind enough to furnish me some years ago with a detailed annotation of this episode.

[2] He is " made up in the castoff mail of a court buck ", U186/177, in allusion to Stephen wearing Mulligan's castoff shoes.

[3] Cf. Stephen on the English dean: " His language, so familiar and so foreign will always be for me an acquired speech ", P221/215.

anything of Joyce's. It is simply one of the devices by which Stephen's hopeless misorientation is characterized. It is to Shakespeare, the author, playing the Ghost at the *Globe*, that the episode explicitly gives the words, " Hamlet, I am thy father's spirit." Joyce likewise studied Stephen all the years of his life which were not vanity in order to play the part of spectral author.

THE WANDERING ROCKS

Framed between the mild " whatever is, is right " of Father Conmee[1] and the viceregal cavalcade, this section juxtaposes events in space as " The Oxen of the Sun " juxtaposes events in time. As the mechanical linkages between the nineteen sections imply, this labyrinth of shadow-selves, small talk, mistaken identity, epiphanizes communal death. The citizens are, almost literally, wandering rocks; nothing unites the simultaneous events but the pavements on which they occur, as we are made to realize every time a fragment from some distant happening is interpolated. The viceroy's procession is the mirror of this Dublin: there isn't a trace of unanimity in the three closely-written pages cataloguing the greetings he receives. One man is indifferent, another doffs his hat, another stares coldly, another is almost run over; and there seems no incongruity in the inclusion, among these quasi-human responses, of Poddle River hanging out in fealty a tongue of liquid sewage, or Eugene Stratton grinning in effigy from a billboard.

THE SIRENS

After non-communal ethos, communal pathos, via music, counterpointed with expressions of utter loneliness. We have already described Bloom's union with Stephen's father in this episode: the " Siopold! ", U271/262, of the climax combines Simon and Leopold via the Lionel of the song, and both men have in different ways lost their wives.

The prose of the " Wandering Rocks " is adapted to brisk notation of externals, though as points of reference we are given one of Stephen's richest meditations, U238/228, and some interior monologue by Tom Kernan, almost indistinguishable

[1] "Father Conmee reflected on the providence of the Creator who had made turf to be in bogs where men might dig it out and bring it to town and hamlet to make fires in the houses of poor people ", U218/209.

from that of Bloom. The prose of the " Sirens " is a polyphonic notation of internal events. This juxtaposition postulates the wide technical oscillations of the second half of the book.

Like the mirror in " Telemachus ", Bloom's rubber band gathers up a complex cluster of themes. (1) It is the instrument upon which he performs, U272/263, amid the vocal exhibitionism going on all round him. (2) As " Love's old sweet *sonnez la gold* " gyving his fingers fast, U269/260, it is a marriage symbol. (3) " Looped, unlooped, noded, disnoded ", U270/260, it enacts the ebb and flow of his relations with Molly, and the dance of the wooers around Penelope. (4) Stretched and snapped, it enacts disaster after pleasure too far prolonged: " Yet too much happy bores. He stretched more, more. Are you not happy in your? Twang. It snapped ", U273/263. (The stretching comically duplicates the prolonged tenor note at the end of the song, U271/262, the snaping the abrupt ending amid applause.)

The marvellously varied thematic index with which the episode opens lists atoms of fractured passion, not of concept; the objection that they are meaningless until the episode has been read is irrelevant. When isolated in a list, phrases like " Warbling. Ah, lure! Alluring." and " Tink cried to bronze in pity " and " Jingle jingle jaunted jingling " and " Boomed crashing chords. When love absorbs. War! War! The tympanum ", U252/242, grind a comic edge on verbal sonorities that are after all the banalities of a hundred tenth-rate operas. It is from such stuff that Dublin's great fugue of passion rises, gravely " per canonem ".

CYCLOPS

The final technical devices are once more being postulated before exploitation: this episode anticipates the " Circe " interruptions of clock-time by comic dilation, and the " Oxen of the Sun's " concatenation of parodies.

The parodies, in line with the art (politics) of the episode, are varieties of public rhetoric; legal jargon, U287/277, a newspaper account of an execution drenched in novelese, U301/291, an account of a Gaelic Athletic Association meeting, U311/301, a fashionable wedding, U321/311, etc.; and varieties of nationalist literature: Ireland's idyllic past, U288/278, the Ossianic hero, U291/281, a journalistic version of

an Ossianic *geste*, U337/327. The key to the presence of the
latter kind of material is simply that the pseudoheroics of books
like O'Grady's *Cuculain: An Epic* were oriented toward the
creation of a national consciousness, and as such were part
of the art of politics.

They are decidedly parodies, not pastiches; dignity passes
into bathos *within* the passage, and then is jolted into further
bathos. From a serious beginning—" There sleep the mighty
dead as in life they slept, warriors and princes of high renown "
—we descend to lame gestures like " . . . and other denizens
of the aqueous kingdom too numerous to be enumerated ", and
the fairy-tale world is suddenly falsified by the verbal poverty
of the narration: " Lovely maidens sit in close proximity to the
roots of the lovely trees singing the most lovely songs while they
play with all kinds of lovely objects as for example . . .",
U289/279. By displaying the relationship of its techniques
to those of journalism, Joyce delivers a critique of the entire
neo-Celtic movement.

Contrary to first impression, there is no repetition of effect
in the episode. The details are precisely grouped toward an
anatomization of every kind of political action and sentiment.
At the execution of the revolutionist, for instance, Kathleen ni
Houlihan wipes her eyes and accepts on the spot the proposal
of a wealthy Englishman who presents his " visiting card,
bankbook, and genealogical tree " (social, financial, and
ancestral credentials), while the Irish mob cheers and regards
the whole thing as a great show. The hangman dominates the
episode, the wolfhound growls in Gaelic, U306/296, and
running metaphors drawn from the cattlepens and the slaughterhouse permeate the whole.

Bloom comes into focus as the helpless humanitarian vis-à-vis
political reality; his feeble definition of Love (" I mean the
opposite of hatred ") is echoed by nursery prattle opening with
a tautology: " Love loves to love love. Nurse loves the new
chemist. Constable 14A loves Mary Kelly. . . . You love a
certain person. And this person loves that other person because
everybody loves somebody but God loves everybody ",
U327/317. His evocation of Christ (" Your God was a jew.
Christ was a jew like me ", U336/326) prompts a new crucifixion (" By Jesus, I'll crucify him so I will ") which Bloom
escapes on the jaunting car, " And they beheld Him even Him,
ben Bloom Elijah, amid clouds of angels ascend to the glory

of the brightness at an angle of forty-five degrees over Donohoe's in Little Green Street like a shot off a shovel ", U339/329.

This is one more " comparison in which two things are measured by each other ". As remarks about the sinhedrim, U317/307, the lost tribes, U320/310, and the land of bondage, U324/314, indicate, the Irish are analogous to the Jews in captivity, and their rejection of Bloom is analogous to the demand for Barabbas. The ironies of this superimposition are inescapable. But Bloom is not entitled to sentimental regard as the champion of the plain man. He is the most inadequate Messiah imaginable.

The lawcourt paragraph, U317/307, is worth attention; it marks the first appearance of a technique that is to dominate the rest of the book: systematic enumeration of instances in the mode of a Renaissance " anatomy ". The account of a court session is inflected with a large variety of nationalities and times: Greek (" oxeyed goddess "), Catholic (" Holy and Undivided Trinity "), Old English (" gave his rede "), modern English (" Justice Andrews . . . in the probate court "), Mediaeval (" Sir Frederic the Falconer "), Irish and Jewish (" the law of the brehons . . . the high sinhedrim of the twelve tribes of Iar "), Feudal (" lead forth from their donjon keep "), French (" ne bail ne mainprise ").

NAUSICAA

The techniques of anatomization go on full exhibition with this episode. In a letter to Frank Budgen we hear of the preliminary labour, " notation of flappers' atrocities and general plan of the specially new frigging style "[1] which in another letter Joyce designated as " a namby-pamby jammy marmalady drawersy (alto la!) style with effects of incense, mariolatry, masturbation, stewed cockles, painter's palette, chitchat, circumlocutions, etc., etc."

We have already explained the metaphorical implications of the opening paragraph. Amid this twilight of civilization, the masculine world consists of four-year old twins and a baby, surrounded by nursemaids. In their sailor caps with H.M.S. Bellisle, U340/330, (Ireland), insignia, they battle over a sand-castle like Irish revolutionaries differing on policy, and succeed in demolishing the sand-castle (Ireland) itself.

Gerty is introduced via the conventions of the love novel,

[1] Joyce to Budgen, Feb. 13, 1920 (Slocum collection).

U342/331, and we learn that Madame Vera Verity (the bright-eyed Athena of the opening of the sixth book of the *Odyssey*) has advised her to try eyebrowleine. Her thoughts pass through the modes of medical ads, U343/332, *Vogue* and *Vanity Fair*, U344/334, Social news, U345/335, the recipe pages, U346/335, *Better Homes and Gardens*, U346/336, prophylactics for "those raging splitting headaches, U349/338, and a wide variety of sentimental novels.

The qualifications of a desirable male in a feminized culture are set forth early in the chapter, U343/333: he is handsome, looks like a gentleman, has an unusually shaped head, rides his bike with no hands, smokes perfumed cigarettes, and is no taller than she. But the drawback of this sort of chap is that he is "too young to understand. He would not believe in love, a woman's birthright". The ideal husband is really a father: " a manly man with a strong quiet face who had not found his ideal, perhaps his hair slightly flecked with grey, and who would understand, take her in his sheltering arms, strain her to him in all the strength of his deep passionate nature and comfort her with a long long kiss ", U345/335. Female pathos and whimsicality are balanced by male subservience and irrationality; the mother's-boy goes berserk to manifest his maleness: "The temper of him! O, he was a man already was little Tommy Caffrey since he was out of his pinnies ", U346/336.

Gerty is a secular perversion of " the Virgin most powerful, Virgin most merciful ", U348/337. Her intercession consists of wishing that her father had " avoided the clutches of the demon drink, by taking the pledge or those powders the drink habit cured in Pearson's Weekly. Over and over she had told herself that . . . gazing out of the window dreamily by the hour at the rain falling on the rusty bucket, thinking ", U348/337.

> The Blessed Damozel leaned down
> From the gold bar of Heaven. . . .

She keeps, like Pope's Belinda, a dressing-table altar with sacramental objects like the confession album (penance), the child of Mary badge (confirmation), the whiterose scent (Eucharist), and an alabaster pouncetbox (anointment of Holy Orders—Luke vii.37).

She is a massive epiphany of second-hand living. The men who pass through her mind as she examines Bloom, U358/347, are classified according to the types in novels, and the only question for Gerty is which novel she is stepping into. Her every gesture has its sanction in her world of erotic fiction, and she feels secure so long as her environment responds according to the book, which it generally does. Bloom is reassuring because she can "type" him, U359/348: a judgment on Bloom. Gerty in that way epiphanizes not merely Dublin adolescent womanhood but the male society which has never behaved in such a way to shake her belief in the reliability of her paradigms.

The religious ceremonial synchronized with this episode is the Benediction: the sacrament, like Gerty, is exhibited but not eaten.

OXEN OF THE SUN

This episode juxtaposes events in time as the "Wandering Rocks" juxtaposes events in space. By a tremendous extension of the basic Homeric device, the 1904 situation is projected through a variety of alien sensibilities against a series of alien backgrounds. Joyce's account of the technique is worth full transcription:

> Am working hard at Oxen of the Sun, the idea being the crime committed against fertility by sterilizing the act of coition. Scene, lying-in hospital. Technique: a nineparted episode without divisions introduced by a Sallustian-Tacitean prelude (the unfertilized ovum), then by way of earliest English alliterative and monosyllabic Anglo-Saxon ("Before born the babe had bliss. Within the womb he won worship" "Bloom dull dreamy heard: in held hat stony staring") then by way of Mandeville ("Then came forth a scholar of medicine that men clepen &c") then Malory's *Morte d'Arthur* ("but that franklin Lenehan was prompt ever to pour them so that at the least way mirth should not lack"), then the Elizabethan chronicle style ("about that present time young Stephen filled all cups"), then a passage solemn uses Milton, Taylor, and Hooker, followed by a choppy Latin-gossipy bit, style of Burton-Browne, then a passage Bunyanesque ("the reason was that in the way he fell in with a certain whore whose name she said is Bird in the Hand"), after a diarystyle bit Pepys-Evelyn ("Bloom sitting snug with a party of wags, among them Dixon jun., Ja. Lynch, Doc. Madden and Stephen D. for a languor he had before and was now better, he having dreamed tonight a strange fancy and mistress Purefoy there to be delivered, poor body, two days past her time and the midwives hard put to it, God send her quick issue") and so on through Defoe-Swift and Steele-Addison, Sterne and Landor-Pater-Newman until

it ends in a frightful jumble of Pidgin English, Nigger English,
Cockney, with Bowery slang and broken doggerel. This progression
is also linked back at each part subtly with some foregoing episode
of the day and besides this, with the natural stages of development
in the embryo and the periods of formal evolution in general. The
double-thudding Anglo-Saxon motives recur from time to time
(" Loth to move from Horne's house ") to give the sense of the
hoofs of oxen. Bloom is the spermatozoon, the hospital the womb,
the nurses the ovum, Stephen the embryo.

How's that for high? . . .[1]

There are, it may be added, after the lightning-flash of conception, U379/368, forty paragraphs corresponding to the
forty weeks of gestation, climaxed, U415/404, by the "utter-
ance of the Word ".

It is funny enough that this immensely laboured virtuosity
should attend the birth of Mrs. Purefoy's insignificant baby.
What really gets born, however, is primarily the Pandemonium
of the ten final paragraphs: modern Dublin: the end-product
of 1900 years of Anglo-Saxon culture. The unfertilized ovum
is pre-Christian Roman and Teutonic culture; the lightning-
flash the Incarnation. As the mention of " the crib in Bethle-
hem of Juda long ago ", U415/404, implies, what gets born
during the chapter is also " Christ the tiger: " the wrath of
Homer's Apollo, the Second Coming murkily foreshadowed
in the advent of " Alexander J. Christ Dowie ", U421/409, at
the end of the episode. The waters, too, flood the Waste Land,
U416/404; there has been a long drought, Pepys tells us,
U390/379, and Purefoy père is exhibited as the Fisher King,
U391/380. Death by Water, as always, is ambivalent: it
brings life to a new little Purefoy and rain to parched Dublin,
but Stephen and company go out and drown themselves in
drink.

CIRCE

Faced by the choice of giving either a full commentary on this
episode or none at all, we shall note only (1) that it is an
apocalypse climaxing in the Black Mass and the burning of
Dublin, U582/565; (2) that the apparition of Bloom's father,

[1] Joyce to Frank Budgen, March 20, 1920. The curious reader may consult
Mr. A. M. Klein's labyrinthine schematization of this episode in *Here and Now*,
Toronto, I–3, 28–48. It probably isn't necessary to suppose that Joyce was quite
so fantastic a mathematician as Mr. Klein would like to believe.

the suicide Virag, U500/485, with his rattling speech, his animal gestures, his anthropoid commentary, and his departure with his unscrewed head beneath his arm, U511/496, is in many ways the most important epiphany in the episode. The animality over which he cackles is endemic to the whole of Dublin as it has been exhibited to us, and as it is pre-eminently exhibited now on Mabbot Street.

It seems absurd to find an apotheosis in Stephen's gesture at the light with his ashplant, U567/550. He doesn't even, as is so often stated, smash the chandelier; he breaks the glass chimney and dents the paper shade, U569/551. All he does is epiphanize his own Luciferian sin against the light. His collapse to the pavement is in line with the Plotinian symbolism he himself employs, U494/479:

> By sinking down in matter and glutting itself with it, the soul can die while yet plunged in the body; likewise when she has quitted the body her death is to lie in Matter until such time as she can escape upwards and by some means lift her face from the mud. This is " the descent to Hades and the after-sleep ".[1]

EUMAEUS

As the cosmic delirium of Rimbaud's *Bateau Ivre* is deflated to a paper boat in a mud-puddle, so, with very different significance since Stephen has learned nothing, Circe's phantasmagoria is deflated to the dull walk home by way of the cabman's shelter, amid a hilariously pedantic heaping up of every verbal cliché in current usage. Like " The Oxen of the Sun ", the episode has incurred the displeasure of those who don't read closely, and imagine that Joyce is conveying the sense of exhaustion by exhausting the reader for fifty pages. This is the old form-content dichotomy. The " sense," by such a reading, is the peregrination and conversation of Stephen and Bloom; the " effect " is something superimposed on the " sense " by the use of " style." On the contrary, Joyce invites close critical attention to the thousands of absurd locutions he employs. The author's mind is working with its usual energy. The Bloom-Stephen situation is sufficiently simple to be a critical *point d'appui* for a great many particular acts of critical discrimination, and that is how Joyce uses it. A sense of the exquisite absurdity of cliché after cliché is never lacking:

[1] Plotinus, *Enneads*, I.viii.13.

[Bloom] fell to woolgathering on the enormous dimensions of the water about the globe. Suffice it to say that, as a casual glance at the map revealed, it covered fully three fourths of it and he realized accordingly what it meant, to rule the waves. On more than one occasion—a dozen at the lowest—near the North Bull at Dollymount he had remarked a superannuated old salt, evidently derelict, seated habitually near the not particularly redolent sea on the wall, staring quite obviously at it and it at him, dreaming of fresh woods and pastures new as someone somewhere sings. U614/592.

The old salt staring at the sea is " ruling the waves " about as effectively as its maritime emperors; and the tag from *Lycidas* (cf. the earlier quotation, " Through the dear might of Him that walked the waves ", U27/23), is charmingly malapropos.

ITHACA

This seems to at least one reader the funniest episode of all: the only comment it requires is a repetition of the advice given above. The questions and answers are designed for separate contemplation; they do not constitute simply an indefensibly circumlocutory way of telling a story. Their periphrastic absurdities are sometimes pathetic:

> Did either openly allude to their racial difference?
> Neither, U666/642,

sometimes solemnly funny:

> Why was the chant arrested at the conclusion of this first distich?
> In consequence of defective mnemotechnic, U673/649,

sometimes wildly absurd:

> Which domestic problem as much as, if not more than, any other frequently engaged his mind?
> What to do with our wives, U670/646,

and sometimes engaged in an oddly cathedralized poetry. The immense catalogues of the junk in which Bloom's hopes, emotions, and present way of life are invested complete the epiphanization of industrial man.

PENELOPE

Mrs. Bloom's monologue, as Joyce said, " turns slowly, evenly, though with variations, capriciously, but surely like the huge earthball itself round and round spinning. Its four cardinal points are the female breasts, arse, womb and cunt expressed by the words *because, bottom* (in all senses bottom button, bottom of the glass, bottom of the sea, bottom of his heart) *woman, yes.* Though probably more obscene than any preceding episode it seems to me to be perfectly sane full amoral fertilizable untrustworthy engaging shrewd limited prudent indifferent *Weib.   Ich bin das Fleisch das stets bejaht!* "[1]

Some readers have over-sentimentalized the final pages of her monologue. They are in key with the animal level at which this comic inferno is conceived: and they are the epiphany of all that we have seen and heard during the day. The " Yes " of consent that kills the soul has darkened the intellect and blunted the moral sense of all Dublin. At the very rim of Dante's funnel-shaped Hell is the imperceptible " Yes " of Paola and Francesca; they are blown about by the winds, but Molly lies still at the warm dead womb-like centre of the labyrinth of paving-stones. Her " Yes " is confident and exultant; it is the " Yes " of authority: authority over this animal kingdom of the dead.

[1] Joyce to Budgen, August 16, 1921 (Slocum collection)

PART THREE

The Dream of the West

*Back we were by the jerk of a beamstark, backed
in paladays last, on the brinks of the wobblish,
the man what never put a dramn in the swags but
milk from a national cowse. That was the prick
of the spindle to me that gave me the keys
to dreamland*

★

Chapter 15

THE STUFFED PHOENIX

Barass! Pardon the inquisition, causas es quostas? It is Da
Valorem's Dominical Brayers. Why coif that weird hood?
Because among nosoever circusdances is to be apprehended the
dustungwashed poltronage of the lost Gabbarnaur-Jaggarnath.

Finnegans Wake (F342)

By dim delty Deva. Forget!

Finnegans Wake (F614)

" A MEDICAL student, an oarsman, a tenor, an amateur actor,
a shouting politician, a small landlord, a small investor, a
drinker, a good fellow, a storyteller, somebody's secretary,
something in a distillery, a taxgatherer, a bankrupt, and at
present a praiser of his own past ", P284/274, John Stanislaus
Joyce had receded, since these words were spoken, twenty-five
years further from the past he praised. " Oh dear, dear God,
those were great times." Bright and sharp and oddly circum-
scribed, the past leaped into a queerly vivid life before his
frequent scrutiny, like the vague furnishings of his bedroom
jumping into focus within the circular rim of the monocle he
still screwed into his eye. His health was increasingly poor,
his heart pounded, he lay long abed. From thirty, from forty,
from fifty years away, across a quarter-century of virtual
stagnation, came crowding in high colours images of sport and
song and drink and electioneering, a kaleidoscopic world to
step into which was oddly like passing through a mirror into a
dream. He would advance toward the bright framed past, his
own image would come forward to meet him, younger,
straighter, less florid, the hands not grey like those that now
gripped the counterpane, he would merge into the advancing
image, and stride, twice himself, a hero through a Dublin full
of life.

The city in the mirror of memory was active and bright;
himself moving through it gay and triumphant. " We beat
Dollymount and I made a big score; and by God I was carried
around the place and such a time we had. I beat my man two

love—anyway I gave him a good beating. I was made a lot
of and was taken around by the boys on their shoulders; and
my God the quantity of whiskey that I drank that night! It
must have been something terrible for I had to go to bed."
His mind rang with song. "Perkins was a baritone; Foley
was a Corkman and he had the grandest bass voice. He was
from Cloyne, County Cork, and my God he had a splendid
voice. I heard him in Opera and he would delight your heart
to hear him. . . ."

He had moved among giants; dead friends' voices joined
in praise:

"—McGuckin heard you singing in the Antient Concert
Rooms and said that you had the best tenor voice in Ireland;
and begor he ought to be a judge.—

"Anyway I had a divil of a good tenor in those days—and
they were great days, My God! they were. . . .

". . . I won the election in Dublin and I was the man that
put in Maurice Brooks and Lyons, and put out Arthur Guinness as he then was, the sitting member. . . . they make damn
good porter—I wish I had a pint of it now. . . . Of course I
didn't know the Dean because he was in Hell long before my
time. The Dean had one of the Van Esses as a sweetheart and
he had a second one but I don't know her name. . . . We all
went in and by God Almighty such drinking of champagne I
never saw in my life. We could not wait to draw the corks, we
slapped them against the marble-topped counter. . . . The
Turkish bath came into my mind and there I went after having
any God's quantity of champagne. Oh dear, dear God, those
were great times."

For anyone who would come near the bed (for he was bedridden now, year in year out) the great days flowed into talk.
On and on and on: "We used have great times then. There
was a bowling-green at the back of his hotel and I was considered a celebrated bowler; and I remember winning a prize at
the time I was secretary to the Distillery Coy. . . . Begor I
told them to clear out to Blazes. . . . I was cock of the walk
that day and I will never forget it; I was complimented by
everybody. . . ."

Sometimes Jim sent a visitor in from Paris: "Van Homrig
who the hell was he? my God I could not tell you. Why does
he want to know these things, Jim must be getting mad. . . .

"Father Charles of Mount Argus—he was the Priest out

there. What in the name of God does he want to know these things for? . . . Holy St. Peter! May God be merciful to him. Holy Father! Jim must have gone mad—he has overworked himself. My God what is coming over him!"

But he sat up in bed on the eve of Jim's forty-ninth birthday to write his eldest son a sheet or two of the florid calligraphy of which he was so vain:

I wonder if you remember the good old times at Brighton Square when you were Baby Tuckoo. And I would often take you walking in the square and I would tell you how the moo-cow comes down the mountains to wake up little boys. . . .

There had been great days for Jim too; John Stanislaus glowed to share, in recalling it, a lethal self-control that had never been his own:

". . . There was a debate and Kennedy if you please took exception to something Jim said. The cool, calm and calculating Jim putting his hand on the table took a note of what Kennedy said. At last Jim stood up and my God he spoke for half an hour and he left Kennedy in a condition that he was not fit to be washed. I often told Jim to go for the Bar, for he had a great flow of language and he speaks better than he writes. However he has done very well.

" Every night of my life and in the daytime too I think of all these things—they all come back to me and my God when I think of the times I used to have and here I am now—well I had a good time, anyway. There is not a field in County Cork that I don't know, for I hunted them all and I now go through all these hunts and the jollifications we used to have after them. They were great. I was one of the best men after the harriers. I used hunt with the Southern Harriers. We had a great pack and I was one of the best on foot. . . . Lord Justice Ronan was with me in Queen's College and he must be nearly 80 years of age. He was lop-sided at that time. His feet were paralysed at one side but he was a great fellow for cricket. I had a happy time of it then. I remember I used to buy cigars from the father of the present Postmaster General of the Free State. He had a shop in Parliament Street and sold papers and tobacco."[1]

Just when Joyce had issued, in *Ulysses*, his certificate of demise on that paralysed world, it suddenly began to assume,

[1] Quotations from the stenographic report of an unidentified interviewer, printed in the *James Joyce Yearbook*, Paris, 1949.

in his father's nocturnal monologues, a particularly vivid factitious life. It began to pass into myth. And in the very year *Ulysses* was published, contemporary Ireland achieved, as the Free State, factitious resurrection, with the same Tim Healy whom Joyce at the age of nine had excoriated for betraying Parnell (" Et Tu, Healy? ") as its first governor-general. Thirty-one years ago John Stanislaus Joyce had walked proudly round to a printer with his eldest son's philippic. Now John Stanislaus was recumbent among visions while Healy exuded frigid hospitality from the governor's mansion, apotheosis nearly in his grasp.

> His aim was to make the peace treaty between England and Ireland a success and his boyhood's dream of a free and independent Ireland a reality. It is not out of keeping with his life—for he was ever a devout man—to say that in his last days he could have breathed his *Nunc Dimittis* with gratitude and sincerity.

To that sort of obituary fame the pious betrayer of Parnell, " always a priests' man ", was moving. Plainly, the New Ireland was no more than an old man's dream; and what had been the dreams of the ubiquitous Healy?

As Joyce contemplated these events, a guiding image thrust itself forward insistently. It was reinforced by trivial accidents of the sort that so often played into his hand: the arrival of a post-card showing in the silhouette of the Hill of Howth the unmistakeable outlines of a sleeping giant; a pamphlet by an English village priest describing the discovery of a giant's grave in the parish lot.

He had written " The Dead ", and he had written, in *Ulysses*, of Dublin as an immense human form in a state of volitional paralysis, hallucinations whirling through its cogwheeling brain. These images were as Irish as they were contemporary; as far back as record reaches, the Irish bards have told of lost heroes sleeping; the gods belong to the past, *fuerunt dei;* unlike Odysseus who is a live man for Homer and, to the newest reader, a live man to-day, unlike the Achaean deities whose blood was heated by the quarrels of men, Celtic gods and heroes alike inhabit an underground dream-kingdom of the Dead.

> The men of the present are turned towards the men of the past. And the men of the past look contemptuously on these stunted descendants. They themselves, however, are only a survival. They pass their time in reminiscences—how touching this becomes in romantic elegy!—and they know that they have reached the period

of their decrepitude: for after all, Finn himself had been allotted two hundred years of full vigour, and thirty years of declining strength. In complete awareness, they are tending towards their downfall.—How much this resembles a twilight of heroes!—Thus, the best are doomed. The weak shall inherit the earth. Fatality drives on to destruction. Unless one takes the plunge into the underground world whose inhabitants enjoy eternal youth. How much this also resembles a religion of death! [1]

It is impossible, in fact, to enumerate the motifs that rushed concurrently into Joyce's mind in the months following the publication of *Ulysses*. A new book was taking shape, polarized between the dreams of his recumbent father and the phantasmagoric actualities of the Healy regime, with the legendary displacement of gods and heroes by mortals as an archetypal action. His father, in whom so much of the past of Dublin was incarnated, became the theme of sketch after sketch:

> An imposing everybody he always indeed looked, constantly the same as and equal to himself and magnificently well worthy of any and all such universalisation. . . . F32.

Attending a Dion Boucicault play:

> this folksforefather all of the time sat, having the entirety of his house about him, with the invariable broadstretched kerchief cooling his whole neck, nape and shoulderblades and in a wardrobe panelled tuxedo completely thrown back from a shirt well entitled a swallowall, on every point far outstarching the laundered clawhammers and marbletopped highboys of the pit stalls and early amphitheatre. . . . F33.

Meeting a tramp in Phoenix Park:

> when the tried friend of all creation, tigerwood roadstaff to his stay, was billowing across the wide expanse of our greatest park in his caoutchouc kepi and great belt and hideinsacks and his blaufunx fustian and ironsides jackboots and Bhagafat gaiters and his rubberised inverness, he met a cad with a pipe. . . . F35.

Attending to his amorphous affairs:

> . . . business, reading newspaper, smoking cigar, arranging tumblers on table, eating meals, pleasure, etcetera, etcetera, pleasure, eating meals, arranging tumblers on table, smoking cigar, reading newspaper, business; . . . those were the days and he was their hero. . . . F127.

This protean figure (" O dear, dear God, those were great

---

[1] Clémence Ramnoux, " The Finn Cycle ", translated by Maria Jolas in *James Joyce Yearbook*, Paris, 1949, 136.

times! ") expanded in Joyce's notes into irrepressible incarnate Ireland, antipodal to the Free State's " scrupulous meanness ". " And the cut of him! And the strut of him! How he used to hold his head as high as a howeth, the famous eld duke alien, with a hump of grandeur on him like a walking wiesel rat. And his derry's own drawl and his corksown blather and his doubling stutter and his gullaway swank ", F197. " Howeth ", fuses him with the Hill of Howth, " duke alien " with Deucalion the Ovidian survivor of the deluge. The Norse spirit, itself obliterated by "scrupulous meanness" in the Norway contemplated by Ibsen, is alive in him; he comes, a storm from Scandinavia, " umwalloped in an unusuable suite of clouds ", F324, or thrusts the phallic prow of his Viking ship up the Liffey, "till with his runagate bowmpriss he roade and borst her bar. . . . When they saw him shoot swift up her sheba sheath, like any gay lord salomon, her bulls they were ruhring, surfed with spree. Boyarka buah! Boyana bueh! He erned his lille Bunbath hard, our staly bred, the trader. He did. Look at here. In this wet of his prow.[1] Don't you know he was kaldt a bairn of the brine, Wasserbourne the waterbaby? Havemmarea, so he was! ", F197–8. Sailor and river coupled and a city was born (" and they were great days, My God! they were "):

> But I was firm with her. And I did take the reached of my delights. . . and I bade those polyfizzyboisterous seas to retire. . . and I abridged with domfine norsemanship till I had done abate her maidan race, my baresark bride, and knew her fleshily when with all my bawdy did I her whorship. . . And I cast my tenspan joys on her, arsched overtupped, from bank of call to echobank,[2] by dint of strongbow (Galata! Galata!) so streng we were in one, malestream in shegulf . . . and the singing sands for herbrides' music. . . . F547.

The same indiscriminate energy went into decking his city-bride with the geegaws of trade: " soft goods and hardware (catalogue, *passim*) and ladderproof hosiery lines (see stockinger's raiment), cocquette coiffs (see Agnes' hats) and peningsworths of the best taste of knaggs of jets and silvered waterroses and geegaws of my pretty novelties and wispywaspy frocks of redferns and lauralworths . . .", F548, —laying out parks and buildings:

---

[1] Adam earned his bread by the sweat of his brow. " Staly " assimilates " stale " and " daily " bread to " steely-bred ".

[2] The bridging of the Liffey at the city site.

my selvage mats of lecheworked lawn, my carpet gardens of Guerdon City, with chopes pyramidous and mousselimes and beaconphires and colossets and pensilled turisses for the busspleaches of the summiramies and esplanadas and statuesques and templeogues ...,

—and streets:

and I laid down before the trotters to my eblanite my stony battered waggonways, my nordsoud circulums, my eastmoreland and westlandmore, running boullowards and syddenly parading. ... F553,

—and bringing a legendary good life into being:

for days there was no night for nights were days and our folk had rest from Blackheathen and the pagans from the prince of pacis: what was trembling sod quaked no more, what were frozen loins were stirred and lived: gone the septuor, dark deadly dismal doleful desolate dreadful desperate, no more the tolvmaans, bloody gloomy hideous fearful furious alarming terrible mournful sorrowful frightful appalling: peace perfect peace: ... F549.

("I was cock of the walk that day and I will never forget it; I was complimented by everybody. ...")

No such invader sails up the Liffey now; contemplating the debaters of the "devil era" in the Dail Eireann, "and all the greedy gushes out through their small souls", the river-woman thinks back with longing toward the aristocratic sea-lord whose extinction she has unthinkingly accepted: "If I seen him bearing down on me now under whitespread wings like he'd come from Arkangels, I sink I'd die down over his feet, humbly dumbly, only to washup", F628.

If the great past, the abolition of the "dark deadly dismal doleful desolate dreadful desperate," sounds a little inflated, the New Era of 1922 is plainly as hollow as the finale of a pantomime, "the whole ... to be wound up for an afterenactment by a Magnificent Transformation Scene showing the Radium Wedding of Neid and Moorning and the Dawn of Peace, Pure, Perfect, and Perpetual, Waking the Weary of the World", F222. Dublin town had been painted a "wearing green ridinghued", F411, and "on that surprisingly bludgeony Unity Sunday Irish eyes of welcome were smiling daggers down their backs, when the roth, vice and blause met the noyr blank and rogues and the grim white and cold[1] bet

[1] Red, white and blue: the British soldiery: also the literary pirate Samuel Roth and the Society for the Suppression of Vice. Green, white and gold: the tricolor of the Free State. Black and tans: English policing troops.

the black fighting tans ", F176, but the criss-crossing gunfire wove in the air, for Joyce, not fireworks of liberation but the familiar spectre of cold jesuitic violence.

> Down the photoslope in syncopanc pulses, with the bitts bugtwug their teffs, the missledhropes, glitteraglatteraglutt, borne by their carnier walve. Spraygun rakes and splits them from a double focus : grenadite, damnymite, alextronite, nichilite: and the scanning fire-spot of the sgunners traverses the rutilanced illustred sinksundered lines. Shlossh! A gaspel truce leaks out over the caeseine coatings. Amid a fluorescence of spectracular mephiticism there caoculates through the inconoscope stealdily a still, the figure of a fellowchap in the wohly ghast, Popey O'Donoshough, the jesuneral of the russuates.... Dumble down, looties and gengstermen! Dtin, dtin, dtin, dtin! F349.

Missledhropes, misled hopes, flying missiles, and ultimate hangman's ropes. The hail of bullets is no more meaningless than the spatter of electrons in a television tube. A ghostly apparatus of valves, carrier waves, iconoscopes, scanners and six-hundred-line screens educes out of the spatter an intelligible form, the General of the Jesuits, alias Father Dolan with his familiar pandybat. A thin-faced bespectacled teacher of mathematics was to supplant Si Dedalus as symbol of Ireland, inaugurate the " devil era ", F473, and transform Dear Dirty Dublin into " dim, delty Deva ", F614.

Eamon DeValera,[1] " Dev " or Kev, " sair sair sullemn and chairmanlooking ", F416, " a conformed aceticist and aristo-taller ", F417, is disclosed " making chilly spaces at hisphex affront of the icinglass of his windhame, which was cold antitopically Nixnixundnix ", F415. He rebukes the " grace-hoper " in the guise of the prudent ant (Joyce spells it " Ondt ", a Danish neuter meaning " evil "). He coaches " rebellium-tending mikes " at " Backlane Univarsity ", F287, in the rudiments of " nucleuds and alegobrew ", F283 (Joyce glosses this episode, HYPOTHESES OF COMMONEST EX-PERIENCES BEFORE APOTHEOSIS OF THE LUS-TRAL PRINCIPIUM), wends him to " Amorica " in quest of cash for the rebellion, recites his creed:

> Never back a woman you defend, never get quit of a friend on whom you depend, never make face to a foe till he's rife and never get stuck to another man's pfife.

[1] De Valera's presence in the *Wake* was first noted by Mr. Andrew Cass in an article in the *Irish Times*, April 26, 1947.

—protests his piety:

> But believe me in my simplicity I am awful good, I believe, so I am, at the root of me, praised be right cheek Discipline! And I can now truthfully declaret before my Geity's Pantokreator with my fleshfettered palms on the epizzles of the apossels that I do my reasonabler's best to recite my grocery beans[1] ... regular, genuflections enclosed.

—boasts of his exploits in the Post Office fighting,

> Down with the Saozon ruze! ... See! blazing on the focoal. As see! blazing upon the foe. Like the regular redshank I am. Impregnable as the mule himself. ...

—and proclaims the Nova Hibernia:

> But it is grandiose by my ways of thinking from the prophecies. New worlds for all! F412.

In his hour of apotheosis we behold him wrapped in the Free State's tricolour, " of all the green heroes everwore coton breiches, the whitemost, the goldenest ", " his smile likequid glue ", surrounded by popular laudations, " in neuchoristic congressulations, quite purringly excited ":

> Hymnumber twentynine. O, the singing! Happy little girlycums to have adolphted such an Adelphus! O, the swinginging hopops so goholden! They've come to chant en chor. F234.

It is a jerrybuilt paradise in Suburbia that they envisage:

> Should in ofter years it became about you will after desk jobduty becoming a bank midland mansioner we and I shall reside with our obeisant servants among Burke's mobility at La Roseraie, Ailesbury Road. Red bricks are all hellishly good values if you trust to the roster of ads but we'll save up ourselves and nab what's nicest and boskiest of timber trees in the nebohood. [The mountain of the burial of Moses comes in here with suspicious patness.] We'll have our private palypeachum pillarposterns for lovesick letterines fondly affianxed to our front railings and swings, hammocks, tighttaught balletlines, accomodationnooks and prismic bathboites, to make Envyeyes mouth water and wonder when they binocular us from their embrassured windows in our garden rare. ... F235.

This bourgeois paradise, the dreams of Gerty MacDowell and Leopold Bloom fused and raised to an infinite power, a

---

[1] Rosary beads.

mere alteration of political arrangements looked to for the apocalyptic gratification of the most vulgar tastes, is appropriately devalued in a terse mathematical metaphor:

> The logos of somewome to that base anything, when most characteristically mantissa minus, comes to nullum in the endth:

to which Joyce appends an unequivocal footnote:

> Neither a soul to be saved nor a body to be kicked.   F298.

" Dev " metamorphoses readily into his enemy Kev, Kevin O'Higgins, the nephew of viceroy Tim Healy and vice-president of the Free State; this dubious trinity is held together by a pun.   In the regime of their abstract hypocrisies the aged recumbent city-founder is forcibly prevented from bestirring himself:

> Now be aisy, good Mr Finnimore, sir.   And take your laysure like a god on pension and don't be walking abroad.   Sure you'd only lose yourself in Healiopolis now. . . .   'Twould turn you against life, so 'twould.   And the weather's that mean too. . . . You're better off, sir, where you are, primesigned in the full of your dress, bloodeagle waistcoat and all, remembering your shapes and sizes on the pillow of your babycurls under your sycamore by the keld water. . . .   F24.

Heliopolis the Egyptian sun-city contained the temple where the Phoenix performed his demimillenniar resurrection from ashes, or according to Herodutus' version brought his embalmed parent for burial.   It was only a stuffed phoenix that was to be seen there, in any case; Herodotus saw only a picture.   Tim Healy occupied the vice-regal lodge in Phoenix Park, and the guide-books boast of the phoenix-like resurrection of Dublin from the ashes of rebellion, but it wasn't, the reborn state, a fire-bird to gladden the heart of John Stanislaus.

> . . . the silence speaks the scene.   Fake!
> So This Is Dyoublong?
> Hush!   Caution!   Echoland!
> How charmingly exquisite!   It reminds you of the outwashed engravure that we used to be blurring on the blotchwall of his innkempt house.   F13.

The old man lay in Dublin, his memory ringing with wine and song and spacious times (" We could not wait to draw the

corks, we slapped them against the marble-topped counter ")
while in the vice-regal lodge and in the Dail scrupulous meanness was organized and consolidated as it had never been in a
thousand years.   Books were proscribed by edict instead of, as
formerly, being burned sporadically by treacherous printers,
the backstage power of the church moved forward into govern-
ment, bill after bill was enacted, signed, and enforced, the
Free State's abstractions overtook the old gossipy personal
finagling of municipal politics, traditions of generous eloquence
receded before the new parliamentary wrangling:

> The Taoiseach had started off his speech by telling the House
> that if he could be convinced that this bill was outraging any prin-
> ciple, then he would consider what could be done, Mr. Morrissey
> added.   Did anybody, inside or outside the House, ever convince the
> Taoiseach of anything?   The Taoiseach was getting from the
> Opposition the cooperation he deserved.   Was not the real reason
> why they were faced with this bill the fact that the Taoiseach never
> co-operated with anybody in the country?[1]

That sort of thing had always gone on in Westminster; now
it was installed in Dublin.

" Every night of my life and in the daytime too I think of
all these things—they all come back to me and my God when
I think of the times I used to have and here I am now—well I
had a good time, anyway."   Joyce in Paris worked on at his
dream-monologue of a garrulous recumbent Ireland, with his
father's cadences guiding his pen and his father's anecdotes
shaping his material.   After eight years his father died, while
the book forged on.   The spectre of his bedridden parent
projecting a dream-past into a nightmare present never shifted
from the centre of his attention.   He wrote to the Alf Bergan of
Ulysses, from whom he was asking to commission a monument to
John Stanislaus, " The Lord knows whether you will be able
to pick the Kersse-McCarry story out of my crazy tale.   It was
a great story of my father's and I'm sure if they get a copy of
Transition in the shades his comment will be ' Well, he can't
tell that story as I used to and that's one sure five! ' "

[1] *Irish Times*, April 26, 1947.

Chapter 16

ALICE IN CHAPELIZOD

In lone and silent hours,
When night makes a weird sound of its own stillness,
Like an inspired and desperate alchemist
Staking his very life on some dark hope,
Have I mixed awful talk and asking looks
With my most innocent love . . .
. . . and, though ne'er yet,
Thou hast unveiled thy inmost sanctuary,
Enough from incommunicable dream,
And twilight phantasms, and deep noonday thought,
Has shone within me. . . .

Alastor

It darkles, (tinct, tint) all this our funnaminal world. Yon
marshpond by ruodmark verge is visited by the tide. Alvem-
marea! We are circumveiloped by obscuritads.

Finnegans Wake (F244)

" Once," said the Mock Turtle at last, with a deep sigh, " I was
a real Turtle."

Alice in Wonderland

" THE UNPURGED IMAGES OF DAY RECEDE "

"THERE was a time ", Wordsworth commences his Ode; and
in a parallel Ode (*Dejection*) Coleridge echoes him:

There was a time when, though my path was rough,
This joy within me dallied with distress,
And all misfortunes were but as the stuff
Whence Fancy made me dreams of happiness. . . .

" There was a time "; the time when the Mock Turtle was
real, when the flowers in the rose-garden did not need to be
painted (" ' Why, the fact is, you see, Miss, this here ought to
have been a *red* rosetree, and we put a white one in by mistake ' "), when babies did not turn into pigs (". . . it was
neither more nor less than a pig, and she felt that it would be
quite absurd to carry it any further "), and when being large
enough to reach the key yet small enough to go through the

276

garden door were not incompatible states; this time, the loss of which involved for Milton Adam's transgression and impious war in heaven, was for Wordsworth and Coleridge quite appropriately figured as childhood, and its loss as the process of growing up. This transfer of the Fall from theological to psychological coordinates is for the student of popular mythology the definitive psychic event (as the emergence of Holmes and Watson is the definitive political event) of the nineteenth century. It polarizes everything from best-selling fiction (*David Copperfield, Tom Brown's Schooldays*) to the dim red-curtained womb-world of the Victorian drawingroom, from the pursuit of Little Eva by Legree's bloodhounds to the pursuit of the skylark soul of Adonais by the dusk-encircled vultures of " envy and calumny and hate and pain," from Lear's and Carroll's anarchic nursery-wisdom to Huxley's notion that the spirit in which the scientist confronted fact was irreproachable because that of a little child.

Healiopolis in the devil era was not a human projection but an abstract nightmare of irrational egoisms and prohibitions, a mirror-lined house called " Nixnixundnix ". The Dublin of 1904 had cohered, the ghost of an eighteenth-century city, threatened by mechanization but dominated still by Si Dedalus; even the symbol of disintegration, Bloom, was humane, cautious, sympathetic. In 1922 Si Dedalus was recumbent amid dreams; the very Dublin of 1904 existed only via talk in pubs, ghost of a ghost; and a political cataclysm comparable to the spiritual cataclysms that had swept the rest of Europe a hundred years before had launched eighteenth-century Ireland, with twentieth-century thoroughness, into the nineteenth century.

In Bella Cohen's brothel in 1904 a dream-version of Simon Dedalus had scratched at a swarming " multitude of midges ": " By the hoky fiddle, thanks be to Jesus those funny little chaps are not unanimous. If they were they'd walk me off the face of the bloody globe ", U513/498. Nineteenth-century maggotry was unanimous now, organized by an implacable mathematics teacher. As in Victorian England, respectability had suddenly become an unquestioned fetish:

... all who have received tickets, fair home overcrowded, tidy but very little furniture, respectable, whole family attends daily mass and is dead sick of bread and butter, ... shares closet with eight other dwellings, more than respectable, getting comfortable parish relief, wageearner freshly shaved from prison, highly respectable, . . . bangs kept woman's head against wall thereby disturbing neighbours, private chapel occupies return landing, removal every other quarter day, case one of peculiar hopelessness, most respectable, . . . serious student is eating his last dinners, floor dangerous for unaccompanied old clergymen, thoroughly respectable, many uncut pious books in evidence, nearest watertap two hundred yards' run away, . . . one foot of dust between banister and cracked wall, wife cleans stools, eminently respectable, . . . travels always with her eleven trunks of clothing, starving cat left in disgust, the pink of respectability, . . . copious holes emitting mice, . . . as respectable as respectable can respectably be. . . . F543.

The tone of the case-worker's report had suddenly become appropriate for describing Cormac's dilapidated house. The sea of matter in which Bloom floated was no longer funny nor sensuously stimulating, it was the very vehicle of respectability. Feelings, memories, unfulfilled hopes (" Have we cherished expectations? Are we for liberty of perusiveness? ", F614) were suddenly banished from " life " into dreams: exactly as had happened to the rest of Europe when it underwent the freezing death of Locke and Hartley, and the Industrial Revolution.

> Locke sank into a swoon;
> The Garden died;
> God took the spinning-jenny
> Out of his side.

So the idiom of nineteenth-century England suddenly became appropriate for rendering twentieth-century Dublin. That idiom was largely the speech of dreams, with a thousand kaleidoscopic facets.

'THOSE IMAGES THAT YET FRESH IMAGES BEGET"

The nineteenth century, preoccupied with its own psychic malaise (" There was a time "), embodied its obsessive problems in everything it touched. Being " sunk into a swoon ", into an unprecedented concern for material production, into a flood of

> . . . burst loveletters, telltale stories, stickyback snaps, doubtful egg-shells, . . . reversibles jackets, blackeye lenses, family jars, falsehair shirts, Godforsaken scapulars, neverworn breeches, cutthroat ties,

...convertible collars,... unloosed shoe latchets, crooked strait waistcoats, fresh horrors from Hades, globules of mercury, undeleted glete, glass eyes for an eye, gloss teeth for a tooth,... F183.

the mind of the age threw up a matching unprecedented spate of novelized and poetized disguises for the popular daydream of tortured innocence, the child gone down into the prison-house.

"Disguises" is the operative word. The nineteenth-century poet or novelist is careful to conceal from his audience and from himself what he is writing about, simple—in fact, naive—though his subject is. Bird, cloud, fire, moon, poet, rose, maiden, are all disguises for Shelley; frost, death, birds of prey, chains, are disguises of " the world " unheeding, and also of a maturity in which this sort of poetry would be less easy to write. To write a stanza Shelley has only to juggle these symbols to the rhythm of an appropriate passion; if one metaphor gets into trouble it can be instantly exchanged for another of the same series without anyone's noticing. Thus in the ninth stanza of *Adonais*, " The quick dreams, / The passion-winged ministers of thought." desert their postulation as winged Hellenic beings (a sense of their embodied autono-mousness having been registered) to become " his flocks, whom near the living streams / Of his young spirit he fed " (pastoral innocence, plus the poet as Good Shepherd, implied in a way that uses the religious feelings without shocking the inatten-tive). The sheep two lines later have become the " unextin-guished sparks " of the West Wind's scattering: they " Wander no more, from kindling brain to brain " (meta-morphosis caught half-way, " wandering " because sheep and " kindling " because sparks); but another shift distracts our half-notice of this—" But droop there, whence they sprung." The sparks having done their momentary duty, they are exchanged for blighted plants as more appropriate vehicles of pathos: pathos instantly screwed a pitch higher by the evoca-tion of orphaned infants with a full set of Freudian compulsions, memories of the birth-trauma and desire to re-enter the womb: " and mourn their lot / Round the cold heart, where, after their sweet pain, / They ne'er will gather strength, or find a home again." " Cold heart " seems a sort of pun on " cold hearth "; one wonders if Shelley intended it.

Nothing in *Finnegans Wake* even looks as chaotic as inspec-tion shows this to be. One can imagine what Dr. Johnson would have said, and it is no wonder the Romantic poets had to begin by repealing his laws as tyrannical and exorcising his insistent presence, dream-fashion, by turning him from an admonitory parent into a ridiculous character in a book by Boswell: a neat piece of ritual father-slaughter. " Poetry turns all things to loveliness," wrote Shelley; " it adds beauty to that which is most deformed." And wrote Freud, dreams are the protectors of sleep.

MATHEMATICIAN THE DAY-SELF OF THE DREAMER

A philosophy of mechanical sensation and an aesthetic of anarchic passion go invariably hand in hand. They are the Tweedledum and Tweedledee of the psychic forest, the " Contrariwise " of the poet countering with automatic idiocy the implacable " Nohow " of the logician. From time to time Tweedledee repeats a nonsensical poem, containing oysters with shoes, a boiling sea, and sun at midnight; from time to time Tweedledum enters a ritual protest at the offhandness exhibited by his Dionysiac brother toward his nice new rattle, the perfectly rationalist universe; the poet having unsuccessfully tried to fold up the umbrella with himself in it, a terrific sham battle ensues, Defenses of Poetry and Essays Concerning Human Understanding being bandied about with deceptive recklessness:

> " We *must* have a bit of a fight, but I don't care about going on long," said Tweedledum. .... " Let's fight till six, and then have dinner."

Tweedledum and Tweedledee are, of course, Dodgson and Carroll, the Oxford recluse and his *alter ego* the shy spinner of children's fantasies; their alternation is the most eloquent parable of their age. They inhabit opposite sides of the Victorian parlour looking-glass. The looking-glass, mirror of memory through which to step back into childhood, Narcissus-pool in which to contemplate one's own image, is the central image of the time: " Nircississies are as the doaters of inversion. Secilas through their laughing classes becoming poolermates in laker life ", F526. " Secilas " are " Alices " spelled as in a mirror; " poolermates " are introverted parlourmaids, laughing child's drab maturity solaced by self-absorption; one recalls the nixieish Polly of *Dubliners* luxuriating in " secret, amiable memories " while awaiting her mother's word that the fly has been trapped:

> Her hopes and visions were so intricate that she no longer saw the white pillows on which her gaze was fixed or remembered that she was waiting for anything. D84/75.

" She no longer saw. . . ." Thus the Romantic poet, absorbed in his own fantasies. The world borne on the shoulders of the post-Lockean Atlas is his own head:

> Since the mind, in all its thoughts and reasonings, hath no other immediate object but its own ideas, which it alone does or can contemplate, it is evident that our knowledge is only conversant about them. *Human Understanding*, IV. i. 1.

Hence the affinity between quasi-mathematical logic and quasi-nonsensical art. " Since the mind . . . hath no other immediate object but its own ideas ", the private world of Carroll and the logical world of Dodgson are identical, or related as systole to diastole. Dodgson pushed mathematics toward the ambiguous zone of puzzles in which he had already located poetry. It is not that one is a refuge from the other; both together shield the mind from things; and the mind under this umbrella becomes steadily more whimsical, steadily more dissociated, oscillates with steady acceleration from the one mode to the other. *Jabberwocky* and *Symbolic Logic* are not related as the real to the unreal; both are unreal, both are mental constructions, related only as one nightmare to another, as Dodgson makes plain in bringing all the resources of his logical science to the irrefutable proof of such propositions as " My writing-desk is full of live scorpions " and " Guinea-pigs never really appreciate Beethoven." He also proved the non-existence of Hell: as the Joycean twin has it, " Bet you fippence anythesious there's no purgatory, are yous game? ", F266.

Dodgson thought of logic as a set of rules for connecting conceptual boxes in which anything might be found: guinea-pigs, scorpions, waltzing kangaroos. He kept this up for a lifetime—indeed, transformed it into a way of life—by allowing his mind to feed on nothing external to itself. Not only did he abhor " sensuality ", he abhorred the world toward which the senses letched for contact. He contrived to turn the visible world into a neutral diffusion of stimuli, to be dealt with by the indifferent Lockean eye and *tabula rasa* of his celebrated camera.[1]

Then, locked up in his skull-box with his Symbolic Logic, exacerbated, like a Kafka hero, by the incapacity of a chain of syllogisms, however prolonged or directed, to achieve a relation other than asymptotic with felt and handled reality, he dissociated himself into Dodgson the mathematician and Carroll the fantasist, and sublimated the latter into a poised girl-child interrogating grotesques in a dream-wood. The sensible world once atomized, the personality cannot long cohere: " The logos of somewome to that base anything . . . comes to nullum in the endth:" neither a soul to be saved nor a body to be kicked.

So with the whole century. The Albert Memorial and *The Blessed Damozel*, Manchester slums and *Prometheus Unbound*, express facets of the same soul. Just as the author of *Alice* stuttered violently when caught by one of his Dodgson acquaintances in a Carroll state, and invariably refused mail addressed to his pseudonymous self at Oxford, so Lamb wrote with exemplary detachment the obituary of " the late Elia ", " Fiona McLeod " wrote letters in a feminine handwriting to unsuspecting friends of " her " alter ego William Sharp, Arnold doubled as prose ironist and wistful poet, Tennyson as roaring squire and maidenly laureate, Yeats as exponent of plangent twilight and of systematized *Vision*. It was Dodgson the mathematician who wrote *Alice in Wonderland*, not Dodgson taking a holiday from mathematics. Shem and Shaun, the Joycean twins, are equally Earwicker the dreamer. The two worlds are one.

THE DREAM GROWS

If one man sums up the nineteenth-century psychic world, that man is Dodgson. During the first five years of work on his Irish dream-book, however, Joyce was virtually unaware of the mine of material afforded by Dodgson's career and works. The relevance of the nineteenth-century psychic world revealed

[1] Maritain shows at great length (*Formal Logic*) that the reduction of thought to algebra depends on the nominalistic view of the middle term as a collection of singulars—precisely, a box, an " x ", containing indifferently anything—rather than as a common nature into which, in a particular case, the mind bites. As in Locke's psychology, a common nature is just a common classification, imposed for convenience by the mind.

itself only gradually. He had his attention fixed on contemporary Ireland.

That Ireland had entered a dream-state was obvious; the Dublin he had known as a young man had become a memory, and continuity with all the Dublins before that was for the first time broken. The emerging Dublin of the new order was, correspondingly, a nightmare. So the new book should be a dream-book, and a dream-language would have to be invented. The language developed slowly. Drafts published after he had been at work on the *Wake* for nearly half the time he took to write *Ulysses* show relatively few puns or odd spellings. In the first two fragments printed (*Transatlantic Review*, April 1924; *Criterion*, July 1925) there are virtually none; in the first published draft of the famous Anna Livia episode (*Le Navire d'Argent*, September, 1925) a few portmanteau river-names are cautiously introduced. The possibility of turning figures of speech into objects had been on his mind ever since, in *Dubliners*, he had described Mr. O'Madden Burke's "magniloquent western name" as "the moral umbrella upon which he balanced the fine problem of his finances ", D183/163. He had played the sight of words against their meaning as far back as the *Stephen Hero* MS., when Simon Dedalus' sense of wonder was awakened by the name beneath Ibsen's photograph, "the upright line of the ' b ' running so strangely beside the initial letter as to suspend the mind amid uncertainties for some oblivious instants ", S88/75. As for the pun, it was a Dublin tradition; Swift is credited with a mock treatise on it. And as for the contrapuntal use of foreign languages, had not Joyce at college, fascinated by the cultural cycles compressed into a few lines of etymology, "read Skeat's *Etymological Dictionary* by the hour ", S26/20? He experimented tirelessly. He composed a phrase, "with half a glance of Irish frisky from under the shag of his parallel brows ", F470, and sent it to Harriet Weaver with the note, "these are the words the reader will see but not those he will hear." He laboured to compress into a draft of an opening paragraph all the archaic themes 108 words could possibly contain, and mailed it to Miss Weaver with an explanation.

The work of finding a language went slowly forward. ". . . in the Paris jungle, stampede of omnibuses and trumpeting of taxielephants etc and in this caravanserai peopled by American loudspeakers I compose ridiculous prose writing on a green suitcase which I bought in Bognor." "... It is a bewildering business. Complications to right of me, complications to left of me, complex on the page before me, perplex in the pen beside me, duplex in the meandering eyes of me, stuplex on the face that reads me. And from time to time I lie back and listen to my hair growing white."[1]

The blocking-out of themes was more rapid. He began by simultaneous work on the first and third parts of the four-part structure: past and present, the genuine and the fake, the city-builder who incorporated many traits of John Stanislaus, and the plausible sham composted of Healy, De Valera, and his own brother Stanislaus, now a professor of English at Trieste: middleman incarnate.

The city-builder/dreamer was named Earwicker (Eire-wicker, Eire-dweller, with an overtone of Earwig, the insect whose severed halves will fight one another). Humphrey Chimpden Earwicker—Humphrey: Hump: the burden of guilt, the curse of fallen man, with a glance at Humpty Dumpty who was so shattered by his fall that not all the political resources of the kingdom could reconstruct him. Chimpden: a cage full of chattering monkeys, man's bodily ancestors. That Earwicker should be an innkeeper, symbol of traditional hospitality, was inevitable; talk flows at an inn. That his inn should be in suburban Chapelizod, equally inevitable. Chapelizod is neither Dublin nor not-Dublin; it borders on Phoenix Park, an admirable Garden of Eden complete with zoo and President's House; it was the legendary birthplace of Iseult (Chapelle d'Iseult), and more lately of Tim Healy.

Earwicker's wife Anna (Joyce's great-grandmother was named Ann McAnn: Ann daughter of Ann) performs the faithful, self-effacing, conserving feminine role. As her husband merges with the recumbent giant silhouette of the

[1] Letters to Harriet Weaver from transcripts in Slocum Collection. Miss Weaver, who at Ezra Pound's instigation had settled on Joyce a sum of money on which to live and support his family, was promoted by Joyce, whom dignified archaisms delighted, to the eighteenth-century role of patroness, entitled to continual progress reports, and so played during the years of work on *Finnegan* the part of confidante that had been Frank Budgen's during the *Ulysses* period. Since he worked surrounded by frenetic expatriate aesthetes in Paris, who eagerly expanded every ironically dropped hint into a corybantic essay (some of them collected in 1929 under the title *Our Examination Round his Factification for Incamination of Work in Progress*), the need for regular correspondence with a non-writer who was not feverishly promoting " the Revolution of the Word " was real and deep.

Hill of Howth above Dublin Bay, so she merges with the river
Liffey, born from a cloud, refreshing the city, and carrying its
drainage off to sea. To the name of Anna Liffey (Anna Livia)
Joyce added an evocation of multiple beauties, Plurabelle; the
river-woman's initials, ALP, point toward the German word
for nightmare, and toward the name of Coleridge's sacred
dream-river, Alph, which ran

> Through caverns measureless to man
> Down to a sunless sea.

The initials of HCE and ALP are woven through the text as
the archetypal characteristics of husband and wife, Adam and
Eve, through civilization.

What is directly presented, however, is the consciousness of
the dreamer; and like the consciousness articulated in *Exiles*,
it undergoes a four-pole dissociation. These have real-life
counterparts, twin sons and a narcissistic daughter doubled by
her mirror, but these persons barely exist in the book except
as loci of attraction for the disintegrated portions of the
dreaming mind. Earwicker at war with himself splits into
Shem the Penman and Shaun the Post, Iseult and the mirror-
Iseult: two male parts, two female parts.

Shaun, " the fine frank fairhaired fellow of the fairytales ",
F220, with his metamorphoses Juan and Yawn, is the point
d'appui for the Healy-deValera material ; he is the go-ahead
organizer of the New Order. Shem, " poor acheseyeld from
Ailing ", F148, a comic re-processing of Stephen Dedalus, is
the introverted champion of the dark Within.

Iseult (Isobel) and her alter ego, " doaters of inversion ",
are twin vampires. " Night by silentsailing night " she lies
calmly in her cot, " quietly, all the woods so wild, . . . neath
of the whitethorn, child of tree, like some losthappy leaf ",
F556, but her placid face masks dreams of " the strangle for
love and the sowiveall of the prettiest ", F145: " Move your
mouth towards minth, more, preciousest, more on more! To
please me, treasure. Don't be a, I'm not going to! Sh!
nothing! ", F146.

All these movements of malaise, sadism, petty triumph,
blarney, worry, introversion, and affection belong to the Irish
soul; they are uncoordinated thrustings within the dreamer
himself, imprisoned in his nightmare world of endlessly
intersecting corridors,

... trying to undo with his teeth the knots made by his tongue, retelling humself by the math hour, long as he's brood, a reel of funnish ficts apout the shee, how faust of all and on segund thoughts and the thirds the charmhim girlalove and fourthermore and filthily. . . .   F288.

" Shee " = *she* + Celtic *sidhe*, fairy; the conjunction with " the math hour " is suggestive.   Faust (" how faust of all ") when Mephisto called was like Dodgson a student of logic perplexed by the failure of his studies to bite into his experience.   From the Dodgson complex the sentence trails off into the logician's secondly, thirdly, fourthly, with repressed matter turning up far along the series (" filthily ").

By 1927, Joyce had brought his material to this degree of organization without having considered Dodgson at all.   In April of that year *Transition* published in Paris an extract from the manuscript which showed, for the first time, the dream language at a fairly full stage of development . . .

... lift we our ears, eyes of the darkness, from the tome of *Liber Lividus* and, (toh!), how paisibly eirenical, all dimmering dunes and gloamering glades, selfstretches afore us our fredeland's plain! Lean neath stone pine the pastor lies with his crook; young pricket by pricket's sister nibbleth on returned viridities; amaid her rocking grasses the herb trinity shams lowliness; skyup is of evergrey. . . . F14.

On May 31 Joyce described to Harriet Weaver the public response:

Another (or rather many) says he is imitating Lewis Carroll. I never read him till Mrs. Nutting gave me a book—not *Alice*—a few weeks ago—though of course I heard bits and scraps. But then I never read Rabelais either though nobody will believe this. I will read them both when I get back. I read a few chapters in a book called *La Langue de Rabelais*. . . .

" Bits and scraps " has a perhaps deceptively unimportant sound.   One of Joyce's college nicknames was " The Mad Hatter ", and he presumably knew what it signified.   And it is difficult to imagine a connoisseur of pun and parody not having run across *Jabberwocky*:

'Twas brillig, and the slithy toves
　　Did gyre and gimble in the wabe:
All mimsy were the borogroves,
　　And the mome raths outgrabe. . . .

—with Humpty Dumpty's pedantic explanation:

"Well, '*slithy*' means 'lithe and slimy.' 'Lithe' is the same as 'active.' You see it's like a portmanteau—there are two meanings packed up into one word.

"I see it now," Alice remarked thoughtfully: "and what are '*toves*'?"

"Well, '*toves*' are something like badgers—they're something like lizards—and they're something like corkscrews."

At any rate, Joyce now turned his full attention on the life and works of the Rev. Charles Lutwidge Dodgson. He acquired the Rev. Stuart Dodgson Collingwood's *Life and Letters* of his uncle (1898),[1] and on March 28 of the following year wrote, "I have been reading about the author of 'Alice'...."

No more useful body of material could have come his way. Writing from the very thick of Pope's universal darkness, Dodgson with a sort of lucid innocence articulates the whole nineteenth century.

DODGSON IN THE *WAKE*

The romantic night-world was his unquestioned element. That is why Joyce found him indispensable. It was as though, in the midst of writing *The Forsaken Merman*, Arnold had been able to interrogate a fish. Dodgson attached great importance to his night-mind. He preserved epigrams from his dreams for literary use (two examples are noted in his preface to *Sylvie and Bruno*) and invented a complicated system, called the "Nyctograph", for taking notes in the dark, and was puzzled not to have it acclaimed as an invention of great general usefulness. He was a poor sleeper, his biographers agree. His intricate spiritual agonies, like those of H. C. Earwicker, took place in bed; apparently he used to evade "anxious thoughts, worrying thoughts, uncharitable thoughts, unholy thoughts" by repeating poems and passages from the Bible. Joyce had only to cross Dodgson's complexes with the verbal élan of his garrulous bedridden father to confer on his cityfounding HCE elaborate symbolic density.

Thus on page 57 of the *Wake* we are given an image ("exegious monument, aerily perennious") of HCE as

[1] This was still among his books when they were catalogued after the war, but had disappeared when the library went on exhibition in 1949. A copy of the catalogue is in the Slocum collection.

Dodgson, which can be checked with numerous photographs of the latter:

> . . . that exposure of him by old Tom Quad, a flashback in which he sits sated, gowndabout, in clericalease habit, watching bland sol slithe dodgsomely into the nethermore, a globule of maugdleness about to corrugitate his mild dewed cheek and the tata of a tiny victorienne, Alys, pressed by his limper looser.

On the previous page, a composite description of HCE moves from the walrus-moustached Joyce père, " the doomed but always ventriloquent Agitator . . . silkhouatted, a whallrhos-mightiadd " to another Dodgson-image complete with the emblematic tear: " while olover his exculpatory features, as Roland rung, a wee dropeen of grief about to sillonise his jouejous, the ghost of resignation diffused a spectral appealing-ness, as a young man's drown o'er the fate of his waters may gloat, similar in origin and akkurat in effective to a beam of sunshine upon a coffin plate ", F56.

All the symbols of the nineteenth century turn up in Dodgson's life with wonderful literalness. Not only did he send his heroine through the looking-glass, but the mirror-girls, innocent and vampire, flit through his biography. Alice Liddell, gentle daughter of the lexicographer, to whom *Wonderland* was dedicated, was supplanted in Dodgson's affections by the emotionally precocious Isa Bowman, who played the part on the stage. Joyce transferred Dodgson's ambivalent relations with Isa to the *Wake* almost unaltered, as HCE's incestuous infatuation with his daughter Iseult. It was, in fact, a relationship of symbolic incest: Dodgson saw in Isa an incarnation of Alice, and Alice was his creation. Iseult's unconcealed disrespect for her father has its analogue in the book of anecdotes Isa published about Dodgson (he used to shower her with " passionate kisses ", and his stories always climaxed in a " deep dark wood " at the mention of which she would snuggle closer.) As authoress, she styled herself " The Real Alice in Wonderland ", in cheeky usurpation of Alice Liddell.

Odd details of these affairs find their way into Joyce's text. On page 226 Iseult is referred to as " Isa " in line 4, and a pun on " beauman " occurs in line 7. On the next page, " the widow Magrievy " in the catalogue of Iseult-avatars is probably Alice Hargreaves, the married name of Alice Liddell.

She was widowed in 1926, but in another sense widowed at the time when she was sundered from Dodgson by the distant politeness that overtook all his relations with his child-friends at their puberty. Isa appears again as " this bountiful actress " in the next line.

The White Knight's innocent spontaneity turns up on page 373: " We just are upsidedown singing what ever the dimkims mummur allalilty she pulls inner out heads." (*Mummur allalilty* = lilting mother/mummer/murmurer Anna Livia.)

> " How can you go on talking so quietly, head downwards? ", Alice asked, as she dragged him out by the feet and laid him in a heap on the bank.
>
> The Knight looked surprised at the question. " What does it matter where my body happens to be? " he said. " My mind goes on working all the same. In fact, the more head-downwards I am, the more I keep inventing new things."

The White Knight, with his pathos of incompetent ingenuity, is pretty clearly Dodgson himself; and Dodgson with apparently no idea of the psychic drama he was articulating imagined that the Alice books were " whatever the dimkims mummur allalilty " pulled out of his head. " I had sent my heroine straight down a rabbit-hole, to begin with," he recalled happily years later, " without the least idea what was to happen afterwards." It is pretty clear that Joyce has the White Knight in mind in the upsidedown sentence; three lines later he shifts to Dodgson's adroit unconscious evasions :

> All old Dadgerson's dodges one conning one's copying and that's what wonderland's wanderlad'll flaunt to the fair. A trancedone boyscript with tittivits by. Ahem. . . . In preplays to Anonymay's left hinted palinode obviously inspiterebbed by a sibspecious connexion. F374.

Dodgson's dodges (his books) are flaunted to the fair (noun and adjective; regressive saturnalia plus the little girls to whom he used his books as calling-cards to scrape up impromptu acquaintances.) The titillating bits of his " trancedone boyscript " are ascribable to ("Ahem! ") inscrutable pressures. The " sibspecious connexion " (sibling + specious + suspicious) who disowned the books was his caustic professional self; but the books disguise their connection with this day-self so successfully that the palinode can be " left hinted " as well as, like the author, left-handed.

Humpty Dumpty, the accredited expositor of *Jabberwocky*, turns up throughout the *Wake*; we hear on the first page of HCE's "humptyhillhead" and "tumtytumtoes," in connection with the Fall which not all the king's men, F47, could repair. And as his fall in *Through the Looking-Glass* is followed immediately by the appearance first of the two Messengers, then of the Lion and the Unicorn fighting for the Crown (the crown of the White King, who is an avatar of the fallen Humpty Dumpty), so the fall of the father in Joyce's book is instantly followed by the Civil War of his twin successors (" for O'Cronione lags acrumbling in his sands but his sunsunsuns still tumble on ", F415). One of the Carrollean Messengers carries a postbag in which he keeps ham sandwiches and hay; the apparition of Shaun the Post, F404, is followed by a thousand-word account of his immense eating habits (cf. " Oop, I never open momouth but I pack mefood in it ", F437). The other messenger, like Shem, is in disgrace:

> " ... He's in prison now, being punished: and the trial doesn't even begin till next Wednesday: and of course the crime comes last of all."
> " Suppose he never commits the crime? " said Alice.
> " That would be all the better, wouldn't it? " the Queen said. ...[1]

Shaun's " beamish brow " and " jehovial oyeglances ", F405, connect him with the " beamish boy " who slew the Jabberwock and was clasped in his father's arms; he execrates " the strangewrote anaglyptics of those shemletters patent ", F419, the jabberwock writings, " penmarks used out in sinscript with such hesitancy " by his " cerebrated brother ", F421, toward whom he makes slaughterous gestures:

> " ... He has encaust in the blood. Shim! I have the outmost contempt for. Prost bitten! Conshy! Tiberia is waiting on you, arestocrank! ... Go o'er the sea, haythen, from me and leave your libber to TCD. Your puddin is cooked! You're served, cram ye! Fatefully yaourth ... Ex.Ex.Ex.Ex.
> — But for what, thrice truthful teller, Shaun of grace? weakly we went on to ask now of the gracious one. Vouchsafe to say. You will now, goodness, won't you? Why?
> — For his root language, if you ask me whys, Shaun replied, as he blessed himself devotionally. ... F424.

[1] Tenniel drew this imprisoned messenger as the Mad Hatter of the earlier book; " The Mad Hatter " was one of Joyce's college nicknames (according to *A Page of Irish History: Story of University College, Dublin,* 1883–1909, compiled by the Fathers of the Society of Jesus, Dublin, 1930, 286). This is one of the most curious of the Joyce-Shem analogues.

(This skirmishing with the Jabberwock went on in Dodgson's life continually. He projected a Shakespeare expurgated for girls, and generally refused to acknowledge the existence of Carroll.)

There are other cross-lights. The Red King, of whose dream Alice is told she is an ingredient (" ' If that there King was to wake,' added Tweedledum, 'you'd go out—bang!—just like a candle!' ") parallels of course the sleeping father, who to the panic of everyone is almost wakened at least once, F255. The Mookse and the Gripes are, besides other things, the Mock Turtle and the Griffin. Joyce is as fond as Carroll of deflating sententious verses by parody. The playing cards, the farcical trial, the animated banquet, the talking flowers, the endless argumentations at cross-purposes, the reversals of time and space, those and other Carrollean motifs recur and recur throughout Joyce's text. There are references to " A liss in hunterland ", F276, to " One of the most murmurable loose carollaries ever Ellis[1] threw his cooking class ", F294, to Alice Liddell to whom the story was originally told:

> Though Wonderlawn's lost us for ever. Alis, alas, she broke the glass! Liddell lokker through the leafery, ours is mistery of pain. F270.

There is even a glance at Dodgson's clerical brother who spent eight years as Vicar of Tristan da Cunha.[2]

Finally, one entire section of the *Wake*, the one most

---

[1] Collaborator with Yeats in a three-volume edition-and-commentary of Blake (1893): another mathematical dream.

[2] Page 159: " I could love that man like my own ambo for being so bailey-cliaver though he's a nawful curillass and I must slav to methodiousness. I want him to go and live like a theabild in charge of the night brigade on Tristan da Cunha, isle of manoverboard, where he'll make Number 106 and be near Inaccessible." This comes from the first paragraph of the professor's explanation of the fable of the Mookse and the Gripes. Tristan da Cunha, a volcanic rock in the mid-Atlantic near Inaccessible Island, had a population of around 100. The " bally clever " brother is wished there by the professor for being a " nawful curillass " (curate plus skirt-chaser); a Shaunian denunciation of the lubricious Shem is superimposed on Dodgson's presumable jealousy at his brother's success in stomaching the holy orders which he himself took only out of professional necessity and which proved a lifelong torture to his conscience. The " bailey-cliaver " (Balaclava) victor over this particular Jabberwock is wished out of sight by the unhappy mathematics lecturer, " slav to methodiousness." In addition, of course, we have Dodgson's official self wishing his Carroll self behind him; it is the professor himself who has just related the fable.

crammed with *Alice* allusions, is a scurrilous mathematics lesson with tittering footnotes by the Isa Bowman-like girl, and another entire section, that containing The Mookse and the Gripes and the Tristan da Cunha reference, consists of intricate riddles of the kind Dodgson delighted in asking his little playmates and worrying at with his apparatus of rule of three and Symbolic Logic. And it is the riddle that touches most sorely the antinomy of his two selves (pp. 148–9) that provokes from the professor the violent oscillation between the Carrollean fable (pp. 152–9) and the interminably Dodgsonian explanation (pp. 159–68).

DODGSON A ROMANTIC EPIPHANY

We have seen how the Trivium died. The key to the literature of the English nineteenth century is the philosophy, and the related *Weltanschauung*, of the late seventeenth century. By this philosophy the "great tradition" as it survived in the eighteenth century was crippled and killed, against this philosophy the "great Romantics" erupted, in truce with its cadres the heirs of the great Romantics settled down to exploit various anxiously-watered tap-roots into their own adolescence. The *gegenschein* of their evasive strategies was the nineteenth-century popular novel (and its poetic avatars like *The Princess*) to which Joyce in *Ulysses* had paid so much attention. The transposition of the popular novel into dream-states was performed by Lewis Carroll. The novels and poems were regarded by their readers as somehow "solving the problems of the age." Carroll regarding himself as solving the problems that still protrude from the novels. Meanwhile the valid confrontation of those problems was going on in France, in the *agon* performed at one level by Flaubert,[1] at another by Gérard de Nerval, Baudelaire, Verlaine, Rimbaud,

[1] Who contains a good deal more than readers of *Madame Bovary* often suppose. The phantasmagoria of the *Tentation*, the exoticism of *Salammbô*, the mock initiation ritual of the *Education*, the catharsis of the Encyclopaedists' Augean Stables in *Bouvard*, comprise a strikingly complete inventory of symbolist modes. He wrote a *Voyage en Enfer* at 14, a *Rêve d'enfer* at 16. The *Tentation*, which went through draft after draft between his seventeenth and fifty-third years, continuously polarized his other work. The relation of *Alice* or *Sylvie and Bruno* to the English popular novels of Carroll's time is a pale parody of the relation of *La Tentation de Saint Antoine* to *Bouvard et Pécuchet*: see Paul Valéry's "La Tentation de (Saint) Flaubert" in *Variété V*, pp. 201 et circa. Joyce claimed to have read every word in Flaubert's complete works.

and Mallarmé. Carroll is a parody of a parody, the sort of material with which, because of its inherent leverage, Joyce delighted to work. Hence the analogies he opens up between the symbolist *agon* and the new dream-Dublin.

Dodgson regarded as his chef d'oeuvre the two-volume novel *Sylvie and Bruno*, which was given to the world, after twenty years' gestation, at Christmas, 1893.[1] As usual, he laboured to conceal from himself the meaning of his labours: here is his own version of the import of the work:

> It is written . . . in the hope of supplying, for the children whom I love, some thoughts that may suit those hours of innocent merriment which are the very life of childhood; and also, in the hope of suggesting, to them and to others, some thoughts that may prove, I would fain hope, not wholly out of harmony with the graver cadences of Life.

The Childhood/Life antithesis turns out, of course, to be an identity. *Sylvie and Bruno* turns out to be an oblique exegesis on, simultaneously, *Alice* (the cult of nonsense, the cult of childhood) and *Wonderland* (the emotional dishonesties of the adult world). Greater dishonesty, by the mature standards he claimed, than is exhibited in Dodgson's sermonizing prefaces would be difficult to find. His milieu could achieve a degree of integrity only in its dream-worlds; and that is what he succeeded in proving.

In the Alice books he had turned loose in the grown-up world of jealousies, ambivalences, and evasions the Child as incarnation of innocent wisdom, logical acuity, and anarchic directness. (Alice isn't taken in by the Duchess, gives no points in her verbal duel with Hare and Hatter, and at the end of each book abolishes the card-game and the chess-game in which she was involved by scattering the counters.) That the little girl of " seven and a half exactly " is pre-sexual was equally important to Dodgson: passion-flowers, pig-babies, and the slaughterous proclivities of the Queen of Hearts are among the " signatures " she is cheerfully unequipped to read,

---

[1] The second volume, that is, of which the author tells us that the final paragraph was first drafted in 1873. The first part appeared in 1889. His account in the two prefaces of his mode of composition—the jotted fragments, the ten years spent " classifying these odds and ends sufficiently to see what sort of story they indicated," the elaborately manipulated parallels and correspondences—must have struck Joyce as a comically earnest adumbration of his own procedures.

and she can the more readily sense their corruption in being
uninterested in their claims.   In *Sylvie and Bruno* as we might
expect the strategy is a good deal more deliberate.   Dodgson
carries on an elaborate counterpoint between a sadly laboured
fairy-story and an excruciating " adult " novel, which as he
implies at the outset *is* to be thought of as a book, not a
transcription from " life ".

Here is the introduction of the heroine: " ' —a young and
lovely lady ! ' I muttered to myself with some bitterness. ' And
this is, of course, the opening scene of Vol. I.   *She* is the
Heroine.   And *I* am one of those subordinate characters that
only turn up when needed for the development of her destiny,
and whose final appearance is outside the church, waiting to
greet the Happy Pair ! ' " It *is* the opening scene of Vol. I,
and she *is* the heroine, and he *is* the pathetic observer.   The
scene takes place on a train, where Dodgson often struck up
acquaintance with the little girls whose friendships and curls
he collected.   The significance of his insistence on the novelistic unreality is plain enough: for him a real grown-up
heroine *would* be unreal.   The " grown-up " part of *Sylvie and
Bruno* is a fantasy spun out of Dodgson's relations with
children, and the " fairy " part is the same fantasy spun small.
The inter-relations take place between two " mocking mirrors,"
not between dream and reality: a characteristic Dodgsonian
evasion.

In the preface to the second volume Dodgson outlines as its
structural convention an elaborate theory of multiple planes
of consciousness, the observer being more or less or entirely
or not at all aware of the presence of fairies.   The " fairy "
and " adult " incidents systematically tally, however.   The
impotent narrator, afflicted with " three score years and ten,
baldness, and spectacles "[1] and (the suppressed pun is telling)
heart trouble, is the meeting-place of two worlds, the correspondences between which are, for the rational observer, of
the most sinister description.   The high-born girl and the
handsome young physician who courts her with intimidated
reverence are equated with the fairy princess and her lisping
six-year-old brother who *won't* stick to his lessons and is
always begging to be smothered with kisses.   On the one hand,
romance is de-sexed by transposition into the pre-adolescent

---

[1] Cf. H.C.E.: " Hairs hoar mummery failend, snowdrift to my ellpow, deff
as Adder ", F535.

affection of brother and sister; on the other hand, innocence is corrupted by the analogies of incest and the reversal of male and female roles. It doesn't need much perspicuity to discover the coordinates of Dickens in the first of these modes of emphasis, and those of Byron in the second: Joyce's allusions to " Doveyed Covetfilles," " the old cupiosity shape ", F434, and the " pillgrimace of Childe Horrid ", F423, depend on an analysis which Carroll's unconscious epiphanizing of a whole century makes it especially easy to perform.[1]

The way in which *Sylvie and Bruno* provides the complete exegesis of a whole dimension of, for instance, Dickens is neatly brought out by a remark of Mrs. Q. D. Leavis (*Fiction and the Reading Public*):

> The peculiarity of Dickens, as any one who runs a critical eye over a novel or two of his can see, is that his originality is confined to recapturing a child's outlook on the grown-up world, emotionally he is not only uneducated but also immature.

The badness of Dickens' well-bred love-scenes has been conceded so often that their resemblance to the " novel " half of *Sylvie and Bruno* can hardly embarrass his most fervent admirers. Nor does the similarity between the fairy-adult convention of *Sylvie and Bruno* and the way Dickens interweaves his love-plot and child-plot require comment. When, as in *David Copperfield* or *Great Expectations*, the love-interest is represented as happening to the child-character grown up, the Carrollean implications are still more marked. Not only does the " reality " of these novels lie in the first half and evaporate as the protagonist ages, Dickens plainly intends the romance both to betray the child-world and to fulfil it (this is especially explicit in his furnishing Copperfield with two wives, one for each function). And the petulance of an Estella vis-à-vis the hurt innocence of a Pip is only a dramatic underlining of the way Dodgson exhibits the male-female as a

[1] That Childe Harold fled from an incestuous attachment is a critical commonplace that doesn't need biography to sustain it. In the fifth stanza of the first Canto, for instance, we read that he " Had sighed to many, though he loved but one, / And that loved one, alas! could ne'er be his. / Ah, happy she! to 'scape from him whose kiss / Had been pollution unto aught so chaste. . . ." Carroll, of course, has it both ways: " ' Pleasure first and business afterwards ' seemed to be the motto of these tiny folk, so many hugs and kisses had to be interchanged before anything else could be done."

pupil-schoolmistress relation.[1] Estella is the young-love metempsychosis of Miss Gargery and her rod Tickler.

It is easy to see how Carroll's grown-up world and his fairy-world are identical: the cross-references are innumerable. Still more revealing is the Dickensian quality of sentiment that informs both. Here is Arthur's image of Lady Muriel:

> " She was like that star to me—bright, beautiful, and pure, but out of reach, out of reach! . . . try as I may, I *cannot* read her feelings towards me. If there *is* love, she is hiding it! No, I must wait, I must wait!

Here is the nemesis of Bruno shirking his lessons:

> . . . but at last Sylvie's sharp eyes detected him, swinging on a tendril of ivy, and Sylvie's stern voice commanded his instant return to *terra firma* and to the business of life.

Estella and Miss Gargery: from the " unattainable she " to *femina imperatrix* is but a step. And when Arthur and Lady Muriel do achieve a conversational intimacy, the overtones of Bruno's lessons and big-sister-indulging-infant-precocity persist:

> " I quite foresee that *we*—I mean this clever little boy and myself — " Lady Muriel said to me, evidently with the kind wish to bring me into the conversation, " —are going to become famous—of course all our inventions are common property now—for a new Code of Rules for Letterwriting! Please invent some more, little boy."

This method of playing a dream-version against a novelistic account of events has possibilities manifested in much of *Ulysses*, especially the " Cyclops " episode. If Dodgson had possessed either the perceptions or the techniques to separate the two worlds, however, he would not have undertaken the book; to his naive belief that he is writing all the time for children (what children!) may be attributed a production of the greatest symptomatic interest. Here, to have done with quoting, is his charade of the Fall:

> Sylvie was arrranging some letters on a board—E-V-I-L. " Now Bruno," she said, " what does *that* spell? "

[1] Cf. the Shaunian Professor's image of the generic heroine " sitting on all the free benches avidously reading about ' it ' but ovidently on the look out for ' him '. . . or on the verge of the gutter with some bobbedhair brieffrocked babyma's toddler . . . held hostage at arms length, teaching His Infant Majesty how to make waters worse ", F166.

Bruno looked at it, in solemn silence, for a minute. " I knows what it *doesn't* spell! " he said at last.

" That's no good," said Sylvie. " What *does* it spell? "

Bruno took another look at the mysterious letters. " Why, it's ' LIVE,' backwards! " he exclaimed. (I thought it was, indeed.)

" How *did* you manage to see that? " said Sylvie.

" I just twiddled my eyes," said Bruno, " and then I saw it directly. Now may I sing the King-fisher song? "

This could very easily be butchered to make a Freudian holiday. It is important to see, however, upon what, in so naked an instance, the strategy for convoking without tension so many feelings depends. The technique is to destroy all perspective, to reduce everything to the same level of playful triviality (whether Evil is meant to be inseparable from Life, for instance, or whether you get Evil by reversing normal life, is pointedly left in suspension.)

Joyce's dreamer does this all the time. The whole nineteenth century *is* his dream. At the psychological level, Earwicker's gestes (as Tristram, or Archangel) are projections of his feelings about and empathy with his children. He slavers incestuously over his daughter (" Would one but to do apart a lilybit her virginelles and, so, to breath, so, therebetween, behold, she had instantt with her handmade as to graps the myth inmid the air. . . . Approach not for ghost sake! It is dormition! ", F561) and projects his shame on one of his sons (the infantile guilt-archetype of clandestine defecation—" When some bugger let down the backtrap of the omnibus ", F 47—is polarized toward Shem in all its recurrences: cf. pp. 185 and 563) and his preferred swashbuckling self-image on the other. But this orthodox application of Freudian mechanisms is only the beginning. Joyce exhibits Earwicker constantly transposing into childish terms the realities with which he is pestered. The dreaming mind adopts the stratagem suggested by the presence of the children; serious problems constantly metamorphose into infant faults and children's games. Imagining himself being crossexamined on his voyeurist escapade, Earwicker turns to babytalk and finger-doodling:

— Recount!

— I have it here to my fingall's ends. This liggy piggy wanted to go to the jampot. And this leggy peggy spelt pea. And theese lucky

puckers played at pooping tooletom.　Ma's da.　Da's ma.　Madas.
Sadam.　F496.

And in the first episode of section II the conflict of Michael
and Satan for the soul, which has been impressed on the
dreamer night after night by the engraving over his bedroom
mantelpiece, forces its way into the dream and is virtually
cauterized by transformation into a childrens' game.

THE HOMEOPATHIC ROMANTIC

Joyce lived through a time when his Ireland was plunging into
the night-world, after fading for more than a century on its
fringe.　To Ireland's delayed immersion can be attributed its
greatest writer's unique eminence.　He was the only man who
ever went through that dark wood armed with the maps and
reports of previous travellers.　The maps did not spare him
the journey, or the agonies of the journey, but they enabled
him to manifest every romantic mode with an unprecedented
degree of consciousness, and to encompass the entire recent
career of the European mind in a single lifetime.　Very early
in his career he saw himself performing for his contemporaries
" My holy office of Katharsis ":

> That they may dream their dreamy dreams
> I carry off their filthy streams. . . .

That broadside of 1904 is not as simple as it looks: The Holy
Office of course was the Inquisition.　The poet pretends to be
a public servant relieving the " timid arses " of the " mumming
company " by actually performing the psychic drama towards
which they gesture.　But his real function is inquisitorial.　He
inspects and utilizes their every manifestation, collects their
phrases, adopts their every posture; and while they imagine
they are sending him down the drain, he is actually pulling the
chain on them and all their works.

That is how, for instance, he handles a Shelley's habits with
language; he looks them in the face and turns them to service.
His images stream, but writer and reader are not being borne
along.　(The Anna Livia episode is to some extent an exception, for structural reasons; it is unfortunate that it has come
to be thought of as representative of the entire book.)　Many
of Joyce's revisions of the earlier drafts consist of interpolated
parentheses in altered tones, against which the reader who has
lapsed from the *qui vive* may bark his shins.　The " streaming "

stratagems of the dream are used to epiphanize at once the evasions they commonly serve and the irreducible meanings by which they are controlled.

Had so innocently comprehensive a figure as Lewis Carroll not existed, he would have had to be invented. Joyce was in process of inventing him when in 1927 Dodgson came sharply to his attention. Dodgson unites all the themes of the dream-bound intellect shifting its channels like a river in flatlands, and relieves each theme of the personal intensity which characteristically occults the significance of a Shelley's or a Tennyson's words. With the personal tensions gone the thematic tensions take over. That was the situation Joyce wanted. Carroll did the antiseptic work for the Joycean operation.

The career of Joyce is that of a man enacting all the romantic patterns—mother-guilt, Byronic exile, infant as anarch, poet as heresiarch—in order to find out and exhibit what they mean. It is precisely because his " characters " are of the most conventional outline—Shaun the Post lifted from Dion Boucicault's cardboard play, Stephen a stock bohemian with an extra dimension, Bloom a bagful of clichés—that they are so efficacious. The same is true of his situations, chiefly antitheses taken from the worst discoverable operas and melodramas. Joyce's perpetual assumption of roles is equally central to his work: Byronic hero, Zolaesque novel, Shelleyan stream-of-images, Carrollean infantilism are phases traversed by him and his artist's consciousness; phases, analogically, traversed by his work. He contains all these things, and he explicates them. His work is the mimetic and cathartic gesture that brings the nineteenth century, with its nightworld in every sense, to an end. After him, every romantic seems spurious.

Portrait-Ulysses-Finnegan: nature as dream and mirror, nature as arena for confrontations with the not-self, nature as matrix of *vestigiae Dei* to be traversed in traversing oneself drop by drop. The history and catharsis of the Romantic Movement is there. " Wait till Finnegan wakes ", Joyce used to admonish Paul Leon in allusion to the unwritten *recorso* of his trilogy.

After seventeen years of toil the last words of the book were revised and copied for the last time:

> . . . and it's old and old it's sad and old it's sad and weary I go back to you, my cold father, my cold mad father, my cold mad feary

father. . . . Yes, tid. There's where. First. We pass through
grass behush the bush too. Whish! A gull. Gulls. Far calls.
Coming, far! End here. Us then. Finn, again! Take. Bussoftlhee,
mememormee! Till thousendsthee. Lps. The keys to. Given!
A way a lone a last a loved a long the   F622.

" I felt so completely exhausted," he told a friend, " as if all
the blood had run out of my brain. I sat for a long while on
a street bench, unable to move."

But he could not save his companions. For they perished by their
own madness, because they killed and ate the cattle of Hyperion the
sun-god, and the god took care that they should never see home
again.

Chapter 17

THE PALE OF WORDS

... And keep them in the pale of words till death.
Pope

L ɪ ᴋ ᴇ a spider among tombstones, the mind of Leopold Bloom
scuttles over the surface of the indecipherable given. If he
doesn't read the signatures of all things, he at least recognizes
that he is surrounded by things, and that they bear signatures.
He has virtually the only such mind in Dublin. The mind of
Simon Dedalus is turned toward the past, that of Stephen upon
himself, those of the Dedalus camp-followers on gossip and
self-interest.

Bloom is a stranger and a naive. He is impressed by the
existence, the there-ness, of things. For Europeans whose
sensibilities lay within the traditions of Europe, things faded
in the eighteenth century with the departure of the light.

Thus at her felt approach, and secret might,
Art after *Art* goes out, and all is Night.

In the dream-world of *Finnegans Wake* the mind is detached
from responsibility toward things, cut loose in the nowhere—
the not quite trackless nowhere in which words remain. It can
occupy only the points other minds have occupied before, and
can get from one point to another only along the track ripped
through space by a quotation, or the fading trail of an *idée
reçue*.

Literally nothing is left but words: slogans, speeches,
maxims, captions, quotations, jingles, familiar phrases, borrowed rhythms, puns, puzzles, parodies, " quashed quotatoes,
messes of mottage ". Thought, feeling and action are carried
on by unrealities in a totally unreal context which only language
makes plausible. " I cannot form the least notion of a brick,"
said Tennyson, " I don't know what it is. . . . But I have more
distinct ideas of God, of love and such emotions. . . . The
human soul seems to me always—in some ways, how we do
not know—identical with God. That's the value of

prayer."[1] Art in the nineteenth-century night-world flourished
when the poet didn't have to cope with bricks:

> Life, like a dome of many- coloured glass,
> Stains the white radiance of eternity :

which is more exciting than

> we see him as he moved,
> How modest, kindly, all-accomplished, wise,
> With what sublime repression of himself,
> And in what limits and how tenderly ;

though neither really has any more bite on the world outside
the dictionary than

> Came whiffling through the tulgy wood
> And burbled as it came.

Humpty Dumpty was right; if you want a word to " mean "
more than usual, you have only to pay it extra; it has no
responsibility except to its employer.   Indeed, the characteristic poetic effects of the time stay wholly within language in a
peculiar fashion:

> A cry that shivered to the tingling stars.

It is no use trying to explain that " tingling " as metaphor,
synaesthesia, or anything else; but among the reasons for
accepting it as indubitably right may be listed the prompting
of " shivered " and the assonance of the word one expects in
its place, the suppressed " twinkling ".   Tennyson at his
purest moved closer to the pun than he would ever have wanted
to admit.

Nothing but words.   The thunder that re-echoes through
Finnegans Wake is the inchoate speech of the universe of
language; it comes decades after the last leap of lightning
from charged cloud to solid ground, as a tremor of readjust-
mant shakes all the molecules of the air.

> The   fall   (bababadalgharaghtakamminarronnkonnbronntonner-
> ronntuonnthunntrovarrhounawnskawntoohoohoordenenthurnuk!) of
> a once wallstrait oldparr is retaled early in bed and later on life down
> through all christian minstrelsy.   F3.

[1] Quoted by Sir Charles Tennyson, in his *Alfred Tennyson*.   The report goes
on: " Then he turned to morality.   Moral good he thought the crown of man,
but what is it without immortality of the soul? "

" Early in bed " is characteristic. " Early and late " is what the phrase starts to say; but " early " slips into a proverbial groove and pulls a bed into the context, while " late " equips itself with a corresponding " life ". " Fall ", the subject of the sentence, prompts " wall " via assonance and Humpty Dumpty (who in fact appears in the next sentence); " wall " drags after it " street ", and the sense recovers its equilibrium by the modification " wallstrait " (once strait, but now fallen). The echoes of " Wall Street ", however, are a moment dying down; the stock market suggests " par ", which worms its way in via Old Parr (1483–1635), and " retail ", which duly modifies " retold ". This is Freudian dream-work, if one likes, but it is also a universe of independent words obeying their chemical affinities with no restraint from things.

The things in *Finnegans Wake* exist only at the prompting of words: Mookse, Gripes, Ondt, Gracehoper, Healiopolis, the house of Atreox, Anonymoses. Hero and heroine are a concurrence of initials. Blazed trails of quotation route a forty-page sermon (" . . . where it is nobler in the main to supper than the boys and errors of outrager's virtue ", F434: Cupid's bow and arrow grafted onto Hamlet's soliloquy). Catches from songs set Shaun and his postman's lamp before our eyes:

> . . . and O, the higher on high the deeper and low, I heard him so! And lo, mescemed somewhat came of the noise and somewho might amove allmurk. . . . Whom we dreamt was a shaddo, sure, he's lightseyes, the laddo! Blessed momence, O romence, he's growing to stay! F404.

It is never the exigency of a reality other than verbal, but always some verbal mechanism on the page, some chain of puns, some waft of rhythm, that produces the next word. If anything is " swift ", that syllable will call up the ghosts of Stella and Vanessa:

> . . . his onsaturncast eyes in stellar attraction followed swift to an imaginary swellaw, O, the vanity of Vanissy! All ends vanishing! F449.

If a vowel is deformed into " a ", the copresence of alpha and omega ensures that it will recur as " o ":

> Heat wives rasing. They jest keeps rosing. He jumps leaps rizing. Howlong! F363.

The contemplation of a Dublin that existed only in his father's reminiscences sharpened Joyce's lifelong sense that the civic reality of Dublin existed in its talk alone. *Finnegans Wake* mines that perception to its depths. Never did a book contain such virtuosity, such inventive, thorough, and minute exploitation of rhythm, gesture, association, song, oration, small talk, cliché, every—literally every—facet of discourse except substance. Yet never for a moment does Joyce's mind shift from his Dublin; its reality *was* in talk, and such is the leverage of his maturest double-writing that from phrase to phrase and from page to page a sense of that reality comes powerfully through. We are overwhelmingly aware of old Kate dancing in the pantomime though the language contains only puns and incantations:

> Whisk! There's me shims amd here's me hams and this is me juppettes, gause be the meter! Whisk! What's this? Whisk! And that? He never cotched finer, balay me, at Romiolo Frullini's flea pantamine out of Griddle-the-Sink or Shushies-with-her-Soles-Up or La Sauzerelly, the pucieboots, when I started so hobmop ladlelike, highty tighty, to kick the time off the cluckclock lucklock quamquam camcam potapot panapan kickakickkack. Hairhorehounds, shake up pfortner. Fuddling fun for Fullacan's sake! F531.

And we acquire a weirdly exact sense of the interaction of Dublin religion and Dublin conviviality from language that hangs in space half way between:

> When, pressures be to our hoary frother, the pop gave his sullen bulletaction and, bilge, sled a movement of catharic emulsipotion down the sloppery slide of a slaunty to tilted lift-ye-landsmen. F310.

It is worse than useless to push this toward one or the other of the meanings between which it hangs; to paraphrase it, for instance, in terms of porter being uncorked and poured. It is equally misleading to scan early drafts for the author's intentions, on the assumption that a " meaning " got buried by elaboration. Joyce worked seventeen years to push the work away from " meaning ", adrift into language; nothing is to be gained by trying to push it back. He had his attention fixed on people talking, not on what the words " really " meant. Frank Budgen reports how

> He was always looking and listening for the necessary fact or word; and he was a great believer in his luck. What he needed would come to him. That which he collected would prove useful in its

time and place. . . . At intervals, alone or in conversation, seated
or walking, one of these tablets was produced, and a word or two
scribbled on it at lightning speed as ear or memory served his turn.

The phrases so scrupulously collected drag with them roots
and soil, the dramatic contexts from which they were extracted:
tensions between mind and object, between speaker and
audience, between the mind and a self-conscious fraction of
the mind. "Pilate! Wy don't you old back that owlin
mob?", U216/207, is a function not merely of "Father
Bernard Vaughan's droll eyes and cockney voice" but of his
showman's relation to the Gospel, his kinesthetic conception
of preaching, and his twofold relation with his audience: genial
rapport at the level of sensibility, unawareness of their latent
antipathy to his accent and nationality. All this emerges from
nine words, three of them phonetically deformed. In the
Wake Joyce carries this principle to its end; he sets up within
each paragraph a drama of strophe, antistrophe, and parabasis
turning on the interactions of juxtaposed contexts, personae,
and gestures.

> Shsh shake, co-comeraid! Me only, them five ones, he is equal
> combat. I have won straight. Hence my nonation wide hotel and
> creamery establishments which for the honours of our mewmew
> mutual daughters, credit me, I am woowoo willing to take my stand,
> sir, upon the monument, that sign of our ruru redemption, any
> hygienic day to this hour and to make my hoath to my sinnfinners,
> even if I get life for it, upon the Open Bible and before the Great
> Taskmaster's (I lift my hat!) and in the presence of the Deity Itself
> andwell of Bishop and Mrs. Michan of High Church of England as
> of all such of said my immediate withdwellers and of every living
> sohole in every corner wheresoever of this globe in general which
> useth of my British to the backbone tongue and commutative justice
> that there is not one tittle of truth, allow me to tell you, in that
> purest of fibfib fabrications. F36.

These phrases are items, not statements: items of talk. The
tones of the Audenesque public-school man of action vibrating
with embarrassed friendship ("Shsh shake, co-comeraid!"),
of the clean-living cricketer ("I have won straight"), of the
challenged Tory ("I an woowoo willing to take my stand,
sir"), of the correct Christian gentleman ("before the Great
Taskmaster's (I lift my hat!)"), of the legal precisionist ("as
of all such of said my immediate withdwellers"), of the
reverberating orator ("every living sohole in every corner

whatsoever of this globe in general "), all these are so many juxtaposed aural observations organized with comprehending detachment. Character is elucidated by rapidly synthesizing the voices and locutions of many persons.

Here is a longer passage; quotation will be continuous, but commentary interspersed. The reader should first read it as an unbroken whole. (F112.)

> Lead, kindly fowl!

[Academic dive after an appropriate apostrophe. The passage comes in the middle of the professor's textual essay; figures of emotion aren't part of his stock-in-trade, and he uses them badly. He reaches into his religiose-hortatory stockpile and comes up with Newman.]

> They always did: ask the ages.

[Modulation toward political oratory; attempt to get back on the track via an enthymeme.]

> What bird has done yesterday, man may do next year, be it fly, be it moult, be it hatch, be it agreement in the nest.

[Blend of popular science—evolutionary; political gesture—automatic progress; and cheap oratory.]

> For her socioscientific sense is sound as a bell, sir, her volucrine automutativeness right on normalcy:

[Psych. lab. jargon being self-consciously popular (" sound as a bell, sir "); the country-doctor facets of the insufficiently sophisticated pedant are emerging. His lack of any genuine sense of an audience leads him to lunge heartily for rapport toward various quarters, now professional, now sentimental, now popular.]

> she knows, she just feels she was kind of born to lay and love eggs (trust her to propagate the species and hoosh her fluffballs safe through din and danger!);

[He finds rank nursery sentimentality, wonders of mother-love, etc., easy to slip into; the parenthesis marks first a recovery of dignity (" propagate her species "), then a new plunge into the grownup's notion of the Mother Goose world.]

> lastly but mostly, in her genesic field it is all game and no gammon; she is ladylike in everything she does and plays the gentleman's part every time.

[Rapid permutation of professional jargon, proverbial wisdom, and Emily Post.]

> Let us auspice it! Yes, before all this has time to end the golden age must return with its vengeance. Man will become dirigible, Ague will be rejuvenated, woman with her ridiculous white burden will reach by one step sublime incubation, the manewanting human lioness and her dishorned discipular manram will lie down together publicly flank upon fleece.

[Parabasis. The stream of malapropisms signals that the ironic critical consciousness has taken control. The innocent joy of the scientist contemplating so happy an augury topples into bathos. " *Its* vengeance " is the first false note. Then the pedantic " dirigible " (= capable of *being directed* by woman; also phallic flying-dreams) implies a ludicrous image of man as transcendental floating gas-bag which corresponds to the sensibility underlying much advocacy of the " air age " as pseudo-apocalypse. Her ridiculous white burdens (overtones of the " white man's burden," familiar rationalization of colonial rapacity) are her husband and child. The clause sounds as though it were going to end with " apotheosis; " " incubation," which comes instead, combines " incarnation " (the wrong word, as usual when the professor is flying high, but iconographically related) with hints of civic nurseries (the incubator liberates the hen from the chore of hatching her own) and of the egg-life reserved for husbands and children, plus the pampered hothouse existence which luxury advertisements continually incite women to claim as their due. The concluding parody of Isaiah XI.6 and the hint of public copulation (cf. 239: " When every Klitty of a scolderymeid shall hold every yardscullion's right to stimm her uprecht for whimsoever, whether on privates, whather in publics. And when all us romance catholeens shall have ones for all amanseprated. And the world is maidfree ") clinch this current of emotion as a sort of popular erotic eschatology; compare the factitious gusto with which the press exhorts us to await startling developments in next season's decolletages and skirt-lengths.]

No, assuredly, they are not justified, those gloompourers

[Among whom, despite our inadvertent reservations, heaven forbid that we scientists should be numbered; do we not labour constantly for progress on this as on all other fronts?]

who grouse that letters have never been quite their old selves again since that weird weekday in bleak Janiveer (yet how palmy date in a waste's oasis) when to the shock of both, Biddy Doran looked at literature.

[The accents of the literary supplements are now intruding themselves; in the next paragraph the hen becomes a lady novelist whose sympathetic critic (still the professor, in yet another role) asks, " But how many of her readers realise that she is not out to dizzledazzle with a graith uncouthrement of postmantuam glasseries from the lapins and the grigs." As " she knows, she just feels " her maternal mission, so she just writes right out of her heart: " she feel plain plate one flat fact thing." A moment later she is writing memoirs of her husband.]

Joyce's syncretic techniques of characterization depend on this sort of rapid surveying of allotropic forms of the same personality, a method peculiarly adapted to the rendering of a society marked by metamorphic personae, rapidly altering roles assumed by persons who act from no centre. By constantly exhibiting the number of tones that can, by a slight adjustment of the knob, be gotten out of the same loud-speaker he underlines both the essential stability of human actions and passions and the morphologies social malaise, lack of communal rapport, and emotional illiteracy can cause them to undergo.

That is why, for instance, a sudden interpolation from the ad-man's loud-speaker glosses the rectitude of the Mookse:

> The Pills, the Nasal Wash (Yardly's), the Army Man Cut, as british as bondstrict and as straightcut as when that brokenarched traveller from Nuzuland . . .

Orthodox contemporary rhetoric has its prefabricated *mot juste* for the condition of the Gripes' breath also:

> Unsightbared embouscher, relentless foe to social and business succes! (Hourihaleine) It might have been a happy evening but . . . F156.

The Mookse and the Gripes contemplate one another for a moment through the hortatory jungles of middle-class magazines. The tobaccos and toiletries of the advertising pages of *Punch*, Bond Street mixture, Yardley soaps, Navy Cut cigarettes, the " bondstrict " strait-coats of quasi-military

respectability, ensure to their possessor the " vacticanated "
Mookse a permanence coterminous with the spiritual warrant
of his Church, outlasting the rival institution of St. Paul's
whose ruins Macaulay's New Zealander sketched from a
broken arch of London Bridge.[1]   Halitosis, B.O., unruly hair,
and other invisible and/or unsightly (*unsichtbar* plus un-sight-
bared) impediments to success are the contrasting lot of the
Gripes.   This sudden expansion of reference into the purlieu
of popular mythology's angels and devils focusses in yet
another way the essential unreality of the Mookse-Gripes
conflict, the factitious splitting-up of the human psyche that
has secured these perennially lucrative social and political
oppositions.   The Latinate artificiality of their dispute is
underlined throughout the episode.   If one says " Efter
thousand yaws " the other is careful to say " Ofter thousand
yores "; they are far more concerned with differing, in the
most mechanical way, than with getting the words right.

GUIDANCE OF THE SPEAKING VOICE

Every mode of deformation has its distinct purpose; one must
observe the plane at which whole passages are canted.   The
parts of the *Wake* that are usually conceded to succeed are the
parts that approximate the effects of romantic poetry.   The
other parts, however, aren't trying to do this and failing; they
have quite different objectives.   This brings us to the way dark
passages acquire a preliminary luminousness when read aloud.
One of Joyce's modalities of composition is to keep in constant
touch with the normal pace of breathing: one use to which he
put his musical training.   If we fail to come upon a comma or a
parenthesis before we run out of breath, it is because a great
tumulus of garrulity is being erected; if on the other hand a
sentence three pages long is conveniently broken, it is because
not superhuman oratory but interminable conversation is there
being imitated.   If the tone shifts rapidly from phrase to
phrase, we are in the presence of a strophic and antistrophic
structure of yet another kind.   Joyce's list of some 600 misprints

---

[1] " And she (the Catholic Church) may still exist in undiminished vigour when
some traveller from New Zealand shall, in the midst of a vast solitude, take his
stand on a broken arch of London Bridge to sketch the ruins of St. Paul's."
Joyce has given " Nuzuland " the backward colonial connotations of Zululand,
and, presumably in recognition of the distance the chap has come, transferred the
broken arches from London Bridge to the traveller.

in the first edition concerns itself mainly with supplying or deleting commas; and a comma appropriately encountered guides us not merely to the grammatical but to the rhetorical structure of what would otherwise baffle completely.

The " linguistic phenomenon," which Joyce insisted should, in comparative disregard of the proliferating allusions, be apprehended for its own sake, manifests itself in the special local strains of careful reading. The number of shifts of tone into which the passage just quoted forces us in our effort to keep the feeling and syntax simultaneously clear is the most insistent key to its meaning we can have. Here, for instance, is a professional disquisition on the *Chamber Music* period of the hapless Shem's career:

> We now romp through a period of pure lyricism of shamebred music (technologically, let me say, the appetising entry of this subject on a fool chest of vialds is plumply pudding the carp before doevre hors) evidenced by such words in distress as *I cream for thee, Sweet Margareen*, and the more hopeful *O Margareena! O Margareena! Still in the bowl is left a lump of gold!* F164.

These accents of perfunctory deprecation are immediate enough; the sentence rattles on briskly, and such unobtrusive deflections as " shamebred music " and " words in distress " introduce with the slyest of grins now and then an unwonted *mot juste* into the lecture-room prose. But the parenthesis, like others in the chapter, intrudes material with which the professor is, for a change, emotionally involved; his controversial snarl is signalled by a stream of puns; our effort of attention and (when reading aloud) of articulation, directed toward making the underlying motifs—entrée, chest of viols, plum pudding, carp, hors d'oeuvres, putting the cart before the horse—break through, compels us to experience a constriction of verbiage, a deformation of sensibility, corresponding to the motivations of this Olympian snub. This is a normal principle: the more deformed the language—the more it plays malapropisms against the easy flow of brogue or epigram—the more some compelling inward pressure, some twist of lubricity or ferocity or shame, is poking up its snout. The thorns in the path of easy reading are not idly sown. Seventy pages later we encounter the same theme as experienced by the guilty poet himself; what was in the former instance a scholastic datum for external description presents itself now as a violent series of emotional twists and wrenches. Here is the anguish of the outcast Glugg[1]

> *— My God, alas, that dear olt tumtum home*
> *Whereof in youthfood port I preyed*
> *Amook the verdigrassy convict vallsall dazes.*
> *And cloitered for amourmeant in thy boosome shede!*

His mouthfull of ecstasy (for Shing-Yung-Thing in Shina from Yoruyume across the Timor Sea), herepong (maladventure!) shot pinging up through the errorooth of his wisdom (who thought him a Fonar all, feastking of shellies by googling Lovvey, regally freytherem, eagelly plumed, and wasbut gumboil owrithy prods wretched some horsery megee plods coffin acid odarkery pluds dense floppens mugurdy) as thought it had been zawhen intwo. Wholly sanguish blooded up disconvulsing the fixtures of his fizz. Apang which his tempory chewer med him a crazy chump of a Haveajube Sillayass. Joshua Croesus, son of Nunn! Though he shall live for millions of years a life of billions of years, from their roseaced glows to their violast lustres, he shall not forget that pucking Pugases. Holihowlsballs and bloody acres! Like gnawthing unheardth! F231.

The way to approach such a passage as this is not to begin as it were with a lexicon disentangling the jabberwocked materials, but to attend to the way it compels itself to be read. Three parentheses in the first sentence jerk us violently three times off the track; the dislocation it describes, the poetic *faux pas* introducing a painful disequilibrium into perilously-poised adolescent " wisdom," is enacted by the syntactic switchbacks and triply reinforced by the headlong metaphors (an explosion blowing off the roof, the lyrical mouthful gushing up scalding into the brain, the tongue suddenly rigid and running through the roof of the mouth); if " thought " was " zawhen intwo " (sawed in two, seen into = put on public display) by the poem, a convulsion equally drastic has overtaken the poet.

The content of the disruptive parentheses is far from accidental. The first (" for Shing-Yung-Thing in Shina from

[1] Glugg and Chuff are the Shem and Shaun of the *Mime*. " Glugg "—a strangling and drowning sound—indicates the self-conscious inadequacy of the frustrated amorist, not yet artist but resolving to seek " compensation " through a confessional art. Glugg corresponds to the Stephen Dedalus stage of self-tortured sensitivity. Shem the Penman of I–7 is from Shaun's point of view " a low sham," but he has at least gotten himself somewhat in hand. Glugg's Shaunian opposite is Chuff: steam-engine noises of express-train efficiency, plus " chaff " (worthless husk of exhibitionist virtue) plus " chaff " (his easy badinage with the girls.) The thousands of proper names in the Wake are all emblematic in this way.

Yoruyume across the Timor Sea "), recalling the dedication of a verse-book or a love-letter, sharpens with its pseudo-oriental innocence of the " Three Little Maids from School " variety Glugg's comically posturing notion of the polite conventions governing his verses. The third, with its reduction of " feastking of shellies by googling Lovvey " to " dense floppens mugurdy," writhes across the path of the main sentence in an agony of ptomainic violence. " Feastking of shellies by goggling Lovvey " (Shelley, Lovelace, the Feast-king, the Festy King theme from elsewhere in the book, the poet as child of nature—a shell by the gurgling Liffey— serenading a " Lovvey " not merely ogling but in her rapture " googling ") contains the sort of notion of the essence of poetic achievement that might be expected to come to this sort of grief (though Shelley seems to have been immune to self-doubt). The specific deformations of phrases are contrived with an eye to their violence: *gumboil owrithy, coffin acid odarkery*, and *dense floppens mugurdy* do not merely inflect the names of typical heart-on-sleeve Irish poets (John Boyle O'Reilly, Kevin Izod O'Doherty, Denis Florence MacCarthy) with Glugg's scathing conviction of their and his unworthiness, they enact the pronunciation of those names with explosive scorn. *Like gnawthing unheardth* prolongs in the same contemptuous way the initial syllable of *nothing* and lends aspirate emphasis to *on earth*. The *pong, ping, pang* of snapping lyre-strings and twinging psychic nerves counterpoints the *prods, plods, pluds* (= plus) of an aroused and jabbing self-respect. The protective preoccupation of his mind with a mechanical and inane figure of speech (" though he shall live for millions of years a life of billions of years ")—like Bloom at the sight of Boylan rapidly thinking of something else—holds off for only two lines the measured beat of accusation: " He shall not forget that pucking Pugases." (A puckish Pegasus puking gas.)

It doesn't therefore really matter that we don't, inevitably, catch a fraction of the detailed implications in a passage of *Finnegans Wake*; Joyce is employing language so resourcefully as dramatic gesture, introducing so consistently his least mellifluous deflections of plain sense at moments of maximum intensity, strewing the text so liberally with so many clues to the articulation of local clusters of feeling, that we can afford to miss a great deal and still, within certain limits of indetermination, possess the work.

DEFORMED TAGS

The seriousness of the moral analyses packed into Joycean phrases consorts inevitably with the insouciance of the techniques. This is itself a technique; an expression like " . . . as he displaid all the oathword science of his visible disgrace ", F227, sounds like a mild deformation of a tautology but proves to contain a tense volitional drama with which the glib expression is counterpointed. The theme over which this phrase draws its brisk glissando is the catechism's definition of a sacrament: an outward and visible sign of an inward and spiritual grace. The " oathwords " are the outward signs of a lack of grace, and their use in polite company incurs disgrace. " Disgrace " however doesn't mean loss of grace but loss of prestige; the displayer of " oathword science " has transposed the context in which he contemplates his own guilt from the theological to the social; he isn't concerned about God but about the figure he cuts. He has made a Byronic banner of his unacceptability ; the oaths are dis-*plaid* like tartan emblems and have been changed from involuntary signs to a studied science. If we recall how a few decades served to housebreak the Byronic hero without in the least altering his orientations (it was possible for a Sherlock Holmes to become a household idol by a *modus vivendi* that had made Byron's name anathema to respectable ladies) we can see the dramatic significance of the innocuous tag Joyce here bends to his uses. The household saying, the tag of verse, the Mother Goose gesture, function in the *Wake* like the Augustan rhyme.

THROUGH THE *DAILY MIRROR*

This brings us round again to the paradox of Joyce's subject; the nullity behind the words, the reality in the words. Both surround any newspaper reader. If John Stanislaus Joyce stepped through the mirror of memory, and Charles Lutwidge Dodgson through that of Narcissus, the looking-glass through which the reader of *Finnegans Wake* is conducted is the *Daily Mirror*.

> – Christ in our irish times! Christ on the airs independence! Christ hold the freedman's chareman! Christ light the dully expressed!
> – Slog slagt and sluaghter! Rape the daughter! Choke the pope! F500.

Marathon dances merge into drunken and rapidly dissolved international marriages:

> And it's high tigh tigh. Titley hi ti ti. That my dig pressed in your dag si. Gnug of old Gnig. Ni, gnid mig brawly! I bag your burden. Mees is thees knees. Thi is Mi. We have caught one-selves, Sveasmeas, in somes incontigruity coumplegs of heoponhur-rish marrage from whose I most sublumbunate. A polog, my engl! Excutes. Om still so sovvy. Whyle om till ti ti. F607.

Apocalyptic emotions are summoned by police alarms:

> Calling all downs. Calling all downs to dayne. Array! Sur-rection! Eireweeker to the wohld bludyn world. O rally, O rally, O rally! Phlenxty, O rally! F593.

The trends of fashion—

> How the fictionable world in Fruzian Creamtartery is loading off heavy furses and affubling themselves with muckinstushes. The neatschknee Novgolosh. F345.

—bear the same stress as the promises of morticians:

> Phone for Phineal toomellow aftermorn and your phumeral's a roselixion. F345.

Pontifical rhetoric issues in a shameless commercial:

> We have highest gratifications in announcing to pewtewr publikumst of pratician pratyusers, genghis is ghoon for you. F593.

" Liberal " clergymen are the ventriloqual outlets of hygienic advice:

> Such, he says, is how the reverend Coppinger, he visualises the hide-bound homelies of creed crux ethics. Watsch yourself tillicately every morkning in your bracksullied twilette. F525.

Life-insurance becomes the modality of salvation (" the Loyd insure her ", F413), Imperial Rome becomes an exhibit for tourists (" chalkfull of masterplasters ", F152), the highest poetry is quoted as vehicle for the most commonplace emotions (" For a burning Would is come to dance inane ", F250), death is exorcised with the spurious heartiness of cracker-barrel philosophy:

> Toborrow and toburrow and tobarrow! That's our crass, hairy and evergrim life, till one finel howdiedow Bouncer Naster raps on the bell with a bone and his stinkers stank behind him with the sceptre and the hourglass. F455.

PSEUDO-METAPHYSICS OF POST-KANTIAN MAN

But *Finnegans Wake* is neither simply a highly compressed mirroring of the newspaper reader's reality, nor simply its *reductio ad absurdum*. The critique cuts a great deal deeper, as we can illustrate from one of the nodal passages where the threads of the book are suddenly compressed into " the eye of a noodle ":

> 9. Now, to be on anew and basking again in the panaroma of all flores of speech, if a human being duly fatigued by his dayety in the sooty, having plenxty off time on his gouty hands and vacants of space at his sleepish feet and as hapless behind the dreams of accuracy as any camelot prince of dinmurk, were at this auctual futule pretcriting unstant, in the states of suspensive exanimation, accorded, throughout the eye of a noodle, with an earsighted view of old hope-inhaven with all the ingredient and egregiunt whights and ways to which in the curse of his persistence the course of his tory will had been having recourses, the reverberration of knotcracking awes, the reconjungation of nodebinding ayes, the redissolusingness of mind-mouldered ease and the thereby hang of the Hoel of it, could such a none, whiles even led comesilencers to comeliewithhers and till intempestuous Nox should catch the gallicry and spot lucan's dawn, byhold at ones what is main and why tis twain, how one once meet melts in tother wants poignings, the sap rising, the foles falling, the nimb now nihilant round the girlyhead so becoming, the wrestless in the womb, all the rivals to allsea, shakeagain, O disaster! shakealose, Ah how starring! but Heng's got a bit of Horsa's nose and Jeff's got the signs of Ham round his mouth and the beau that spun beautiful pales as it palls, what roserude and oragious grows gelb and greem, blue out of the ind of it! Violet's dyed! then *what* would that far-gazer seem to seemself to seem seeming of, dimm it all?
>
> Answer: A collideorscape! F143.

When you jiggle a kaleidoscope (" shakeagain, O disaster! shakealose, Ah how starring! ") the coloured objects at the end of the tube of mirrors assume more or less beautiful hexagonal patterns. You are always looking at the same few beads, buttons, and bits of paper, but the arrangement is never twice alike, is always symmetrical, and is always far more complicated than inspection of the raw materials would lead one to suppose possible. The shapes, while they resemble those of crystals and snowflakes, are ontologically meaningless; and the " reconjungations " and " redissolusingnesses ", however complex, offer no nutriment to the intellect. They are

fortuitous rather than dramatic actions; the efficient cause is
the motion of the experimenter's hand, but the formal and final
causes belong wholly to chance

The kaleidoscope's mirror-lined tube is the Bloom-like
Carrollean mind of post-Kantian man, " as hapless behind the
dreams of accuracy as any camelot prince of dinmurk." The
cloud that Hamlet said had the shape of a camel, then of a
weasel or a whale, the dream-city of Camelot to which the
nineteenth century attached so many irridescent emotions,
took their forms from the perceiving eye. In rejecting the
hylomorphic doctrine that things are intrinsically intelligible,
post-Cartesian philosophy placed itself in H. C. Earwicker's
posture of " suspensive exanimation ", producing by a twist of
the hand an infinite succession of private geometrically-
ordered worlds (everything in the kaleidoscope seems hexagonal)—the pseudometaphysics of Malebranche, Descartes,
Hume, Kant, and Locke[1] and the phenomonological
dazzle of Times Square. Into his image of this somatic
universe Joyce poured, like scraps into the kaleidoscope, load
after load of old iron, broken furniture, scraps of reading,
shreds of philosophy, " once current puns, quashed quotatoes,
messes of mottage ", F183.

In another passage the philosophical alignments are still
more explicit. Old Kate the maid-of-all-work has dumped the
household rubbish in storied Phoenix Park, where already
" fossil footprints, bootmarks, fingersigns, elbowdints, breech-
bowls " and other signatures of all things were " all successively
traced of a most envolving description ". " What subtler
timeplace of the weald," Joyce asks, to hide " a loveletter,
lostfully hers, that would be lust on Ma, than then when
ructions ended, than here where race began: and by four
hands of forethought the first babe of reconcilement is laid in its
last cradle of hume sweet hume ", F80.

" Hume " is humus, but also a philosopher; we are attending the interment of the hylomorphic babe. At the moment
when Hume denied causality the intelligible signatures of
things began to be obliterated by impenetrable detritus, and

---

[1] Whose dualistic absolutes will never oblige by remaining existentially distinct:
" but Heng's got a bit of Horsa's nose and Jeff's got the signs of Ham round his
mouth ": montage of Hengist and Horsa, ancestors of Saxon Britain, and of
Japhet and Ham, sons of Noah. Overtones of equine British noses and canni-
balistic fratricide: Jeff hasn't applied his napkin to the traces of Ham.

the accumulation of inscrutable terminal moraines of dates, treaties, documents, legends, counterpurposes, and memories supplanted the historical drama of the divine will unfolding in time which the middle ages had contemplated. The entire fifth section of *Finnegans Wake* is given over to the erudite puzzlings of a scientific scholar over the meaning of one tattered letter on Kate's midden-dump (Kate = Kathleen ni Houlihan; the letter is both human history and any intelligible object). What Hume did was deny not merely efficient causality but any intelligible connection between adjacent things. He initiated, for philosophy, the kaleidoscope-world of discrete inscrutables,[1] continually rearranged. Professor Gilson gives us Hume in a strikingly Finneganistic context:

" There are two principles which I cannot render consistent," Hume says in the Appendix to his *Treatise of Human Nature*, " nor is it in my power to renounce either of them, namely, *that all our distinct perceptions are distinct existences*, and *that the mind never perceives any real connection among distinct existences*." We do not know with certainty what, exactly, Kant had read of Hume, but there is little doubt that this sentence was the very one that aroused him from his dogmatic slumber. It shows at least what a tremendous charge of existential explosive was introduced by Hume into the Wolffian universe of nicely concatenated essences in which Kant himself was slumbering. The ontological world of Wolff was at once blown to pieces in the mind of Kant, and it almost immediately dawned upon him that his own philosophical problem was going to be: What are we to do with existence, if all our perceptions are distinct existences, and if the mind never perceives any real connection between them? To this question, his own answer was finally to be:. The mind does not *perceive* such connections, it *prescribes* them.[2]

The mind prescribing connections does the kaleidoscope-mirrors' job for itself. The intelligible universe has been fragmented into a " collideorscape " of private worlds, and " meaning," apart from the specific intentions of the particular unifying intellect you happen to be talking with, has become meaningless. It is difficult to imagine what modalities of language, other than those invented by Joyce, could obey the contours of the irrationally prismatic result.

[1] " The first babe of reconcilement " is also the Christ-child, mediator between visible and invisible. Hume laid Him in his " last cradle " also in performing what turned out to be a philosophical annihilation of the meaning of his mission.

[2] Étienne Gilson, *Being and Some Philosophers*, Toronto, 1949, 122.

It is curious that Gilson should employ for Hume's effect on the slumbers of Kant the image of " a tremendous charge of existential explosive "; as a matter of fact the voluntaristic Kantian world is presented by Joyce in the very paragraph after " hume sweet hume " under the image of Viconian thunder:

> For hear Allhighest sprack for krischnians as for propagana fidies and his nuptial eagles sharpened their beaks for prey: and every morphyl man of us, pome by pome, falls back into this terrine: as it was let it be, says he!

[The Humeian propositions in effect signal the return of the ntelligible world to primeval chaos: " as it was." The first fall, which involved an apple (*pomme*), is repeated in this new voluntary darkening of the intellect; as one of the harbingers of the new age, Newton too watched an apple falling, and shifted the law of falling bodies (Leopold Bloom's bête noir) from theology to mechanics. In Joyce's multivalent phrase, as surely as mortal dust returns to dust (" this terrine ") and as men and apples obey the gravitational law, so surely all men, in the warped gravitational field of the postlapsarian moral universe, repeat the original fall: especially in moments of irrational terror.]

> And it is as though where Agni araflammed and Mithra monished and Shiva slew as mayamutras the obluvial waters of our noarchic memory withdrew, windingly goharksome, to some hastyswasty timberman torchpriest, flamenfan, the ward of the wind that lightened the fire that lay in the wood that Jove bolt, at his rude word.

[We are returned to the first Viconian age of veneration of Jove and altar-fires; the past has been obliterated by a second flood. Like the sea in *Ulysses* that receives the fallen Dedalus, the flood is an obliteration of the intelligible species of things.]

> Posidonius O'Fluctuary! Lave that bloody stone as it is! What are you doing your dirty minx and his big treeblock way up your path? Slip around, you, by the rare of the ministers'! And, you, take that barrel back where you got it, Mac Shane's, and go the way your old one went, Hatchettsbury Road! And gish! how they gushed away, the pennyfares, a whole school for scamper, with their sashes flying sish behind them, all the little pirlypettes! F80.

[The categorical imperative of Kantian voluntarism replaces

the rational image of the structure of the moral act. The
context of social custom is replaced by the bawling fiats of
irascible authority, internal as well as external. The " whole
school for scamper " sets off on its competitive scramble; it
was one of G. K. Chesterton's profoundest observations, that
the dominant social images had shifted since the middle ages
from the dance to the race. Cf. Joyce's " here where race
began; " as the human race took its biological origin after the
first fall, so the race for wealth and honours begins, as a respectable modus vivendi, after the second. The ancient
conception of Fortune's Wheel was abolished as embarrassing
from the post-Kantian world. Joyce restores it, at a very deep
level of generalization, in the temporal cycle that dominates
one dimension of *Finnegans Wake*.]

As the museum of prose styles in " The Oxen of the Sun "
epitomized the sterilization of the act of coition between the
mind and things, so the collage of fragments in *Finnegans Wake*
epitomizes the post-Kantian world in which all connections are
prescribed, rather than perceived, by the mind. Some validity
continues to adhere to the cardinal precept of the classical
rhetoricians, that the choice and arrangement of words
indicates invariably who is speaking to whom and under what
circumstances; but language is cut totally loose from things,
and a pale of words imprisons the mind. Words, as the
rationalist of this tradition conceives them, have " denotations "
(which are at bottom arbitrary though sometimes explicable,
and which, like the value of pi or the cube root of 2, can be
looked up in a table) and " connotations " accessible only to the
dubieties of irrational sensibility, independently visible like
the solar corona only when " denotation " goes into eclipse
(hence the spectroscopes of semasiology are rushed into
action whenever an event like *The Waste Land* or *Finnegans
Wake* occurs), and in no case to be relied on for anything but a
flickering, green, and will-o'-the-wispish light. Hence poems
are *statements* made by joining denotations together with *plus*
and *equals* signs, the inevitable connotations being adjusted
into some sort of innocuous conformity with the equations so
produced. That feelings, for inscrutable reasons, coexist with
thoughts and require to be hustled into line with them is thus
the capital difficulty of writing—or reading—a poem.

Joyce broke through this pale by looking at what was before
him: people talking. He placed the reality of words where

Dublin placed it: rooted in particular contexts of action, passion, and speaker-audience manoeuvre. Recovering in this way the first principle of classical rhetoric, he aligned himself with the eighteenth century rhetorician Giambattista Vico, for whom such perceptions held the key to all civilization.

Chapter 18

VICO AND HISTORY

... but it is historically the most glorious mission, secret or profund, through all the annals of our—as you so often term her—efferfreshpainted livy, in beautific repose, upon the silence of the dead, from pharoph the nextfirst down to ramescheckles the last bust thing. The Vico road goes round and round to meet where terms began. Still onappealed to by the cycles and unappalled by the recoursers we feel all serene, never you fret, as regards our dutyful cask. ... We only wish everyone was as sure of anything in this watery world as we are of everything in the newlywet fellow that's bound to follow.

Finnegans Wake (F452)

" THERE are plenty of other versions of the resurrection story," Joyce told Frank Budgen, " but this was the most suitable to my purpose." " This " was " Finnegan's Wake ", the most suitable because a popular song, the work of an unknown Irishman. Sufficiently exfoliated, it would touch and include everything in the mind of Dublin. At the turn of the century Joyce had captured the material he would never afterwards desert by carefully polishing to ironic elegance the parlour songs of fin-de-siècle Ireland. A third of a lifetime later he was applying the essential method of *Chamber Music*, with every technical resource at his command, to a single ballad.

> Tim Finnegan lived in Walker Street,
> An Irish gintleman, mighty odd.
> He'd a bit of a brogue, so neat and sweet,
> And to rise in the world Tim carried a hod.
>
> But Tim had a sort of tippling way;
> With a love of liquor Tim was born,
> And, to help him through his work each day,
> Took a drop of the creature every morn.

CHORUS: Whack. Huroo. Now dance to your partners,
> Welt the flure, your trotters shake;
> Isn't it all the truth I've told ye,
> Lots of fun at Finnegan's Wake?

On page 4 of the book is an elaborate rescription of this first stanza of the ballad; on page 6, of the second:

> ... wan warning Phill filt tippling full. His howd feeled heavy, his hoddit did shake. (There was a wall of course in erection) Dimb! He stottered from the latter. Damb! He was dud. Dumb! Mastabatoom. ...
> Shize? I should shee! Macool, Macool, orra whyi deed ye diie? of a trying thirstay mournin? Sobs they sighdid at Fillagain's chrissormiss wake, all the hoolivans of the nation, prostrated in their consternation, and their duodisimally profusive plethora of ululation. ... And the all gianed in with the shoutmost shoviality. Agog and magog and the round of them agrog. ... E'erawhere in this whorl would ye hear sich a din again? ... They laid him brawdawn alanglast bed. With a bockalips of finisky fore his feet. And a barrowload of guenesis hoer his head. Tee the tootal of the fluid hang the twoddle of the fuddled, O! F6.

This fallen man stretched out between Genesis and apocalypse becomes, a paragraph later, the whole Dublin landscape, serenaded by winds and waters:

> From Shopalist to Bailywick or from ashtun to baronoath or from Buythebanks to Roundthehead or from the foot of the bill to ireglint's eye he calmly extensolies. And all the way (a horn!) from fjord to fjell his baywind's oboboes shall wail him rockbound (hoahoahoah!) in swimswamswum and all the livvylong night, the delldale dalppling night, the night of bluerybells, her flittaflute in tricky trochees (O carina! O carina!) wake him.

A few lines later his flesh is the sacramental meal of Christianity:

> But, lo, as you would quaffoff his fraudstuff and sink teeth through that pyth of a flowerwhite bodey behold of him as behemoth for he is noewhemoe. Finiche! Only a fadograph of a yestern scene.

Via the fish-image of Christendom, he turns into the sacred salmon of Ireland:

> Almost rubicund Salmosalar, ancient fromout the ages of the Agapemonides, he is smolten in our midst, woebecanned and packt away.

The mourners were mistaken, however, in thinking him "packt away". In the midst of a quarrel that broke out at the wake ("'Twas woman to woman and man to man"):

Mickey Malony raised his head,
  When a gallon of whisky flew at him;
It missed him, and hopping on the bed,
  The liquor scattered over Tim.
" Och, he revives.   See how he raises."
  And Timothy, jumping from the bed,
Cried, while he lathered round like blazes,
  " Bad luck to your sowls.   D'ye think I'm dead? "

    . . . Isn't it all the truth I've told ye,
    Lots of fun at Finnegan's Wake?

So Joyce's Finnegan turns into the distant giant Finn Mac-
Cool, who faded in the Christian dawn of St. Patrick, and who
lies, like England's Arthur or France's Roland, lapped in
hero's sleep until the day of resurrection and return:

> Olivers lambs we do call them, skatterlings of a stone, and they shall
> be gathered unto him, their herd and paladin, as nubilettes to cumule,
> in that day hwen, same the lightning lancer of Azava Arthurhonoured
> (some Finn, some Finn avant!), he skall wake from earthsleep,
> haught crested elmer, in his valle of briers of Greenman's Rise O,
> (lost leaders live! the heroes return!) and o'er dun and dale the
> Wulverulverlord (protect us!) his mighty horn skall roll, orland, roll.
> For in those deyes his Deyus shall ask of Allprohome and call to
> himm: Allprohome! And he make answer: Add some. Nor
> wink nor wunk. *Animadiabolum, mene credidisti mortuum?* . . . F74.

Mene credidisti mortuum? Finnegan's " D'ye think I'm dead? "
resounds through the text: " Anam muck an dhoul! Did ye
drink me doornail? ", F24. " Your saouls to the dhaoul, do
ye. Finnk. Fime. Fudd? ", F499.

Finnegan's recumbency is the sleep of every superannuated
hero, his resurrection every resurgence, his wake every hurly-
burly of the practical world. A witness to the Easter Rebellion
is cross-examined:

> I want you, witness of this epic struggle, as yours so mine, to recon-
> struct for us, as briefly as you can, inexactly the same as a mind's eye
> view, how these funeral games, which have been poring over us
> through homer's kerryer pidgeons, massacreedoed as the holiname
> rally round took place. F515.

GRAMMARIAN VICO

As a very small boy, as he tells us in his *Autobiography*, Giambattista Vico, reaching for a book in his father's library, fell off

the ladder on which he was stretching tiptoe, crashed to the floor, and was given up for dead. His subsequent resurrection, no less startling than that of Finnegan when the whiskey was splashed, restored to the world the potential author of *La Scienza Nuova*, which was to furnish nearly two hundred years later both the method and many of the dominant motifs for Joyce's virtuosic rescription of the ballad of Finnegan's Wake.

That Vico should have commenced his career with a miniature re-enactment of Finnegan's fall, wake, and rise must have delighted Joyce when he came to perform the Viconian tale-into-archetype operation on that ballad. He had, by the time he started to write *Finnegans Wake*, been familiar with Vico's work for some fifteen years. He had first read it in the Trieste days, when he was labouring on the *Portrait* and commencing to intuit its sequels, a day-book of the " vast indifferent dome " dominated by earth's fecundity, and a night-book " new, fantastic, dim, uncertain as under sea, traversed by cloudy shapes and beings," P200/196. As every day for two years, commencing in the spring of 1907, he crossed the Piazza Giambattista Vico to reach his Trieste house, reminded each time of the Vico road in the Dublin suburb Dalkey, he could scarcely have repressed curiosity about this Neapolitan philosopher of whom the Anglo-Saxon world had never heard. Nor was the key book inaccessible; the first edition since 1860 had been published at Milan in 1903. By 1911 Joyce was working at the final draft of the *Portrait*, surrounded by a Viconian renaissance: in that year Benedetto Croce's treatise on Vico's philosophy was published, and the volumes of the authoritative Nicolini edition began appearing.

It took very little reading in Vico to convince Joyce of his relevance to the Joycean projects. For Vico, a professor of rhetoric and law, was the last of the great grammarians. He projected into undreamed-of dimensions the Joycean pre-possession with linguistic analogy that had been fed by Skeat's *Etymological Dictionary* and the Trivium at Clongowes. He read the book of universal history as the mediaeval grammarians had read the Book of Nature and the Book of God— the traditional Two Scriptures. From events, legends, traditions, etymologies, linguistic freaks, he educed patterns of eschatological significance.

Ulysses is very largely " about " its own audience; that is an important level of meaning in the failure of contact between

Bloom and Stephen, or between Stephen and his father. Failure of communication is so salient a contemporary pheno- menon that Joyce could scarcely have omitted it from his compendia. *Finnegans Wake*, in the lay sense Joyce's most unreadable book, is very largely " about " the art of reading, which is, in its fullest extension, the basic human art. Hence Joyce's interest in the mystique of names, and in the pre- lapsarian talents of Adam.

THE TWO SCRIPTURES

Plato was Vico's elected philosopher, and Plato's supposition in the *Cratylus*, that some power more than human gave things their first names, and that names are therefore mys- teriously related to essences, was obviously congenial to the early Christian fathers, who read in Genesis II.19 how the Lord God brought all the beasts and fowls before Adam, "and whatsoever the man called every living creature, that was the name thereof ". Adam, as Joyce has it, " first said goo to a goose ". He possessed a high degree of metaphysical insight, and could read the book of nature easily. But the Fall cut language off from its perceptible contact with the world of essences, and Solomon alone of all the sons of men, as Mr. Bloom at one point confusedly recalls apropos of the universal language of music, U281/271, has ever recovered the power to read the Book of Nature. Since the Fall and since Babel (though there was an odd tradition that the Irish enjoyed, without intervention of Babel, a language descended from the Adamite speech) artists have had to strain their attention on fleeting " epiphanies ", and the interrelation of the Two Scriptures, the Book of Nature and the Book of the Word, has had to be painfully reconstructed by exegetical technique.

Joyce tells us repeatedly that his ability to write *Finnegans Wake* depends on his having learned to " read " the things he puts into it :

> The prouts who will invent a writing there ultimately is the poeta꞊ still more learned, who discovered the raiding there originally. That's the point of eschatology our book of kills reaches for now in soandso many counterpoint words. What can't be coded can be decorded if an ear aye sieze what no eye ere grieved for. F482.

Furthermore, the traditional Two Scriptures are explicitly incorporated into the work. They are the letter and the barrow of rubbish, the Word and the World.[1] The wheelbarrow turns up constantly as a creation-symbol: " he dumptied the wholebarrow of rubbages on to soil here ", F17. This is not only the refuse of Earwicker's house, it is Dublin itself and it is the world created by God in time (left " to soil " and requiring to be refreshed by Grace). It is also the barrowload of rubbish (equated with the " barrow " of Finn's entombment—Christ allegorically entombed till the Last Day, significance locked up in material opacity since the Fall) from which the hen retrieved the letter (pp. 80, 110–11). As is made plain on p. 19, reading the letter is equivalent to reading, like an archaeologist slicing through a kitchen-midden or a stratified city, the contents of the barrow itself: " (Stoop) if you are abcedminded, to this claybrook, what curios of signs (please stoop), in this allaphbed! " The " middenhide hoard of objects " contains " Olives, beets, kimmells, dollies, alfrids, beatties, cormacks, and daltons " (=aleph, beth, gimel, daleth; alpha, beta, gamma, delta.) The letter and the barrow, that is, are the two scriptures, to which identical exegetical techniques are applicable. Both, furthermore, are analogous with *Finnegans Wake* itself. " The world, mind, is, was and will be writing its own wrunes for ever, man, on all matters that fall under the ban of our infrarational senses . . . ", F19. On page 13 we see the past transformed into a book for our contemplation " idler's wind turning pages on pages . . . the leaves of the living in the boke of the deeds ". On page 20 the very relics of the past turn into writings under the supervision of a shadowy Gutenberg (" Gutenmorg ": tomorrow: the future: the final causes toward which the past and present are polarized): " A bone, a pebble, a ramskin; chip them, chap them, cut them up allways; leave them to terracook in the muttheringpot: and Gutenmorg with his cromagnom charter,

---

[1] The Word turns up in another way, as the Anna Livia Plurabelle chapter itself. This is at one level the work of art created by Shem: " He lifts the lifewand," we read at the end of the previous chapter, " and the dumb speak." The dumb are the tree and the stone whom Shem metamorphoses into garrulous washerwomen. This phrase unites three levels of meaning for Shem: the phallic " lifewand " of artist as *creator;* the healing of the dumb as a miracle of *Christ;* the releasing of floods of intelligibility from insentient matter in his capacity as *grammarian and rhetorician.* At another level, the Anna Livia Plurabelle is an analogue of God's second Scripture, the Bible: the book of Life (Liffey, Lifé) as it is called at one point. In the parallel with the Mass that runs through the book, it corresponds to the Gospel as the fifth chapter (the hen's letter) does to the Epistle.

tintingfast and great primer must once for omniboss step rubrickredd out of the wordpress else is there no virtue more in alcohoran." This "wordpress" is a winepress; writing is allied to fermentation, and a scripture (The Koran) emerges. "So you need hardly spell me how every word will be bound over to carry three score and ten toptypsical readings throughout the book of Doublends Jined . . . till Daleth, mahomahouma, who oped it closeth thereof the. Dor.", F2o. [Daleth = Delta; the pile of detritus heaped at the mouth of time's river; the Scripture of Nature again. What is closed at the end is the golden door (d'or) of true dreams. The "three score and ten" readings introduce the pattern of human life itself as another analogy for the pattern of history and eschatology. "Doublends Jined" (the closed cycle) is Dublin's Giant, the Hill of Howth, the City itself, and its collective genius.] Finally, the "Scripture" is any collective writing ; in the second chapter of Book II it is a schoolroom scribbler with marginal comments by the two boys and footnotes by the girl. "Really, it is not I who am writing this crazy book," Joyce told a party of friends. "It is you, and you, and you, and that man over there, and that girl at the next table."

TRISMEGISTINE ALCHEMY

Creeping up such a web of relationships, the human mind chronically forgets which end is tied to earth, like the meteorologist in *Rasselas* who came to imagine that he was controlling the weather. During the reign of the trivium, whenever manipulation got on top of contemplation, allegory shaded into alchemy. In our own time, reading in Sir Thomas Browne about the ghost of a rose, Mr. Eliot put the image into a poem; while Yeats' brotherhood, afire with the same notion, solemnly attempted to make the spectre manifest itself above the burnt flower's ashes in the jar of an air-pump. Dublin, during Joyce's years there, was a-twitter with such stories: symbolic grammar was coming back, feet foremost.

Joyce, always interested in the popular parodies of great traditions, put this component of his Dublin's clumsy intellectualism to delighted use. In the geometry-lesson in *Finnegans Wake*, Dolph performs for the scandalized Kev a lewd grammatical exegesis of a diagram strikingly like the alchemical formula quoted by Jung: "Fac de masculo et foemina circulum rotundum, et de eo extrahe quadrangulum et ex quadrangulo triangulum; fac circulum rotundum (of the triangle) et habebis lapidum Philosophorum."[1]   Joyce's diagram is based on the construction for an equilateral triangle (Delta = ALP), and all the secrets of the universe are extracted from it, F293.   Allegory gets out of control in this way the moment we cease to *see* the relationships and start walking blindfold a logical plank.   The red triangle on the label of a bottle of Bass gets mock-anagogical exegesis in *Ulysses*, "writhing in the skies a mysterious writing till after a myriad metamorphoses of symbol it blazes, Alpha, a ruby and triangled sign upon the forehead of Taurus ", U407/396, and two pages later fixes Bloom's attention in a way that causes Mulligan to remark on his look of theosophical abstraction.   The charms and talismans of the " Secret of all secrets.   Seal of King David ", U239/229, depend on the Star of David or double triangle.

The people in Joyce's works who fuss with triangles depend umbilically from the Ellis-Yeats exegesis of Blake (1893), the editorial excesses of which are not altogether un-Blakean. Blake himself, who so to speak thought there ought to have been a grammatical tradition but had no direct way of making contact with it, got a lot of Blavatskyesque lore out of Swedenborg and Boehme (whose *Signature of All Things* indicates his affiliation with the esoteric wing of grammar).   Blake's geometrical ferocity links their cabbala-world with Locke, who effected what proved to be a lethal codification of rationalist *idées reçues* with the urbanity of Sanson of the Terror mounting the scaffold with a rose between his teeth.   The diagrams, the Lockean component, represent the tragic flaw in everything Yeats and his poetic brotherhood undertook.   In the tailpiece to *A Vision* we find Yeats day after day contemplating a symbol, " attempting to substitute particulars for an abstraction like that of algebra " until " it seems as if I should know all if I could but banish such memories and find everything in the symbol.

" But nothing comes—though this moment was to reward me for all my toil."

But if Cabbalism and Theosophy are the bargain basement of classical grammar, the great tradition itself stocked con-

[1] C. G. Jung, *The Integration of the Personality*, trans. Dell, London, 1940, 145.

siderable foolishness on its dimmer shelves.   It contained no
inner check; when all things are aspects of one reality, one
can never be sure what one may not need to know, or what
information is relevant.   Quintilian found it necessary to warn
teachers not to attempt omniscience.   That the written book,
the author's mind, language itself as a collective human product, are all in analogical relation to the visible world and to
the unifying Logos, has been one of the most fecundating
conceptions in the history of the west; but its fecundity verged
on the cancerous.   If it underwrote the profuse analogical
patterns of the imagery of Shakespeare, or the elaborate witty
analogies discerned and manipulated by Donne (whose sermons reveal him as an orthodox patristic divine), it contained
nothing to balk the most extravagant allegorical commentaries
on Homer and Virgil, or the most tedious conceits of *Euphues*
and *Arcadia*.   Its denizens could allegorize that microcosm the
human body till they could no longer see it, and the Word of
God till they could no longer read it.   The Hexameron was a
favourite theme for exegesis because the seeds of all things were
gathered together in the Six Days' Work of God, but only
a distinguished mind like St. Augustine's can devote a
whole chapter (*Confessions*, xii) to a single verse without the
reader's reflecting that the line between the commentator's
meditations and the content of the text has been thinned to
invisibility.

VICO AND THE ANALOGY OF LANGUAGE

The weakness of all such exegetical enterprises is that they
offer to probe divine intentions, a limitless undertaking.   When
Philo of Alexandria turned the methods of the grammarians
onto history itself, he regarded the events of history as a
gigantic and complex statement for exegesis: but a divine
statement.   Vico's great insight was that the materials of
history, if not its directions, are of human origin.   The sphere
has two poles; myths, languages, customs, events, may meet
in the Logos; but they also meet in the human mind.   And the
human mind is accessible to investigation, the Logos to
speculation only.

   " It follows ", Vico announces near the beginning of Book I,
" that the first science to be learned should be mythology or
the interpretation of fables, which were the first histories of the

gentile nations."[1] And again, near the beginning of his Introduction:

> In the present work, with a new critical art that has hitherto been lacking . . . philosophy undertakes to examine philology (that is, the doctrine of everything that depends on the human will; for example, all histories of the languages, customs and deeds of peoples in war and peace). . . . (p. 6).

In describing Philology as " the doctrine of everything that depends on the human will," Vico registers his understanding of language as a social product whose morphologies simultaneously link and harmonize the mind itself, the external world as perceived by the mind, the human community of minds and wills, and the artifacts and deeds of all peoples. From this he proceeds to his fullest statement of principle:

> But in the night of thick darkness enveloping the earliest antiquity, so remote from ourselves, there shines the eternal and never-failing light of a truth beyond all question: that the world of civil society has certainly been made by men, and that its principles are therefore to be found within the modifications of our own human mind. Whoever reflects on this cannot but marvel that the philosophers should have bent all their energies to the study of the world of nature, which, since God made it, He alone knows; and that they should have neglected the study of the world of nations or civil world, which, since men had made it, men could hope to know. This aberration was a consequence of that infirmity of the human mind . . . by which, immersed and buried in the body, it naturally inclines to take notice of bodily things, and finds the effort to attend to itself too laborious; just as the bodily eye sees all objects outside itself but needs a mirror to see itself. (p. 85.)

Vico's title is an explicit allusion to the *Novum Organon* of Francis Bacon; but Bacon, working as he was in the traditions of Franciscan science, was concerned with application to the Book of Nature of principles which Vico immediately saw were more impressively applicable to the book of human actions. He is quite explicit (p. 61) about this transferral of co-ordinates. The allegories derived by grammarians from the Book of Nature were, Vico readily saw, not philosophies but psychologies. Like their blandly unsophisticated cousin, the naturemystique of Wordsworth, they ministered to psychic order and a high degree of social and moral wisdom; but in default of a

[1] Giambattista Vico, *The New Science*, trans. T. G. Bergin and M. H. Fisch, Ithaca, 1948, 31. All references to this edition.

basis in Adam's or Solomon's immediate perception of essences, it was an order rather in the mind than in things that they both perceived and furthered:

> The human mind is naturally inclined by the senses to see itself externally in the body, and only with great difficulty does it come to attend to itself by means of reflection.
>
> This axiom gives us the universal principles of etymology in all languages: words are carried over from bodies and from the properties of bodies to express the things of the mind and spirit. (p. 70.)

Rational nature being equal in all men (p. 16),

> There must in the nature of human things be a mental language common to all nations, which uniformly grasps the substance of things feasible in human social life, and expresses it with as many diverse modifications as these same things may have diverse aspects. A proof of this is afforded by proverbs or maxims of vulgar wisdom, in which substantially the same meanings find as many diverse expressions as there are nations ancient and modern. (p. 60.)

There is the key to Joyce ransacking libraries for proverbs, folk-tales, children's singing games, etc. It is the key to much more:

> This common mental language is proper to our Science, by whose light linguistic scholars will be enabled to construct a mental vocabulary common to all the various articulate languages living and dead. (p. 60.)

Since Vico's time, the " common mental language " has manifested itself impressively in the work of Frazer and the comparative mythologists, and Jung has made claims for the collective unconscious as a store not only of mental forms but of racial memories that would have staggered the methodical Neapolitan. Vico is quite un-mystical in his account of how a poetically animated universe comes to be framed:

> When [the vulgar] wonder at the prodigious effects of the magnet on iron, even in this age of minds enlightened and made erudite by philosophy, they come out with this: that the magnet has an occult sympathy for the iron; and they make of all nature a vast animate body which feels passions and effects. . . . (p. 106.)

Such conceptions, he never tires of reminding us, deserve scrupulous and whole-hearted exegetical attention, expressing as they do the most complex human, if not physical, truths.

Far from being discouraged by the fabulous quality of primitive Greek and Latin historical records, Vico simply turns them inside out. If they do not give us " facts ", they give us the essential dynamics of a whole situation, often compressing a long development into the work of one hero:

> The snakes joined in the head of Medusa, whose temples bear wings, are the high family domains the fathers had in the state of the families, which later went to make up the civil eminent domain. This head was nailed to the shield of Perseus, which is the same as that borne by Minerva, who, among the arms (that is, in the armed assemblies) of the first nations ... dictates the frightful punishments that turn the spectators to stone. We noted above that one of those snakes was Draco, who is said to have written his laws in blood. ... And among the Chinese, who still write in hieroglyphics, the dragon, as we have said above, is the sign of civil authority. (p. 203.)

Draco, that is, by etymological exegesis, becomes something more than a legendary man of blood mentioned by an old author in passing.

Thus Vico employs the allegorical and etymological principles of interpretation to a carefully defined area of research in which there can be no doubt of their validity. It is natural that he should regard language as a midden-heap of history:

> The vulgar tongues should be the most weighty witnesses concerning those ancient customs of the peoples that were observed at the time when the languages were being formed.
>
> A language of an ancient nation, which has maintained itself as the dominant tongue throughout its development, should be a great witness to the customs of the early days of the world. (p. 58.)

Thus the verb *legere* contains in the etymology supplied by Vico the entire course of society from forests through huts, villages, and cities to academies:

> Thus we observe in the Latin language that almost the whole corpus of its words had sylvan or rustic origins. For example, *lex*. First it must have meant " collection of acorns." Thence we believe is derived *ilex*, as it were *illex*, " the oak " (as certainly *aquilex* is the " collector of waters "); for the oak produces the acorns by which the swine are drawn together. *Lex* was next " a collection of vegetables," from which the latter were called *legumina*. Later on, at a time when vulgar letters had not yet been invented for writing down the laws, *lex* by a necessity of civil nature must have meant " a collection of citizens " or the public parliament; so that the presence of the people was the law that solemnized the wills that were made

calatis comitiis, in the presence of the assembled *comitia*. Finally collecting letters and making as it were a sheaf of them in each word, was called *legere*, " reading." (p. 70.)

THE THREE AGES

We are making no attempt either to give a summary of Vico's book or to list passages from which Joyce borrowed directly. (He seems in fact to have borrowed very little.) What we are trying to do is give the reader a conspectus of Vico's method, exhibiting its affinities with Joyce's patristic studies and etymological interests. The cardinal principle, that since history is a human creation its causes are to be sought in the human mind, gives us the rationale of *Finnegans Wake*, in which the past, present and future of the human race are made to emanate from the brain of a sleeping Dubliner.

It should now be possible to see that the three ages which have impressed most writers on Vico are in many respects simultaneous. They are the successive temporal manifestations of a single human nature. The *semina motuum* of the Age of the Gods are present in twentieth-century man; and of the Age of Heroes; and of the Age of Men. Vico's very conception of an eternal ideal history discoverable by psychological analysis of existing men and etymological analysis of existing languages illustrates this principle. This is not an aspect of his theory that Vico is much concerned to establish; rather, he takes it for granted. It is the temporal succession, not the simultaneous orientation of the three ages that takes up most of his space, for the excellent reason that its ability to clear up the order and sequence of events in Greek and Roman legendary history afforded the best possible proof of the validity of the New Science. Yet his constant sense of the continual co-presence of all the phenomena of which he treats peeps through many of his formulations:

> ... Our new Science must therefore be a demonstration, so to speak, of the historical fact of providence, for it must be a history of the forms of order which, without human discernment or intent, and often against the designs of men, providence has given to this great city of the human race. For though this world has been created in time and particular, the orders established therein by providence are universal and eternal. (p. 91.)

" The orders established therein by providence " include, of course, the rational nature itself of man.

Thus when Vico describes the natures and customs proper to each of the three ages:

> The first customs were all tinged with religion and piety, like those of Deucalion and Pyrrha, fresh from the flood.
> The second were choleric and punctilious, like those related of Achilles.
> The third are dutiful, taught by one's own sense of civil duty. (p. 303.)

—no one is going to pretend that these are to be confined in chronological cubbyholes. They are, like the passions and humours of mediaeval character-writing (with the assumptions of which Vico displays a real affinity) potentialities held in some sort of balance in each individual; and if, say, modern England is permeated by a sense of civil duty, the pious and the choleric are not thereby excluded. What happens during the course of the " ideal eternal history traversed in time by every nation in its rise, development, maturity, and fall " (p. 71) is that these customs (rooted, as Vico's phraseology shows, in psychological orientations) achieve successive predominance in the body politic. Similarly, if of the three kinds of languages, the third, articulate speech, is " used by all nations to-day ", the first, " a divine mental language by mute religious acts or divine ceremonies ", is retained today by religions, and the second, " heroic blazonings with which arms are made to speak ", survives in military discipline. As Vico himself remarks, the ceremonial language " belongs to religions by the eternal property that it concerns them more to be reverenced than to be reasoned "; it survives, that is, not as a fossil but as the living manifestation of an intrinsic order.

VICO AND JOYCE

In turning to Vico for the alignments of his final work Joyce displayed no shifting of his former interests. A Viconian drama was the logical conclusion of his *oeuvre*. The psychological clue provided by Vico both to histories and to cultural patterns simply generalized the mythical method Joyce had already used in *Ulysses*. He had been concerned there with the Homeric situation as a form not merely recurrent but eternal: a tension between man's unshakeable rational nature and his ineluctable fallen condition. Vico's three ages, far from being schemae imposed upon material, grow out of axiomatic observations of human nature and behaviour, and are used by him not to schematize but to guide perception of a vast array of particularized persons, events, and postures of fact. He illustrates them as readily by orthodox allegorical exegesis of an introductory engraving as by considering the nature of the true Homer, the meaning of the story of Cadmus, or the etymology of the word *orbis* (p. 174). Such rapid alterations of scale, so disconcerting to present-day historical method, make perfect sense in terms of the traditions of grammar toward which Joyce was oriented from the time when he wrote schoolroom essays adducing the moral configurations of ancient myth and history in inculcation of some Dublin virtue.[1] For Vico as for Joyce, language, myth, and human actions and passions were aspects of a complex analogical whole. For Vico as for Joyce, human events obeyed the contours of human situations; the static artifact educes intelligible form from an almost literally infinite number of particular cases; Stephen and Bloom act according as they are, and they are as are all confrontations of action and passion, pride and virtue, rebellion and orthodoxy, or tradition and the individual talent: these are not identical but analogous relationships. In *Exiles*, by a dramatic exfoliation of the pressures of *Chamber Music*, Joyce had tried to epiphanize the situation of four Dubliners as the eternal form at once of rebellious man, un-communal man, and fallen man. In *Finnegans Wake*, he broke the claustrophobic walls of the earlier drama, to make a convincing superimposition of hilarity and pathos, the life of the family and the life of nations, Dublin politics and warring angelic powers, all educed from the human and therefore indefinitely capacious brain of a middle-aged father drowsing above his sawdust-strewn pub. That from the convolutions of the human brain all human societies and all human works and deeds take their origin is Vico's claim; that their seeds are present in any human brain is his corollary; that all time obeys the paradigms present in any instant, that all languages are akin and intrinsically related to all other things human, that gossip and eloquence, paternal

[1] A comical list of 52 essay topics, one for each week, begins on page 306 of *Finnegans Wake*, with classical analogues listed in the margin. Aristotle exemplifies " A Place for Everything and Everything in its Place ", Prometheus appears as an archetypal " Santa Claus ", Noah suggests " A Visit to Guinness' Brewery ", and Ajax, " The Dublin Municipal Police Sports at Ballsbridge ". The week he was assigned " Your Favourite Hero ", Joyce, it will be remembered, wrote on Ulysses.

gestures and heroic gestes, the schooling of children and the lawgiving of nations, obey common intelligible contours, are not assumptions alien to his method. Since Eden, in the night of the darkened intellect, human affairs have gone a continual round, to each man, fixed in his time and place, a treadmill, perhaps, or a prison, but to the philosopher of the *New Science* in its totality an adumbration of " the great city of the nations founded and governed by God ". Plato's ideal commonwealth, he tells us, is here and now. It was brought into being by providence from the first beginnings of nations (p. 377); the resplendent civic virtues even of Athens and Rome " were of short duration and even of small extent as compared with the universe of peoples, which was constituted by such orders and secured by such laws that even in its decay it assumes those forms of states by which alone it may everywhere be preserved and perpetually endure " (p. 382).

La! Lamfadar's arm it has cocoincidences. You mean to see we have been hadding a sound night's sleep? You may so. It is just, it is just about to, it is just about to rolywholyover. Svapnasvap. Of all the stranger things that ever not even in the hundrund and badst pageans of unthowsent and wonst nice or in eddas and oddes bokes of tomb, dyke and hollow to be have happened! The untireties of livesliving being the one substance of a streamsbecoming. Totalled in toldteld and teldtold in tittletell tattle. Why? Because, graced be Gad and all giddy gadgets, in whose words were the beginnings, there are two signs to turn to, the yest and the ist, the wright side and the wronged side, feeling aslip and wauking up, so an, so farth. Why? On the sourdsite we have the Moskiosk Djinpalast with its twin adjacencies, the bathouse and the bazaar, allahallah-allah, and on the sponthesite it is the alcovan and the rosegarden, boony noughty, all puraputhry. Why? One's apurr apuss a story about brid and breakfedes and parricombating and coushcouch but others is of tholes and oubworn buyings, dolings and chafferings in heat, contest and enmity. Why? Every talk has his stay, vidnis Shavarsanjivana, and all-a-dreams perhapsing under lucksloop at last are through. Why? It is a sot of a swigswag, systomy dystomy, which everabody you ever anywhere at all doze. Why? Such me. F597.

Chapter 19

THREE DREAMS

I: THE SLEEPER

> A cry off.
> Where are we at all? and whenabouts in the name of space?
> I don't understand. I fail to say. I dearsee you too.
>
> *Finnegans Wake* (F558)

THE four-part dream-book is in seventeen sections, the rhythms and techniques of which differ so markedly that the accomplished reader can place a quotation within a few pages by simply listening to it.

[I–1] It opens in mid-sentence (" riverrun . . . ") with a swirl down into tossing visions. The movement of the opening section is very rapid, the transitions sharp and frequent, the pace of the language brisk:

> The movibles are scrawling in motions, marching, all of them ago, in pitpat and zingzang for every busy eerie whig's a bit of a torytale to tell. F20.

The situations are all clearly recognizable; so is their relevance to recent daytime events: a glimpse of a bricklayer at work, F4, city traffic, F5, a funeral, F6, a walk in the park, F7, a visit to the museum, F8, a hen pecking in the rubbish-heap, F10, a letter from relatives in Boston with four x's scrawled at the end, F11, an encounter with an archaeologist or perhaps an archaeological article in the daily paper:

> (Stoop) if you are abcedminded, to this claybrook, what curios of signs (please stoop), in this allaphbed! Can you read (since We and Thou had it out already) its world? It is the same told of all. Many. Miscegenations on miscegenations. F18.

These items convey a social tone (lower-middle-class suburban village) with great accuracy; they also serve to mark, in the first moments of unconsciousness, disturbances against which the dreaming mind is struggling to stay asleep. Memories of the drunken evening just ended attach themselves to a funeral mentioned in the letter, F6. The recurrent " tip " of a bough knocking a pane is masked as the museum-keeper's demand for gratuities, F8. Bedbugs ("Fleppety! Flippety! Flea-pow! Hop!") become 400,000 Dubliners thronging the torso of the landscape's sleeping giant "hopping round his middle like kippers on a griddle, O, as he lays dormont from the macroborg of Holdhard to the microbirg of Pied de Poudre", F12—from Howth Head to the Powder Magazine in Phoenix Park. An erotic impulse transforms itself into the upthrust of Bygmester[1] Finnegan's tower: "his roundhead staple of other days to rise in undress maisonry upstanded (joygrantit!), a waalworth of a skyerscape of most eyeful hoyth entowerly, erigenating from next to nothing and celescalating the himals and all, hierarchitectitiptitoploftical, with a burning bush abob off its baubletop. . .", F4.

As sleep gradually confirms its grip on the dreamer, the materials of this vivid whirl become in successive episodes less and less clearcut, sinking deeper and deeper into the swamp of the night-mind, joining the mud-encrusted memories of earlier months and years, and allying themselves with obscurer psychic forces.

[I–2] With the second episode the pace suddenly slackens and the sentences grow interminable. Gradually the dreamer hears turned against himself the derision that had greeted the fall of English power in Ireland ("O here here how hoth sprowled met the duskt the father of fornicationists", F4), a derision culminating in the *Ballad of Persse O'Reilly*:[2]

> He was onetime our King of the Castle
> Now he's kicked about like a rotten old parsnip. . . .
>
> He was fafafather of all schemes for to bother us. . . .
>
> We had chaw chaw chops, chairs, chewing gum, the chicken-pox
>   and china chambers
> Universally provided by this soffsoaping salesman.
> Small wonder He'll Cheat E'erawan our local lads nicknamed him
> When Chimpden first took the floor
>   (CHORUS)   With his bucketshop store
>   Down Bargainweg, Lower.
>
> And not all the king's men nor his horses
> Will resurrect his corpus. . . .   F47.

[I–3] " Therewith was released in that kingsrick of Humidia

---

[1] Big Mister + *Bygmester Solness*, the Norwegian title of Ibsen's *Master Builder*.
[2] *Perce-oreille* is the French for "earwig". Pearse and O'Rahilly (the former a poet) died in the Easter Rebellion they did much to instigate. Persse was Lady Gregory's maiden name.

a poisoning volume of cloud barrage indeed ", F48. The dreamer, alternately elated and deflated, imagines himself quoted by a biographer (" Life, he himself said once, . . . is a wake, livit or krikit, and on the bunk of our breadwinning lies the cropse of our seed-father ", F55), accused by three soldiers of indecent exposure before two girls in the park, F34, canvassed in copious interviews [1–4] (" Have you evew thought, wepowtew, that sheew gweatness was his twadgedy? ", F61), pursued by hounds, F97, and belaboured for two and a half hours with indecent epithets shouted through the keyhole by an American hog-caller, F70.

As the embarrassment of the affair in the park recedes, the vignettes of episode 1 begin to combine into the cloudy metaphors that permeate the book. [1–5] The letter, for instance, fuses with the middenheap of hen and archaeologist to become a mysterious document out of the past, a Book of Kells the exegesis of which receives some twenty pages of pedantic discussion. Behind the academic doubletalk we can hear De Valera's lofty repudiation of the treaty his pleni-potentiaries brought back from London in 1921 (" Closer inspection of the *bordereau*[1] would reveal a multiplicity of personalities inflicted on the documents or document[2] and some prevision of virtual crime or crimes . . . ", F107) and the December Dail debate that ended in Civil War.

The dream once fairly launched, one hallucinated re-staging of the material follows another. At the end of each a few calm moments whose rhythm is the pace of troubled breathing marks the descent to a still deeper level of sleep:

> Liverpoor? Sot a bit of it! His braynes coolt parritch, his pelt nassy, his heart's adrone, his bluidstreams acrawl, his puff but a piff, his extremeties extremely so: Fengless, Pawmbroke, Chilblaimend and Baldowl. Humph is in his doge. Words weigh no no more to him than raindrips to Rethfernhim. Which we all like. Rain. When we sleep. Drops. But wait until our sleeping. Drain. Sdops. F74.

Or later [1–8]:

> Night now! Tell me, tell me, tell me, elm! Night night! Telme-tale of stem or stone. Beside the rivering waters of, hitherand-thithering waters of. Night! F216.

[1] The French word has punning overtones of the row about the Ulster border. We hear elsewhere of " borderation ".

[2] During the Treaty Debate De Valera produced a " Document Number Two " whose contents added to the confusion by leaking into the press.

By the end of I–8 the dirty linen of the affair in the Park is washed clean by the famous gossiping women on the banks of the Liffey, and Earwicker's dream switches to a new phase. [II–1] The language grows suddenly denser, the psychological drama cloudier, and the confused affair of how Buckley shot the Russian General (an incident from the Crimean War, superimposed on the Irish Civil War to dramatize the deep-seated inner scission of HCE himself) moves toward the foreground. [II–2] He searches back to childhood memories of pantomimes, games, and school-books; and fusing them with the actions of his own children the previous afternoon, moves insensibly forward to the events of the evening before. [II–3] A long dense recollection of the evening's talk in his pub closes with the recollection of his stumble up to bed after drinking up what the customers left in their glasses; the room had swung round his fuddled head like a moving ship:

> . . . he came acrash a crupper sort of a sate on accomondation and the very boxt in all his composs, whereuponce, behome the fore for cove and trawlers, heave hone, leave lone, Larry's on the focse and Faugh MacHugh O'Bawlar at the wheel, one to do and one to dare, par by par, a peerless pair, ever here and over there, with his fol the dee oll the doo on the flure of his feats and the feels of the fumes in the wakes of his ears our wineman from Barleyhome he just slumped to throne. F382.

[II–4] This bedding recalls his wedding-night; he is Tristram bringing back Iseult on the bride-ship, deceiving her affianced King Mark while four censorious old men peek at the windows: The Evangelists, the Four Masters who wrote the annals of Ireland, and his bed-posts.

[III–1] A striking clock initiates the third part. The edge has been taken off his sleep, and as the half-roused dreamer slumps back into the night-world a more or less syntactic connection overtakes the scrambled motifs of the dream. The turgidities of the pub-talk, like the confusions of the Civil War, are over; [III–2] Shaun the Post, harbinger of the New Day, delivers an immense lubricious sermon, pedantic as a De Valera public address, and takes his farewell amid keenings:

> But, boy, you did your strong nine furlong mile in slick and slap-stick record time and a farfetched deed it was in troth, champion docile, with your high bouncing gait of going and your feat of passage will be contested with you and through you, for centuries to come. The phaynix rose a sun before Erebia sank his smother! Shoot up

on that, bright Bennu bird! *Va faotre!* Eftsoon so too will our own sphoenix spark spirt his spyre and sunward stride the rampante flambe. Ay, already the sombrer opacities of the gloom are sphanished! Brave footsore Huan! Work your progress! Hold to! Now! Win out, ye devil ye! The silent cock shall crow at last. The west shall shake the east awake. Walk while ye have the night for morn, lightbreakfastbringer, morroweth wheron every past shall full fost sleep. Amain. F473.

It is in the third part of the book that De Valera comes into his own; in this paragraph we have his youthful prowess at footracing, the " feat of passage " by which he slipped off to America on a fund-raising mission, a feat which did not fail to call forth acrimony and panegyric from factions evenly matched in bitterness, his Spanish ancestry (" sombrer opacities . . . sphanished "), and the smothering of the sunbird.

[III–3] Yawn, the new order, reappears as a corpse undergoing senatorial inquest; the great speech of the cityfounder breaks through their deliberations, in part a broadcast, in part a spirit-voice from a seance:

> . . . Seven ills so barely as centripunts havd I habt, seaventy seavens for circumference inkeptive are your hill prospect. . . . The chort of Nicholas Within was my guide and I raised a dome on the wherewithouts of Michan: by awful tors my wellworth building sprang sky spearing spires, cloud cupoled campaniles: further this. By fineounce and imposts I got and grew and by grossscruple gat I grown outreachesly. . . . I was merely out of my mint with all the percussors on my braincap till I struck for myself and muched morely by token. . . . F541.

It is a self-vindication much impeded by stammering and double-entendre; the city that is being defended against the new order grew amid as much corruption as foresight, and Shaunian politics derive from it with (he fears) no less legitimacy than did the dreamer's go-ahead son.

[III–4] This effort of assertion and vindication is his last; the dreamer drifts exhausted (" What was thaas? Fog was whaas? Too mult sleepth. Let sleepth ", F555) into halfconsciousness of his mean bedchamber and the sleeping family round him:

> Salmonpapered walls. . . . No curtains. Blind drawn. . . . Chair for one. Woman's garments on chair. Man's trousers with crossbelt braces, collar on bedknob. . . . Over mantelpiece picture of Michael, lance, slaying Satan, dragon with smoke. . . . F559.

A child cries, the mother rises to comfort him:

> You were dreamend, dear. The pawdrag? The fawthrig? Shoe! Hear are no phanthares in the room at all, avikkeen. . . . Sonly all in your imagination, dim. Poor little brittle magic nation, dim of mind! F565.

And in contrast to the stirring moments of the first descent into sleep, the dreamer lies lapped in dim awareness of the hush before the first light, to the rhythm of a magical refrain:

> While elvery stream winds seling on for to keep this barrel of bounty rolling and the nightmail afarfrom morning nears. F565.

> While the elves in the moonbeams, feeling why, will keep my lily-gem gently gleaming. F566.

> It's only the wind on the road outside for to wake all shivering shanks from snorring. F578.

> . . . flispering in the nightleaves flattery, dinsiduously, to Finnegan, to sin again and to make grim grandma grunt and grin again while the first grey streaks steal silvering by for to mock their quarrels in dollymount tumbling. F580.

[IV] At last the dawn breaks (" Scatter brand to the reneweller of the sky, thou who agnitest! Dah! Arcthuris comeing! Be! Verb umprincipant through the trancitive spaces! ") amid imagery of Easter rebellion (" Array! Surrection! ") and washing up (" Guld modning, have yous viewsed Piers' aube? . . . Lever hulme! "); and the new light moves " amid the semitary of Somnionia. Even unto Heliotropolis, the castellated, the enchanting."

The New Ireland has emerged with the new day:

> Good safe firelamp! hailed the heliots. Goldselforelump! Halled they. Awed. Where thereon the skyfold high, trampatrampatramp. Adie. Per ye comdoom doominoom noonstroom. Yeasome priestomes. Fullyhum toowhoom. F613.

The chant is " Per Jesum Christum filium tuum "; but " Yeasome priestomes ", yea-saying clerics, are the reality; filial to whom? " God save Ireland " is transformed into cries of safety and of selling for gold. The " skyfold " is a scaffold, resounding with an ominous tramp: " Adie! "

As for Ireland, so for the dreamer: the tensions of the previous active day have been nulled by sleep and its materials gathered into the ideal order of all previous days, a few more ounces of soil for the Liffey. The awakening is an ambiguous regeneration. " Yet is no body present here which was not there before. Only is order othered. Nought is nulled. *Fuitfiat!* ", F613. Former aspirations and preoccupations return like clothes from the laundry of night: " . . . all your horodities will incessantlament be coming back from the Annone Wishwashwhose . . . Themes have thimes and habit reburns. To flame in you ", F614. The active hopes of radical renovation are abandoned:

> What has gone? How it ends?
> Begin to forget it. It will remember itself from every sides, with all gestures, in each our word. Today's truth, tomorrow's trend.
> Forget, remember!
> Have we cherished expectations? Are we for liberty of perusiveness? Whyafter what forewhere? A plainplanned liffeyism assemblements Eblania's conglomerate horde. By dim delty Deva.
> Forget! F614.

So with one regretful lapse into the tranquillity of night (" But Still. Ah diar, ah diar! And stay. It was allso agreenable in our sinegear clutchless, touring the no placelike no timelike absolent ", F609) H.C. Earwicker awakes; and in the moments of waking the ideal union of mountain with river, of wind with tree, of husband with wife, is dissolved as a worn flesh-and-blood woman takes form by his side and the dream of Anna Livia slips away:

> Soft morning, city! Lsp! I am leafy speafing. Lpf! Folty and folty all the nights have falled on to long my hair. Not a sound, falling. Lispn! No wind no word. Only a leaf, just a leaf and then leaves. . . .
> But I'm loothing them that's here and all I lothe. Loonely in me loneness. For all their faults. I am passing out. O bitter ending! I'll slip away before they're up. . . . A way a lone a last a loved a long the   F619-28.

II: KING OEDIPUS

> – God save you king! Muster of the Hidden Life!
> – God serf you kingly, adipose rex! I had four in the morning and a couple of the lunch and three later on, but your saouls to the dhaoul, do ye. Finnk. Fime. Fudd?
>
> *Finnegans Wake* (F499).

Drama follows epic, and *Finnegans Wake* with characteristic prodigality makes dozens of gestures towards drama of every kind. Shem the Penman and Shaun the Post are lifted from Victorian plays;[1] there is a whole section of washerwoman's dialogue, a whole section of questions and responses, a recurring Mutt-Jute colloquy, and a continual reliance on set speeches recalling the classical tragedy via the operatic aria; the pantomime furnishes the explicit conventions for another section, televised drama for twenty pages of yet another, and the voice of the movie director resounds through pages on end (e.g. 558–560, 565, 501, etc.).

And as *Ulysses*, finally, exploited analogies with the Greek epic, so *Finnegans Wake* is rooted in Greek drama. There is a tissue of reminiscence from the *Oresteia* of Aeschylus and the *Alcestis* of Euripides, but the central situation is that of the Sophoclean *Oedipus*, already transferred to contemporary axes by Freud.

The *Oedipus* correspondence hasn't the episode-by-episode linearity of the Homeric ground-plan to *Ulysses*, and consequently isn't easy to summarize in a few pages. Without quoting masses of evidence, however, we can indicate the main resemblances with sufficient precision. Both works turn around the creation, fall, and redemption of the City: Thebes, and Dublin. As HCE is the eponymous city-founder, so is Oedipus fourth in line of descent from, and as King the surrogate of, Cadmus founder of Thebes. " Creator he has created for his creatured one a creation ", F29. The city, however, lies under a mysterious curse: " What then agent-like brought about that tragoady thundersday this municipal sin business? ", F5. And an agonizing enquiry proves Oedipus to be responsible: " he is ee and no counter he who will be ultimendly respunchable for the hubbub caused in Edenborough ", F29. Each ruler has a symbolic deformity: Oedipus his swollen foot, HCE his hunchback. Oedipus has unwittingly slaughtered his father: HCE has mysteriously replaced Finnegan. Oedipus answered the Sphinx's riddle about four legs, two legs, and three legs. Joyce uses this motif in various ways. The riddle-motif runs through the book from the moment of HCE's encounter with the Cad with a Pipe,

---

[1] Sir Charles Young's *Jim the Penman* and Dion Boucicault's *Arrah-na-Pogue*, respectively. For some curious notes on the latter, see J. S. Atherton, " Arrah-Na-Pogue and Finnegans Wake," *Notes and Queries*, CXCIV.20 (Oct. 1, 1949), 430–432.

F35; a whole section (I–6) consists of riddles and answers, and the *Mime* (II–1) turns on Shem's inability to guess a riddle; Shem however does, like Oedipus, know the answer to " the first riddle of the universe ", F170, and delights in pestering his brothers and sisters with it. 432, the date of St. Patrick's arrival in Ireland, receives continual salience, F486, and the numbers 4, 3, and 2 (four old men, three soldiers, two temptresses) are buried on virtually every page. Oedipus has inadvertently married his mother, and Anna chatters through Earwicker's dream as " our turf-brown mummy ", F194, and near the end addresses her man as " sonhusband ", F627. Oedipus thus became brother to his own daughters; Earwicker projects through his Shaun-self a lubricious spate of brotherly advice to his daughter Iseult. Oedipus when the truth is known blinds himself; HCE after an evening of embarrassment in the pub gets himself blind drunk and staggers up to bed, F381. Oedipus leaves matters in the hands of his wife's brother Creon, a diplomat who parades his virtue, makes much show of his desire to hush the matter up, and becomes the tyrant of the *Antigone*. Earwicker's mantle descends on his go-ahead son Shaun. Oedipus in the sequel is mysteriously translated into the other world; Earwicker/Shaun vanishes amid ambiguous glory, U471.

This exceedingly sketchy survey takes no account of the thematic richness in which Joyce invests the Sophoclean materials. As in the Homer-parallel in *Ulysses*, he is exploring a situation, not unwinding a plot. From this point of view, *Finnegans Wake* may be regarded as an immense allegorical commentary on the ideal tragic stasis manifested by Sophocles. One or two points about Sophoclean drama may be noted in this connection. The *Oedipus* is conceived, like *Finnegans Wake*, as a prolonged *agon* for one character. The other figures are introduced, with marvellous economy of means, as interlocutors; with each dialogue the action is advanced, and a new aspect of Oedipus' predicament is explicated. The Chorus of Theban Elders (variously, Joyce's four old men and his " bundle of a dozen of representative locomotive civics ", F221) have a complex function. They project the audience onto the stage; they assist in the interrogation[1]

---

[1] It is worth noting how much of *Finnegans Wake* is taken up with interrogations and investigations of a vaguely law-court kind. The whole of III–3 and most of I–3 and I–4 may be instanced. HCE appears to have committed some

of Oedipus; they spin a continuous web of commentary on the action.   The parts of *Finnegans Wake* that look like narration are based, at several removes, on these choric conventions:

> What then agentlike brought about that tragoady thundersday this municipal sin business?   Our cubehouse still rocks as earwitness to the thunder of his arafatas but we hear also through successive ages that shebby choruysh of unkalified muzzlenimiisslehims that would blackguardize the whitestone ever hurtleturtled out of heaven. Stay us wherefore in our search for tighteousness, O Sustainer.... F5.

The habitual second person plural should be noted: " We " as members of the chorus, and " We " as chorus and reader. It is a municipal " We ": the fraternal note of the citizens of Dublin.

III: THE PRIEST VICTIM

> *Muta:* Quodestnunc fumusiste volhvuns ex Domoyno?
> *Juva:* It is old Head of Kettle puffing off the top of the mornin.
> *Muta:* He odda be thorly well ashamed of himself for smoking before the high host.
> *Juva:* Dies is Dorminus master and commandant illy tonobrass.
>
> *Finnegans Wake* (F609)

Against *Oedipus*, the psychological drama of antiquity which more than any other provides Aristotle with instances of exemplary dramaturgy (chiefly in connection with peripeteia and anagnorisis, the dramatic mechanisms of epiphany) Joyce counterpoints the Mass, the metaphysical drama of Christendom.   The drama of the Fall and the drama of Redemption are superimposed.

Earwicker as protagonist and chorus becomes, or is simultaneously, Earwicker as priest/victim and congregation.   Like Oedipus, he expiates his sins in the interests of the whole people: Christ as Priest offers up Himself as victim for the sins of the world.   The sin of Adam, like that of Oedipus, was against the Father, and Christ as new Adam expiates to His Father the burden of sin inherited by Adam's children: the burden symbolized, in the mode of *Pilgrim's Progress*, by the hump on HCE's back.

offence against the by-laws of the park, probably unauthorized defecation among the bushes.   The " poisoning volume of cloud barrage indeed " released " in that kingsrick of Humidia ", F48, is both the clouding of the facts and of his reputation, and the pestilence fallen on Thebes.

The traditions gathered around the central Christian sacrifice during its over 1900 years' history gear admirably with the artistic assumptions of *Finnegans Wake*. The *Wake* is at one level an eschatological exegesis of a set of commonplace familial actions whose very familiarity confers on them a ritual quality; drinking in a pub, children's games, an arithmetic lesson, a woman aroused before dawn to comfort a child who has wet his bed. These actions as explicated by Joyce not only mime the psychic and biological life of the person and the race, they enact the anagogical drama of creation, fall, redemption, and resurrection. The mass, similarly, for the lower-class Dubliner, is a familiar, almost domestic action for daily or weekly observance, elaborate, central to his psychic and religious life, mysterious, commonplace. Liturgical histories describe its slow elaboration during the centuries, as dramatic accessories, connecting this or that mystery of the faith or this or that communal custom to the central eucharistic sacrifice, were added to the rubrics and the prayers. The analogical relations of its parts to every mode of experience are unbelievably complex; so much so that to most worshippers the meaning of the accessory actions, like much of the meaning of the central action, is completely opaque.

The Viconian analogies are obvious. God, the Saints, and today's communicants are brought together in its symbolism: the Three Ages in chronological sequence are telescoped into a single complex action. God as God, God as crucified tragic hero, God as Man, unite Vico's three ages in anagogical radiance. The worshipper as Divine image, the worshipper as heroic contender with the Devil within the Church Militant, the worshipper as sinner imploring grace, unite the three ages in temporal simultaneity: Gods, Heroes, Men.

Joyce's researches led him into the local rituals of obscure corners of Christendom. The peculiarities of the " Old Catholic " *Augustiner Kirche* are woven into the plight of the " shapewrucked " Gripes,[1] and as we shall see the Maronite

---

[1] According to a letter to Frank Budgen from Lucia Joyce (evidently at her father's instigation), Sept. 3, 1933. (Slocum Collection.) " They separated from Rome in '71 when the infallibility of the pope was proclaimed a dogma but they have since gone much more apart. . . . Most important of all they have abolished the Filioque clause in the creed concerning which there has been a schism between western and eastern christendom for over a thousand years. Rome saying that the Holy Ghost proceeds from the father and the son. Greece and Russia and the East Orthodox Churches that the procession is from the father

liturgy underlies the ceremonial connected with the departure of Shaun, F469–471. So we should not be surprised to find that the ancient Celtic (" Mooksian ") liturgy underlies much of the epiphanic and Viconian conception of the entire work.

What is curious about the symbolic structure of the ancient Scotic (Irish) Eucharist is its simultaneous enactment of a concentrated redemptive drama (the Passion of Christ) and a diffuse historical drama extending from the Creation to the Last Judgment.[1] A priest-victim, like Earwicker or Oedipus, enacts the atoning agony of Christ against the entire panorama of human history.

The elements to be consecrated were carried ceremoniously into the Church at the very beginning of the mass, and gradually unveiled as the service proceeded. So the objects in the bedroom are revealed to the reader only 69 pages before the end of the book. So the doctrine of the Incarnation existed in the mind of God from the beginning, but was brought to light only at the birth of Christ. So Finnegan lies during his Wake, " with a bockalips of finisky fore his feet. And a barrowload of guenesis hoer his head ", F6, stretched out between the apocalyptic *finis* and the wheelbarrowload of potentialities dumped into the world in Genesis. Yet it is at the *finis*, with the sprinkling of whiskey, that he rises; in his end, in each of the Eliotic senses, is his beginning.

Like Vico, the ancient Gael recognized three ages or laws or dispensations: the patriarchal age of Nature, the Mosaic age of the Letter, the Christian age of the Holy Ghost. According to tradition, the Gaelic-speaking peoples alone of the Gentile races possessed the Mosaic Law until the coming of the Faith (*iris*).[2] They brought it with them from Egypt, having been converted to the fear of the Lord by Moses MacAmram,

alone, ex patre without Filioque. . . . See the Mookse and the Gripes, that is west and east, paragraph beginning While that Mooksius and ending philioquus, F156. All the grotesque words in this are russian or greek for the three principal dogmas which separate Shem from Shaun. When he gets A and B onto his lap C slips off and when he has C and A he loses hold of B. . . ."

[1] The following material is paraphrased from the Rev. Duncan Macgregor, " An Ancient Gaelic Treatise on the Symbolism of the Eucharist, with Translation and Notes ", *Transactions of the Aberdeen Ecclesiological Society*, XI, Aberdeen, 1898, 291–340.

[2] That the Gaelic word for Faith is the name of the Greek rainbow-goddess enables Joyce to tie God's pledge to Noah, which throughout the *Wake* accompanies the Viconian motifs of thunder and deluge, with another divine pledge on another time-scale.

foster-child of the daughter of *Forannan Cinchris* (Pharoah).[1]

The vertical levels of Finnegans Wake corresponding to the three strands in the Celtic Liturgy are easy to list. The last Supper corresponds to the evening dispensing of food and drink in the Earwicker pub; the life, works, agony, death, burial and resurrection of Christ, to the *agon* of Earwicker; the historical panorama to the Viconian perspectives.

Horizontally, the Mass is divided into three main sections: The Introit or Proanaphora, which runs up to the reading of the Gospel; the Anaphora; and the Communion. The Proanaphora corresponds part by part with the first Book of *Finnegans Wake* (pp. 1–218). The correspondence of Anaphora and Communion with Books II and III is roughly demonstrable, but for various reasons not particularly important: Joyce telescopes the liturgical unfolding of events in the interest of freely-disposed exegesis.

Book I. (Proanaphora) has eight chapters:

1. INTROIT. The Communion theme—the eating of the father/ whale—is a dominant image of this section: upper half of pp. 7 and 12, bottom of p. 13, last eight lines of p. 23, etc. The Wake motif is firmly established, and the bride of the deceased (Mother Church) distributes portions of his body to the mourners: " he is smolten in our mist, woebecanned and packt away." F7.

2. CONFITEOR AND GLORIA. The span of history is covered here in the mode of oral tradition, from the encounter with the Cad in the Park (at one level a confused recollection of Adam's embarrassed meeting with God in the cool of the day, and subsequent shame and expulsion) to the apotheosis of the hero in a scurrilous ballad. The former is a stammering Confiteor, F36, the latter an inverted Gloria, F44, decrying the Old Adam as the Christ celebrated by the Gloria in the Mass is the new Adam. Note the explicit signal to the choir: " . . . ' Ductor ' Hitchcock hoisted his fezzy fuzz at bludgeon's height signum to his companions of the chalice for the Loud Fellow, boys' and *silentium in curia!* (our maypole once more where he rose of old) and the

---

[1] Compare the intertwining of Irish and Jewish material in the " Aeolus " and " Cyclops " episodes of *Ulysses*, and the tradition about the kinship of Hebrew and Gaelic, " both having been taught on the plain of Shinar 242 years after the deluge in the seminary instituted by Fenius Farsaigh, descendant of Noah, progenitor of Israel, and ascendant of Heber and Heremon, progenitors of Ireland ", U672. There was a tradition too that Gaelic was descended from the only tongue to escape the miscegenation of Babel, and was consequently traceable by uninterrupted etymology back to Adam's speech which corresponded with the essences of things.

canto was chantied there chorussed and christened where by the old tollgate, Saint Annona's Street and Church."

3. The Trial and Incarceration, and

4. The Death and Resurrection of the hero are discernible through clouds of gossip. It sounds like the same old story still more embroiled, but the accent has been shifted from the lapsarian to the expiatory, from a vague guilty worry to judicial process, from Adam to Christ. We enter the New Testament with:

5. EPISTLE. The letter ("a polyhedron of scripture," 107), ambiguously ascribed to the wife (mother church, the Church instructing the faithful on points of belief as distinguished from the Gospel, God imparting the essential story to mankind), and emanating from Boston across the sea (St. Paul in Rome writing to churches on the far side of the Mediterranean). The decipherable fragments of the text are cited on p. 111; the rest of the chapter is Higher Criticism (exegetical fuss has always surrounded the epistles rather than the gospels).

6. CATECHISM AND SERMON. (The Riddles, the Mookse and the Gripes, the Professor's lecture). Formerly the first part of the Mass (up to the Gospel and Creed) was oriented toward the Catechumens (converts awaiting baptism). Only the baptised were allowed to participate in the rest of the service. The Mass of the Catechumens is a prayer service up to the epistle, then an instruction service up to the Creed. This usage is recalled by Joyce's introduction of catechetical material, and a misplaced sermon, at this point in the book.

7. The character and vindication of Shem the Penman, amanuensis of the gospel, cloudily recalls the " munda cor meum " (" purify me that I may be allowed worthily to announce Thy holy Gospel "). The evocation of the inspiring Mother, " running with her tidings, old the news of the great big world ", F 194, leads us to

8. THE GOSPEL (The Anna Livia Plurabelle chapter). The chronicle of her redeeming waters (baptism, regeneration of the Waste Land) and her gifts to her children (pp. 210–212) closes the Mass of the Catechumens. It isn't a wholly reassuring gospel. She is distributing unlucky gifts to the people who made fun of HCE.

The parts of the first section of the Mass—Introit, Confiteor, Gloria, Epistle, Sermon, Gospel—appear in the *Wake* in order, with remarkable exactness of correspondence. And corresponding to these preparatory services, the dream, its meanings lying relatively near the surface, plays over past materials in which some degree of sequence is readily traced. The second part now plunges into a dense multi-layered continuous present in which correspondences are far less easily unravelled. The sequence of episodes—children's games, children's evening studies, feasting in the pub, and the vision of the bride-ship and gulls (HCE drunkenly abed with his wife, scrutinized by the four bed-posts)— reproduces the events of the immediate evening; but as the far greater complexity of language indicates, psychological and eschato- logical relevance is to be sought now at numerous simultaneous levels. It is impossible even to summarize the eucharistic relationships in a reasonable space; suffice it to point out the cor- respondence of the long, complex tavern episode (pp. 309–382) with the intricate sequence of events at the altar running from the Offertory through the Canon to the distribution of Communion and the priest's consumption of the purification.[1]

With the third part of the *Wake* (the four watches of Shaun the Post) the correspondences become those of the Mass for Good Friday, the one day in the year when no Host is con- secrated. This is connected on one level with the Shaun motif of sterility, on another level with the mourning gap between crucifixion (HCE slumping to the floor) and Resurrection (Part IV), on yet another level with the return to linear his- torical succession after the intersection of eternity with time during the life of Christ (the dense simultaneous present of Part II) and the fading of meaning from subsequent com- memorative events.

At one time-level of course there has been a substitution; the Christ of the agony has been superseded by his minister, the jovial Irish cleric who patters through his " ghee up, ye dog, for your daggily broth, etc., Happy Maria and Glorious Patrick, etc., etc. In fact, always, have I believe. Greedo! ", F411. At another level Shaun as officiating priest enacts the agony himself.

The events of the Good Friday liturgy appear in the text somewhat transposed. Shaun's lenten sermon to the twenty- nine convent girls is a *Via Crucis* of 14 stations ending with a litany based on the Maronite ritual for Good Friday. On May 24, 1924, Joyce wrote to Harriet Weaver that the episode was

---

[1] This is one of the most evident landmarks in the text. After communion the priest rinses the chalice with wine which he then drinks that no drop of the consecrated fluid may be lost. HCE (pp. 380–381) after the departure of the customers drinks up everything that remains in their glasses and bottles and then slumps in a heap to the floor.

... a description of a postman travelling backwards in the night through the events already narrated. It is written in the form of a via crucis of 14 stations, but in reality it is only a barrel rolling down the river Liffey.

(The 14 stations correspond to this and the 13 preceding episodes.) As for the finale of the episode, here is part of Joyce's letter of August 8, 1928.

The Maronite (Roman Catholic) liturgy the language of which is Syrian is at the back of it. On Good Friday the body of Jesus is unscrewed from the cross, placed in a sheet and carried to the sepulchre while the girls dressed in white throw flowers at it and a great deal of incense is used. The Maronite ritual is used in Mount Lebanon. Shaun departs like Osiris the body of the young god being pelted and incensed. He is seen already a Yesterday (Gestern, Guesturning back his glance amid the wails of " Today! " from To Morrow—tomaronite's wail, etc.). The apostrophe balances the hyphen Guesturn's, To-maronites.

Joyce goes on to explain how the incident is prepared for by references to incense in several languages, how the litany (" Oasis, cedarous esaltarshoming Leafboughnoon . . .", F470) is based on the Latin quoted in the *Portrait* (" Quasi cedrus exaltata sum in Libanon . . .", P118/118), the girls dividing into two groups, those who pronounce *Oah*sis and those who pronounce *Oeye*sis, and how in imitation of the Maronite and Latin " pax " given with embrace of arms, the girls turn toward one another and (apparently calling one another's names) exclaim " Peace " in twenty-nine languages: he lists German, Dano-Norwegian, Provencal, French, Greek, French variations, Malay, Echo, Gypsy, Magyar children's, Armenian, Senegalese, Latin variation, Irish Diminutive, N. Breton, S. Breton, Chinese, Pidgin, Arabic, Hebrew, Sanscrit, Hindustani, and English, and adds that the word was actually signalled around the world in that way in 1918.

We are not yet through with this episode. As he conducts his girls on a *via crucis*, Shaun manages simultaneously to run through a mixed-up Mass of his own. He hastily consults the calendar, F433, after completing the Introit, F432, launches directly into the sermon, and helps himself to an immense communion, F455–456, and purification, F462; phrases like " Sussumcordials all round ", F453; " Shunt us! Shunt us! Shunt us!", F454, and " Eat a missal lest ", F456 (sursum

corda, sanctus, ite missa est), protrude from time to time, sometimes in sequence and sometimes not, to give us a hazy idea
of our bearings. " I truly am eucherized to yous," he
announces, " his chalished drink now well in hand ", F461.
Promising to leave behind for their consoling his " altar's ego
in miniature ", F463, (the altar sacrament plus the Holy
Ghost) he disappears with a *benedicat vos omnipotens Deus*
(" Bennydick hotfoots onimpudent stayers! ", F469), the
Last Blessing of the Mass. The dramatic function of this
garbled ceremonial " in slick and slapstick record time ",
F473, is not unlike that of the parody-mass performed by Buck
Mulligan in the first section of *Ulysses*. In its perfunctory
formularization, its melange of parish gossip, worldly wisdom,
and completely un-supernatural motivations it epiphanizes
both a corrupt clericalism and a verbalised and superficial
culture playing with shells.

The next episode of this section parallels the Good Friday
Adoration of the Cross. " Yawn " lies low on the hillock
(Golgotha); the priest lays the unveiled cross on a cushion in
the centre of the sanctuary. On p. 486 the Cross (" that
initial T square of burial jade ") is applied to Shaun's forehead,
lips, and breast (Cf. the custom of making a sign of the cross
on each of these places before the reading of the Gospel). The
Improperia (" O my people, what have I done unto thee? ") is
echoed by HCE's long speech at the end of the episode (pp.
532–534). The elaborate account of the Tree of Life on pp.
504–505 is aligned with traditional patristic exegesis of the
meaning of the Cross.

Book IV of *Finnegans Wake* corresponds, in ways too obvious
to require enumeration, to the Resurrection at the climax of the
lenten sequence, and to the Last Gospel (John I) at the close
of the mass proper.[1]

[1] According to a note to Frank Budgen written apparently at Joyce's dictation
(Slocum collection), " In Part IV there is in fact a triptych—though the central
picture is scarcely illuminated. Namely the supposed windows of the village
church gradually lit up by the dawn, the windows i.e., representing on one side
the meeting of St. Patrick (Japanese) and the (Chinese) Archdruid Bulkely (this
by the way is all about colour) and the legend of the progressive isolation of St.
Kevin, the third being St. Lawrence O'Toole, patron saint of Dublin, buried in
Eu in Normandie. (See note 8, page 307.) "

Chapter 20

TWO SELVES

A king and a prince at last in death, with incidental music. And, what though murdered and betrayed, bewept by all frail tender hearts for, Dane or Dubliner, sorrow for the dead is the only husband from whom they refuse to be divorced. . . . He found in the world without as actual what was in his world within as possible. . . . Every life is many days, day after day. We walk through ourselves, meeting robbers, ghosts, giants, old men, young men, wives, widows, brothers-in-love. But always meeting ourselves.

Ulysses, U210/201

JOYCE spent his life playing parts, and his works swarm with shadow-selves. He was the young Rimbaud in Dublin, a Svevo-like accountant of ethical balances in Trieste, and a pallid disciple of Huysmans and Lautréamont in Paris, according as his imagination was absorbed by Dedalus, Bloom, or Shem the Penman. He was photographed in a gamut of roles from wild-eyed Irishman through Mephistopheles to stolid *père de famille*: one would scarcely guess that the portraits illustrating the Gorman biography are all of the same man. Against Irish respectability he was a wild youth in tennis shoes and a yachting cap who laughed so heartily in the streets that passers-by turned to stare. Against avant-garde Paris he was the dean of a super-graduate-school, harnessing the adulatory energy of the *Transition* cénacle for secretarial work; we hear of them searching " through numerous note-books with mysterious reference points to be inserted in the text ", or transcribing reports on assigned readings into note-books which Joyce condensed to a line or a paragraph.

Stephen Hero's " taste for enigmatic roles ", S77/64, was partly accountable for these mutations; it was more important for Joyce to palliate the curiosity of perforce intimates with a ready-made role than to obviate popular distrust by a façade of polite conformity. There was more to it than public relations, however. Parody was the medium of his art, and he played these parts that he might better write them. To make Bloom an authentic parody of himself, Joyce turned himself for long

354

periods into a parody of Bloom.   And with a nervous sense at
once of himself, his material, and his way of working, he
allowed himself to be haunted throughout his life by a sort of
Doppelgänger metaphysic.   His first alter ego was his father,
and the rest of his life was full of shadow-selves.

The shadow-self was a Dublin theme.   From the boy in
" The Sisters " who is shaken more deeply than he can
understand by the death of his friend the paralysed priest, or
Little Chandler the nascent poet rushing to a rendezvous with
his inflated counterpart Gallaher the journalist, or Mr. Duffy
visited by the chill spectre of a passionate life he might have
elected, to Gabriel Conroy's vision of the consumptive face of
a pale boy standing in the rain " at the end of the wall where
there was a tree ", his wife's dead lover, evoked by a phrase
and a song, now gone as his own passionate self is gone and his
present self is going—throughout *Dubliners* people are jostled
by incarnations of what they would like to be, or really are, or
never were.   The songs of *Chamber Music* tremble with a
vague yearning for other lives and profounder loves.   In
Exiles Richard Rowan meets, in Robert Hand, his Doppelgänger, and not by wrestling with that dark angel but rather
by refusing to wrestle with him, by disdaining him, receives a
Jacob's wound in the hollow of his thigh, " a deep wound of
doubt that can never be healed ".

Richard abstains from conflict with Robert, but the pride he
takes in his magnanimity disguises contempt for Robert, and
through Robert for Bertha.   Robert proposes to Richard a
spiritual battle with Bertha as prize, not because he loves
Bertha or respects Richard, but because he desires to feel
himself real enough to fight and love.   The one is contemptuous, the other unreal, and the unreal is the perpetually
hidden side of the white austere unheated contemptuous, a
satellite mistaking himself for a sun, turning one face always to
that around which he circles, and the other to the black void.
That is how Joyce by 1914 had sized up the Romantic's
quarrel with his age, and that is the key to the sparring with
shadow-selves in his later work.

So Stephen Dedalus in the *Portrait* fancies to revenge himself on his schoolmates by dying (" And Wells would be sorry
then for what he had done ") and crossing the narrow gap
between humility and pride transforms in imagination his tiny
corpse into that of his elected other self, a hero:

– He is dead.   We saw him lying upon the catafalque.
A wail of sorrow went up from the people.
– Parnell!   Parnell!   He is dead!
They fell upon their knees moaning in sorrow.   P26/30.

So Stephen in *Ulysses*, toying with another heroic alter ego,
Shakespeare, transforms his meeting with Synge in Paris into
St. Patrick's meeting in the forest with the archaic Ossian,
whom it is his destiny to supersede:

> Oisin with Patrick. Faunman he met in Clamart woods, brandishing
> a winebottle. *C'est vendredi saint!* Murthering Irish. His image
> wandering, he met. I mine. I met a fool i' the forest. U197/188.

So Stephen, having spoken of how we meet always ourselves,
Stephen who had modelled himself upon Monte Cristo,
returning avenger, meets in Nighttown the archetypal returning avenger, Ulysses of the great bow, now in 1904 by metempsychosis incarnate as a timid cuckold, and joins him in
micturition beneath " the apathy of the stars." He has met
himself, he has met his spiritual father, having rejected in
contempt his consubstantial father, and that morning in still
more fascinated contempt having wrestled with the stage
Irishman, his spiritual brother.

In *Finnegans Wake* the battle with the alter ego goes on.
Mutt and Jute: tourist meets caveman, F16. Mookse and
Gripes, pope meets heretic; mock turtle / moocow encounters
griffin, unreality battling unreality over unreal questions in
hairsplitting Latin; fox snaps at unattainable grapes and
pronounces them sour; all the while Nuvoletta the cloud-girl,
avatar of the Bertha of *Exiles*, looks on, F152. Glugg, the
drowning man going down for the third time, his very name a
strangling sound, is worsted three times at riddle-guessing by
the chaffing " sky sheraph " Chuff, around whom the twenty-
nine month-girls join hands, F234. Butt the victim is
belaboured by Taff the Welshman, F338, as Joyce by Wyndham Lewis (" Taffy was a thief "). The Ondt, an industrious
nullity with a " chairmanlooking " smile, legislates out of
existence the Gracehoper, " hoppy on akkant of his joyicity ",
F414.

None of these conflicts embodies much passion. Shem and
Shaun are a " musichall pair ", F418, who bandy stage
epithets and belabour one another with noisy slapsticks,
"after which they are both carried off the set and brought home

to be well soaped, sponged and scrubbed again " by Anna
Livia, F220. The emotion in *Finnegans Wake* is contained in
the permanent plight of the unmoving Earwicker, recumbent
prey of many inner voices; the battle of self with shadow-self
which had fueled the emotion not only of Joyce's earlier works
but of western art for 150 years is reduced in the last drama
to comic byplay. The Romantic Agony of the post-Renais-
sance West becomes what it always was, the noise of a few
bursting bubbles in the foam of Finnegan's wake.

All these books are about people who cannot read them;
they all contain therefore, apparently labelled " Author ", a
Joyce who could not have written them. Hence on the one
hand Robert Hand, Buck Mulligan, and Shaun the Post; on
the other Richard Rowan, Stephen Dedalus, and Shem the
Penman. The name of Jim the Penman is lifted from a
Victorian drama about a forger; that of Shaun the Post, from
an Irish melodrama about a stage Irishman. Shaun contains
traits, assimilated to the stock convention of genial blarney, of
Eamon de Valera, Stanislaus Joyce, and Wyndham Lewis.
The Penman with whom he contends is " a sham and a low
sham ". That is what de Valera presumably would have
thought of Joyce, and what Lewis and brother Stanislaus did
think of his last phase; Shem the Penman isn't Joyce, he is
their image of Joyce. But he is the Joyce of Joyce's friends as
well as of Joyce's enemies: the image of Joyce put forward,
from 1922 on, by Joyce's upholders on the eminently factitious
battleground of literary politics.

DE VALERA AS ALTER-EGO

De Valera must have appeared to Joyce as if divinely appointed to go into *Finnegans Wake* as an *alter ego* for the author.
He and Joyce were born in the same year; both were tall,
both bespectacled, both ex-schoolmasters, both pedantic of
speech and chary of intimacy. Confronted by " Dev " the
Shem-figure postures impotently; it is Little Chandler *vs.*
Gallaher over again. " Dev " in the Dáil with his Spanish
aloofness, " Man Devoyd of the Commoner Characteristics of
an Irish Nature ", F72, " protesting to his lipreaders with a
justbeencleaned barefacedness ", F91; or presiding over a
League of Nations session, " a fingerhot of rheingenever to
give the Pax cum spiritututu ", F406, or addressing the Free

State by wireless," a voice, the voce of Shaun, vote of the Irish, voise from afar ", F407, or granting a cheerfully evasive interview:

> – Yet one minute's observation, dear dogmestic Shaun, as we point out how you have while away painted our town a wearing greenridinghued.
> – O murder mere, how did you hear? Shaun replied, smoiling the ily way up his lampsleeve (it just seemed the natural thing to do), so shy of light was he then, F411,

or seeking the inner light in moments of crisis:

> Sometimes he would keep silent for a few minutes as if in prayer and clasp his forehead and during the time he would be thinking to himself and he would not mind anybody who would be talking to him or crying stinking fish, F482,

—Dev the inscrutable administrator made an admirable foil for the equally inscrutable author of the *Wake*. Dev is simply Joyce's outward aspect translated into public life. Though he upholds the Free State's list of prohibited books, repudiates the productions of his " cerebrated brother " as " Puffedly offal tosh ", F419, and describes with distaste "jameymock farceson " " making his pillgrimace of Childe Horrid ", " always cutting my prhose to please his phrase ", F423, he is pleased to imply that he could, if he felt like it, make a good job at the same sort of thing himself:

> . . . and by the power of blurry wards I am loyable to do it (I am convicted of it!) any time ever I liked (bet ye fippence off me boot allowance!) with the allergrossest transfusiasm . . . I'd pinsel it with immenuensoes . . . and my trifolium librotto, the authordux Book of Lief, would, if given to daylight, (I hold a most incredible faith about it) far exceed what that bogus bolshy of a shame, my soamheis brother, Gaoy Fecks, is conversant with in audible black and prink. F425.

The notion of Eamon de Valera setting himself in confidence to write another *Finnegans Wake* is sufficiently funny to justify itself. Conceivably, three volumes of candid memoirs by the chameleon Free State casuist, " spickspookspokesman of our specturesque silentiousness ", F427, might far outbalance in scandalous revelation the proscribed Punman's mild collection of

> blasphematory spits, stale shestnuts, schoolgirl's, young ladies', milkmaids', washerwomen's, shopkeepers' wives', merry widows', ex nuns', vice abbess's, pro virgins', super whores,' silent sisters',

Charleys' aunt's, grandmothers', mothers'-in-laws', fostermothers', godmothers' garters. F183.

THE PARIS JOYCE AS ALTER-EGO

The worst Joyce has to say of de Valera, in fact, is that he resembles to a nicety the image Parisian idolators, after *Ulysses*, constructed of Joyce. He was praised for the pedantic way in which he made everything *fit*, Bloom's potato of page 56 called into play on page 428; nobody thought Bloom's use for the potato was funny. He was praised for the courage with which he made intimate revelations without reserve; nobody considered that he might have been making them up. He was praised for having composed a scientific document (" I have learned more psychology and psychiatry from it than I did in ten years at the Neurological Institute ", wrote the doctor to whom the *New York Times*, typically, consigned the book for review). He was praised for the profundities of Molly Bloom, who commanded an unapologetic chorus of lyrical assent from the moment the shrewd amazed whistle of Arnold Bennett, hard-headed man of the world, invited a book-review audience to " talk about understanding feminine psychology! " He was praised for being Stephen Dedalus, smasher of chandeliers, disgusted with everyone and everything; which disgust insured his having no particular axes to grind, like a white-coated Frankenstein, above politics, devoted to pure science, standing behind the wreckage of Hiroshima, inscrutable, paring his fingernails.

While in the genteel press Alfred Noyes was finding omitted from these " imbecile pages " " no foulness conceivable to the mind of man ", and *The Pink 'Un* (officially known as *The Sporting Times*[1]) was reporting to the pub-and-darts fraternity that " The main contents of the book are enough to make a Hottentot sick ", the Dedalian anti-genteel were belabouring with their ashplants the salon chandeliers of middle-class London. *Ulysses*, like the Irish Free State, rapidly became undiscussable except as a fiat of its anarchic creator: apotheosis of (*a*) scientific method (the presentation of Bloom); (*b*) protean poetry disguised as a-moral Nature (Molly), and (*c*)

[1] Joyce was later to introduce an indecency narrated in Latin with the words, " Let manner and matter of this for these our sporting times be cloaked up in the language of blushfed porporates than an Anglican ordinal, not reading his own rude dunsky tunga, may ever behold the brand of scarlet on the brow of her of Babylon and feel not the pink one in his own damned cheek ", F185.

the alchemist intellectual as enemy of the bourgeois (Stephen.) When in 1927 the magazine *Transition* took over this reputation and began to surround the monstrous birth of *Finnegans Wake* with the voodoo rites of the Revolution of the Word, Joyce's Stephen Dedalus *persona* became a major literary racket.   Mobilized against the hated bourgeoisie, it was pumped full of " the new magic " and used to focus a cult, sustain a bookstore, and sell a magazine.

Joyce didn't rebel as he might have ten years earlier.   At forty-five, almost blind, remembering the wrangle with Grant Richards, the printers who refused to set up the *Portrait* " even though it may be a classic ", the confiscation of *The Little Review*, and the burning of *Dubliners* at Dublin and *Ulysses* at Folkestone, he needed a publishing arrangement for the new book that wouldn't strain his nerves.   So he admitted the amazing Gene Jolas to his friendship, withheld comment while the jitterbugs of the night-world processed his reputation, and sardonically contemplated the creation of a legend.

In addition, he had learned by 1927 the value of sitting still and letting new material come to him; if he didn't fend it away he could occupy the observer's point of vantage at its centre. And the legend that had formed round his name created unforeseeably favorable conditions for the crystallization of exactly the sort of material he wanted.   He had only to sit tight, and the twentieth century, as was its nature, would recreate the nineteenth.   It did: Shelley's great age began anew, its golden years returned.   Material for the anatomy of romanticism came swarming round his flat; he was back in the nineteenth century to which he had devoted so much meditation; it was like living in the heyday of Byron.

Bliss was it in that dawn to be alive.   " We want the imagination huge and free ", wrote Mr. Jolas in 1928, and proceeded to draw up manifestoes reminiscent in their extremely conventional naughtiness of Baudelaire's cats and mulattoes:

VERTIGRAL:

HYPNOLOGUES AND PARAMYTHS
ONEIROMANCY AND EXORCISM
DEMONS AND SERAPHIM
PHANTASMATA AND CHIMERAE
THE LANGUAGE OF THE NIGHT

Joyce was acclaimed as the Svengali of the new dispensation, bell-wether of " a populace released to fuller realizations because permitted to express themselves individually in a mass " (!) He was, the chorus announced, achieving what Mr. Jolas called " the ecstatic way of thinking . . . the struggle for a phantasmagoric reality ". In *Ulysses* he had expressed their horror of the quotidian; in *Work in Progress* he gave them back their rapturous identity with a banality into which he had now pumped laughing-gas. " A complete symbiosis of writer and reader ", as one Transitionist put it; " A Cyclopean picture of humanity and the gods ", affirmed another; " the furth-Radex of a Device's insidicostal-complexivate-the-FORM-flow-of-SoneRich-TumbleDisplay, in the PunPass-DuoMeans of ince-possi-halt>rcsuming-the-CONTEXT's SetUpAddit-Impliqs-Bouquet ", stammered a third.

Joyce took all the details for Shem the Penman he needed from the panegyrics so lavishly provided. He studied the dreamwork of the recumbent Earwicker from an articulate collective model. He also appears to have taken revenge in the most elaborate legpull of his career: he permitted a *Transition* fellow-traveller, Stuart Gilbert, to believe that his useful book was the authorized exposition of *Ulysses*. Beneath the thickly-lensed eye of the Master, Mr. Gilbert's gaze swung to and fro from the riddling text to the typewritten table of themes. " The bliss of ignorance is a short and sorry affair beside the studious delectation of the connoisseur," wrote Mr. Gilbert in his Introduction, and Joyce nodded grave assent when the chapter was read to him. " It is in absence of mind, when he is up in the clouds or on his way to Cythera, that man achieves the energy of happiness ", pursued Mr. Gilbert, and Joyce did not disagree. He quoted five times from Madame Blavatsky's *Isis Unveiled*, and nine times from her dupe A.P. Sinnett's *Esoteric Buddhism* and *Growth of the Soul*, with unsuspecting deference. He wrote earnestly of The Seal of Solomon, with acknowledgments to *Les Croyances Fondamentales de Bouddhisme* and The Smaragdine Table of Hermes Trismegistus, found " the spirit of the original " in Butcher and Lang's *Odyssey*, and described Gerty MacDowell's seventh-hand magazine sentiment as " a bonnetful of truelove knots and favours incorruptible by moth or rust ", without a hand raised in caution.

" Wipe your glosses with what you know ", F304, Joyce advises his scholiasts; your glasses, that is, with what you know,

and your glosses with you know what (or perhaps vice versa;
one recalls the smeared microscope in Blake's *Island in the
Moon*). He provided a title for a 1929 collection of *Transition*
Joyce-essays—" Our Exagmination round his Factification for
Incamination of Work in Progress "—and later inserted it in
the book itself to precede a comical account of the flocking-
round of " Cabraists and Finglossies ", climaxing with a generic
celebrant " riding lapsaddlelonglegs up the oakses staircase on
muleback like Amaxodias Isteroprotos, hindquarters to the fore
and a kick to the lift ", F498. As none of the twelve Exag-
minators seems to have noticed (they rushed into print with
only a fraction of the final text available, and the very title a
secret), a sequence of long words ending in " -ation " is the
trademark of the perennial jury of twelve who keep getting in
the way of the action of the *Wake* while they participate in its
" shoutmost shoviality " as a *modus vivendi*. " Exagmination " is " examination " corrupted by " agmen " (Lat.
road); " factification " joins defense-works to a way of making;
freely translated, the title reads, " Our sight-seer's stroll round
the fortifications behind which he maintains the meaning of
his Work in Progress *in camera*."

Meanwhile *Transition* streamed on, praising Joyce in every
issue as the man who set the moustaches of the bourgeois on
fire, abolished the past, cauterized the present, jazzed the
future, and proclaimed the esperantic millennium. A tone of
continual scorn for the fuddy-duddies who would " deny him
the right " to his liberties with language characterizes the self-
defensive aggressiveness of this campaign. Upon this situation impinged Wyndham Lewis.

WYNDHAM LEWIS: THE ENEMY AS ALTER-EGO

Lewis appeared grimacing in his professional role of The
Enemy: enemy of this Joyce-shadow thrown by the *Transition*
spotlights. Joyce, after his first irritation at the " Analysis of
the Mind of James Joyce " in *Time and Western Man* (1927),
the most brilliant misreading in modern criticism, must have
been elated to realize how articulate the circumjacent vacuum
was getting. Concept, not comprehension, was invading
chaos, knowing over-reaching what was there to know.

Lewis' critique had the disturbing merit of being neither
impressionistic nor irrelevant. He took a few quick sights at

the object, extracted from their living tissue with a surgical eye
four or five salient facts which no one else had been able to see
—a mole, a cheekbone, an ear—set them down on his canvas
in abridged relationship, and turning away from the model
(since he knew more than he could see) filled in the composition
brilliantly with the sallow planes of a plausible parchment
mask: a Portrait of the Artist as Susceptible Drudge.

He saw, for instance, that the characters of *Ulysses* were
clichés: " . . . a stage Jew (Bloom), a stage Irishman (Mulligan), or a stage Anglo-Saxon (Haines)." He thought, however, that Joyce didn't see it too. He saw that Bloom oddly
resembled Stephen, but he supposed that this was only because
they were both self-portraits of Joyce, *aetat*. 38 and 22. He
saw that the interior monologue wasn't an instrument of
psychological revelation but an epiphany of experiential
constriction—" some figures for a moment bump against you,
and you certainly perceive them with great distinctness—or
rather some fragment of their dress or some mannerism; then
they are gone. . . . That is all that the ' telling from the
inside ' amounts to "—but he failed to reckon this among the
meanings of the book.

He saw two other things, of indisputable salience: that the
book was concerned, in an unprecedented way, with the flux of
matter, and that Stephen Dedalus was a hopeless farce. Here
we had better quote *in extenso*:

Matter:

> . . . an Aladdin's cave of incredible bric-a-brac in which a dense mass
> of dead stuff is collected. . . . a circumscribed psychological space
> into which several encyclopaedias have been emptied. . . . a suf-
> focating, moeotic expanse of objects, all of them lifeless, the sewage
> of a past twenty years old, all neatly arranged in a meticulous se-
> quence. . . . It is the voluminous curtain that fell, belated (with the
> alarming momentum of a ton or two of personally organized rubbish),
> upon the victorian scene. So rich was its delivery, its pent-up out-
> pouring so vehement, that it will remain, eternally cathartic, a
> record diarrhoea. No one who looks *at* it will ever want to look
> *behind* it. It is the sardonic catafalque of the victorian world.

Stephen:

> He is the really wooden figure. He is " the poet " to an uncomfort-
> able degree, a dismal, a ridiculous, even a pulverising degree. His
> movements in the Martello-tower, his theatrical " bitterness ", his

cheerless, priggish stateliness, his gazings into the blue distance, his Irish Accent, his exquisite sensitiveness, his " pride " that is so crude as to be almost indecent, the incredible slowness with which he gets about from place to place, up the stairs, down the stairs, like a funereal stage-king; the time required for him to move his neck, how he raises his hand, passes it over his aching eyes, or his damp brow, even more wearily drops it, closes his dismal little shutters against his rollicking irish-type of a friend (in his capacity of a type-poet), and remains sententiously secluded, shut up in his own personal Martello-tower—a Martello-tower within a Martello-tower—until he consents to issue out, tempted by the opportunity of making a " bitter " —a very " bitter "—jest, to show up against the ideally idiotic background provided by Haines. . . .

With these master-keys in his hand Lewis might have written the definitive exegesis. It pleased him however to use *Ulysses* rather than seek to reveal it. So he convinced himself that a flood of matter coursed through the book because Joyce had a bourgeois appetite for dated rubbish, and that Stephen was " slow " and " quiet " and " sensitive " because the under-privileged Joyce meant him, in awkward Dickens-fashion, for a " gentleman ". He complimented Joyce on the ideally-organized case-material he had provided for a Lewisian commentary on the *Zeitgeist*. The Irish drudge had managed to do this by not mixing his secretions with thought: " There is not very much reflection going on at any time inside the head of Mr. James Joyce. That is indeed the characteristic condition of *the craftsman*, pure and simple."

No indeed, " There was not very much windy Nous blowing at the given moment through the hat of Mr. Melancholy Slow! ", F56, echoed Joyce, apropos of Shem the Penman, " lazy skald or maundering pote ", lifting " wearywilly his slowcut snobsic eyes . . . and lengthily lingering along ". " Windy Nous " is the plenary diagnosis: it is thought à la Wyndham Lewis, a νοῦς, a *Geist*, blowing where it listeth, not a searchlight playing over fact but a stiff breeze through the head. Grasp of the whole, Joyce saw, had yielded to " insight ", and insights constellated in the void, or connected by schematic planks, perverted in Lewis' polemic books the function of a rarely accurate eye for fact. The eye for fact dominated such writings as a story Joyce much admired, *Cantelman's Spring Mate*, but the Windy Nous and the butcher's axe had taken over its functions in the past ten years:

Johns is a different butcher's. Next place you are up town pay him a visit. Or better still, come tobuy. You will enjoy cattlemen's spring meat. John is now quite divorced from baking. Fattens, kills, flays, hangs, draws, quarters and pieces. Fell his lambs! Ex! Feel how sheap! Exex! His liver too is great value, a spatiality! Exexex! COMMUNICATED. F172.

Lewis incarnated and rendered superbly articulate an old Joyce theme, the theme of *Exiles*, Ibsenite rectitude in a vacuum. He transferred the theme, however, from will to idea. It was not liberated action but independent thought that he imagined himself to exemplify, as though thought could be liberated from fact any more than action from context. Joyce didn't attempt to dislodge him from mid-chaos. He left him there as a listening-post. With an amused reference to " that most improving of roundshows, *Spice and Westend Women* (utterly exhausted before publication, indiapepper edition shortly) ", F292, he permitted Lewis to supply numerous tones and locutions for the portrayal of Shaun the Post. He also accepted gratefully, for Shem the Penman purposes, everything Lewis had to say about Stephen Dedalus and about Joyce himself. Here is a peep inside the head of Mr. James Joyce:

> ... an you could peep inside the cerebralised saucepan of this eer ill-winded goodfornobody, you would see in his house of thoughtsam (was you, that is, decontaminated enough to look discarnate) what a jetsam litterage of convolvuli of times lost or strayed, of lands derelict and of tongues laggin too. ... F 292.

Here is Shem trying to pretend that he is a gentleman:

> the evilsmeller ... used to stipple endlessly inartistic portraits of himself in the act of reciting old Nichiabelli's monolook interyerear ... a heartbreakingly handsome young paolo with love lyrics for the goyls in his eyols, a plaintiff's tanner vuice, a jucal inkome of one hundred and thirtytwo dranchmas per yard from Broken Hill stranded estate, Camebreech mannings, cutting a great dash in a brandnew two guinea dress suit and a burled hogsford hired for a Fursday evenin merry pawty, anna loavely long pair of inky Italian moostarshes glistering with boric vaseline and frangipani. Puh! How unwhisperably so! F182.

Here is the militant Lewis (Taff the Welshman) under the sign of the spatializing Eye, " his bulgeglarying stargapers razzle-dazzlingly full of eyes, full of balls, full of holes, full of buttons, full of stains, full of medals, full of blickblackblobs ", attacking Joyce/Shem:

> Grozarktic! Toadlebens! Some garmentguy! Insects appalling, low hum clang sin! A cheap decoy! Too deep destroy! Say mangraphique, may say nay por daguerre! F339.

It was Lewis who assigned the eye to himself and the ear to Joyce. It was also he who assigned time to Shem and space to Shaun. *Ulysses*, he wrote, was a time-book, a midden-heap of *temps retrouvé*, a lingering over what had long faded from the world.

> There is nothing for it today, if you have an appetite for the beautiful, but to *create new beauty*. You can no longer nourish yourself upon the Past; its stock is exhausted, the Past is nowhere a reality. The only place where it is a reality is in *time*. . . . So the metnal world of time offers a solution. . . . The local colour, or locally-coloured material, that was scraped together into a big variegated heap to make *Ulysses*, is—doctrinally even more than in fact—the material of the Past.

" There is nothing for it but to create new beauty." Joyce must have pricked up his ears at this unbelievably pat echo of Stephen Dedalus' election of " the loveliness that has not yet come into the world ". The Lewisian toughness concealed, it seemed, its quota of Romance. It was aperçus like this that led Joyce to make Shem and Shaun periodically exchange roles. Swaggering aficionado of the hard outside and sedentary epigon of the dark fluid within, space-fanatic and time-lackey, Enemy and poltroon, like Dodgson logician and Carroll dreamer, or like Holmes Übermensch and Watson Burgher, or like Stephen son and Bloom father, were at bottom one because at bottom purveyors of mental worlds in despite of the inexhaustible real.

Innumerable details of the *Wake* have their key in Lewis: the Gracehoper making his meal of Time (" He had eaten all the whilepaper, swallowed all the lustres, devoured forty flights of styearcases, chewed up all the mensas and seccles, ronged the records, made mundballs of the ephemerids and vorasioused most glutinously with the very timeplace in the ternitary ", F416), while the Ondt " made spaces in his psyche "; the Mookse who lived " eins within a space and a wearywide space it wast ", F152, setting out from Ludtown *a spasso*, girded with his *lanzia spezzata*, to encounter a Dubville Gripes,

" having the juice of his times ", F153, who cannot tell him " whose o'cloak you ware ", F155; the footling Butt, " his spent fish's livid smile giving allasundery the bumfit of the doped ", F339, " slinking his coatsleeves surdout over his squad mutton shoulder so as to loop more life the jauntly-man ", F343; and most extensively the incorrigible Professor Jones (another Welsh name) who lectures for twenty pages on " the dime-cash problem ", F149, expresses confidence in his " own spacious immensity ", F150, and accuses his squalid *alter ego* of being " a barefooted rubber with my supersocks pulled over his face which I publicked in my bestback garden for the laetification of siderodromites and to the irony of the stars ", F160 (Lewis thought that his *Enemy of the Stars* had engendered some of the " Circe " techniques).

Jones has the Shaunian obsession with food and a Lewisian penchant for the elusively intricate theory, the continental authority, and the striking word. He expounds the generic Richard-Robert-Bertha or Shem-Shaun-Iseult relationship in terms of Burrus (" full of natural greace . . . obsoletely unadulterous "), Caseous (" not an ideal choose by any meals ") and the " cowrymaid " Margareen. Directing his " grope-sarching eyes[1] through the strongholes of my acropoll " onto the mutations of butter, cheese, and margarine, he observes " in the dairy days of buy and buy " a " most tantumising state of affairs " about which he is " working out a quantum theory " in opposition to " Bitchson ", " Winestain ", and numerous other philosophers with whom he quarrels from phrase to phrase. He recalls to our admiring attention the intrepidity with which he has trespassed " on the space question where even michelangelines have fooled to dread ", alludes to one of his own paintings, " my goulache of Marge . . . which I titled *The Very Picture of a Needlesswoman* ", and dwells with satis-faction on its geometrical idiom:

> The hatboxes which composed Rhomba, lady Trabezond (Marge in her *excelsis*), also comprised the climactogram up which B and C may fondly be imagined ascending and are suggestive of gentlemen's spring modes. . . .

[1] " Buck Mulligan ' turned abruptly *his great searching eyes* from the sea,' etc. Great searching eyes! Oh, where were the great searching eyes of the author, from whom no verbal cliché may escape, when he wrote that? "—*Time and Western Man*, p. 115.

Cantelman's Spring Mate again; a page later he is blasting a group of patent Lewis targets, the child-cult, Charlie Chaplin, and the simpering Loos-like female.

Jones' prose is like Lewis' without the epithetic sparkle: heavily parenthetical, digressive, quarrelsome, constantly promising the future ordering of vast tracts of material, syntactically loose and locally rapid. Striking configurations of image abound, with little indication of a main line of argument. Lewis delights in staging elucidative dialogues with principles under attack; Jones relates the fable of the Mookse and the Gripes. Lewis swings paragraphs about with an energetic contempt for order, characteristically opening with a trenchant phrase and allowing the rest of the sentence to settle as it will; Jones hurls into motion the terms " quality and tality " with a parenthetic (" I shall explex what you ought to mean by this with its proper when and where and why and how in the subsequent sentence ", F149) Lewis made his persona Tarr say in a 1918 novel,

> I see I am boring you. The matter is too remote! But you have trespassed here and you must listen.—I cannot let you off before you have heard, and shown that you understand. If you do not sit and listen, I will write it all to you. YOU WILL BE MADE TO HEAR IT! And *after* I have told you this, I will tell you why I am talking to a fool like you!

Jones has a similar measure of respect for his " foibleminded " audience:

> As my explanations here are probably above your understandings, lattlebrattons, though as argumentatively uncomparisoned as Cadwan, Cadwallon, and Cadwalloner, I shall revert to a more expletive method which I frequently use when I have to sermo with muddle-crass pupils. Imagine for my purpose that you are a squad of urchins, snifflynosed, goslingnecked, clothyheaded, tangled in your lacings, tingled in your pants, etsitaraw etcicero. F152.

And with a trenchant allusion to Lewis' blasting and bombardiering military background, Jones in a single parenthesis manages to dispose of himself with incomparable neatness:

> This soldier-author-batman for all his commontoryism is just another of those souftsiezed bubbles who never quite got the sandhurst out of his eyes so that the champaign he draws for us is as flop as a plankrieg. F162.

Sandhurst is a military school. The champagne he draws is flat beneath its specious sparkle, and his sketch of the champaign is ultimately a bodiless two-dimensional map, a conceptual pattern in chaos, not even disinterested but a war-plan (Kriegsplan), flat as a pancake.

Lewis hoped that the endlessly susceptible Joyce of his account would in turn be influenced by the Lewis critique: " I hope it may be so, for he would be a most valuable adherent." Joyce took the hint, glossed his every word, and reproduced his every configuration of thought. Why should he bother inventing shadows and counter-shadows when they invented themselves?

STANISLAUS JOYCE AS ALTER-EGO

As for Joyce's brother Stanislaus, the third major component of Shaun the Post around whom the girls cluster to chant " Enchainted, dear sweet Stainusless ", F237, Joyce apparently supposed him to be covetous of the affections of Joyce's wife Nora; something of the sort peeps from behind Stephen's *Ulysses* theory of Shakespeare's brother's amours with Ann Hathaway ("a brother is as easily forgotten as an umbrella ", U208/199). Stanislaus played Shaun the Post to the hilt, assuming the status of professor of English in the Trieste to which in 1905 he had followed his brother. The " stanidsglass effect ", F277, of his rectitude (" He still had the same intemperate habits, and I set about deliberately to break him of them ") assimilated easily to the " smile likequid glue " of Shaun / De Valera surrounded by the flower-girls (" Unclean you art not. Outcaste thou are not.... You are pure. You are pure. You are in your puerity", F237). He thought Paris a bad influence on his brother (" I argued with him ... that a work of art must have an outer meaning clear to the simple man "). The epiphany of the fraternal relationship may be given in his own words:

> The admirers of the book always cite the same passages and repeat the same explanations. It is palpable that they only report what has been explained to them. By themselves they don't understand very much. ... Let them admire away. I know that they admire what they don't comprehend—the most humiliating form of intellectual servitude. ...

When *Finnegans Wake* was published ... on the author's fifty-eighth birthday, my brother wrote to me offering a copy in homage. I refused it.

He retrieves this confession with magisterial aplomb:

There is little need to tell how much regret this refusal has since cost me—even less need when the uselessness of all regret is considered. He told me that there would be a third part, *The Reawakening*. I found myself hoping that after so many years of ingenious experiment ... his style would achieve a suggestive efficacy such as to surpass even the best pages of *Ulysses*. I could hardly wait for the light to break, for the day when a language would be spoken that all could understand. The work must remain forever incomplete now that the author is immersed in a sleep that knows neither dreams nor reawakening.

Epilogue

FOUR BURIALS

... Hunchback and Saint and Fool ...
W. B. Yeats

Zürich, den 13 Januar 1941, Schwesternhaus Rotkreuz. Heute morgen um 2 Uhr starb im Rotkreuzspital unerwartet rasch unser lieber Mann, Vater und Grossvater James Joyce in seinem 58 Lebensjahr. Stille Bestattung im Friedhof Allmen Fluntern Mittwoch, den 15 Januar, nachmittags 2 Uhr. Es wird gebeten, von Kondolenzbesuchen abzusehen.

Nora Joyce, Giorgio Joyce, Lucia Joyce, Stephen Joyce.

JOYCE, JAMES (1882–1941), Irish author, was born in Rathgar, Dublin, on Feb. 2, 1882, to John Stanislaus Joyce, a witty but improvident Corkonian, and Mary Jane Murray, originally of Longford ... left Ireland for the continent to work out his destiny as an artist independently of family, country, and religion ... meagre livelihood at various occupations until subsidized by friends ... a detailed, if not always accessible parallel with the *Odyssey* which implies an unflattering view of both the modern world and the classical ... endlessly blending ... leaves the reader floundering ... extreme of obscurity in modern literature. A measure of his total achievement, however, may well be T. S. Eliot's remark that Joyce was the greatest master of the English language since Milton.

Encyclopaedia Britannica

James Joyce used to write regularly to his sisters in Dublin. " He always expressed his love of Dublin and of the Dublin people, and often said that he would love to live here again," said Miss Eva Joyce.

"WAS OUR IDOL"

" He suffered much from rheumatic fever, though, and the climate would not suit him.

" However some people may criticise what he wrote, he was our eldest brother and our idol, and to us, at least, his writings had the stamp of genius.

" He had the kindest disposition, hated show and publicity, and spent all his spare time with his family, enjoying trips with them in the French countryside."

Irish Press, 14th Jan., 1941

And it was a ghastly winter day with a lot of slush coming down from the sky, and there were no taxis any more, as the petrol rationing was very strict . . . . I took a tram, and in this tram, going up the hill very slowly, there was assembled almost the whole funeral party. . . .

We arrived at the cemetery, and were directed into a chapel, but as James Joyce did not want to have a priest at his funeral, there was nobody there. . . .

Meanwhile in the distance there was the faint roar of the wild animals in the zoo, and we stood round the grave, and again didn't quite know what to do, because again there was no priest, and this time not even an official funeral speech. So we hoaxed each other in a very embarrassed way until a very, very old man turned up—obviously a man who hovers over the grave, as one sees in almost every churchyard, men who seem to just wait till they are buried themselves. A tiny man who obviously was deaf, because he went to one of the attendants of the mortician, who was holding the rope which went under the coffin, as the coffin was not sunk yet into the grave, and he asked " Who is buried here? " And the mortician said " Mr. Joyce." And again in front of the whole assemblance of mourners he seemed not to have understood it. He again asked " Who is it? " " Mr. Joyce " he shouted, and at that moment, the coffin was lowered into the grave.

Eyewitness account, broadcast by the BBC, March 22, 1950.